U.S. History

An Enthralling Guide to America's Major Events, Including the Revolutionary and Civil Wars

Free limited time bonus

We forget 90% of everything that we've read in 7 days...

Get the free printable pdf summary of the book you've read AND much, much more... shhhh...

Enter Your Most Frequently Used Email to Get Started

DOWNLOAD FREE PDF SUMMARY

© Enthralling History

Stop for a moment. We have a free bonus set up for you. The problem is this: we forget 90% of everything that we read after 7 days. Crazy fact, right? Here's the solution: we've created a printable, 1-page pdf summary for this book that you're reading now. All you have to do to get your free pdf summary is to go to the following website: **https://livetolearn.lpages.co/enthrallinghistory/**

Or, Scan the QR code!

Once you do, it will be intuitive. Enjoy, and thank you!

Table of Contents

PART 1: AMERICAN HISTORY 1

INTRODUCTION..2

SECTION ONE: NORTH AMERICA COLONIZATION (1492-1776) 3

CHAPTER 1: EXPLORATION AND FIRST SETTLEMENTS.......................4

CHAPTER 2: THE THIRTEEN COLONIES..11

CHAPTER 3: THE FRENCH AND INDIAN WAR.......................................15

CHAPTER 4: CAUSES FOR REVOLUTION..19

SECTION TWO: THE UNITED STATES ARE BORN (1776-1861) 24

CHAPTER 5: THE AMERICAN REVOLUTION 25

CHAPTER 6: THE CONSTITUTION AND THE BILL OF RIGHTS 35

CHAPTER 7: THE LOUISIANA PURCHASE AND THE WAR OF
1812..43

CHAPTER 8: EXPANSION IN THE WEST AND SOUTH........................50

CHAPTER 9: THE MEXICAN-AMERICAN WAR, THE OREGON
TREATY, AND THE GOLD RUSH 59

SECTION THREE: THE CIVIL WAR AND THE
RECONSTRUCTION (1861–1877)..68

CHAPTER 10: WHAT CAUSED THE CIVIL WAR? 69

CHAPTER 11: KEY BATTLES AND CAMPAIGNS OF THE CIVIL
WAR 73

CHAPTER 12: SLAVERY, EMANCIPATION, AND THE
AFTERMATH...86

CHAPTER 13: THE RECONSTRUCTION (1865-1877)..............................91

SECTION FOUR: FROM RECONSTRUCTION TO WWI (1877-1917) 96

CHAPTER 14: FROM RECONSTRUCTION TO EXPANSION 97

CHAPTER 15: THE PROGRESSIVE ERA 102

CHAPTER 16: THE FATE OF THE NATIVE AMERICANS 109

CHAPTER 17: POLITICAL AND ECONOMIC CHANGES 118

SECTION FIVE: WWI, GREAT DEPRESSION, AND WWII
(1914-1945) 129

CHAPTER 18: WORLD WAR I AND THE ROARING '20S 131

CHAPTER 19: THE GREAT DEPRESSION AND THE NEW
DEAL 138

CHAPTER 20: WWII: AMERICA BECOMES A SUPERPOWER 143

SECTION SIX: THE COLD WAR AND THE SPACE RACE BEGIN
(1945-1969) 156

CHAPTER 21: THE TRUMAN YEARS: THE COLD WAR BEGINS 157

CHAPTER 22: THE IKE YEARS: COUP D'ÉTATS AND CIVIL
RIGHTS 163

CHAPTER 23: THE KENNEDYS AND THE '60S: DREAM UP
A BETTER WORLD 172

SECTION SEVEN: DÉTENTE AND THE END OF THE COLD
WAR (1968-1992) 185

CHAPTER 24: THE NIXON-FORD YEARS: DÉTENTE AND
ECONOMIC CHANGES 186

CHAPTER 25: JIMMY CARTER: THE END OF DÉTENTE 192

CHAPTER 26: REAGAN AND REAGANOMICS 198

CHAPTER 27: GEORGE H. W. BUSH: THE END OF THE COLD
WAR 205

SECTION EIGHT: FROM CLINTON TO TRUMP (1992-2021) 212

CHAPTER 28: THE CLINTON YEARS: THE SWIFT AND
SCANDALOUS '90S 213

CHAPTER 29: THE GEORGE W. BUSH YEARS: 9/11 AND THE
WAR ON TERROR 221

CHAPTER 30: BARACK OBAMA: THE FIRST BLACK PRESIDENT 227

CHAPTER 31: DONALD TRUMP: A CONTROVERSIAL
PRESIDENT 234

CONCLUSION: LOOKING FORWARD 242

PART 2: THE AMERICAN REVOLUTION 243

INTRODUCTION 244

CHAPTER 1: PRELUDE TO A REVOLT 246

CHAPTER 2: GROWING DISCONTENT 254

CHAPTER 3: BOSTON UNDER SIEGE 265

CHAPTER 4: THE SHOT...275

CHAPTER 5: EARLY SUCCESSES 285

CHAPTER 6: A DECLARATION AND INVASIONS 295

CHAPTER 7: THE MIRACLES OF TRENTON AND SARATOGA 306

CHAPTER 8: ALLIES AND ADVERSARIES 318

CHAPTER 9: TRYING TIMES...328

CHAPTER 10: THE SOUTHERN CAMPAIGN 339

CHAPTER 11: YORKTOWN 352

CHAPTER 12: THE FINAL DAYS...360

CONCLUSION 367

PART 3: THE AMERICAN CIVIL WAR..369

INTRODUCTION...370

CHAPTER 1: 19TH-CENTURY AMERICA....................................372

CHAPTER 2: THE NORTH AND THE SOUTH...........................381

CHAPTER 3: RISING TENSIONS 391

CHAPTER 4: THE REPUBLICAN PARTY....................................411

CHAPTER 5: THE 1860 PRESIDENTIAL ELECTION 414

CHAPTER 6: OUTBREAK OF THE WAR.....................................424

CHAPTER 7: AMERICA AT WAR 434

CHAPTER 8: THE WAR GROWS 441

CHAPTER 9: THE WAR IN 1863 460

CHAPTER 10: THE FINAL CAMPAIGNS....................................473

CHAPTER 11: AFTERMATH 482

CONCLUSION 491

HERE'S ANOTHER BOOK BY ENTHRALLING HISTORY THAT
YOU MIGHT LIKE..494

FREE LIMITED TIME BONUS..495

SOURCES 496

Part 1: American History

An Enthralling Overview of Major Events that Shaped the United States of America

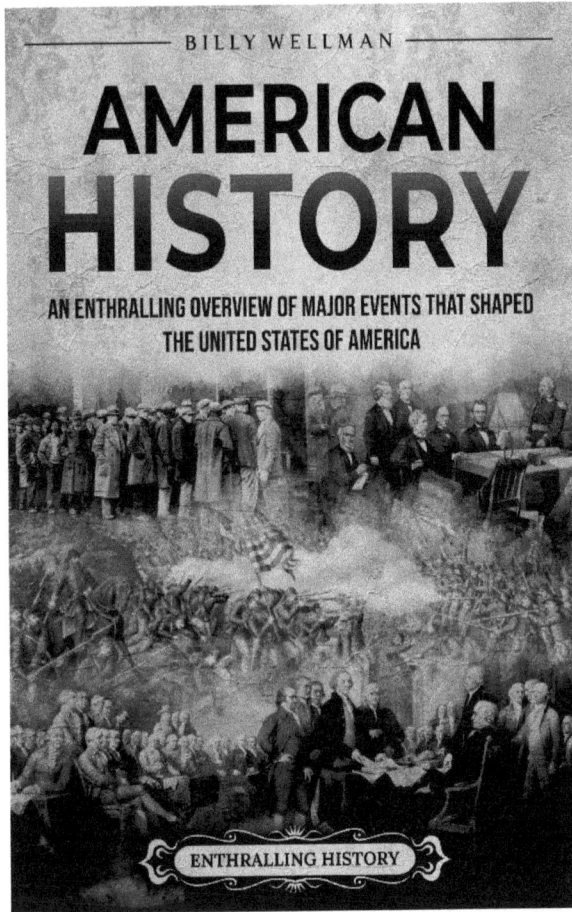

Introduction

The United States is, without a doubt, one of the world's superpowers. It has played a significant role in international politics and has been an example that other nations have looked up to for many years.

It's almost impossible to imagine that, once upon a time, America was nothing but a handful of colonies settled by people trying to carve out a life from nothing in the unfamiliar lands of North America. This powerful nation was colonized by Europeans and has a long, complicated, rich, and often bloody history dating back centuries.

So, how did America *become* America? How did it gain such power? And how did it become a leader in the global world? This book answers all those questions and more.

For those looking for a basic introduction to American history, from its earliest colonial roots to the present day, this guide is the perfect start. This book provides a comprehensive and simple overview of some of the most critical moments and events in American history and talks about how it developed from a colony into one of the biggest and most powerful nations in the world. This topic is massive, so this will not be an all-encompassing, in-depth book on the full history of the United States. Instead, we will be giving the broad strokes, leaving you with a better understanding of how the nation evolved over time.

Turn the page to learn about America, and discover for yourself which part of American history fascinates you the most.

SECTION ONE:
North America Colonization
(1492–1776)

Chapter 1: Exploration and First Settlements

Christopher Columbus

The man commonly associated and credited with "discovering" America is Christopher Columbus. Today, the United States continues to celebrate the famous explorer with a federal holiday held on the second Monday in October. The date is meant to celebrate the moment Columbus arrived in the Americas in 1492.

However, as we all know, Columbus did not discover a brand-new country or continent. In fact, the Americas had already been inhabited by Native Americans for hundreds of years. They were descendants of hunter-gatherers who made their way to the continent tens of thousands of years ago.

Christopher Columbus likely would have been surprised to discover that he wasn't even the first European to land in the Americas. One thousand years before his arrival, Vikings had made their way to what is present-day Canada.

But in 1492, when Columbus excitedly set foot on American soil, neither he nor the people back in Europe knew this. His discovery opened the door for Europeans to begin migrating en masse to this new land.

When Columbus set sail from Spain, his goal was to find a shortcut to the East Indies. King Ferdinand and Queen Isabella of Spain agreed to fund his voyage, and in 1492, he set off with dreams of finding the perfect spice route.

Christopher Columbus.

He ended up in The Bahamas instead, although he believed he had found India. Columbus continued his explorations and found Cuba and eventually Hispaniola. When Columbus and his men encountered natives, it created friction and problems. Columbus's arrival would be the start of the ongoing conflict between settlers and the Native Americans. The Europeans also brought a host of diseases and illnesses with them, such as smallpox, influenza, and typhus, just to name a few. These diseases had a devastating impact on the indigenous population, as they easily succumbed to these diseases since they had no built-up immunity.

Between 1492 and 1504, Columbus made four trips to the Americas. Each voyage resulted in new discoveries. And each discovery inevitably led to more violence and bloodshed.

The arrival of the explorers was the beginning of the end of life as the Native Americans knew it. Subjected to foreign diseases and unimaginable brutality and violence at the hands of the colonists, they were treated as less than human. Before the colonists arrived in North America, Native Americans already had a way of living. They had communities with diverse cultures and ethnicities.

When the Europeans first landed in what would become the United States, their survival in the harsh, unfamiliar terrain depended largely on the generosity and help of the Native Americans. However, that generosity was often not reciprocated, and as colonists became more familiar with and settled in their new land, they turned on the very people who had helped them. Native Americans were pushed out of their land, often through force and violence. Both Native Americans and settlers committed terrible atrocities during this tense period of history.

Spanish Expeditions

As news of Columbus's discoveries spread across Europe, a series of expeditions quickly began, with kingdoms clamoring to expand their domains.

Several years after Columbus's death, King Ferdinand asked Juan Ponce de León to search for more land. He eventually discovered modern-day Florida and a passage through the Florida Keys to the Gulf of Mexico.

Explorers continued to travel to the New World as the years passed. They mainly focused on exploring Central and South America and the Caribbean. But the 16th century also saw an influx of Spanish explorers conquering parts of North America and establishing settlements on the land.

One of the better-known explorers was Francisco Vázquez de Coronado. Coronado was the governor of Nueva Galicia, a province in New Spain (present-day Mexico). He was also a conquistador. Coronado had heard stories of the Seven Golden Cities in the southwestern US and was determined to find them.

He put together an expedition, in which he invested heavily with his own money, and set off in 1540, traveling up the western coast of Mexico. He and his men ended up in the southwestern US. For the next two years, he explored the land between Mexico and Kansas. Although Coronado was the first to find Kansas, he was not the first Spaniard to venture deep into the US, as Hernando de Soto traveled as far as Arkansas, becoming the first documented European to cross the Mississippi River.

Coronado never found the treasure he was seeking, though his expedition did lead to the discoveries of the Colorado River and the Grand Canyon. However, for all intents and purposes, his expedition had been a failure. When he returned to New Spain, charges were brought against him for his conduct on the expedition against the Native Americans. He was eventually cleared of the charges and resumed his position as governor. He stayed in Mexico City until his death in 1554.

In time, other European countries began to also look toward North America.

Jacques Cartier

When Jacques Cartier, the famous French explorer, set out from France, it was hoped that he would have great success in discovering what Columbus had set out to do all those years ago. King Francis I of France wanted Cartier to find the elusive Northwest Passage: the westward route that would lead directly to Asia.

In April 1534, Cartier set out with a crew of sixty-one men and two ships, intent on discovering the Northwest Passage. Instead of a route to Asia, he stumbled upon North America and explored the coast of the St Lawrence River. He ended up discovering the Gulf of St. Lawrence, the west coast of Newfoundland, and Prince Edward Island.

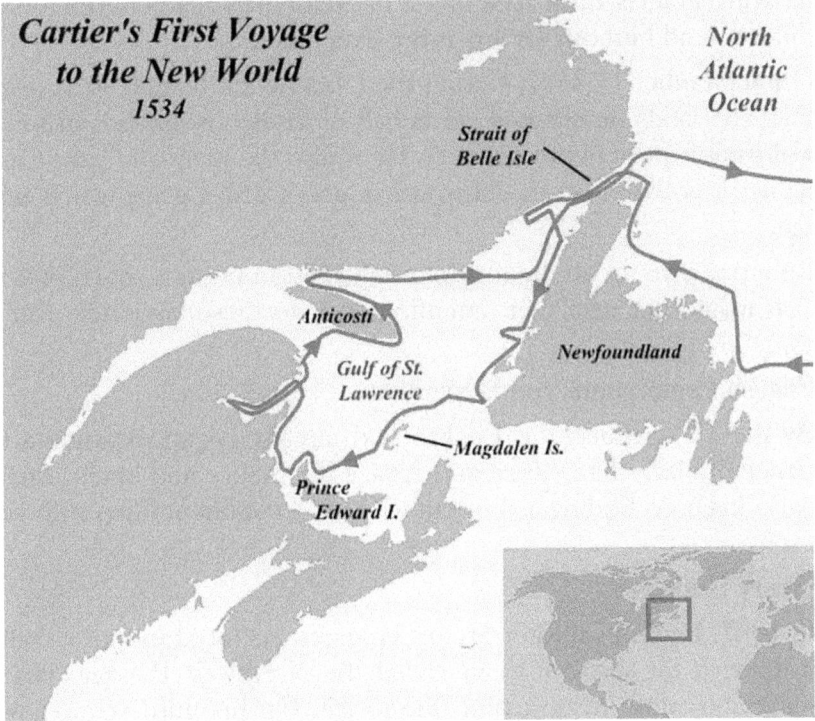

Cartier's first voyage.

When Cartier returned to France after the first expedition, he brought two Native Americans with him that he had captured. For Cartier's next expedition, King Francis I gave him 110 crew members and an additional ship. When they reached North America, Cartier used the captive Native Americans as guides to further explore the St. Lawrence River. The explorations led them to Quebec, where a base camp was established.

Tensions started to rise with the Iroquois. On top of this, many of Cartier's crew became sick. When spring came, Cartier once again returned to France. This time, he went back with Iroquois chiefs who had been taken by force.

Cartier's final expedition took place in 1541. King Francis asked Jean-François de Roberval to lead the charge this time. He was tasked with building a permanent colony in the lands discovered by Cartier.

Cartier left a few months before Roberval. While in Quebec, he found what he believed were precious gems and gold. He immediately headed back to France, only to discover that his treasure was not treasure at all. King Francis must have been displeased by his behavior because he did not send him out for any more expeditions.

On September 1ˢᵗ, 1557, Cartier died, but he left behind an enormous legacy. The lands he claimed on behalf of France would go on to form part of what is present-day Canada. He is also the man who gave Canada its name; it is based on the Huron-Iroquois word *kanata*, which means village.

Roberval gave up on the idea of establishing a permanent colony. The French would not turn their attention back to these lands for over fifty years.

English Explorations and Settlements

By the 16ᵗʰ century, the English had already begun expanding their influence in places like Africa and Asia. Like France and Spain, England was also keen on finding a shortcut to Asia, a continent filled with riches and spices.

Henry Hudson

In 1607, English explorer Henry Hudson was hired to find a route to Asia through the Arctic Ocean called the Northwest Passage. His first two attempts were unsuccessful due to ice. On his third voyage, which took place in 1609 and was sponsored by the Dutch, he chose to go a different route.

He ended up on the Atlantic coast and sailed on a river initially called the North River. This would later become known as the Hudson River. On September 11th, his ship sailed into Upper New York Bay. By the end of September, he decided to return to Europe. His mission to find the Northwest Passage had been unsuccessful.

He regrouped and attempted another voyage the following year. The voyage would be his last one, but it would also be one of his most memorable. On August 2nd, he and his men sailed into Hudson Bay. They believed they had found the Pacific Ocean at last, but Hudson eventually realized he had not found the Northwest Passage after all. The winter months were harsh, and the expedition was unsuccessful.

When Hudson and his crew eventually headed back to England, tensions continued to mount until the crew turned on Hudson and his son. They, along with some other men suffering from scurvy, were set adrift in the Hudson Bay on a lifeboat with scant supplies.

The world never heard from them again.

Hudson's voyages provided the foundation needed to establish Dutch colonies along the Hudson River Valley. He also opened the door for the English to claim land in Canada. Like Jacques Cartier, he left behind an enduring legacy.

Other Explorers

Once the door was opened to the New World, many explorers, like John Cabot, Sir Walter Raleigh, Martin Frobisher, and John Davis, began to embark on expeditions of their own.

John Cabot was one of the earliest explorers, setting sail not long after Columbus. Although he was Italian (his real name was Giovanni Caboto), he moved to England sometime in his late thirties and carried out explorations commissioned by King Henry VII. He felt certain there was a better way of reaching Asia.

Cabot arrived in North America. Historians believe he landed in the Newfoundland or Cape Breton area. After exploring the area, he claimed the land for the English and returned to England, excited at his discovery.

His second voyage ended in catastrophe when the ships were caught in a storm. Cabot's exact fate remains unknown, but it's believed he likely died at sea.

Sir Walter Raleigh was a later English explorer. He set out on his expedition in 1587 (almost one hundred years after Cabot had set sail). Raleigh explored the territory from Florida to North Carolina, naming it Virginia after the Virgin Queen, Elizabeth I. He also set out to find the legendary El Dorado but instead discovered tobacco and potatoes. Raleigh introduced these two products to Britain.

Although Raleigh led an impressive life filled with adventure, he was eventually charged with treason by King James I and beheaded.

Each expedition led to the discovery of another part of North America, eventually shaping it into the continent we know today.

Roanoke – The "Lost Colony"

The earliest attempt at establishing a proper and permanent colony in North America was known as Roanoke Colony. Situated off the coast of present-day North Carolina, this English colony was founded in 1585 by Raleigh. The colony was a failure, but Raleigh attempted the endeavor again a few years later, in 1587.

A small group of 115 settlers arrived on the island, intent on creating a permanent English outpost. However, they faced many hardships. Namely, they didn't have enough supplies, they had poor harvests, and they had a difficult time adjusting to the land.

John White, who was made governor of the colony, returned to England the same year to stock up on supplies. He left his wife, daughter, and granddaughter (the first English child born in the New World) behind on the island.

When White arrived in England, the country was engaged in a naval war with Spain. Queen Elizabeth I stated the priority was for all ships to fight against the Spanish Armada. White wouldn't be able to return to Roanoke until August 1590. When he did, he found that all traces of the colony had vanished. One lone clue was left behind carved into a post: the word "Croatoan."

To this day, nobody knows what happened to the colony or its inhabitants. Some speculate that they were killed by a tribe of Native Americans from an island called Croatoan, while others believe that when John didn't return, they tried to sail back to England and were lost at sea. It is also possible they went to Croatoan Island. However, nobody knows for sure what happened to the "Lost Colony."

Chapter 2: The Thirteen Colonies

What we know as the present-day United States, a massive country boasting fifty states, initially started off as thirteen British colonies grouped together to form British America.

In the early 17th century, the colonies began to be established by Queen Elizabeth, who was keen on growing the British Empire and who wanted to keep pace with Spain.

Some of these colonies had already been around since the early 17th century. Each had a specific history of its own and was founded for a wide range of reasons, such as overpopulation in Europe, more religious freedom, and business ventures.

During the 17th century, most European countries were competing with one another for power and wealth. Wealth was associated with trade, resulting in trading companies running a mad race to get colonies. The hope was that colonies in America would allow England to establish trading ports along the coast, which would lead to jobs and money. Colonists also hoped they would find precious minerals, such as gold.

Pilgrims and Puritans also sought to settle in the New World. About one hundred people sailed on the *Mayflower* to find a new life. Many of those on board were Pilgrims who wanted to escape religious persecution in England and separate from the Church of England.

This group eventually arrived in Plymouth, Massachusetts, in 1620. The people set up trading posts in Maine and Cape Cod and received the freedom to worship as they wished. Like the other colonists, they also ran into difficulties with the Native Americans. However, they maintained a better relationship with them than other colonists.

A decade later, Puritans, who were non-separatists but still wished to change the practices of the Church of England, also migrated to the New World. They established the Massachusetts Bay Colony. The Puritans were pious people looking for economic benefits in a new land. They were also very literate and were known for writing sermons and poetry.

The Puritans founded Harvard in 1636. The university was initially established as a Congregationalist institution designed to train ministers. Over the centuries, it evolved to become what it is today, one of the most well-known and respected universities in the world.

The Puritans also founded a printing press and emphasized the importance of education. Their beliefs and influence eventually led to the American school system.

Overview of the Colonies

Many of the Thirteen Colonies were named after British royals or notable figures (for instance, Pennsylvania was named after William Penn's father) and are typically divided into three regions:

- The Middle Colonies
    - Delaware
    - New York (this colony was originally part of a Dutch colony and was called New Netherland)
    - New Jersey
    - Pennsylvania
- The Southern Colonies
    - Maryland
    - Georgia (named after King George II)
    - North Carolina
    - South Carolina (both are named after King Charles I)
    - Virginia (named after the Virgin Queen, Elizabeth I)
- The New England Colonies.
    - Massachusetts Bay
    - Connecticut
    - New Hampshire
    - Rhode Island

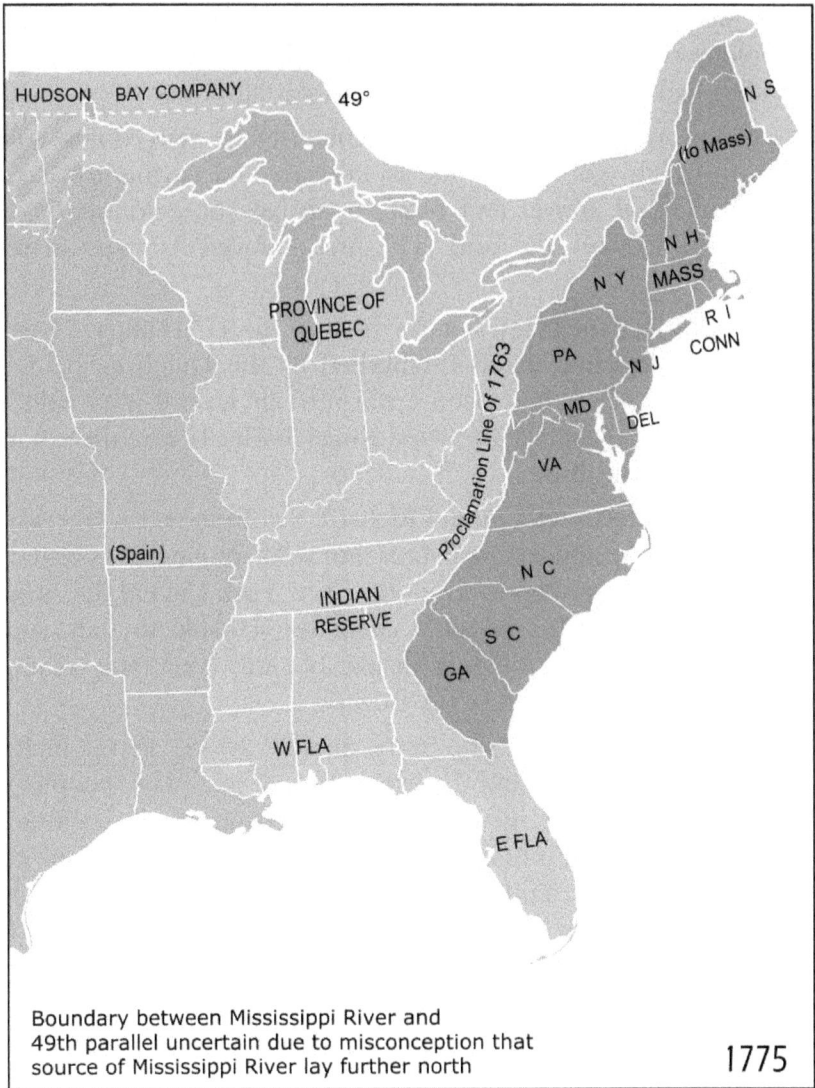

The Thirteen Colonies in 1775. The colonies fluctuated over the years, though; their borders
weren't always so well established.

Life in the colonies was extremely difficult, and conditions were often
very harsh and primitive, especially during the winter months. Things got
better as time passed, but Jamestown, the first permanent English
settlement in North America (and the first permanent settlement in what
would become the United States), was established in what would become
Virginia in 1607. The colony had a very rough start. The winter of

1609/10 was called the Starving Time. There were five hundred people in the colony at the start of winter; by the end, there were only sixty-one. The settlers had to resort to cannibalism to stay alive.

It took nearly a decade for the colonists to start doing well in Jamestown, which was mostly due to growing and trading tobacco. As tobacco plantations spread and began to thrive, the colonists began to bring in slaves to work the land. The first enslaved Africans arrived in 1619.

New York was a melting pot as far back as the 17th century. Originally called New Netherland, it was established by the Dutch in 1614. The Dutch and the English had been embroiled in several wars with each other and were enjoying a truce when King Charles II gave the colony to the duke of York, his brother.

The duke of York sent Colonel Richard Nicolls to go to America and seize the colony. Armed with warships and soldiers, he did as asked and sailed into New Amsterdam (present-day New York City) in the spring of 1664 and demanded the colony's surrender. Unable to rally support from the people because of their dislike of him, Peter Stuyvesant, the Dutch governor, surrendered to the English.

Most of the population who were already settled there, including Germans, Scandinavians, and Belgians, stayed put. The people were quickly absorbed by the English, and the name of the colony was changed to New York. From its very inception, New York was one of the most diverse colonies, eventually becoming one of the most multicultural cities in the world.

The colonies in North America remained a part of the British Empire for almost 170 years. Eventually, though, the Founding Fathers broke away from the British Empire. The Thirteen Colonies became a new nation called the United States of America.

Chapter 3: The French and Indian War

French and Indian War (1754-1763)

The continued struggle and tension between France and Great Britain eventually escalated into another war in 1754. The French and Indian War is viewed as the North American theater of the Seven Years' War, which began later in 1756.

What caused the war? When France expanded its territory into the Ohio River Valley in North America during the early 1750s, it conflicted with some of the territory claimed by the British. There were also disputes over waterways, trading, and religious differences. In 1754, the royal governor in Virginia sent a group of men from the Virginia Regiment to secure the Forks of Ohio.

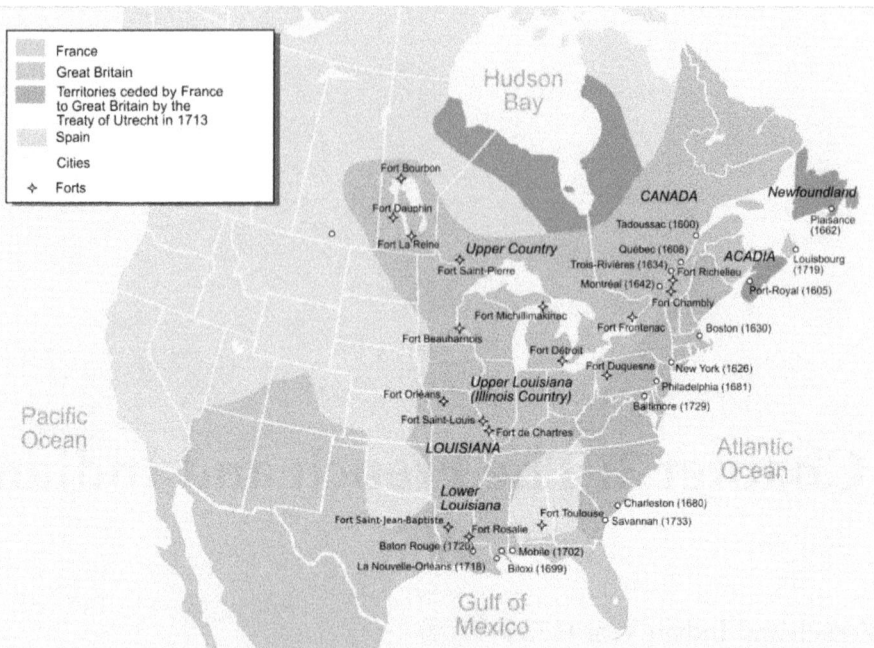

European colonies in North America in 1750.

When the Virginians arrived, they discovered the French had already started to build Fort Duquesne in what is present-day Pittsburgh, Pennsylvania. Twenty-one-year-old George Washington headed the Virginian expedition to the area; he decided to go on the offensive. Things escalated from there, leading to the Battle of Jumonville Glen.

Also known as the Jumonville affair, this battle was the official start of the French and Indian War. It was also significant in that this was Washington's first armed conflict.

Before the battle broke out, Washington had arrived at Great Meadows in May; it was roughly seven miles (eleven kilometers) away from where the French set up camp. Fearful of an imminent attack, Washington struck the first blow by leading a group of soldiers to the hiding spot of the French.

The French, who were led by Joseph Coulon de Villiers de Jumonville, were decimated. However, it turns out the French were not seeking military action; rather, they were carrying a message to Washington to evacuate the area.

Jumonville was killed, as were most of his men. It's unclear what exactly happened in the battle. According to most accounts, the Native Americans aiding Washington killed and scalped Jumonville. This unexpected attack opened the floodgates for other natives to do the same, and in short order, nine French soldiers were scalped before Washington could do anything.

One soldier managed to escape, and he recounted what happened when he returned to the fort. The incensed French declared Washington to be a war criminal, leading to the Battle of Fort Necessity. That particular battle ended with Washington surrendering; it was the one and only time he would do so in his career.

Role of the Native Americans in the War

Many Native American tribes got involved in the war, but they didn't all pick the same side. The Shawnee, Seneca, Kickapoo, Sandusky, and Wea tribes allied with the French. On the British-American side were the Mohawk, Montauk, Cherokee, Cayuga, Seneca, Chickasaw, Creek, Onondaga, and Tuscarora.

The Native Americans who allied with the French did so because they were getting tired of how much control Britain was exerting on their lands and how much the colonists had already taken from them. They were increasingly being pushed out, and they hoped that if the French defeated the British, this would stop.

The Native American tribes that sided with Britain did so for much the same reason. They hoped that by giving the British support, they would be able to stop the colonists from further encroaching on their lands. The priority for the natives was to keep their tribal lands safe and in their hands.

Two years after the French and Indian War began, war erupted in Europe between France and England, triggering the beginning of the Seven Years' War.

The French were woefully outnumbered by the British, who had over two million settlers in the colonies at the start of the war. The French only had around 60,000 settlers. This made the French particularly dependent on the natives who joined forces with them.

While many in Europe saw America as another theater of the conflict, for the North American settlers, it became their own war that had nothing to do with Europe.

The war in Europe dragged on for seven years. The French and Indian War and the Seven Years' War formally came to an end after the Treaty of Paris was signed in February 1763. Under the treaty, a number of trades took place. France gave Britain its territories east of the Mississippi River. Spain handed over Florida to the British. France was allowed to keep some Canadian islands, while Spain took Louisiana from them.

Even after the war finally ended, territorial disputes continued, especially among the Native Americans, who wanted to get some of their lands back.

Impact of the War on the Colonies

The French and Indian War would become one of the catalysts for the American Revolution. The American colonists were unhappy that they were being made to shoulder the costs of the war, especially when they had no real representation in British Parliament. This created a deep divide between the colonies and the empire of Great Britain. However, the war had also drained Britain of money and resources, which it hoped to recoup from the colonies.

Immediately after the war, there was a sense of unity, purpose, and a feeling of victory amongst the colonists. They had fought in a significant war and came out as victors. However, the sense of euphoria was short-lived, as Britain began to pressure them. The colonists were suddenly feeling resentful and questioning what purpose they served and why they were doing what they were doing.

These feelings of discontent would eventually boil over into a revolution.

Chapter 4: Causes for Revolution

The American Revolution did not happen overnight.

Tensions between the Thirteen Colonies and the British Empire simmered for many years before violent conflicts broke out. Life in the colonies was far from ideal and could often be harsh and difficult. But the colonists had made things work. They prospered, and as time passed and due to certain factors, they simply had enough of the British.

Although the French and Indian War did not directly cause the American Revolutionary War, the consequences of the war triggered a chain of events culminating in the eruption of the revolution. The global conflict had ended in a victory for Britain. The British secured their authority along the Atlantic coast and brought new territories under the Crown's control. However, it would come at a high cost, as it would be the beginning of the end of Britain's control over the region.

In order to recoup the expenses incurred during the war and the many other wars fought in Europe, the Crown decided to impose taxes on the colonies. Less than two years after the war ended, the Crown passed the Stamp Act. The colonists now had to pay taxes on stamped papers, which included legal documents, newspapers, and even playing cards! The colonists fought back against the act, and it was repealed in 1766. However, it wouldn't be the last act to be implemented.

And each new thing served to increase the continuing tensions between the Crown and the colonies, coming to a head in 1776.

A few of the most significant events and causes of the revolution are as follows:

- Colonies were opposed to the British trying to exert control over them. Felt that they were infringing on their rights and freedom.
- Didn't like the taxes that Britain imposed on them in order to pay for their defense during the French and Indian War

Taxes were raised steadily through a series of acts over a period of eight years. Stamp Act of 1765, the Townshend Acts of 1767, and the Tea Act of 1773.

The colonists were fiercely opposed to these rising taxes, especially since they had no representation in British Parliament. The colonists were opposed to the British trying to exert more control over them, as they had enjoyed a lot of freedom and rights beforehand. They also resented the British in the motherland, as they tried to make the colonists pay for the French and Indian War when the colonists had been the ones fighting on the front lines.

The Boston Massacre

Tensions continued to rise, and in 1770, the resistance from the colonists spilled into violence. A small group of British soldiers was protecting the customs house. The colonists came to taunt them, but things escalated, with rocks being thrown at the soldiers. A soldier fired, and some of the other soldiers followed, even though no direct order had been given. Five men ultimately died. This event would become known as the Boston Massacre. The poor relationship between the Crown and the colonies was now on display.

As the relationship between Britain and its colonies continued to deteriorate, Americans felt increasingly frustrated. When the Tea Act of 1773 was passed, the Bostonians were fed up enough to find a way to make their frustrations known.

On December 16th, 1773, at Griffin's Wharf, Bostonians seized 342 chests of tea that had just arrived from the British East India Company and poured it into the Boston Harbor (in today's money, that equates to almost two million dollars). The Boston Tea Party, as it would become known, led to Parliament passing additional laws in the colonies called the Coercive Acts or Intolerable Acts, which were passed in 1774.

Boston Tea Party.

The Boston Tea Party led British Parliament to pass four new acts called the Coercive Acts (they were dubbed the Intolerable Acts in the colonies). They were as follows:

- The Boston Port Act – This act was passed in March 1774 and allowed the British Royal Navy to blockade and cut off commercial traffic from Boston Harbor. Under the act, imports and exports from international ports were forbidden. The only provisions allowed to come through were those used by the British Army and necessities. The blockade would be lifted once Boston paid restitution to the British East India Company for the destroyed tea.

- The Massachusetts Government Act – Under this act, which was passed in May 1774, the Massachusetts government was restructured with people appointed by the British Empire. These people were given more power and authority. It effectively took away the democratic rights of colonists and ensured they had very little say in political matters by not allowing them to vote officials into office. Town meetings also became restricted to just once a year.

- The Administration of Justice Act – This act is also known as the Murder Act and was passed on the same day as the Massachusetts Government Act. The act gave the governor more power to intervene when a British officer was charged with a capital offense. It allowed for the trial to either be moved to another colony or to England so that the offender could have a "fair trial." However, the colonists interpreted this as a way for British officers to get away with crimes, including murder.
- The Quartering Act – This was the final Intolerable Act and was passed in June 1774. Under this act, high-ranking army officers were allowed to demand better quarters for their troops. It also allowed them to refuse accommodations they deemed inconvenient or unacceptable. To add insult to injury, colonists would have to pay for this housing.

The Coercive Acts were implemented to regain control and authority over the unruly colonies. The British sought to punish the rebellious Bostonians and bring the other colonies into line. But the acts did not help. The colonists pushed back and decided to address their concerns head-on with the Crown. They created a delegation to discuss what to do next. In September 1774, the First Continental Congress, made up of George Washington, Patrick Henry, John Jay, John Adams, and Samuel Adams, among many others, met in Philadelphia.

Their demands were simple: they still wanted fair representation (a popular cry was "No taxation without representation") and sought to boycott British goods, hitting the British in their pocketbooks. They wanted the British to ask for their consent, so they sent a letter to British Parliament, asking to rescind the acts.

Before adjourning, the men planned to meet again in May 1775. But by this time, the conflict had turned violent. Only a month before, the Battles of Lexington and Concord had taken place, kicking off the American Revolution.

The biggest causes of strife for the colonists were the lack of representation in the British government and the heavy taxes. The list of grievances was long, but they were angry because their needs and wants were not addressed or represented by the government in Great Britain. They had to pay taxes to a government that did not seem to care about or have any interest in representing them. Britain didn't allow the colonists to trade with other countries. The colonists were completely reliant on the Crown for all their imports. Colonists were also forbidden from expanding beyond the Mississippi River.

With such a long list of complaints, the possibility of armed conflict was high. And eventually, the colonists and British had had enough of the petty bickering and set out to solve the problem through war.

SECTION TWO:
The United States Are Born
(1776–1861)

Chapter 5: The American Revolution

As tensions between Great Britain and the colonies in North America continued to escalate, minor skirmishes and conflicts began to take place, eventually setting off the American Revolutionary War.

Battles of Lexington and Concord

The Battles of Lexington and Concord in Massachusetts, where the first shots were fired, would officially mark the beginning of the American Revolution on April 19th, 1775.

Tensions between the colonists and the British Empire had been simmering for many years and were further heightened following the end of the Seven Years' War. Relations reached a breaking point after the British set out a series of acts and British Parliament declared that Massachusetts was openly rebelling against it.

The stage was set for war to break out at any moment. That moment came on April 18th, 1775, when a doctor named Joseph Warren, who was also a member of the Sons of Liberty, found out that Redcoat troops would be marching into Concord that very night. He sent two men, Paul Revere and William Dawes, to let the residents know.

Revere went to Charlestown, a neighborhood in Boston where Patriots were on the lookout for British troops. Two lanterns were hung in the North Church, located in Boston, to signal that the British were coming by sea.

Meanwhile, Dawes went on a separate route to Lexington, which was located a few miles away from Concord. Revere also traveled to Lexington, beating Dawes there since he was closer. The two were joined by Samuel Prescott, a doctor.

They were successful in warning people, but the British authorities were also alerted. Revere was caught. Dawes and Prescott escaped, but only Prescott finished the ride.

The following day, on April 19th, around seven hundred British soldiers arrived in Lexington to find a Patriot arsenal. Seventy-seven militiamen were waiting to stop the British. The militiamen were in the process of retreating when someone fired a shot, leading to additional shots being fired. When the shooting ended, eight militiamen had been killed, and an additional nine were injured. Only one Redcoat was wounded.

The British continued their march into Concord to seize arms and weapons but were surprised to discover the majority of the weapons had already been dispatched elsewhere. Furious, they burned down what they could get their hands on.

Fearing the whole town would be burned, the militiamen advanced on Concord's North Bridge, where a group of British soldiers was defending it. The British fired, and the militiamen fired in return.

Soon, nearly two thousand militiamen had arrived in the area, ready for a battle. They fought hard and with determination, and the British eventually retreated. At Lexington, a fresh group of Redcoats had arrived to support their troops, but the colonists kept their attacks going. Further reinforcements arrived for the militiamen later that evening.

Even though the colonists fought in a disorganized manner and shot out at random, often missing their mark, it was nonetheless a dizzying victory. They had managed to fight back against the powerful British Army. The American Revolution had officially started.

When the Second Continental Congress met again as planned a month later, the delegation had two notable new members: Thomas Jefferson and Benjamin Franklin.

The First Continental Congress hadn't planned to create a revolution when they decided to meet again in a year, but things had changed. The Second Continental Congress agreed to create a Continental Army, which would be headed by George Washington.

British Allies

Britain tried to form alliances with the slaves in the colonies. Between 1700 and 1775, the population in the colonies had grown from 250,000 people to 2.5 million people. A quarter of this population (one in four people) were slaves. In November 1775, Lord Dunmore, the governor of Virginia, proclaimed that slaves of the rebelling colonists who fought alongside the British would be granted their freedom. The idea of freedom was too good to pass up. Throughout the course of the American Revolution, tens of thousands of Africans fought on the British side. Around five thousand fought on the colonists' side.

Many Native American tribes tried to remain neutral at first, but the majority of the tribes eventually sided with the British, especially when they came under constant attack from the American militia. They were promised great things in return for the services, things that never came to fruition.

Colonial Allies

Surprisingly, the colonists had a lot of allies. The French, the Spanish, and the Dutch eventually helped them fight against the British. Well-known historical figures, such as the Prussian officer Frederick William, the Polish soldier Kazimierz Pulaski, and other notable men helped with the American Revolution.

Perhaps the most well-known personage was Marquis de Lafayette, a French aristocrat who fought with the colonists during the American Revolution. He later played a crucial role in the French Revolution and the July Revolution of 1830.

Born into a noble family, Lafayette became a courtier at King Louis XVI's court, but what he really yearned to be was a soldier. So, he traveled to the colonies on his own at the age of nineteen and became a major general in the Continental Army.

He had no military or battle experience, so Washington took him under his wings, and the two became close friends. Under the guidance of Washington, Lafayette quickly emerged as a man with great skill. He also had great connections to the French court.

Lafayette was eventually given his own division and served the Continental Army well. In 1779, he returned to France and convinced the king to send more supplies, resources, and troops to the colonies to help the Americans, which he did. Lafayette returned to the US in 1780.

Upon Lafayette's return to France in 1782, he was made a brigadier general, and his exemplary performance earned him an honorary citizenship to the US.

George Washington

https://en.wikipedia.org/wiki/File:Gilbert_Stuart_Williamstown_Portrait_of_George_Washington.jpg

The fall and winter of 1775 were tough for Washington's forces, but the capture of Fort Ticonderoga helped to shift the tide in their favor, with British soldiers leaving the city and finding shelter in Canada.

The American Revolution went on for eight years and is peppered with dozens of battles and conflicts, big and small. We don't have the space to look at them all, so we will look at some of the most decisive battles that influenced the war.

The Capture of Fort Ticonderoga – May 10th, 1775

Fort Ticonderoga was located in Lake Champlain in New York, which was an ideal location. It had access to the Hudson River Valley and to Canada, making it a desirable target.

Early in the morning of May 10th, 1775, the British fort was attacked. The surprise offensive was carried out by General Benedict Arnold, who had joined forces with Ethan Allen and the Green Mountain Boys of Vermont.

The attack shook the completely unprepared British soldiers, as it was the first American offensive of the war. Even though it did not escalate into a large-scale conflict, it was a significant victory for the Americans. They captured the fort and took all of the British weapons and artillery.

This was a great moment for General Benedict Arnold and Ethan Allen, both of whom viewed themselves as the hero in the early days of the war. Arnold would go on to betray the Patriots. He defected to the British in 1780 and was planning to give up the US post at West Point to them, but the plot was discovered in time. Allen was captured by the British in 1775 after failing to take Montreal; he was released around three years later.

Benedict Arnold.
https://commons.wikimedia.org/wiki/File:Benedict_Arnold_1color.jpg

Battle of Bunker Hill – June 17th, 1775

Breed's Hill, less than a mile away from Bunker Hill, located in Massachusetts, was the setting of the first real battle of the war. Even though it did not end in a victory for the colonial soldiers, it helped to boost the morale of the Continental Army.

The majority of the colonists had no experience with war and were pitted against experienced British soldiers, yet they managed to hold them off for several hours. The colonists were eventually pushed back by the British, but not before they managed to wound or kill nearly half of the 2,200 soldiers, making it one of the bloodiest battles of the war. Compared to the one thousand Redcoat casualties, only around four hundred Patriots were wounded or killed.

The Battle of Bunker Hill showed the colonists that they could rise to the challenge and do what they needed to do for their country. The British realized the fight wouldn't be as easy as they had initially thought and took less aggressive measures to conserve manpower.

Battle of Fort Washington – November 1776

The Battle of Fort Washington resulted in one of the Patriots' worst defeats during the war. While General George Washington led the Continental Army, Robert Magaw was the man on the battlefield, while General William Howe led the British and Hessian troops. The Americans suffered approximately three thousand casualties (most of whom were captured) and also lost critical supplies and weapons.

Faced with utter defeat, the Continental Army retreated into Delaware, and Howe moved into Fort Washington.

Battles of Trenton and Princeton – December 1776-January 1777

During the American Revolution, Washington won two crucial battles for America within ten days of crossing the Delaware on December 25th, 1776.

One was the Battle of Trenton, which took place on December 26th, 1776. Washington and his troops easily defeated a group of Hessian mercenaries, who were tired and entirely unprepared for Washington's calculated attack. They surrendered quickly with minimal bloodshed. Out of the 1,400 soldiers who made up the Hessian force, only 22 died. Another ninety-two were wounded. On the American side, two soldiers froze to death, and five others were wounded.

Washington realized his men wouldn't be able to hold Trenton against the British Army, so they withdrew into Delaware to bide their time.

On December 30th, Washington crossed the Delaware again and found his army was grossly outnumbered by the British soldiers. Washington managed to raise his number of troops to five thousand and waited at Trenton for the British.

Around 5,500 British soldiers arrived, led by General Charles Cornwallis. The two sides engaged in a series of skirmishes before Cornwallis pulled back for the day, thinking that victory was nearly his.

But Washington wasn't ready to give up. He left behind five hundred troops at the campsite while the rest of the army marched through the night to Princeton, which was located twelve miles away. They walked in the dark without torches and wrapped cloth around the wagon wheels to muffle the noise. Imagine Cornwallis's surprise when he woke up the next morning and discovered their disappearance!

Washington arrived at Princeton, and his troops easily broke through the British defense and won the Battle of Princeton. They continued their march until they arrived at Morristown, where they set up quarters for the winter, away from the British.

These two battles were huge victories for Washington. He had managed to unite soldiers from the different colonies to fight as one, and they had been able to defeat their common enemy as a united force.

Battles of Saratoga – September 19th and October 7th, 1777

Two battles were fought in Saratoga County, New York. During the first battle, the British forces, under General John Burgoyne, emerged victorious. However, the victory cost them dearly. When the British attacked the colonists at Bemis Heights, they were soundly defeated by the Americans and forced to turn back.

This would become the turning point in the revolution. Since 1776, France had been secretly helping the rebel forces fight against the British, with aristocrats like Lafayette supporting their cause. After the victory at Saratoga, France came out from the shadows and publicly pledged its support for the Americans. However, it would be another two years before France formally declared war on Britain.

Soon after these two battles, the British began focusing on the south, as they believed there were more Loyalists there. By late 1778, British troops had taken Savannah, Georgia. In 1780, they took Charleston.

Battle of Yorktown – September 28th–October 19th, 1781

A group of American and French forces cornered the British army in Yorktown. The forces couldn't leave, nor could they receive any additional help because the British fleet had been driven off by the French.

General Charles Cornwallis had no other choice but to surrender. The war was essentially over, even though Charleston and New York City stayed under British control for another few years. Toward the end of 1783, the last of the British soldiers finally left, officially marking the end of the war.

Peace treaties were drafted in Paris in November 1782. The Treaty of Paris was signed on September 3rd, 1783. Britain ceded all control of the colonies and fully recognized them as an independent nation. Under the treaty, Canada remained a British province, which created the northern border of the United States.

However, not all colonists living in America were opposed to the British; they were called Loyalists. The Loyalists mostly stayed out of the war, but once the war officially ended, approximately 100,000 Loyalists left America and either went to Britain or settled in other British colonies, such as Canada.

Post-Revolution Territorial Changes

Founding Fathers

The Revolutionary War ended as a success story for the United States due to the collective efforts of all the colonies and outside nations. However, there were a number of men, known as the Founding Fathers, who are historically seen as having played a key role in securing the country's independence.

There were many men who could be considered Founding Fathers, but seven stand out the most. This is, by no means, a comprehensive list of the Founding Fathers, but it gives you a good idea of what kind of men the nation looked up to.

- George Washington: He led the Continental Army and became the first president of the United States.
- Thomas Jefferson: He was a diplomat to France, where he earned its help in the war. He drafted the Declaration of Independence and was the first secretary of the state, the second vice president, and the third president.
- John Adams: He became the second president of the US and served as vice president twice. He was a prolific writer and lawyer.

- Benjamin Franklin: He was a notable inventor, writer, printer, and intellectual. He served as a diplomat to France and Sweden and was the first postmaster general.
- Alexander Hamilton: Best remembered for his infamous duel with Aaron Burr, Hamilton was the first secretary of the treasury. He promoted the idea of a central bank and was a prolific writer, crafting almost all of *The Federalist Papers*, which were essays to garner support for the US Constitution.
- John Jay: He was the first chief justice. He helped create the Constitution and wrote some articles for *The Federalist Papers*. He helped craft foreign policy after the war.
- James Madison: He became the fourth president of the US. He was a major contributor to the Constitution and Bill of Rights.

The Founding Fathers.

https://en.wikipedia.org/wiki/File:Declaration_of_Independence_(1819),_by_John_Trumbull.jpg

Their writings on life and liberty, as well as their actions and thoughts, provided the foundation upon which the newly independent country was built. What is remarkable is that most of these men were all young men in their thirties and forties by the end of the war. There were a few outliers, like Washington, who was in his early fifties, and Franklin, who was in his seventies.

Their contributions were not simply idealistic. Washington led an army during the revolution, and Thomas Jefferson wrote the Declaration of Independence. John Jay was a chief justice in the Supreme Court, and Hamilton was secretary of the treasury. They didn't just put words on paper; they followed through and tried to achieve what they thought would benefit the country the most.

The Founding Fathers had an idea of what a free, independent country should be like, and they used those ideas to create the American nation. They managed to do what many European colonies dreamed of: independence from the motherland.

Unfortunately, their ideals were not always fair and placed greater emphasis on ensuring the rights and liberties of white landowning men rather than all Americans. Many of them owned slaves and placed a lesser value on their lives. They also weren't always united in their beliefs, which led to friction.

However, the legacy they left behind cannot be denied. Subsequent generations used their foundation for equality to fight for minorities and the disadvantaged. Today, for the most part, Americans enjoy the same liberties, protections, and freedoms.

Chapter 6: The Constitution and the Bill of Rights

The Constitution, written in 1787 and ratified in 1788, is perhaps the most important law in the United States. It is also the world's oldest national constitution still in use today.

James Madison is the Founding Father credited with drafting the Constitution and the Bill of Rights. However, even Madison admitted that many other people contributed to the creation of the documents.

When the Constitution was drafted, the main purpose was to give the government enough power to run the country. However, the government had limits so that it could not infringe upon the people's fundamental rights.

The federal government was separated into three different branches: legislative, executive, and judicial. Checks were put in place to ensure that the power of all three branches would stay balanced. The powers of each branch are vested by the Congress (legislative branch), the president (executive branch), and the Supreme Court and federal courts (judicial branch). A clause was also put into the Constitution so it could be amended should the need arise.

Roman Influences

Ancient Rome was one of the biggest sources of inspiration for the Founding Fathers when they were deciding on the best form of government. Rome was initially ruled by a king, but once the monarchy was abolished, the country became a republic.

The Roman Republic was a sort of golden era, especially in terms of democratic principles, as it saw Rome rise in prominence. As many of you know, Rome became a power to be reckoned with. This period of history was studied extensively in the Western world. Most educated Americans' studies included ancient Roman literature and the philosophies around liberty, power, and freedom.

Therefore, it is not surprising that the Founding Fathers had similar views on what an ideal American government would look like. Similarities were often drawn between Rome and America since both fought to become free from tyrannical rulers. As such, the political system for the new world was influenced greatly by the Roman Republic.

Constitution

The US Constitution was drafted and finalized on September 17th, 1787. It was signed by thirty-nine of the fifty-five delegates. Some refused to sign it because the Constitution did not include a Bill of Rights (this would be added later). One delegate refused to sign the document because the Constitution protected the slave trade.

The first real form of government was the Second Continental Congress. On July 4th, 1776, after a formal declaration of their independence from the Crown, it acted as an interim government. The Second Continental Congress drafted the Articles of Confederation, which outlined the functions and responsibilities of the government. This was the document that preceded the Constitution.

Once the United States was formed, George Washington soon realized that something stronger than the Articles of Confederation was needed. With his encouragement, the process of drafting a constitution was started. The new document replaced the original Articles of Confederation. The biggest difference between the two documents was the three separate branches of government.

The US Constitution.
https://en.wikipedia.org/wiki/File:Constitution_of_the_United_States,_page_1.jpg

Bill of Rights

Although the Constitution was eventually adopted, it was not a painless process. Support for the Constitution was divided between the Federalists and the anti-Federalists.

The Federalists were in support of the Constitution and pushed to have it ratified. They believed in the need for a strong union and a centralized government. The group was made up of wealthy bankers, businessmen, and other professionals.

Anti-Federalists, on the other hand, did not see a need to create a new document as they thought the Articles of Confederation was enough. They did not want a stronger central government, as they feared an overly powerful government would pose a threat to people's individual rights and liberties. This group was made up of laborers, small farmers, shopkeepers, and others who were understandably worried about not having a voice.

The pushback from the anti-Federalists eventually led to the implementation of the first ten amendments. The amendments were introduced by James Madison, and although twelve were produced, only ten were ratified. These amendments make up the Bill of Rights, and they guarantee the following rights to all American citizens:[1]

- Freedom to practice one's religion, the freedom of speech, and the freedom of the press;
- The right to bear arms;
- No quartering of soldiers;
- Freedom from unreasonable searches and seizures;
- Right to due process;
- Rights to a speedy trial if accused of a crime;
- Right to be tried by a jury;
- Freedom from any cruel or unusual punishments;
- Other rights of the people;
- Powers reserved to the states.

In short, the Bill of Rights ensures individual freedoms and liberties cannot be infringed upon by the government on a whim.

Levels of Government

Under the Constitution, the federal government was separated into three distinct branches to ensure an equal division of power and authority.

---

[1] "Bill of Rights: The Really Short Version."
https://users.csc.calpoly.edu/~jdalbey/Public/Bill_of_Rights.html.

The branches are as follows:

• Legislative (Congress)

This branch is made up of the House of Representatives, the Senate, and special agencies that help with work passed in Congress. These agencies include the Copyright Office, Government Accountability Office, and US Capitol Police, to name a few.

Congress drafts new laws and has the power to declare war. It is also responsible for confirming or rejecting nominees for federal agencies and the Supreme Court. Members of Congress hold debates and investigations to make sure the country's governing apparatus works efficiently and is free of corruption. Members of Congress are voted in by the public.

• Executive

The responsibility for carrying out and enforcing the laws lies with the executive branch. This branch is made up of three key roles, with the most famous role being that of the president.

The president is voted into office by the public, although, technically, the electoral college votes the president in. The public votes, and the party with the most votes wins that state's batch of votes for the electoral college. Different states have different numbers of electoral votes based on the number of people that state has in Congress.

It is the president's job to lead the country and government. They are supported by the vice president and the Cabinet. In the event that the president can't serve, the vice president steps into the role. Today, presidents can only serve a maximum of two terms; however, vice presidents do not have that cap. They can serve for any number of terms.

The Cabinet includes the vice president and other high-ranking public servants and heads of executive departments. Each member of the Cabinet is appointed by the president, although the Senate must approve the nomination with a vote.

The bulk of the work in this branch is carried out by government departments and public servants.

• Judicial

The third branch of the US government is responsible for interpreting and applying the country's federal laws and legislations. The courts also decide if any laws are in violation of the Constitution.

Federal courts and the Supreme Court fall under the judicial branch. According to the Constitution, Congress is the authoritative power that can establish federal courts.

Judges in the Supreme Court are appointed through a nomination from the president. The nomination must be debated and then voted on by the Senate.

As you can see, the three branches of government, while quite distinct and separate, are intertwined and work closely together. The Founding Fathers believed that dividing up power in such a way would ensure that the government would always act in the best interest of the people and society.

The First President of the United States

Once the country was created, the electoral college was faced with a daunting prospect: who was going to lead the country? Today, presidents are voted into office every four years through an election, but no such process was in place back in 1788.

The first election was an extremely simple and straightforward affair, quite unlike the current presidential elections. A few months after the Constitution was ratified on June 21st, 1788, the electoral college took a vote, and a unanimous decision was made to elect George Washington as president.

Washington was not keen to become president. In fact, after the Revolutionary War ended and the Treaty of Paris was signed, his plan was to retire from public life. But the pressures and demands of the public outweighed his own desires, and he took on the mantle. His work as the head of the Constitution committee was especially impressive, as was the way he had conducted himself in battles during the revolution. The delegates were convinced they had their first president.

John Adams, another candidate for the role of president, was elected as the first vice president. (For a time, the vice presidency was awarded to the man who had the second highest number of votes; this changed under Jefferson.) Washington and Adams formally came into office on April 30th, 1789. Because Washington, DC, did not yet exist, the inauguration took place in New York City.

George Washington's inauguration.

It was a great honor and an immense burden all at once. How was he going to lead a brand-new country that was fresh out of a war with Britain? By cutting ties with Great Britain, the United States had embarked on a journey to embrace democracy, which was a rare notion in a world filled with kings, empires, and royals seeking more and more power. Democracy was great in theory, but Washington had to figure out how to show that a country could run on those ideals.

After Washington's first term in office ended, he was elected unanimously once again on February 13th, 1793, to lead the country once more. During his time in office, he helped shape the executive branch and define the roles and responsibilities for the roles in that branch. He knew he would be setting a precedent for how future presidents would conduct themselves, and he was determined to set a stellar example as a fair and honest man with strong principles and integrity. Wishing to keep the US out of any global conflicts, he typically maintained a neutral stance in foreign affairs, even when the French Revolution broke out.

Some men, like Thomas Jefferson, believed the US should help its former ally, especially considering that the French were trying to install their own version of democracy. But Washington believed neutrality was the best option considering the French didn't seem to have a firm plan in place with how to proceed once the revolution was over.

Washington's presidency was marked with several firsts. He was the one who signed a bill to establish a permanent capital city in the US. It was named Washington, DC, after him. He established the first national bank, set up the presidential Cabinet, nominated the first judge for the country's Supreme Court, and signed a law protecting authors' copyrights.

What Americans know as Thanksgiving Day is the national holiday Washington created to celebrate both the end of the Revolutionary War and the ratification of the Constitution. It is held on the fourth Thursday of November every year.

Under his presidency, the Bill of Rights was ratified, and the United States expanded to include five more states: Vermont, Kentucky, North Carolina, Rhode Island, and Tennessee. To this day, Washington remains one of the most influential people in American history. He set an example that was hard to follow for some, and he consistently ranks as one of the best presidents.

Chapter 7: The Louisiana Purchase and the War of 1812

Louisiana

The Louisiana territory was first discovered by Spanish explorer Hernando de Soto in 1541 while he was exploring the Mississippi River. But it was claimed in 1682 by a French explorer named René-Robert Cavelier, although Native Americans had been living in the area by that point for thousands of years. The region was named after Louis XIV.

In 1762, Louisiana went to Spain as part of the negotiations to end the Seven Years' War. Under the terms of the Treaty of Fontainebleau, Louisiana was given to Spain. But in 1800, Napoleon forced the country to give up the territory, which it did under the Treaty of San Ildefonso.

The plan was to build a French force and have it stationed in Louisiana to defend "New France" against British or American attacks. France wanted to expand its empire in North America.

While this was happening, slaves in Haiti began to revolt against the French. While dealing with this revolution, Napoleon was also fighting the Napoleonic Wars in Europe. He desperately needed money for the war, so he made the decision to sell Louisiana, bringing a permanent end to France's desire to expand its North American empire.

The territory was purchased from the French First Republic by the United States for $15 million (around $309 million in present-day dollars). The transaction was negotiated by a treaty confirming the purchase was signed in Paris, France, in 1803.

The land was located to the west of the Mississippi River and was enormous, measuring approximately 828,000 square miles. It included the Rocky Mountains, went up the Gulf of Mexico, and stretched all the way to the Canadian border. It was so big that it doubled the size of the existing country. As you might already know (or have guessed), present-day Louisiana is much smaller than the original territory.

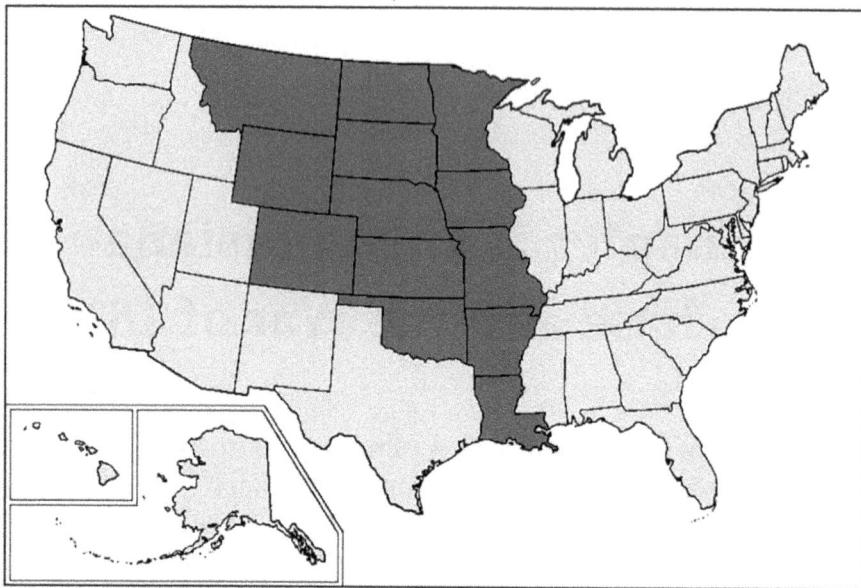

States that likely would have been included in the Louisiana Purchase.
MaGioZal, based on an image by Wikimedia Commons user Brianski, which is itself based on an image by Wikimedia Commons user Roke and Wikimedia Commons user Brianski., CC BY-SA 3.0 <http://creativecommons.org/licenses/by-sa/3.0/>, via Wikimedia Commons; https://commons.wikimedia.org/wiki/File:United_States_Louisiana_Purchase_states.png

What did the purchase of the territory mean for the US? Well, the French only owned a small piece of the territory, as most of it was inhabited by Native Americans. The US government had the right to get the land from the indigenous people either through force or cooperation.

The purchase was a smart decision. The land was rich in natural resources and strategically placed next to an important waterway, the Mississippi River. New Orleans was an important port city that had a rich culture, being influenced by French, Spanish, and African cultures. Now, the US had control of the city, and the country looked to continue its expansion.

The War of 1812

Causes

While the United States tried to stay out of global conflicts to instead focus on expanding and cementing its own nation, petty conflicts continued to rage in Europe. Things were especially tense between Great Britain and France. Despite America's best attempts to stay out of the Napoleonic Wars, they were dragged into the escalating conflict for a number of reasons.

Chief among them was that both France and Great Britain tried to stop the US from trading with each other. Great Britain even went as far as to pass an order in 1807 requiring neutral countries to have a license before they could trade with France or any of its colonies. This did not sit well with the US. The Royal Navy also began to practice impressment, where sailors were removed from US ships and forced to work on British vessels.

President Thomas Jefferson decided to counter Britain by placing restrictions on imports. In 1807, he passed the Embargo Act, which closed all of America's ports to exports. Jefferson's hope was to teach France and especially Britain a lesson by showing them how much they depended on American goods. He wanted them to accept his country's neutral stance, and he wanted Britain to stop the impressment of sailors.

The Embargo Act was a complete failure and only served to hurt America's economy, which saw exports fall from $108 million to $22 million in under a year. Congress decided to repeal the act and replaced it with the Non-Intercourse Act. Under this act, America could trade with any country except France and Britain. This came with its own set of problems.

Finally, a bill was introduced in May 1810 that changed things. The US pledged that if one country removed its restrictions against America, then the US would, in turn, place restrictions against the other country. When France dropped its restrictions against the US, the US resumed its restrictions against Great Britain.

War Begins

While the US was dealing with a potential conflict with Britain, it was also facing issues at home with the Native Americans. The Americans were looking to expand their territory but were met with resistance and hostility from the natives.

In 1809, the Treaty of Fort Wayne was agreed upon. Under the treaty, several Native American tribes had to sell three million acres of land in what is now Ohio, Michigan, Indiana, and Illinois to the US; in return, the Native Americans would receive two cents per acre.

Although the Native Americans involved in the process agreed to the treaty (at least for the most part), not all of the tribes in those lands were consulted, namely the Shawnee. Tecumseh, a Shawnee leader, spoke against the treaty and warned the Americans to stop encroaching on their land. He eventually organized a group of Native Americans to fight back against the relentless expansion of white settlers.

Governor William Henry Harrison (a future US president) organized one thousand troops to march into Prophetstown. This village was named after Tecumseh's brother, who called himself the "Prophet." He believed he was meant to lead the natives to rise up against the settlers, who had introduced evil vices and turned the natives away from their culture.

The fighting that ensued from November 7th, 1811, became known as the Battle of Tippecanoe. Tecumseh was away during the battle, and when he returned home, he found the village in ruins. Angry and defeated, Tecumseh decided to side with the British in the hopes they would stop the Americans from further expanding on their lands.

In the meantime, Congress was being pressured by the War Hawks to make a decision about a war with Britain. The War Hawks were a group of young politicians who were itching for a confrontation with Great Britain. They were hoping that by fighting the British, they could increase territorial gains in Canada and any other British-protected lands.

To their joy, the president, James Madison, finally declared war on Britain on June 18th, 1812. However, not everyone was happy about this decision. But happy or not, in the long run, the war would be a crucial point in America's history and demonstrate its growth as a country.

The Siege of Detroit – August 1812

As a colony of Great Britain, Canada became the first target of the American forces. American troops, led by William Hull, prepared to invade. Their goal was to capture Montreal. However, Hull felt it would be best to use Fort Detroit as their base and attack from there. He expected a swift victory.

However, he soon began to get nervous, especially since he was faced with the indigenous population who would not hesitate to take up arms against the US troops.

The battle was led by Sir Isaac Brock, a British soldier. He was supported by Native American allies led by Tecumseh. Sensing Hull's hesitation, he pressed forward and used Hull's fears about the natives to his advantage.

Brock and Tecumseh played mind games by making him believe they had a bigger army than they actually did and making him feel as if he was surrounded. Hull fell for the bluff and surrendered Detroit, Michigan, as well as his troop. The number of deaths was minimal, and Hull did not put up a big resistance.

The battle ended in a humiliating defeat for the Americans and wasn't a great start to the war, especially considering Fort Mackinac in what is now Michigan had already fallen with a single shot being fired.

The loss of Detroit brought all plans to invade Canada to a standstill. It was a critical point for the Americans because their war strategy had just fallen apart.

The Battle of Lake Erie – September 1813

Although American troops did not fare well in land battles, they excelled in naval fights. The Battle of Lake Erie is a great example of the Americans' might on water. The US Navy, under the guidance of Captain Oliver Hazard Perry, took on the British Royal Navy near Put-in-Bay, Ohio.

The Royal Navy was the largest navy in the world, so it might be surprising to hear that the US Navy was able to defeat them on multiple occasions. However, Britain was fighting against Napoleon in Europe, so most of its resources were concentrated there.

In the Battle of Lake Erie, the US was able to successfully prevent the British from taking control of Lake Erie. It was an important victory for the Americans, both morally and strategically, because they ensured the lake remained theirs.

Bolstered by this victory, they turned their attention to Detroit, which was recaptured after the Battle of the Thames. Tecumseh died in that battle, breaking the Native American confederacy. Although the natives continued to help the British on a small scale, they were no longer united.

The End of the War

Since the start of the war, the US Navy had won a number of victories against the British navy, but by April 1814, Napoleon had been defeated. Great Britain now had the luxury to pour all its efforts into the war against America.

Over the spring and summer, a large number of British troops poured into North America and made their way to Washington, DC. On August 24th, 1814, the British marched into the capital, setting fire to key monuments and buildings, such as the White House and the Capitol building. A few days later, a massive storm swept through (some think it might have been a hurricane), extinguishing the flames and wrecking British ships.

The Treaty of Ghent

Less than a month later, on September 11th, the American navy defeated the British fleet on Lake Champlain. Two days later, Fort McHenry in Baltimore held steady as the Royal Navy bombed them for over twenty-four hours. Discouraged by their lack of progress, the British left Chesapeake Bay and turned their attention toward New Orleans. Francis Scott Key was so moved by the sight of bombs bursting in the air that he wrote the "Star-Spangled Banner."

In the meantime, British officials had already begun talks to negotiate for peace. The negotiations were finalized in the Treaty of Ghent, which was signed in late December 1814. Under the terms, any territory conquered during the war had to be returned to its rightful owner. The boundaries of Canada and the US would also be formally determined. Impressment and the rights of neutral US ships and vessels were not discussed in the treaty. However, the treaty allowed the US to continue expanding in the Great Lakes region.

Because news of the treaty did not reach North America immediately, British forces in America continued their campaign. On January 8th, 1815, a major battle took place in New Orleans. British troops suffered another defeat. The US troops were led by Andrew Jackson, who would eventually become the president of the United States.

Although the treaty had not provided any resolutions to the main causes of the war, the Americans still considered it to be a victory, even though the war was technically a stalemate. However, it is hard to discount what the Americans achieved. They had taken on the greatest navy in the world and came out as the clear winners.

Effects of the War of 1812

In America's long and colorful history, the War of 1812 was certainly not a hugely impactful war. However, it helped shape the country in the years to come.

The Treaty of Ghent helped put an end to partisan infighting and led to the demise of the Federalist Party. Many felt their reluctance to enter the war had been unpatriotic. Winning the war was a huge boost to American nationalism and their sense of not needing anyone else to survive and thrive. It also further solidified their intent to expand and grow, which would become their primary focus in the 19th century.

Chapter 8: Expansion in the West and South

Monroe Doctrine

As the United States continued to expand and began to firmly establish itself globally as an independent nation, it wanted to make sure its future would stay secure. So, President James Monroe issued the Monroe Doctrine in 1823.

President Monroe.
https://commons.wikimedia.org/wiki/File:James_Monroe_White_House_portrait_1819.jpg

The doctrine would form a key part of American foreign policy. It basically made it clear that no outside powers were allowed to meddle in the Americas.

Four key points made up the doctrine. They are as follows:

- The United States would stay out of Europe's affairs.
- The United States would not interfere with any existing colony in the Americas.
- No further attempts at European colonization in the Western Hemisphere would be allowed.
- The US government would view any European power trying to meddle in the Americas as a hostile act.

In short, the US wanted to be left alone, and in exchange, it pledged to do the same. It would be the beginning of America's isolationism policy and its reluctance to get involved in external affairs. It was a policy that would have a significant effect on both world wars.

Over the years, additional changes were made to the Monroe Doctrine. Although the Monroe Doctrine is technically not used today, its principles can still be seen in American foreign policies.

Florida

Much has been discussed in the previous chapters about the British and French colonies, but what about the Spanish colonies?

One of the earliest explorers of what would become the United States, Juan Ponce de León, a Spaniard, discovered the modern-day state of Florida in 1513. Because the land was so vibrant and beautiful, he called it Pascua Florida in honor of Easter (the name means "Flowery Easter"). Early European settlers came to Florida, making it one of the first American frontiers.

Florida would have one of the most colorful histories of the US state, as it changed hands numerous times. For three centuries (from the 16th to the 19th century), Florida was under Spanish rule except for a brief period in the 18th century when it was ruled by Britain due to Spain siding with France during the French and Indian War. Once the American Revolution was over and the Treaty of Paris was signed, Florida was returned to Spain. But things were far from peaceful, and boundary issues continued to plague Spain.

After several years of negotiating, Spain and the US signed the Adams-Onís Treaty. Spain agreed to cede East Florida to the US and gave up any claims to West Florida. In exchange, the US agreed to pay out claims of damages to US citizens on behalf of Spain. The total cost was roughly $5 million.

Florida was initially a Spanish colony. During the Seven Years' War, Spain gave Florida to Britain. The British divided Florida into East and West. They held onto Florida until 1783, when Britain ceded Florida to Spain.

Disagreements over who owned Florida continued for some, but ultimately, the US gained the territory. In 1822, Florida officially became a US territory and then became the twenty-seventh state in 1845.

The Seminole Wars

The Seminole Wars played a significant role in the cession of Florida. It was also not one of the proudest moments in American history since the series of wars basically served to eject an entire group of people from the land.

In 1817, American authorities were on a mission to recapture slaves who had run away from their owners and were living among a group of Native Americans called the Seminoles. The charge was led by General Andrew Jackson, and American troops forced themselves into the lands occupied by the Seminoles. They burned villages and towns and seized Pensacola and St. Marks, two cities held by Spain.

During this first of the three Seminole Wars, the US convinced Spain the best thing for it would be to cede its territory in Florida, which it did under the Adams-Onís Treaty.

In 1835, the Second Seminole War broke out when the majority of the Seminole population refused to relocate to another area near the Mississippi River. They did not want to leave their reservation near Lake Okeechobee, a space that had been specifically established for them. But wanting to expand their territory, the Americans needed the Seminoles to leave. The Indian Removal Act was established to get rid of them and other Native American tribes living in the Southeast.

Seminole warriors, led by their chief, Osceola, valiantly defended their home. The war finally ended when Osceola was captured by the Americans while parleying with them. The Seminoles stopped resisting after that, and most of them eventually agreed to leave the area.

The Third Seminole War lasted for three years (1855-1858), but the American government was determined to get rid of every last Seminole in Florida. There was very little violence or resistance. Most left on their own, and some were paid to leave. A couple of hundred Seminoles remained in the swamps of Florida. However, their numbers were small, and they remained hidden where the settlers couldn't find them. Florida was finally ready for US expansion.

The Trail of Tears (1830–1850)

The Seminole Wars bring to light another important event: the forceful removal of Native Americans from their homes. Native Americans had been living on the land that would eventually become part of the United States for generations. But by the end of the 1830s, most natives had been pushed westward.

The US government wanted the valuable land the natives were living on. The American settlers could grow cotton and other crops in the rich and fertile land. Gold was discovered in some Native American territories, creating a mad rush to stake claims. The settlers were increasingly encroaching on native territories, leading to skirmishes between both sides. It seemed as if the tensions would never be solved. Newspapers and stories painted Native Americans as either noble savages or a menace to civilization. Americans were both scared and resentful of the natives and wanted a solution to the "Indian problem."

One suggestion, which was even made by George Washington, was to Westernize the Native Americans and make them more like white settlers. This way, they could assimilate better. This method was adopted in some southeastern states.

But in other parts of the country, the Americans forced the Native Americans to leave their homes through violence. They destroyed their villages, looted their homes, and committed mass murder. This is not to say the Native Americans weren't guilty of atrocities as well; sometimes, the US troops took violent measures to act against the violence the Native Americans had committed. Regardless, some Native Americans were forcibly and violently pushed out of their homelands.

Andrew Jackson had long been a great advocate of removing Native Americans. When he became president of the US, he signed the Indian Removal Act of 1830. The act officially gave the government the authority to take away the valuable land held by the Native Americans in the Southeast in exchange for a designated Indian Territory in the West. The Native Americans that were targeted were called the "Five Civilized Tribes." They had been greatly Westernized, showing that even the idea of Westernizing tribes would not work in the United States.

Under the act, the government had to negotiate removal and do so in a peaceful manner. However, more often than not, Native Americans were coerced to move west under the threat of violence. The Choctaw were the first to leave. They left during the winter of 1831. Some were placed in chains, and many had no food, water, or basic supplies. The trip was long, and many died. Perhaps none suffered more than the Cherokee. It is thought that nearly four thousand Cherokee died on the Trail of Tears.

Their problems didn't end when they reached their destination of Oklahoma either. The Indian Territory was already inhabited by other tribes. The Native Americans also had to figure out how to eke a living in this new territory. Although the US government and charities gave assistance, their efforts often were not enough. This is especially prevalent with the boarding schools that were established, which stripped native children of their traditional culture (language, clothing, religion, etc.) to make them more European. This led to the erasure of their culture and their ostracization from their native community. They also weren't fully accepted by the white settlers either, making them straddle two worlds they didn't fit into. Native Americans would not become US citizens until 1924.

Second Great Awakening

While the government was focused on expanding the country and dealing with political reforms and changes, a great social reform was also being undertaken. In the late 18th century, a wave of Protestant religious revival swept across the United States. This wave is called the Second Great Awakening. Religious meetings and church became an integral part of people's lives.

The idea of needing to save one's soul took hold of people and led to numerous moral and social reforms. Some of these reforms included temperance, the emancipation of women, and the abolition of slavery. The reforms not only helped shape society and the lives of Americans, but they also had a deep impact on political and government policies. This would be seen clearly with the issue of the annexation of Texas.

Texas Revolution

Like Florida, Texas was initially explored by a Spaniard. Alonso Álvarez de Piñeda was the first to explore what would become Texas.

For the most part, Texas was largely ignored by European settlers until Spain became nervous that France might want to take it over. So, the Spanish tried to set up a few missions. Their attempt was a failure due to resistance from the Native Americans.

The Spaniards went back to Mexico and didn't think of Texas again until French settlers began to arrive in Louisiana. By 1718, San Antonio had been established by Spain, but tensions with the natives continued.

Believing that a bigger population would help their cause, Spain allowed large numbers of Americans and Europeans to immigrate to Texas in 1820. This led to a rapid increase in the population, but it also started to make Mexico, which gained independence shortly after the first immigrants arrived in Texas, worried because many of the new settlers had no respect for Mexican law. The American government also actively tried to purchase Texas. By 1832, many people in Texas began to openly disobey Mexican laws and revolt against the country. Mexico was also dealing with problems of its own, as its government was unstable.

Rising tensions eventually led to the Texas Revolution. For several months, the Texans fought violently against Mexican troops.

The Battle of the Alamo

The Battle of the Alamo was a significant conflict during the Texan Revolution. The battle started on February 23rd, 1836, and ended on March 6th.

In December 1835, a group of volunteer soldiers in Texas decided to occupy the Alamo, a former mission. The mission had been built by Spanish settlers in the early 18th century. It was used to house missionaries and converts for around seven decades before all of the Spanish missions became secularized in 1793.

Soon after, Spanish troops began to make use of the chapel in the former mission as a fort. In 1821, Mexico gained its independence. Soldiers from the Alamo Company (with Alamo meaning "cottonwood" in Spanish) called the fort the "Alamo" after their hometown of Alamo de Parras.

The Battle of the Alamo is probably the most well-known event of the Texas Revolution. When the Texan soldiers made the decision to occupy the fort in late 1835, they knew this would anger the Mexicans. And on February 23rd, an army of Mexican soldiers led by General Antonio López de Santa Anna (who would become president of Mexico several times and played a pivotal role in the Mexican-American War) marched to the Alamo to seize it.

For nearly two weeks, the Texans managed to hold them at bay, but on March 6th, the Mexican forces were able to breach the fort and take down the Texans. Almost everyone was killed; there were only fourteen survivors.

But instead of breaking the Texans' spirit, what happened at the Alamo only solidified their desire to become independent. The battle became a symbol of resistance and courage. On April 21st, when Sam Houston and his men defeated and captured many of Santa Anna's forces in the Battle of San Jacinto, they cried, "Remember the Alamo" while attacking.

The win at San Jacinto cinched the independence of Texas. Santa Anna was taken prisoner. A declaration of independence was quickly signed after defeating Mexico, making Texas a republic on March 2nd, 1836. However, Mexico refused to recognize the independence of Texas and instead viewed it as a rebellious province. The majority of the Texas population wanted to become a part of the United States, and within a year of becoming a republic, Texas was trying to get annexed by the country.

However, friction between opposition parties and differing views on the practice of slavery delayed the process. Abolition was already a hotly debated issue within Congress, and the Democrats and the Whigs were fiercely opposed to adding Texas, a pro-slavery state, to the Union since it would upset the balance of free and slave states. They also did not want to anger Mexico, where slavery had been abolished. The Mexicans also continued to refuse to recognize Texas as an independent state.

By this time, the days of electing a president through a simple vote were long gone, and political parties had emerged. In the late 1820s, the Democratic Party emerged. Members of this party were initially part of the Democratic-Republican Party, which was founded in 1792. Over time, the party began to crumble and was eventually split into two parties: the Democrats and the Whigs. The two parties had their differences of opinion, but they were united behind one cause: Texas should not be a part of the United States.

Annexation of Texas

For almost a decade, the annexation of Texas continued to be a political issue, and the great debate dragged on. The eighth president of the US, Martin Van Buren, saw Texas as a huge liability and rejected the annexation proposal. The matter was laid to rest for some time.

However, annexation came up again when William Henry Harrison was elected president in 1840. He only served for thirty-two days before dying, making his vice president, John Tyler, the president.

President Tyler once again opened up the conversation around annexation as part of his expansionist agenda. Texas became his primary focus because he was convinced it would win him a second term. There were also fears that Texas might threaten American security if it was left to its own devices.

In the meantime, the economic situation in Texas was steadily becoming critical. In the early 1840s, Sam Houston, the president of Texas, decided to try and reconcile with Mexico using Britain as a mediator. He wanted Mexico to officially recognize Texas as a republic or allow them to function independently within the Mexican borders. In exchange, Texas would emancipate its slaves.

As they opened these discussions, talks were also secretly being held with the US to become part of the Union, where the political climate had shifted somewhat. When Mexico got wind of this, it told Congress if the US went ahead with the annexation, all diplomatic ties between the two countries would be broken, and war would be declared.

Texas boundaries after annexation in 1845.

Texas remained a republic for almost ten years, but its annexation finally happened on December 29th, 1845, the same year James K. Polk became the eleventh president of the United States.

Chapter 9: The Mexican-American War, the Oregon Treaty, and the Gold Rush

Causes of the Mexican-American War

As many in the US had predicted and foreseen, the annexation of Texas angered Mexico and led to a breakdown in the relationship between the two countries. In addition to the annexation of Texas, the two countries were also embroiled in a dispute about the borders of Texas. According to the US, the Rio Grande formed the southern border of Texas. But Mexico contended the Nueces River was the boundary.

California also became a hot issue, as President Polk wanted to continue America's expansion all the way to the Pacific Ocean, believing it to be the country's destiny. Manifest Destiny was the idea that the US was destined by God to settle North America.

And on top of all of this, Mexico had defaulted on its payments to the US. It had promised to pay nearly $3 million to Americans whose properties had been damaged or destroyed as a result of the Texas Revolution.

A combination of these issues eventually led to an all-out war. But before the war began, Polk had offered to purchase California and New Mexico. When Mexico refused the offer, American troops moved into the hotly debated area between the Nueces River and the Rio Grande. In the past, everyone had recognized this as rightfully being a part of

Coahuila, a Mexican state.

A series of small-scale skirmishes began on April 25ᵗʰ, 1846. American and Mexican forces fought the Battle of Palo Alto and the Battle of Resaca de la Palma.

The Mexicans were easily defeated in both battles, but Polk made it clear to Congress that they had to do more. On May 13ᵗʰ, Congress approved of declaring war. Some lawmakers were against this declaration, but it was too late, as the US and Mexico were officially at war.

The Mexican-American War

The number of Mexican people living north of the Rio Grande was relatively small. The population was estimated at approximately seventy-five thousand. The US troops advancing into the area were able to conquer the territory easily with little to no resistance. The city of Monterrey was captured just as easily.

Around this time, General Antonio López de Santa Anna came back into the picture. He had been a charismatic and popular leader who headed the government in Mexico eleven times and styled himself as the "Napoleon of the West." In 1835, he repealed the Mexican Constitution, which essentially led to the start of the Texas Revolution. After the revolution ended, he was held captive in Texas for around three weeks. He was forced to sign a humiliating treaty that gave up Texas. He was eventually allowed to return to Mexico.

Santa Anna was soon given control of the army again. He would become president off and on from 1839 to 1844. He ruled like a dictator. In 1844, Santa Anna, who was scared for his life, stepped down from power because of rising tensions over how he ruled. He was captured by a group of Native Americans, who handed him over to the authorities, who then forced him into exile.

He was in exile in Cuba when the war between Mexico and America started. Santa Anna promised Polk that if he came back to Mexico, he would make sure the US came out as the winner in the peace agreements. Mexico had also set aside its anger toward Santa Anna and wanted him to return to lead the charge.

When Santa Anna returned, he took control of the Mexican Army and led it against the US. He had no intentions of honoring his promise to Polk. During the Battle of Buena Vista in February 1847, the American troops crushed Mexico, forcing them to retreat.

There were several significant battles, but every one ended the same. The Mexican troops put up a valiant fight but suffered too many casualties. They suffered from poor leadership and were no match for the American troops.

A year into the war, it was becoming clear that the war was over. It was equally clear who the winners were.

Treaty of Guadalupe Hidalgo

In September 1847, the Mexican government formally surrendered after the fall of Mexico City, and negotiations for peace began. The Treaty of Guadalupe Hidalgo was finalized and signed on February 2nd, 1848. The terms of the treaty outlined that Mexico would have to recognize the annexation of Texas. It defined the US-Mexican border as the Rio Grande, not the Nueces River. Mexico also had to sell all the territory north of the Rio Grande and California to the American government for $15 million.

The US came out of the war the clear winner and with an enormous chunk of land. The land it received was almost as big as Louisiana had been, and its acquisition changed the US completely. For Mexico, the war was disastrous, and the Mexicans came out of it with heavy losses and no gains.

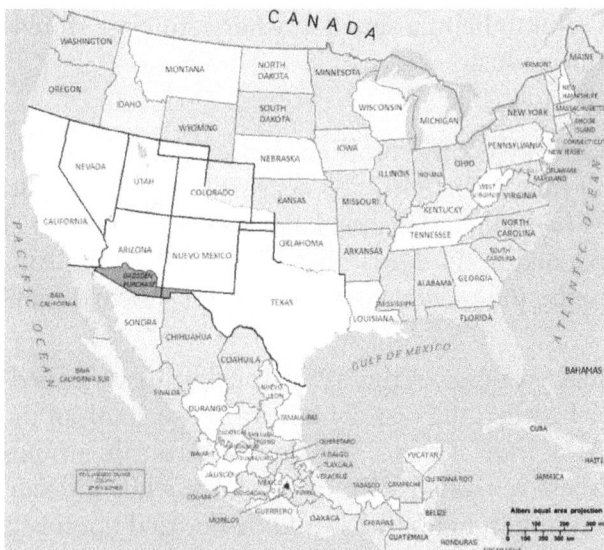

A look at what the US gained after the war. It received everything in white; the area in brown was contested by Mexico after the treaty.

https://commons.wikimedia.org/wiki/File:Mexican_Cession_in_Mexican_View.PNG

Northwestern Territory

The US had its eye on other parts of North America as well. The Pacific Northwest was a coveted tract of land that several countries competed for as early as the 18th century. Spain, Britain, Russia, and the United States all wanted the territory for themselves. It became even more important after the War of 1812 for diplomatic reasons. In 1825, both Russia and Spain signed treaties formally withdrawing their claims to the region, leaving the US and the British with contested control over the area.

An ongoing dispute ensued on who had sovereignty over a specific area of the Northwest Territory. For the British, the region was called the Columbia District, while the Americans called it Oregon Country.

In 1844, the Democratic Party suggested annexing the area. The Whig Party wasn't interested in the dispute, as it felt there were bigger issues to consider.

After some time, Polk offered the British a compromise, the 49th parallel, but the British refused. They wanted the border to be along the Columbia River.

After the offer was refused, Polk was advised to annex all of the Pacific Northwest, but tensions with Mexico over Texas were on the rise. Polk did not want to be in a situation where America would have to fight two wars simultaneously.

Treaty of Oregon

The US came to a compromise with the British and signed the Treaty of Oregon on June 15th, 1846. For nearly three decades, Britain and the United States had jointly occupied the Pacific Northwest. But with US resources stretched in the Mexican-American War, the Americans knew they had to settle the matter in the northwest to avoid fighting a war on two fronts.

The original proposal of the 49th parallel was established in the treaty as the border between the two countries. Those south of the 49th parallel would be American citizens, while those north would be British. Vancouver Island remained a British territory, while the San Juan Islands were left as a question mark that would be decided upon later.

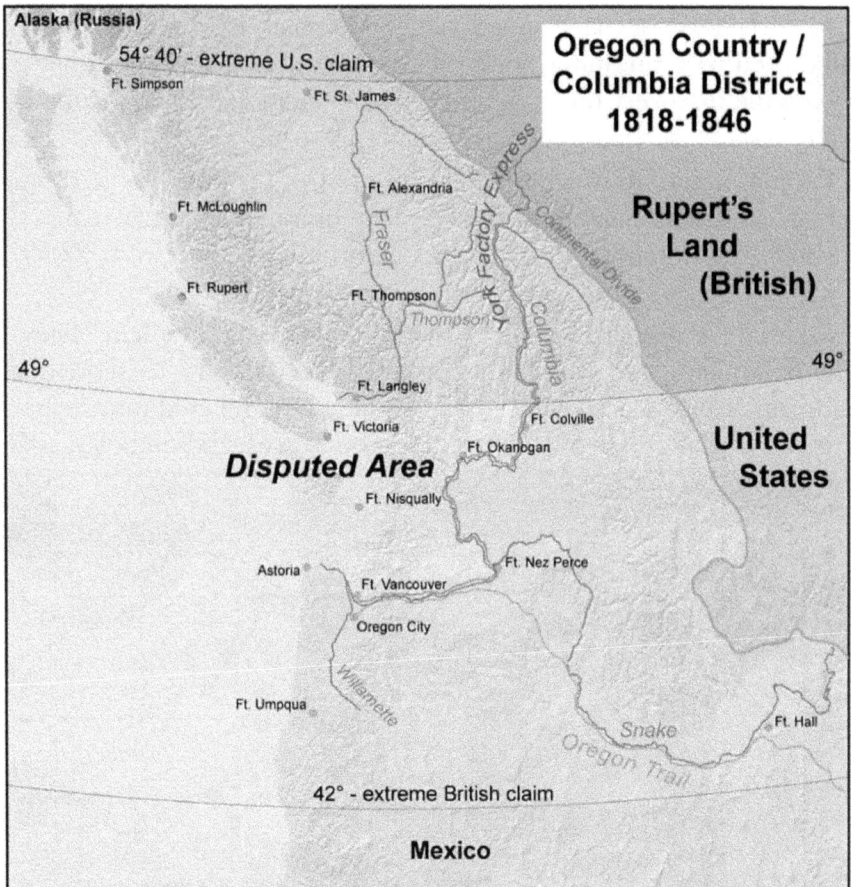

Alaska (Russia)

54° 40' - extreme U.S. claim

Ft. Simpson

Ft. St. James

Oregon Country / Columbia District 1818-1846

Ft. Alexandria

Ft. McLoughlin

Rupert's Land (British)

Ft. Rupert

Ft. Thompson

49°

49°

Ft. Langley

Ft. Victoria

Ft. Colville

Disputed Area

Ft. Okanogan

United States

Ft. Nisqually

Astoria

Ft. Nez Perce

Ft. Vancouver

Oregon City

Ft. Umpqua

Snake

Ft. Hall

42° - extreme British claim

Mexico

49ᵗʰ parallel.

The treaty did not please Upper Canada, as the people there felt that Britain was not doing a good job of looking out for their interests or even taking their opinions into consideration. They were increasingly looking to have more independence, especially when it came to international matters.

California Gold Rush (1848–1855)

As the United States continued to expand, its population grew at a steady pace. Over the years, there would be waves of new immigrants, and the Gold Rush certainly led to such a wave. It was a hugely significant event in America's history and would shape the years to come, especially in the state of California.

In early 1848, a man named James Marshall, who was working in a mill owned by John Sutter, found flakes of gold in California. They tried to keep the discovery quiet, but the word soon spread, sparking the Gold Rush.

People began to migrate there in masses, leading to a dramatic increase in the population of the country. In a matter of ten years (1850 to 1860), the number of people in California increased from 92,597 to 379,994!

Men and even some women gave up everything they had. They left behind families and gambled their life savings to try to score big in California. Known as the Forty-Niners, these hopeful gold miners arrived in droves in California, traveling on foot, on horses, and on boats.

Prospectors during the Gold Rush.

The gold that was easily accessible on the surface went fast, and by 1850, there was hardly any left, leaving people no choice but to start mining for it. Mining was expensive, so companies and rich individuals ran the enterprises and hired help.

Mining was difficult, dangerous, and laborious. Life for the people in mining camps was tough. The mining camps themselves were lawless and unruly. Crime, drinking, violence, and prostitution thrived there.

During the Gold Rush, over 750,000 pounds of gold were found. Thousands of people extracted $2 billion worth of gold, making some people very rich and changing their fortunes forever. However, for most, the Gold Rush led to nothing extra in their pockets. Some died or became destitute in California. Many ended up staying in California, shaping the state's history in ways that could not have been imagined prior to the Gold Rush.

Unfortunately for Mexico, the gold was discovered just a few days before the Treaty of Guadalupe Hidalgo was signed. It was of the utmost importance for the US that it gained control of California.

In late 1849, California applied to become a part of the United States. The application was quickly accepted in large part due to the discovery of gold and the huge population influx. California even skipped the step of becoming a territory! But the people in California had a caveat: they wanted to join as a free state. This caused a crisis in Congress, as slavery continued to be a contested issue.

The Compromise of 1850 saw California admitted as a free state. It also strengthened the fugitive slave laws and banned the slave trade in Washington, DC (although slavery itself was still allowed there).

California Genocide

While the Gold Rush meant riches and good fortune for many, for California's indigenous population, it was anything but. Their fairly peaceful existence was disrupted, and worse still, they were seen as a hindrance by white settlers. What would later become known as the California genocide is seen as one of the state's most heinous and shameful acts.

Soon after becoming a state, the government decided it needed more land to look for more gold and to make room for California's expanding population. To acquire the land, they needed to get rid of the Native American population, and the easiest way to do so was by killing them.

Fueled by bigotry and fear, the white settlers set out on a crusade to "exterminate the savages before they can labor much longer in the mines with security" with the government's blessing and support.[2]

---

[2] Blakemore, Erin. "California's Little-Known Genocide."
https://www.history.com/news/californias-little-known-genocide.

Over a period of twenty years, over 80 percent of the indigenous population in California was eradicated through genocide. Tribal populations and villages were wiped out entirely through massacres.

A law was passed giving Americans the right to enslave Native Americans or take their children. White settlers were also given the authority to arrest the natives or force them into labor. While they were essentially still being kept as slaves, the acts allowed Americans to do it in a "legal" way. Children were often taken away and forced to attend schools to help them assimilate into white culture. The majority of these children never returned home.

It is estimated that of the 150,000 indigenous people who were in California at the start of the Gold Rush, 100,000 were killed in the first two years. Just over twenty years later, only thirty thousand indigenous people remained.

Today, California is one of the most diverse states in the United States and is home to 109 indigenous tribes. A formal apology was offered by the state in 2019 for the atrocities committed during the California genocide.

The Republican Party in 1854

Before we talk about the next major event in US history (the Civil War), it is important to talk about one more notable event that happened during the Gold Rush period: the formation of the Republican Party.

Up until the 1850s, the two dominant political parties were the Democrats and the Whigs. Former members of the Whig Party began to meet to discuss the possibility of creating a new party that opposed slavery. The breakdown of the party came about as a result of the admission of Kansas and Nebraska as states to the Union.

In January 1854, the Missouri Compromise (which set a boundary for which states could be slave states and which could be free) was repealed, and the Kansas-Nebraska Act was introduced. Under this act, the tract of land to the west of Missouri would be divided into two territories, and they would be allowed to decide for themselves whether they wanted to keep or abolish slavery. Essentially, they could join as a free or slave state.

This did not sit well with those who were opposed to slavery because it opened up the door for slavery to exist in territories where it had previously been banned. The politicians who opposed slavery did so more out of fear of slave-owning states gaining all the power rather than morally opposing slavery. If the number of slave states dominated the number of free states, then politically, those states would get their way with the government and hold more power.

As the Whig Party fell apart over this controversy, anti-slavery Whigs continued to meet. On March 20th, 1854, they formed the Republican Party. They quickly gained a lot of support and played a hugely significant role during the American Civil War.

A Republican named Abraham Lincoln would go on to become president. He would be the one to formally abolish slavery in the Confederate States, which set the wheels in motion to abolish slavery in the entire US.

SECTION THREE:
The Civil War and the
Reconstruction (1861–1877)

Chapter 10: What Caused the Civil War?

When the United States was just Thirteen Colonies, it was easy to find common ground and remain united. However, as the country expanded and as more territories joined, differing political views, values, morals, and goals began to cause tensions between the states.

One of the most glaring issues was the glaring economic differences between the North and the South. This, coupled with the continuing debate over slavery, led to increased friction.

By the middle of the 19th century, America was really starting to come into its own. It had defeated European empires, settled its conflicts with neighboring Mexico and Canada, and dramatically expanded its territory. Immigration was booming, and there was growth in almost every sector. However, there were key differences in how Northern states, like New York, and Southern states, like Georgia, made money.

In the North, the economy was driven by manufacturing and industries, and business was booming. The Northern states were rapidly becoming industrialized and enjoying wealth and prosperity, whereas economic growth in the South was less dramatic. In the Southern states, agriculture and farming were the main sources of income. Some people had rolling plantations and endless acres of land, which were used to grow cotton, tobacco, and other crops. But the majority of the South was made up of smaller farms. Of course, the backbreaking work was done almost entirely by black slaves. Plantation owners and even small farmers were dependent on slaves. They worried about what would happen to their source of income and their economy if slavery were abolished.

Early in 1854, the Kansas-Nebraska Act was passed by Congress, which essentially allowed these new territories to have slaves if they wished. This intensified the already heated issue and set off a series of events that ultimately culminated in the Civil War.

First, after the state of Kansas was created in 1854, battles between pro- and anti-slavery forces erupted in the territory and continued sporadically for the next five years. They were vicious, violent battles and became known as Bleeding Kansas.

The Dred Scott Case

The already tense political atmosphere worsened three years later when the Supreme Court handed a ruling in the Dred Scott case.

Dred Scott was a young man who had been born into slavery. When his master took him to a free state, he technically became free, but upon his return to a slave state, he once again became enslaved.

Scott sued for his freedom, arguing that once he had been freed, he could no longer legally be a slave. The courts disagreed, and in 1854, he appealed the decision to the Supreme Court. In 1857, the court ruled against him, and he lost his bid for freedom. The Supreme Court ruled that people with African ancestry could not claim citizenship. It has been labeled as one of the worst decisions the Supreme Court has ever made.

Dred Scott.
https://commons.wikimedia.org/wiki/File:Dred_Scott_photograph_(circa_1857).jpg

The decision seemed to support the Kansas-Nebraska Act. Abolitionists were furious at the decision, and anti-slavery sentiments increased and gained momentum.

Secession of States

In 1860, Abraham Lincoln, a Republican who was firmly against the practice of slavery, was elected as the sixteenth president of the United States. Even though Lincoln had made no plans to free the slaves because doing so would go against the Constitution, the Southern states decided they had had enough.

A convention was called in January 1861, and the delegates decided that South Carolina would secede from the United States. Six additional states also seceded: Florida, Georgia, Louisiana, Mississippi, Alabama, and Texas. Four other states—Tennessee, Arkansas, North Carolina, and Virginia—did the same later that year. Eventually, the group of eleven states would band together to become the Confederate States of America. During the Civil War, they would be known as the Confederacy, while those fighting for the North would be referred to as the Union.

Start of the War

Within a month of the initial states' secession, the states created a government and named Jefferson Davis as the interim president.

The Confederacy began to make moves almost immediately. President James Buchanan, who was leaving office in 1861, refused to surrender any of the Southern ports to them. Confederate troops retaliated by forcefully seizing them. A ship making its way to Fort Sumter with supplies for Federal forces was forced to turn around.

However, the war didn't officially start until Lincoln took office. When Lincoln was inaugurated, he reaffirmed that he had no intention of abolishing slavery in the slave states. He also refused to accept the secession and called for the country to unite and resolve its differences.

Meanwhile, Fort Sumter was still without supplies, so another attempt was made to deliver them. Lincoln hoped to avoid a confrontation, so he advised South Carolina beforehand. Robert Anderson, the man in charge of the fort, was asked to surrender. Anderson again refused to abandon Fort Sumter. On the following day, the militia commander, P. G. T. Beauregard, opened fire early in the morning, around 4:30 a.m., on Fort Sumter.

A few hours later, Abner Doubleday fired back, at which point Beauregard unleashed a barrage of shots, firing three thousand shots in a span of thirty-four hours. On April 13th, cannon fire pierced through the fortress, starting fires in the post. There were no casualties in this first battle, although some Union soldiers died when a cannon exploded in the fort while giving a salute on April 14th. Anderson finally agreed to evacuate the fort. The Civil War had begun.

Chapter 11: Key Battles and Campaigns of the Civil War

Before we delve deeper into the battles and campaigns of the Civil War, let's take a closer look at the opposing groups.

Union Army

Also known as the Federal Army, the Northern Army, or the Yankees, the Union included twenty states:

- New York
- Maine
- Vermont
- New Hampshire
- Connecticut
- Massachusetts
- Rhode Island
- Pennsylvania
- Ohio
- New Jersey
- Indiana
- Illinois
- Kansas
- Wisconsin

- Michigan
- Minnesota
- Iowa
- Nevada
- California
- Oregon

A picture of the Union Army; General George McClellan, who led the Peninsula Campaign, is to the right of the stump.

https://commons.wikimedia.org/wiki/File:GeorgeMcClellan1861a.jpg

The president of the Union was Abraham Lincoln. The Union was anti-slavery, although not everyone was fighting to ultimately abolish slavery. Many fought because they wanted to keep the Union intact.

It should also be noted that residents living in western Virginia didn't want to secede, so that portion of the state became a part of the Union as the state of West Virginia. Even though it was part of the Union, it didn't fight for the Union. It and four other slave states—Delaware, Maryland,

Kentucky, and Missouri—were border states. They maintained a fairly neutral stance throughout the war. They were not as reliant on slave labor as the Southern states but believed leaving the Union was the wrong way to go about things. Many individuals from the border states fought in the war, with most of them fighting for the Union.

Confederate Army

The Confederate soldiers, sometimes referred to as Southerners or Rebels, came from the states that seceded from the United States. They were as follows:

- Texas
- Louisiana
- Arkansas
- Mississippi
- Tennessee
- Georgia
- Alabama
- Florida
- South and North Carolina
- Virginia

Jefferson Davis was the president of the Confederacy.

The Confederate Army planned to fight a defensive war. The Confederates felt confident the North wouldn't want to engage in a full-scale conflict and would agree to a compromise to avoid a prolonged war. Southerners also felt their way of living left them better prepared to be soldiers. They had some great military leaders and a cause worth dying for. A combination of these factors led them to arrogantly believe a war with the North would be short and quick; they also believed they would emerge as the victors.

One of the more important things the Union soldiers had going for them was the North's ability to manufacture and produce weapons. By the time the Civil War started, the North was rapidly growing in industrial strength. The Southern economy was based on farming and agriculture, which wasn't ideal for financing or planning a war. The South also had a much smaller population, which created a significant disadvantage in terms of raising taxes and funds to finance the war. A smaller population also meant that when they suffered losses on the battlefield, they had fewer people to replace the fallen soldiers.

The Union Navy was also much stronger and more capable than the Confederate Navy. When Southern ports were subjected to blockades by the Union, the South was unable to ship its cotton to foreign ports, which dramatically reduced its exporting capacity and affected the Confederacy financially.

In short, the Union Army was better placed to fight the war in almost every way. However, they failed to take into account the South was more passionate about the war's cause and knew the South's terrain better. Both sides expected a short war and a quick victory. What neither side anticipated was the tenacity and determination of their foe.

Confederate Army

Confederate Army.
https://en.wikipedia.org/wiki/File:ConfederateArmyPhoto.jpg

American Civil War

First Battle of Bull Run – July 21st, 1861

The First Battle of Bull Run (also known as the Battle of First Manassas) was the first major full-scale battle of the Civil War. It was an eye-opening experience for the two sides, both of which had naively assumed the war would be over quickly and with limited casualties.

After the Civil War started in Fort Sumter, the Union forces felt confident they could win the war in short order. This led to a premature offensive in Virginia by around thirty-four thousand Union troops, which were led by General Irvin McDowell. Only about eighteen thousand took part in the fight.

When the Confederate Army found out about the advance, General Beauregard gathered around twenty-two thousand troops. General Joseph Johnston also joined him with an additional twelve thousand troops. Again, only about eighteen thousand took part in the battle.

By the morning of July 21ᵗ, both sides were ready for a battle. It started when three Union divisions crossed the Bull Run stream, driving back the Confederate troops to Henry House Hill.

But Beauregard had a strong defensive line, which fired and fought back from a concealed slope. A sudden charge by the Rebels (another name for the Confederates) down the hill broke McDowell's line, and the Union troops were forced to retreat.

This gave way to chaotic, unorganized fighting and bloodshed. Almost three thousand Union soldiers died, went missing, or were wounded. The Confederates had almost two thousand casualties. It was a horrifying thing for civilians and the troops to witness. Wealthy families from DC came to picnic and watch the battle, expecting an easy Union victory. They also had to retreat hastily when the battle did not go their way. It also left the government feeling uncertain about how to proceed. A war they thought would be easily won was now looking far more complicated.

The Civil War began on April 12ᵗʰ, 1861, when the Rebels fired shots at Fort Sumter. It ended on April 9ᵗʰ, 1865, with the Confederacy surrendering to the Union. Over the course of four years, it is estimated that between 620,000 and 750,000 soldiers lost their lives to the bloody and violent battles. This number doesn't account for the thousands of innocent civilians who died as a direct result of the war. Historians estimate that number to be around fifty thousand, although the actual number of casualties is likely quite higher.

However, the Civil War wasn't fought entirely in vain. By the end of the war, the country had been united once more, although tensions were still high. Slavery was also abolished for good by the end of 1865.

While the war featured thousands of battles, only around fifty were significant, with some of those battles being more defining than others. We will take a look at the biggest battles of the war; if you are interested in this time period (or any other time period in US history), we strongly encourage you to check out the references to learn more about what happened in greater detail.

The Battle of Antietam – September 17th, 1862

During the Maryland Campaign, the Union won the Battle of South Mountain, while the Confederates won the Battle of Harpers Ferry. Hoping to secure another win for the Confederates, General Robert E. Lee ordered his forces to converge near Antietam Creek. The topography of the area made it ideal for mounting a defense. Lee's troops went into position on September 15th and waited for the Union troops to arrive.

Union General George McClellan's troops arrived the following afternoon. He sent a corps across the creek, where they found some of Lee's troops. The two divisions fought, and the next morning, at dawn, the Union troops launched an attack. The two sides attacked back and forth, putting up a formidable fight.

By late afternoon, the Union troops had managed to push back the Confederates and claim victory. Even after the battle was over, minor skirmishes continued for another two days before Lee and his men fully withdrew. McClellan decided not to follow Lee, which made Lincoln question his abilities. Feeling unsure about McClellan, Lincoln decided to put the Army of the Potomac under the command of Major General Ambrose Burnside.

Antietam would become the bloodiest one-day battle in the country's history. The battle saw a staggering 22,717 casualties: 12,401 on the Union side and 10,316 on the Confederate side.

After this victory, President Lincoln signed the Emancipation Proclamation, which will be discussed in greater detail in Chapter 12.

The Battle of Fredericksburg – December 11th–December 15th, 1862

Nearly 200,000 men fought in the Battle of Fredericksburg, making it the battle with the highest number of troops. General Lee led the charge with 72,500 Confederate troops against General Burnside, who had 106,000 soldiers. This was one of the earliest major battles of the Civil War, and it ended in a great victory for the Confederates.

Even though Burnside and his troops had arrived in Falmouth, Virginia, by November, they didn't have the pontoons to cross the Rappahannock River. Bad weather and snow further delayed them.

The delay allowed Lee to prepare. He correctly predicted that Burnside would cross the river, so he stationed Rebel troops in defensive positions along the river. When the battle started on December 11th, with Union soldiers crossing into Fredericksburg, they were shot at by Confederate soldiers.

Things continued to go badly for the Union soldiers; they lost twice the number of men compared to the Confederates. On December 15th, Burnside's men retreated, and the Rebels claimed an incredible victory. The win provided a huge morale boost for the Southern states and was a devastating blow for the Union.

A second offensive against Lee was mounted in January 1863, but this, too, was a failure. After this, Burnside resigned from his post and was replaced by "Fighting" Joe Hooker.

The Battle of Chancellorsville – April 30th-May 6th, 1863

After the disastrous Battle of Fredericksburg, the Union Army was left shaken and disorganized. Burnside resigned, and Hooker took over. Hooker's first order of business was to train the troops. His goal was to capture Richmond, Virginia, which was the capital of the Confederacy.

Hooker's plan was simple. He would send two-thirds of his troops near Fredericksburg to trick Lee into thinking they were planning a frontal assault. In the meantime, he would take the rest of his troops across the Rappahannock River.

But Lee, who had thought ahead, also decided to divide his troops and was thus ready for Hooker's army when they arrived near Chancellorsville on May 1st, 1863. Lee decided to split his troops once again. Thomas "Stonewall" Jackson, one of Lee's most trusted generals, marched ahead with twenty-eight thousand troops to attack Hooker's right flank, which had been left exposed.

Jackson destroyed half the Union troops that day. Later that evening, as he and his men went exploring in the forest, a North Carolina regiment started shooting at them, thinking they were Union troops. Some of the bullets struck him, and he broke his arm, requiring his arm to be amputated. He contracted pneumonia and died on May 10th, 1863. The Confederacy hailed him as a war hero.

On May 6th, Hooker and his troops retreated to Washington. The Battle of Chancellorsville lasted a week and ended in a huge victory for the Confederates. Lee seemed nearly unstoppable.

The Battle of Gettysburg – July 1st–July 3rd, 1863

The seemingly unstoppable General Lee's series of victories ended at the Battle of Gettysburg, which is perhaps the most well-known battle of the Civil War. It would be the turning point in the war.

Fresh from his victory at Chancellorsville, Lee made the decision to cross into Union territory. A year ago, Lee had been forced to turn back from the North after a Union victory at Antietam, but he was ready to try again. He also hoped the invasion in the North would divert some Northern troops away from the ongoing siege of Vicksburg, which will be discussed shortly.

Lincoln was having difficulties finding the right commander for the Army of the Potomac. Mere days before the battle at Gettysburg, he appointed General George Meade. Meade's orders were to follow Lee and make sure Union troops prevented him from getting to Washington.

On June 15th, Lee led parts of his army across the Potomac, and by the end of the month, they had reached the Susquehanna River. The battle began on July 1st when a group of Confederate troops made their way to Gettysburg, Pennsylvania, for supplies. They were confronted by a Union cavalry unit, which held them off until more reinforcements arrived.

By the afternoon, the chance encounter at a road junction between the two forces had erupted into a ferocious battle. For three days, the Unions and Confederates continued to battle with heavy losses on both sides. An estimated 51,112 soldiers were killed: 23,049 from the Union side and 28,063 on the Confederate side.

The Battle of Gettysburg.

Adam Cuerden https://en.wikipedia.org/wiki/File:Thure_de_Thulstrup_-_L._Prang_and_Co._-_Battle_of_Gettysburg_-_Restoration_by_Adam_Cuerden.jpg

It was the bloodiest battle of the Civil War. When it became clear the Union Army was winning, Lee retreated and began to head south. Meade made the decision not to go after him, much to Lincoln's displeasure.

Feeling defeated, Lee tried to resign from his post but was refused by President Davis. Even though other battles would still be fought before the Civil War ended, Gettysburg was seen as the final decisive battle where the tide turned in favor of the Union. Gettysburg would be the last full-scale invasion in the North by Confederate troops. Lee's defeat essentially put an end to any hopes of the Confederate States becoming an independent nation.

Within a few months of the battle's end, the Gettysburg National Cemetery was established. On November 19th, 1863, Lincoln delivered his most famous address. In his speech, he highlighted the Civil War as no longer just a fight to preserve the Union. It was a fight for democracy, liberty, and equality. He pledged that the nation "shall have a new birth of freedom and that government of the people, by the people, for the people, shall not perish from the earth."[3]

Vicksburg Campaign – December 29th, 1862–July 4th, 1863

When the Civil War started, the Southern states had control of the Mississippi River, which was an important waterway for the country, as it provided a link to countries outside of the US. The Union would ultimately take control of the vital water route. Vicksburg would end up being a decisive and successful victory for the Union Army, but it would also be the longest campaign of the war.

During the winter of 1862/63, General Ulysses S. Grant tried to take the city, but his campaign was unsuccessful. He tried again in the spring of 1863. This time, he expected a long siege, so he had the army construct trenches to enclose Confederate soldiers, who were led by General John Pemberton.

Twenty-nine thousand troops were trapped within the perimeter, and in a matter of weeks, Vicksburg was captured by Grant and his men. Unsuccessful attempts were made by other Confederate troops to rescue the trapped force.

Pemberton put up a valiant effort and held out for nearly two months. On July 4th, a total of forty-seven days after the siege began, Pemberton finally surrendered to the Union. This defeat was a key event in the Civil War. After the Union Army successfully defeated the Rebels at Port Hudson in Louisiana, control of the Mississippi River was finally in their hands.

The Battle of Spotsylvania – May 8th–May 21st, 1864

After Gettysburg, a series of battles were fought in Virginia. General Ulysses Grant's main objective was to pursue Lee, defeat his army, and capture Richmond, the capital city of the Confederate states. He instructed General Meade and the Army of the Potomac to pursue Lee relentlessly. That pursuit led them toward Spotsylvania; their goal was to get in between Richmond and Lee's army.

As both armies reached the area, they were determined to block the other's progress. A twelve-day battle ensued, with heavy casualties on both sides. Nearly 3,000 Union troops died during the battle, while an

---

[3] "Battle of Gettysburg." https://www.history.com/topics/american-civil-war/battle-of-gettysburg#section_1

additional 15,400 were wounded, captured, or missing. The Confederate Army suffered fewer casualties, with approximately 1,500 dead and another 11,000 wounded or missing.

The end result of the battle remains inconclusive to this day, as both sides declared themselves to be the winners of the battle. The Confederate Army had maintained its defenses, and the Union Army had severely incapacitated Lee's army. Lee lost men he would not be able to replace.

Winner or not, it ended up being a significant and strategic victory for Grant because, little by little, Lee and his army were being run into a corner. He finally surrendered in April 1865 in Appomattox, Virginia.

The Battle of Atlanta – July 22nd, 1864

The Union Army's Atlanta Campaign started in May of 1864. The plan was for the Union Army to make its way from Tennessee into Atlanta, which was strategically important for the Confederate Army because it had a railroad and was a manufacturing hub. It was also close to Richmond, Virginia, which was the capital of the Confederacy.

Capturing Atlanta would be a significant victory. The battle started on July 22nd, 1864. The Union troops were led by Major General James McPherson and Major General William Tecumseh Sherman. During an engagement with Confederate troops, which were led by General John Hood, McPherson was shot and killed.

Unwilling to give up, the Union troops pressed on and continued to fight. They were able to successfully push back against the Confederate offensive, with the Confederates suffering heavy casualties, losing around 5,500 men (roughly 10 percent of their entire force).

Even though Hood and his troops retreated, they did not surrender. Sherman had managed to cut off Atlanta from the railroad to the east, but the Confederate troops held on tenaciously. Sherman continued to shell the city and stationed his army near the west to cut off ties with the railroad there.

The city of Atlanta was successfully captured by Sherman and his men a few months later in September. Following the victory, Sherman and his men traveled out of the city and lay waste to the countryside of Georgia in a campaign that is now called Sherman's March to the Sea.

The march lasted from mid-November to December 21st, 1864. The troops traversed Georgia, pillaging and destroying everything they could get their hands on. They ended eventually surrounded Savannah, Georgia, and demanded its surrender. On December 21st, the mayor formally surrendered.

Native Americans in the Civil War

Nearly twenty thousand Native Americans fought in the Civil War. They chose sides based on their existing loyalties and what they believed in. They fought for their families, their sovereignty, and their tribes.

Many Native Americans wanted the status quo to remain (or for things to get better). Many also fought based on their beliefs about slavery. There were also tribes who were encouraged by wealthy Native Americans who owned slaves themselves to sign treaties with the Confederacy and fight on their behalf. Many tribes sided with the Confederacy, which promised to restore lands.

In the end, none of the Native Americans got what they wanted and instead ended up fighting each other, with nothing to gain from it.

End of the Civil War

The surrender came on the heels of the Battle of Appomattox Court House. By the early spring of 1865, the Confederate soldiers knew they were losing the battle. As the Rebels retreated westward, they were almost entirely surrounded by Union troops. However, unwilling to admit defeat, the Rebels, under Lee, mounted one last offensive on the morning of April 9th. But it quickly became clear to them that the Union soldiers far outnumbered them.

By late morning, without any food or supplies and facing a large number of Union troops, Lee made the difficult decision to surrender. Lee and Grant met at Wilmer McLean's home, where Lee formally surrendered.

Although the war was over, it didn't put an immediate end to the battles, as news traveled slowly back then. After Lee surrendered, six other small battles took place. The last one, the Battle of Palmito Ranch, took place in mid-May. After this, the war was finally and truly over.

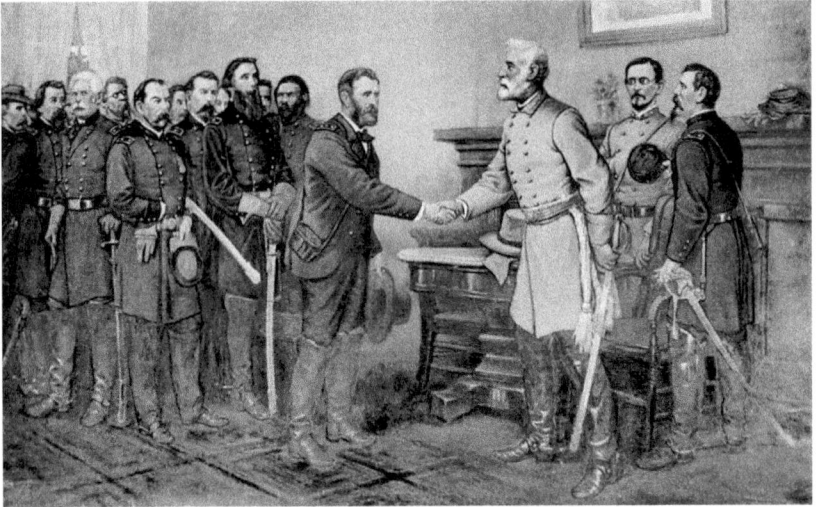

Painting of Lee's surrender to Grant.

Grant was very generous with Lee. He pardoned all the soldiers in the Confederate Army and allowed them to keep their private property, including their horses and sidearms. He even insisted on the Union soldiers sharing their food rations with the Rebels because, in his eyes, they were all Americans.

Chapter 12: Slavery, Emancipation, and the Aftermath

Slavery

From the country's earliest days, slavery had been a source of tension in the United States. as time went on, the divide between those who were for and against slavery deepened.

President Lincoln abhorred the idea of slavery, and he did not believe it had a place in the United States. However, he did not think he could abolish slavery completely since it would go against the constitutional right of slave states. He even says as much in his first inaugural address in 1861. Instead, he tried to educate the nation about it and tried to make sure any new states joining the country would not be allowed to establish slavery.

When the Civil War broke out, slavery was one of the reasons for the South's discontent. Lincoln himself stated the war was not about gaining freedom for slaves; the goal was to prevent the country from splintering into two.

As the war progressed and slaves began to flee from the South, some argued that if slaves in the South were freed, it would weaken the Confederate position since they were so reliant on slave labor. This would help the Union Army's war effort.

In July 1862, Congress decided that black men would be given permission to serve in the American forces. It was called the Militia Act. A second act, called the Confiscation Act, stated that any slaves who were captured from Confederate states or supporters would be given their freedom.

Lincoln appealed to the border states for help with emancipation, but they were not interested. Abolitionists urged him to take a firmer stance on slavery, but Lincoln didn't want to because his main priority was to bring the country back together.

Emancipation Proclamation

In the meantime, Lincoln's Cabinet was working on a document regarding slavery. Lincoln's secretary of state, William Seward, advised him to sit on the document and only release it after the Union Army won a big victory.

The victory came during the Battle of Antietam, where the Union forces crushed Lee and his troops. A few days later, Lincoln's document, which would become known as the Emancipation Proclamation, was announced. The proclamation implored the Confederate States to come back into the Union by January 1st, 1863. If they did not do so, then Lincoln vowed that all "persons held as slaves ... within the rebellious states ... are, and henceforward shall be free."[4]

When January 1st rolled around, the Emancipation Proclamation became law. In the past, when Lincoln encouraged emancipation, he had talked about providing compensation to slave owners or emigration for the slaves, but this was no longer his stance. He viewed the proclamation as a wartime measure.

Contrary to popular belief, Lincoln did not free all the slaves. The proclamation only applied to the slaves in Confederate States. Regardless, the Emancipation Proclamation created a foundation and set the stage for slavery to be permanently abolished. It also gave African Americans a stronger reason to win the war. It made the war a fight for freedom.

The goal of the Civil War began to shift. Although uniting the Union was still at the top of the agenda, abolition began to become more important. Perhaps it was hard for Northern politicians to imagine putting those who had been freed back into bondage. Congress and Lincoln began working on the Constitution to add an amendment that

---

[4] "The Emancipation Proclamation." https://www.archives.gov/exhibits/featured-documents/emancipation-proclamation.

would abolish slavery.

At the end of January 1865, the Thirteenth Amendment was passed. It would not be ratified until December. Lincoln, who had been hesitant to take a firm stance on emancipation initially, declared in February 1865 that he hoped this would become his legacy. It is safe to say that it did.

Border States

Not all slave states left the Union to join the Confederacy. The five states that remained part of the United States included Kentucky, Maryland, Missouri, West Virginia, and Delaware. Throughout the Civil War, they were known as the border states.

At the start of the Civil War, most of the border states were neutral. Some individuals even sided with the Confederacy, as they felt that the North was being unfair toward them. But as the war continued, there was a shift in sentiments.

Kentucky was neutral at the start but shifted its stance to side with the North. Kentucky's support contributed greatly to the war effort for the Federalists.

The same was true for Maryland. It was strategically located between Virginia and Washington, DC. Had Maryland seceded, things may have gone very badly for the Union Army. In 1864, Maryland voted to abolish slavery.

While Missouri was officially neutral, a significant percentage of the population felt that the war against the Confederacy was wrong and sent soldiers to support them. As the war progressed, the state government divided into two: one was pro-Confederacy, while the other was pro-Union.

Delaware was loyal to the Union, and its loyalty did not waver during the Civil War.

Things were a little more complicated for West Virginia, as the Civil War was the catalyst that split Virginia into two. While West Virginia was a staunch Union supporter, many people did not agree and joined the war effort on the side of the Confederacy.

Even though, for the most part, the border states' governments did not engage in active fighting, they were strategic allies for the Union and helped the war effort by providing supplies, materials, and money. Individuals fought in the war, but they weren't sent by the state government. Geographically, their support was also important.

The neutrality of the border states is one of the reasons Lincoln was so hesitant to come down hard on slavery. He didn't want to alienate the border states that were still pro-slavery.

By the time the Civil War was in full swing, a significant majority of the people in the border states had sided with the Union troops. Approximately 275,000 men from the border states joined the war on the Union's side. The Confederate Army had much less support, with approximately seventy-one thousand men from the border states fighting for them.

Aftermath

Once the war was officially over, the country was left ravaged and war-torn, especially in the South. The Thirteenth Amendment of the Constitution, which was ratified in late 1865, further impacted the South, as it led to the abolishment of slavery across the country.

Approximately four million slaves became free. Over the next five years, former slaves were granted equal citizenship, as well as the right to vote. Unfortunately, President Lincoln, the man who had fought so hard for this moment, would never see it happen.

President Lincoln.
https://commons.wikimedia.org/wiki/File:Abraham_Lincoln_O-77_matte_collodion_print.jpg

The Assassination of President Lincoln

The man who pulled the country through the Civil War would not live to see the country united once more.

Even when Lee and his army surrendered, some Southerners firmly held on to the belief that they could still create a Confederate country if Lincoln was killed. A famous actor named John Wilkes Booth was a staunch supporter of the Confederacy. He hatched a plot to assassinate President Lincoln and his successors so the American government would be left without clear leadership or direction. And in that turmoil, the Confederacy could be restored.

On April 14th, 1865, five days after the Confederacy's surrender, President Lincoln was in his private box at Ford's Theatre, watching a performance of *Our American Cousin*. Booth waited for a moment when the audience would be laughing and shot the president in the back of his head. Lincoln died the following day.

No other important figure was assassinated, although there was an attempt on Seward's life. On April 26th, Union troops tracked down and tried to capture Booth. He ended up getting shot by a Union sergeant and died within a few hours. The men and one woman who conspired with Booth were arrested, convicted, and hung to death on July 7th, 1865.

Lincoln may not have lived to see the fruit of his labor, but his legacy would set the foundation for the country the United States would become.

Chapter 13: The Reconstruction (1865–1877)

American history is colorful and volatile. However, back in the mid-1850s, nothing had been as significant, brutal, or as impactful as the Civil War. The country was unified once more, although the process of formally admitting the Confederate States would take some time. The war also traumatized a generation, resulted in hundreds of thousands of lives lost, and created deep resentment.

Once the dust settled, the country was faced with a monumental task. The government had to rebuild the nation. The turbulent decade following the end of the Civil War became known as the Reconstruction. The country was in uncharted territory and found the period difficult to navigate. The Confederate States returned to the Union, and millions of freed slaves struggled to find their place in society.

Congressional Reconstruction

The Reconstruction Acts outlined the terms and conditions for the Confederate States to rejoin the Union. The bills were written in Congress by Radical Republicans and were enacted in 1867 and 1868.

After Lincoln's assassination, Vice President Andrew Johnson was sworn in as the seventeenth president of the United States. He wanted to unify the country, but as a Southerner and former slaveholder, he also didn't want to be too harsh with the Confederate States. His instincts told him to be laxer and more lenient with the South. The Radical Republicans were fiercely opposed to this approach. The anti-slavery group in Congress determined that freed slaves should be given equal rights, and they wanted stricter measures for the Confederate States.

After going back and forth, the Reconstruction Acts were created. A major point in one of the acts was the requirement to create five military districts in the South. For a rebel state to rejoin the Union, they also had to create and draft a new state constitution, which would need to be approved by Congress, and ratify the Thirteenth and Fourteenth Amendments (the Fourteenth Amendment granted citizenship to formerly enslaved people). President Johnson did not agree with these measures, but his concerns were overridden by Congress.

Beginning in 1868, the Confederate States began to come back into the Union. Georgia rejoined the same year but was quickly expelled for removing black people from its state legislature. Two years later, on July 15th, 1870, Georgia rejoined for a second time, and the United States was finally whole again.

The Black Codes

At President Johnson's urging, the Confederate States were granted amnesty. They were also allowed to establish their own governments. It stands to reason that these governments would do what was best for their people and stay true to their values and beliefs. And for these states, slavery was still important.

To them, slavery was a precious institution that generated a lot of money. The South had been built on slave labor, and now the South not only faced much damage from the war but also had to come up with a new way to rebuild its economy.

To prevent African Americans from climbing the political ladder and to essentially force them to work for little wages, they established laws called the black codes, which severely limited African Americans' ability to integrate into society. By creating laws that restricted their lives, the white politicians created a system where a freed slave's life was quite similar to their enslaved life.

Slaves in the South were "free" on paper, but opportunities and privileges enjoyed by white people were denied to them. Their freedom and liberties were severely restricted. In many ways, they were just as trapped as ever.

This was made possible as a result of a loophole in the Thirteenth Amendment, which stated that slavery was forbidden unless it was used as a punishment for a crime. This led to Southern states criminalizing normal activities that could then be used to imprison African Americans. While the codes varied based on the state, some common laws included things like prohibiting African Americans from loitering in areas or engaging in conversations as a large group. Being unemployed was also considered a crime.

Black people had to sign yearly contracts agreeing to receive the lowest pay possible. Anyone who refused to sign the contract or forgot could be arrested and forced to pay a fine. Of course, most black people barely had any money, so their only option was to pay off their debt by working on farms. Nobody was exempt, not even children. This vicious cycle ensured the former Confederate States still had their slaves; they just weren't labeled as such. Such acts enraged many in the Northern states.

In 1866, the Civil Rights Act was passed by Congress, which gave black people some more rights, such as being allowed to own property or rent. They were allowed to enter contracts and even sue someone. It was a good start, but it wasn't nearly enough.

Fourteenth and Fifteenth Amendments

Things got slightly better, at least on paper, with the ratification of the Fourteenth and Fifteenth Amendments.

Under the Fourteenth Amendment, which was adopted in 1868, African Americans were allowed to become citizens. In theory, citizenship meant they had the same rights, protections, and liberties as other American citizens. The Fifteenth Amendment was ratified two years later, in 1870. It entrenched voting rights for black men by prohibiting states from forbidding any male citizen from voting due to race.

Eventually, the Southern states repealed the black codes, but unfortunately, it didn't do much to improve their lives, especially once the Jim Crow laws were established. Systemic racism, hatred, and fear toward African Americans persisted and would continue to persist for decades, allowing white supremacist groups like the Ku Klux Klan to flourish.

Johnson's Impeachment

Johnson clashed heavily with Congress over the Reconstruction Acts. The Radical Republicans despised him, while Democrats in the South marked him as a traitor. Johnson did nothing to enforce the acts, even though they needed a strong hand to make sure they worked. He also frequently pardoned ex-Confederates and openly defied the government he served.

In 1867, the Tenure of Office Act was passed, even though Johnson tried to veto it (he vetoed twenty-nine pieces of legislation, with Congress overriding him fifteen times). The act was designed to curb presidential power by requiring the Senate's permission before the president could dismiss a government official.

Johnson ignored the act and suspended the secretary of war, a man named Edwin Stanton, who was openly supportive of the Radical Republicans. Ulysses S. Grant, the famed Union general, was nominated in his place. Congress overruled the suspension, and Grant resigned from the post, which increased the people's respect and admiration for him. But Johnson would not budge and dismissed Stanton again.

Congress finally had enough. On February 24th, 1868, the House of Representatives passed a measure to impeach him. After an eleven-week trial, he was saved from being thrown out of office by one vote. When his term ended, Ulysses S. Grant, a Republican candidate, won the election and took over the presidency.

Ulysses S. Grant's Laws

When Ulysses S. Grant ran for president in 1868, the Ku Klux Klan's terrorist activities were at their peak, and the nation's political climate was fraught with tension.

Protecting African American rights was one of his top priorities, but he also did not wish to throw the country into another civil war. When he became president, he was faced with an overwhelming task ahead of him, and he set about trying to create an America for all.

In 1870, the Fifteenth Amendment was ratified, granting African American men the right to vote. He also helped Congress pass a series of acts between 1870 and 1875. These acts were called the Force Acts, and their purpose was to protect the constitutional rights of Americans while guaranteeing the Fourteenth and Fifteenth Amendments for African Americans. Under the Force Acts, the federal government had the right to enforce penalties (including using the military) on any states or officials who interfered in a citizen's right to vote, register, or hold office.

The acts were instrumental in reining in the illegal activities of groups like the Ku Klux Klan. Even though not everyone agreed with his policies, Grant won the 1872 presidential election by a landslide. However, his priorities would shift during his second term from black rights to dealing with the Panic of 1873, when the stock market crashed and plunged the country into a financial crisis.

Even with his attention divided, Grant signed the Civil Rights Act in 1875, which affirmed that all men were equal before the law.

Grant fought the hardest for African Americans out of any other president in the 19th century. He ensured they were given rights and that those rights were protected. He also made it possible for black people to vote, own land, and be seen as equals in the eyes of the law.

However, this would not last. Democrats began to win again, taking back seats in Congress. The government's attention shifted to other issues the country was facing. After Reconstruction ended, the Jim Crow laws were passed in the South. Poll taxes and literacy tests were established, making it more difficult for blacks to vote. Since blacks couldn't vote, their voice wasn't heard on the issues that mattered to them. And since they didn't vote, they couldn't sit on juries. Schools and libraries were underfunded. Segregation was the law of the land, and it would remain so until the civil rights movement in the 1960s.

SECTION FOUR:
From Reconstruction to WWI
(1877–1917)

Chapter 14: From Reconstruction to Expansion

During the last few decades of the 19th century, the United States again turned its attention toward expansion. It focused its expansion efforts on immigration and innovation and annexed places around the world.

Transcontinental Railway

The railroad first came to North America in 1827, and three years later, it started to provide passenger services. By 1831, mail was being carried on the rails.

Over the next few decades, railroads kept expanding. By 1860, trains were running on over thirty thousand miles of railroad in the United States, and in 1863, the ambitious plan to construct the first transcontinental railroad began. It took six years to complete, but when it was done, it transformed America.

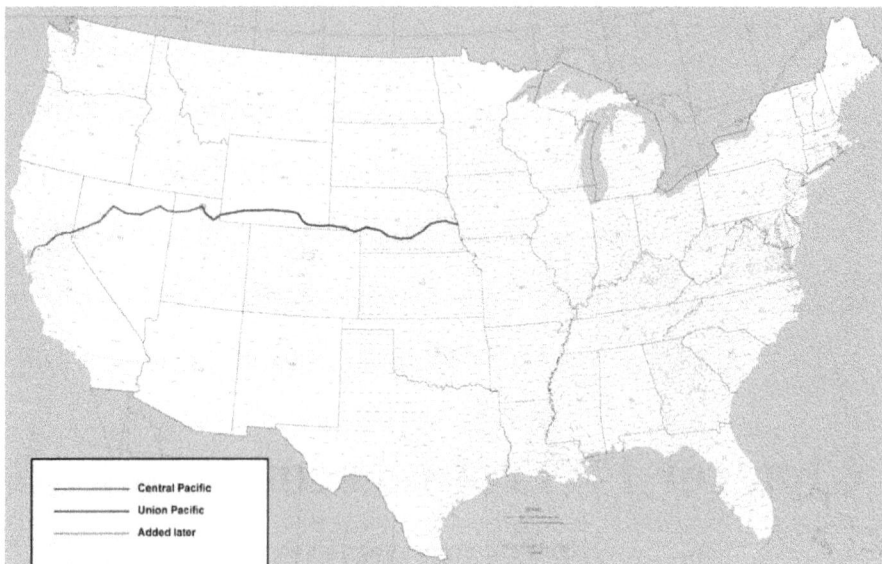

Transcontinental railroad.

The railroad connected the two American coasts. It made traveling more affordable and easier to export resources from one end of the country to the other. Before the transcontinental railroad, it would take nearly six months to go from New York to California and could cost $1,000 ($20,000 in today's money). After the railroad, the travel time was cut to just a week, and the cost was reduced to approximately $150 ($5,300 in today's dollars)!

The ease in transport allowed new businesses, such as mail order catalogs, to flourish and helped with the country's westward expansion, giving people more choices on where they wanted to live. As the country thrived, people in Europe began to look at North America with keen interest, leading to a period of mass migration.

The Industrial Age

The development of railways and other technological advances, such as the inventions of the telephone, electricity, the telegraph, and other things, dramatically changed the way people lived in America.

In Europe, many people were in search of a better life, as they had to deal with land shortages, lack of employment, and poor financial prospects. Many turned to America, hoping for a better life, and over a period of fifty years, from 1870 to 1920, more than eleven million immigrants arrived in the United States. Most of them were southern or eastern Europeans, but there was a significant wave of Chinese people who flocked to the country. Their cultures mixed with those already living in the country, leading to unique traditions. America certainly deserves its title of "Melting Pot."

The African American population also continued to grow, with many moving to the North. The number of immigrants may have continued to rise if not for the outbreak of the First World War, which led to a steep decline in immigration.

In addition to the war, the American government also started to make immigration more restrictive by setting limits on how many Europeans could come into America. In the mid-1920s, Congress passed a law barring all Asians from entering the country except for people from the Philippines.

Alaska

As the United States expanded, there was one tip of the continent that still remained beyond its control: Alaska. The US was keen to bring Alaska into the Union. Alaska would help the nation become a Pacific power, and the possibilities of finding gold or trading furs on a large scale were too tempting to pass up.

Russia was having a hard time managing the territory of Alaska due to the distance and lack of solid settlements. It was worried about losing the territory to Great Britain, so it was eager to sell the land to the US.

After a series of negotiations, Russia agreed to sell Alaska to the United States for $7.2 million. The purchase was finalized on March 30th, 1867. Some people refer to the purchase as Seward's Folly. Secretary of State William Seward pushed for the purchase so the country could gain a foothold in the Pacific. At approximately two cents an acre, most agree it was a good purchase. Alaska has many natural resources and adds to the grandeur of the United States.

Annexation of Hawaii

Ever since the original Thirteen Colonies had banded together to form the US, the government was more preoccupied with matters at home to really consider expanding internationally. By the time they started looking at conquering other lands, most of the world had already been divvied up, except for a few remote islands in the Pacific.

Hawaii was one such island, and the US wanted it. It had wanted the territory since the 1820s but couldn't do much about it. Hawaii had a monarchy, and the people were determined to keep the conquering European powers out of their island.

America gained entrance into Hawaii through the sugar trade. Sugar farmers (mainly white American men) in Hawaii were paid generously for their products. However, in 1890, the McKinley Tariff was approved by Congress. This raised the import rates of sugar coming from outside the US. Sugar growers realized that if Hawaii were annexed by the US, their tariff problems would disappear.

Around this time, Queen Liliuokalani came to sit on the throne. She was not fond of foreign powers interfering in island affairs, which would cause a clash between the two powers. When the sugar growers rose up against the monarchy in January 1893, US Marines were sent by the government to the island and forced the queen to abdicate.

It was up to Congress to figure out how to navigate these uncharted waters. Newly inaugurated President Grover Cleveland (who was serving his second term in office; so far, he is the only president to serve two non-consecutive terms) felt the Marines were in the wrong. He was an anti-imperialist and believed Hawaii should be left alone, even though the majority of the American population supported the annexation.

So, the matter was left in limbo until he left office. After the war with Spain started, Hawaii took on a new importance, as it could provide naval bases in the Pacific. President William McKinley signed a resolution to formally annex the islands. Hawaii became a territory in 1900, and in 1959, it became the fiftieth state of the US.

The Spanish-American War

While the United States was busy with railroads, immigration, and purchasing new territories, Spain was dealing with a rebellion from Cuba, whose people were striving for independence. This would be important for US history because it would lead to a war between Spain and the US.

The Cuban War of Independence and Spain's repressive measures and actions were covered extensively in American newspapers, leading to a lot of sympathy for the Cubans and their plight. The US government began to be pressured to intervene or do something, especially after the USS *Maine*, an American battleship, sank in Havana Harbor. The explosion was blamed on the Spanish, although it is believed there was something wrong with the ship.

Wishing to avoid conflict with the US, Spain announced its intentions to grant Cuba a limited form of self-government, but US Congress declared that Cuba had a right to become fully independent and insisted that Spanish forces leave the island. In retaliation, on April 24th, 1898, Spain declared war against America. The United States responded by declaring war on Spain the following day but making it retroactive to April 21st.

Two months later, American forces arrived in Cuba, and within a matter of days, they were engaged in the Battle of San Juan Hill, where the Spanish troops were soundly defeated. On July 3rd, 1898, the Spanish fleet on Santiago Bay in Cuba was destroyed by the Americans. A little over a month later, Spain formally surrendered.

Hostilities between Spain and the United States officially ended after the Protocol of Peace was signed on August 12th. The war itself came to a formal end on December 10th with the signing of the Treaty of Paris.

Under the terms of the treaty, Spain gave up any and all claims to Cuba, while Guam and Puerto Rico were ceded to the United States. Cuba would remain under American control until 1902 when the country gained its independence and became the Republic of Cuba. The exception was Guantanamo Bay, which had been seized by the Americans during the war with Spain to establish a naval base. A year after becoming a republic, Cuba agreed to let the US lease Guantanamo Bay and continue using it as a base. The US pays for the base every year, but only one payment has been cashed since Cuba's revolution in 1959.

Spain also agreed to accept $20 million from the US in exchange for transferring the sovereignty of the Philippines. This transfer of sovereignty would later turn into another headache for the US, as it led to another war. The US colonized the Philippines for forty-eight years. In 1946, the US formally recognized the Philippines as an independent nation.

But in the immediate aftermath of the Spanish-American War, the United States was feeling pretty victorious and powerful. It was rapidly emerging as a world power with interests and possessions beyond the North American continent. For Spain, losing the war meant its empire was on the decline.

Chapter 15: The Progressive Era

In the 17th century, America's focus was on expansion and building a strong, unified country. By the late 1890s, the country was pretty well established geographically and had enjoyed several decades of economic prosperity and industrial growth.

The bubble of prosperity broke with the Panic of 1893, and the economic depression ended in 1897. By this time, a wave of social activism was sweeping the country. This desire to create a better society became known as the Progressive Era.

Reformers had a vision of an equal and just society. They wanted to get rid of corrupt politicians and unfair or unethical practices. The movement had four aims:

- Protection of social welfare
- Moral improvement
- Creation of economic reform
- Foster efficiency

While industrialization had brought great prosperity to the country, there were many downsides as well, especially in how workers were treated and paid. Many businessmen had no issues with mistreating workers to increase their profits, and politicians did little to nothing to help the lower classes.

Reformers wanted better protections for people, as they believed that humans were capable of improving their conditions and environment. They also believed the government had a role to play to help make that happen. These beliefs slowly led to a shift toward more democratic and liberal values.

In this chapter, we will look at some of the most significant events to come out of an era that would be marked by a number of major reforms and social advancements around labor rights, economic reforms, women's suffrage, and racial inequalities.

First Labor Strikes

One of the earliest strikes to take place was the Great Railroad Strike of 1877. Workers were outraged when their wages were cut by the B&O (Baltimore and Ohio) Railroad. On July 14th, the workers began to protest, shutting down railroads in West Virginia and Pennsylvania. Over 100,000 workers protested in a number of cities and states.

Great Railroad Strike of 1877
https://commons.wikimedia.org/wiki/File:Harpers_8_11_1877_Blockade_of_Engines_at_Martins burg_W_VA.jpg

With half the railroads shut down, state governors called on the militia to put an end to the uprisings. A total of one hundred protestors were killed, with another one thousand put in jail. The workers eventually went back to work. The strike did not lead to any big changes or accomplishments for them.

Coal mining in Pennsylvania started in the mid-1700s, and it quickly became an important part of the economy. The mines relied on hundreds of thousands of men and children. Child labor was one of the many things Progressives worked to fix. Child labor laws were put in place in 1938. Working conditions for miners were extremely dangerous, and the job itself was very hard. Miners did not get paid a lot and were often in a lot of debt. Yet the owners of the mine profited handsomely.

At some point, the workers had enough. On May 12th, 1902, the Coal Strike of 1902 began. Miners wanted better wages, more reasonable working hours, and their union to be recognized. It would be one of the most famous strikes of the Progressive Era. It lasted for a total of five months and deeply affected different sectors of the country. With each passing week, businesses, railroads, and factories started to run out of coal. Even schools and post offices threatened they would have to shut down. The lack of coal had a ripple effect, leading to price increases at restaurants, bakeries, hotel rooms, and even rents.

President Theodore Roosevelt was desperate to fix the situation but couldn't find a way to end the strike. He eventually reached out to J. P. Morgan, a wealthy businessman, who drafted a plan to end the strike. Roosevelt also created a commission to mediate problems and complaints between the miners and their employees.

According to the plan signed by both sides, the miners' workday was reduced to nine hours instead of ten. They were given a 10 percent increase in their salaries, which was retroactive. The employers did not recognize the union but stated their employees had the right to join unions.

This was a huge victory for the miners and spurred the American labor movement. It made workers feel they could make a difference in how they were treated and also showed businessmen that results could be achieved through peaceful negotiations. As the miners went back to work, things slowly went back to normal.

Another strike that had a significant impact on America was the Bread and Roses Strike. Workers at the Everett Mill in the town of Lawrence, Massachusetts, received their pay on January 11th, 1912. They were outraged to discover they had been paid $0.32 less.

The reduction was due to a new law in Massachusetts that cut back work hours from fifty-six to fifty-four hours per week, so employers decided to cut wages accordingly. The $0.32 was hugely significant since the workers made less than $9.00 a week.

The workers walked out, and the next day, workers in neighboring mills began to do the same. Utter chaos reigned, as strikers destroyed machine belts and bolts of clothing. They broke windows with bricks and inflicted other damages on the properties.

Within a day, over ten thousand workers were striking. Thousands more joined over the following weeks, demanding enough wages to give them food and dignity. Many of the banners read, "We want bread and roses, too," giving the strike its name.

Other American laborers had the strikers' backs. They collected money for them, handed out food, and were very supportive. But things became tense between strikers, their employers, and the police. Some parents were so worried that they sent their children away to Manhattan, relying on strangers to care for them.

When President William Howard Taft opened an investigation into the workers' claims, Congress was horrified to hear about the working conditions in the mills, the mistreatment of the workers, and how their life expectancy was dramatically reduced. Working conditions were poor in many other industries as well, such as the meat-packing industry and other factory jobs.

Eventually, the employers agreed to a 15 percent wage increase and overtime compensation. After nine weeks of striking, workers went back to work. This victory helped the Lawrence workers and also paved the way for workers in other industries to receive wage increases.

Many strikes took place in the US, but we can see in each of these examples what an important role the central government plays. It goes back to the reformers' belief that the government can help make lives better for the population.

Women's Suffrage Movement

While women's suffrage had begun in the 1820s, it became more prominent and visible during the Progressive Era. This was the period when women really started to come into their own. They became major leaders in pushing social and political movements forward. They were tired of being told their roles were at home; they wanted to make a difference.

Women's suffrage was a huge priority for many. They wanted the right to a better education and more employment opportunities. They also wanted the freedom to get involved in politics and, most importantly, to have their voices heard through the power of voting.

Even though each group gained some ground in its own way, a few groups felt they would be stronger as a united front. In 1890, two groups, the National Woman Suffrage Association and the American Woman Suffrage Association, joined together to form one group called the National American Woman Suffrage Association (NAWSA).

NWSA, or National Woman Suffrage Association.
https://commons.wikimedia.org/wiki/File:National_Women%27s_Suffrage_Association.jpg

The women in this group were no longer fighting to be given the same rights as men. Instead, they argued that women should be given the right to vote precisely because of how different they were. This approach helped their cause, as different groups saw how women's vote would aid their own political agenda. For example, advocates of temperance were keen to give women the vote because it would add a huge number of votes in their favor.

The fight for women's suffrage would come to a successful end on August 18th, 1920, when the Nineteenth Amendment was ratified. Under this amendment to the Constitution, women were given the right to vote.

Through the tireless work of reformers, American women were eventually allowed to own property and were given the right to control and manage their own money. They were allowed to have custody of their children in the event of a divorce. However, it took decades for all of these changes to take place. For instance, a woman could not have her own bank account until the 1960s.

In addition to getting the right to vote, women also pushed for prohibition and reforms in public health.

Progressivism in Black Communities

During the Progressive Era, the widespread activism and fight for social justice largely excluded black people. Even though they had been given certain rights after the Civil War, they continued to face discrimination, violence, and racial segregation.

The Jim Crow laws were in full effect by the 1920s. They made it illegal for a white person and a black person to marry. The laws made racial segregation legal, suppressed voter rights, and ensured black people remained oppressed.

In order to have their concerns heard, African Americans knew they had to fight against the racial injustice they faced on their own. With that in mind, white and black activists established the National Association for the Advancement of Colored People (NAACP) in 1909. Today, it is the oldest and largest civil rights organization in the United States. The NAACP worked tirelessly to raise awareness about the injustices faced by black people.

After William McKinley's assassination in 1901, Vice President Theodore Roosevelt took office. He strongly advocated for pro-labor laws, fair trade, and reforms to fix racial inequalities.

Theodore Roosevelt.
https://commons.wikimedia.org/wiki/File:ROOSEVELT,_Theodore-
President_(BEP_engraved_portrait)_(cropped).jpg

Roosevelt tried to bring more stability to black employees, who tended to be viewed as disposable by employers. They were typically the first ones to be cut from jobs or fired. Roosevelt also put changes in place to allow people to have equal opportunities for training and jobs, regardless of the color of their skin. When he was the governor of New York, he ended segregation in schools, allowing white and black children to be taught together.

His invitation to black civil rights activist Booker T. Washington to dine with him in the White House was met with stern disapproval and caused a lot of issues. Even though Roosevelt never did something like that again, these little acts helped break down some barriers.

Roosevelt's administration did not push for change as much as it could have due to strong resistance within the political system, but it did try to implement some things that served as stepping stones for African Americans in the decades to come as they continued to fight for equal rights.

Chapter 16: The Fate of the Native Americans

As the United States welcomed hordes of immigrants and continued to develop as a nation, you might be wondering what happened to the original settlers of the land. Violence and conflicts between the settlers and the Native Americans had been a constant problem since the early period of colonization. White settlers were determined to seize the land, as they needed it to expand and for its resources. They did so through treaties, trickery, trade, and violence.

Although this chapter will step back in time a bit, it is important to discuss what the Native Americans endured and how Progressivism failed to take them into account.

Indian Removal Act

When America was expanding, it needed the land that was being used by the tribes, as sharing seemed out of the question due to tensions between the settlers and the native population, who saw the ownership of land differently than the settlers. But in order to get the land, the US needed to remove the Native Americans living there.

The American government came up with the idea of the Native American reservation system in 1786. Under this system, indigenous people would be given land to live on, and they could continue to self-govern and live life under their own social traditions and cultural beliefs. Each tribe would remain its own independent tribe.

For nearly one hundred years, this system stayed in place and provided some form of balance. This isn't to say the conflicts ceased. There were a lot of problems with the reservation system. Brutality against the Native Americans continued, and land remained a source of tension.

Andrew Jackson was very keen on removing the Native Americans even before he became president in 1829. In 1814, he led troops against the Creek nation. After defeating them, approximately twenty-two million acres of Native American land was taken by the states of Georgia and Alabama.

President Andrew Jackson.
https://commons.wikimedia.org/wiki/File:Andrew_jackson_head.jpg

More land was taken by the government in 1818 after Jackson invaded Spanish Florida. The government did not send Jackson there with the implicit purpose of invading, but it did not do much to stop him. Jackson continued in this fashion until 1824, playing a key role in negotiating treaties with the natives for land in the east and trading it for lands in the west. For the most part, the indigenous population agreed to these treaties because they wanted to maintain the peace.

Tensions over land increased when the Supreme Court made a ruling in 1823, saying that while Native Americans could live on the land they occupied, they could never own it because America's "right of discovery" trumped their rights.

Five Native American nations—the Creeks, Cherokee, Chickasaws, Choctaws, and Seminoles—did their best to resist, but they eventually assimilated by learning how to farm in the European style and receiving a Western education. They became known as the "Five Civilized Tribes."

Realizing that something needed to be done, the government created the Office of Indian Affairs in 1824 to settle land disputes. Six years later, the Indian Removal Act of 1830 was implemented as a way of forcing the indigenous people off the coveted lands. They would be moved westward to lands in Oklahoma that weren't as desirable. Over forty-six thousand indigenous people were forced out of their lands. Numerous events, like the Mexican-American War and other conflicts, also hastened the removal of Native Americans from their land.

In 1851, the Indian Appropriations Act was created. This authorized the creation of reservations in several states across the country. According to the US government, the reservations would keep the natives off the desired land and leave it available for white settlers. Additional acts would be passed by Congress under the same name, which we will discuss further later in this chapter.

Conflicts and Wars

Unsurprisingly, Native Americans did not like the idea of reservations, although some moved there with little to no violent resistance. Escalating tensions between natives and settlers led to a series of battles and wars. The two sides had been engaged in conflict for centuries, so this section will focus on significant battles from the mid- to late 19th century.

Dakota War (1862)

The Dakota War, also referred to as the Sioux or Dakota Uprising, began on August 17th, 1862. It took place in southwest Minnesota along the Minnesota River.

A series of treaties between the Dakota and the government, which were signed from the early 1800s to 1858, considerably reduced the amount of land held by the Dakota tribe. To make matters worse, the

US government violated the treaty agreements, made late payments, or paid the money directly to traders who claimed that the tribes had debts.

The Dakota went hungry, and the lack of income and other treaty violations increased their hardships. When the payment was yet again delayed during the summer of 1862, Dakota warriors were determined to retaliate and did so by killing five white settlers. The warriors then visited Chief Little Crow and asked him to lead them into battle so they could get back their land. Reluctantly, Chief Little Crow agreed. The following day, an attack was made on the Lower Sioux Agency. Attacks on settlements continued along the Minnesota River Valley.

The war had officially begun.

Sometime in August, Henry Sibley was appointed to command a troop against the Dakota. This would prove to be very hard for Sibley because of his intimate familiarity with the Dakota. He had known them for decades; he spoke their language, was friends with Chief Little Crow, and even had a Dakota child. But he did as he was told and took his troops into battle.

For five weeks, the two sides fought fiercely. When the US troops soundly defeated the Dakota on September 23rd, 1862, at the Battle of Wood Lake, it was a devastating blow for the tribe. Three days after this defeat, the tribe surrendered to the government.

While the war was over and the fighting had stopped, the men who surrendered were held captive to await a military trial. Non-combatant Dakota were forcefully removed by US troops and taken to Fort Snelling. The first groups arrived at the fort on November 13th and were placed temporarily on the river bottom beneath the fort while the soldiers began to build a concentration camp.

A wooden stockade was used to close off three acres of land. Approximately 1,600 Dakota people, mostly women, children, and the elderly, were moved inside the camp. Their movements were controlled by the guards stationed outside. That winter, several hundred Dakota people died. The prisoners were treated harshly by the Americans. They were abused, tortured, and tormented.

Several months later, in February 1863, Congress decided to annul all its treaties with the Dakota, with all the land and any annuities going to the US government. A month later, a second bill was passed to remove the Dakota people. In May, the remaining Dakota were taken away to a reservation in a desolate part of what is now South Dakota.

By the time the war came to a full end, the Americans had managed to wipe out most of the Dakota from Minnesota.

The Colorado War (1863–1865)

The Colorado War was fought between the Cheyenne and Arapaho tribes against the white settlers for control of the Great Plains in eastern Colorado. The territory rightfully belonged to the Native Americans under the terms of the Fort Laramie Treaty of 1851. However, as waves of new immigrants arrived in the area to settle and as miners began searching for gold, the need for resources and land increased.

At first, the tribes tried to resolve the matter peacefully. They even accepted a new settlement where the indigenous people gave up most of their land in exchange for a reservation and annuity. But it became difficult for the tribes to live off just the reservation, and the government payments and the tension from the Civil War made things worse.

John Evans, the governor of Colorado, wanted to keep the Native Americans away from white communities. He announced that all Native Americans who wanted peace should move closer to military posts to show they were not hostile. The tribes did as they were told, believing themselves to be secure. However, a few months later, on November 29th, 1864, Colonel John Chivington, with the support of Evans, marched his seven hundred men into the Sand Creek area and launched a surprise attack on the peaceful Native Americans.

Women, children, and men were hunted down and killed. Over 148 Cheyenne and Arapaho died, most of them children and women. Volunteers from Colorado went back to the village and made sure to kill the wounded before setting the village on fire.

The massacre was so brutal and atrocious that it led to a public outcry. Once the Civil War ended, the government tried to deal with the tribes in a less horrendous way. The Native Americans involved in this war had had enough. They moved northward, raiding forts and attacking the US forces they came across.

Texas-Indian Wars (1820–1875)

Conflicts with Native Americans had been a long-standing issue in Texas ever since the first Spanish and European settlers moved into the area. As Texas became a part of Mexico, then a republic, and then part of the Union, the conflicts and tensions with the natives continued. Things became particularly tense after the Mexicans left because, as we have seen, the US government was opposed to tribes settling in what it now considered to be its territory.

A series of battles took place from 1820 to 1875 and became known as the Texas-Indian Wars. The Comanche tribe was less concerned with maintaining peace than tribes like the Sioux. This meant the battles were bloody and violent.

One event of particular significance is the Salt Creek massacre, also referred to as the Warren Wagon Train raid. On May 18th, 1871, in the Loving Valley near Graham, Texas, a wagon train was making its way to a fort with supplies. A group of 150 Kiowa was hidden behind a hill, waiting for the wagon train to cross so they could raid it. During the raid, seven men were murdered.

After the successful raid, the natives thought nothing more of it, but for the Texans, this raid would be the straw that broke the camel's back. When the raid was reported to General William Tecumseh Sherman, who had led the March to the Sea during the Civil War and who was inspecting the military outposts of Texas at the time, he began to understand the fear under which Texans lived. Sherman ordered that the tribe's chiefs be arrested.

One chief, Satank, was killed while trying to escape, while the other two, Satanta and Big Tree, were arrested, tried, and sentenced to death. The governor of Texas, Edmund Davis, decided to give them life in prison instead. Chief Lone Wolf eventually negotiated an early release for them on the promise of good behavior. Neither one kept this promise. Satanta committed suicide in 1874 after getting captured, while Big Tree lived a life of confinement at Fort Sill. When he was released, he lived on a reservation and died in 1929.

By 1875, all of the original Native American tribes in Texas had been wiped out or forced to relocate. The Texas-Indian Wars formally ended when the last band of Comanche, led by a Quahadi warrior, surrendered and relocated to the Fort Sill reservation.

Today, Texas has almost no Native American land.

Great Sioux War (1876–1877)

As the conflict in Texas was coming to an end, another was simmering in Montana and Wyoming.

Between 1876 and 1877, the Lakota, Sioux, and Northern Cheyenne fought with US troops. Settlers tried to encroach on and seize their lands after gold was discovered in the Black Hills.

Once the gold was discovered, the US government wanted the land, which went against the terms of the Treaty of Fort Laramie of 1868. Under this treaty, the Sioux had exclusive rights to a portion of the territory, which included the Black Hills area. It also gave them land to be used for hunting. But after the discovery of gold, Americans began rushing to the Black Hills area, and there was nothing the government could do to stop them.

In 1875, a group of Sioux went to meet President Ulysses S. Grant. They requested that he honor their treaties and stop the miners. Grant suggested paying the tribes for the land and helping them relocate to Indian Territory. This was unacceptable to the Sioux. The series of battles that ensued is known as the Great Sioux War or the Black Hills War.

An important battle during this war was the Battle of the Little Bighorn. Fought near the Little Bighorn River, this battle was a decisive victory for the Native Americans. When George Custer's 7th Cavalry was tasked with scouting the area for enemies, they made their way to the Little Bighorn Valley. The Native Americans rallied together, and Custer's seven hundred men were met with over two thousand Native Americans. Custer himself commanded about 210 US troops; every man who fought with Custer died. The two messengers he sent out earlier were the only survivors of his unit. While it was a victory for the Native Americans, the killings further cemented the image white settlers had of natives being vicious and violent.

While battles were being fought, efforts were being made to resolve the matter through diplomacy. Congress stopped providing rations to the Sioux until they agreed to cede the land. The tribes began to divide, and in the spring of 1877, some groups began to surrender to the US.

However, Chief Sitting Bull, a Hunkpapa Lakota (also known as the Teton Sioux), refused to surrender. He led a group of Sioux to Canada, but in the summer of 1881, they came back. With no other options, they surrendered. The Black Hills was ceded to the American government.

Wounded Knee Massacre

One of the final events of the Sioux Wars took place at Wounded Knee, where a group of natives practiced the Ghost Dance. They believed that if they did the Ghost Dance and turned away from the white settlers' way of life, their gods would create a fresh world and destroy the enemy.

The Americans stationed there did not feel comfortable with such beliefs. On December 29th, a cavalry of American troops surrounded Ghost Dancers near Wounded Knee Creek. The US troops were worried the Ghost Dance meant the natives were going to attack. So, on that morning in December, they confiscated the natives' weapons. It is believed that a deaf Lakota man refused to surrender his gun. It went off, and the US troops started to attack. The Native Americans attacked to defend themselves, but they didn't have their guns.

The American troops slaughtered the natives. It is believed that between two hundred and three hundred Lakota died, most of them civilians. On the American side, thirty-one men died. Back then, it was called a battle, but today, we refer to this event as a massacre.

After the end of all the wars, the American government got what it wanted. It was successful in its attempts to remove and relocate the majority of the indigenous people onto established reservations.

Indian Appropriations Acts

As part of the "Indian problem," Congress passed a series of acts called the Indian Appropriation Acts. The first one, passed in 1851, established the creation of the reservation system and allowed the government to send the indigenous people to reservations. The act passed in 1871 stated that the US would no longer recognize indigenous people as members of a sovereign nation. Thus, the government no longer had to work on treaties with them. In 1885, the Indian Appropriations Act stated that tribes could negotiate the sale of land that was not occupied by anyone.

The Dawes Act

The Dawes Act of 1887 brought yet another dramatic change for the Native Americans. Under this act, the federal government broke up the lands given to the tribes into smaller plots. The tribes or people who accepted the plot of land would have the right to become US citizens.

The end goal of the act was to eradicate Native American cultural practices and traditions. The government's point of view was that the best way of solving the continued indigenous dilemma was to "convert" them into Americans. Politicians wanted to assimilate the natives into American society and "civilize" them.

After the Dawes Act went into effect, over ninety million acres of tribal land were taken away from the indigenous people and purchased by settlers. The Dawes Act ended when President Franklin Roosevelt's administration drafted the US Indian Reorganization Act in the 1930s. The new act allowed Native Americans to form their own government and stopped the parceling of land.

In June 1924, President Calvin Coolidge signed the Indian Citizenship Act, which granted all Native Americans citizenship to the United States. However, they were not granted full citizenship rights until the late 1940s.

The reformers wanted the Native Americans to be treated better by society, and they felt the best way of accomplishing this was to integrate them into American culture. They discouraged tribal landholding and encouraged Native Americans to give up their traditional way of living to adopt the American way. While some Native Americans were amenable to assimilation, others were less keen and resisted.

Chapter 17: Political and Economic Changes

Constitutional Changes

The Progressive Era saw more involvement from the government with regard to societal issues. The push for progress saw the establishment of several constitutional reforms and changes designed to make society fairer and more equal. The reforms also improved the life of the general public.

Three constitutional changes stand out during this time period.

Sixteenth Amendment

Present-day laws regarding paying federal income tax began with the ratification of the Sixteenth Amendment.

Under Article 1, Section 8 of the Constitution, Congress is authorized to collect taxes on income from American citizens. That money would be used by the federal government for the upkeep of the country for things like building bridges, maintaining the armed forces, enforcing laws, and other things.

The amendment was passed in Congress on July 2nd, 1909, and was ratified on February 3rd, 1913.

Seventeenth Amendment

In 1912, a change was proposed to Article 1, Section 3 of the Constitution, which allowed senators to be appointed by state legislatures. Under the amendment, people would be allowed to vote directly for

American senators in each state.

The amendment passed Congress on May 13th, 1912. It was ratified almost a year later, on April 8th, 1913. This reform was seen as a solution to the electoral process, which was increasingly seen by the public as corrupt and ineffective. The amendment also ensured that big businesses, industrialists, and other wealthy people could not influence the process of selecting senators.

Nineteenth Amendment

The Nineteenth Amendment was a significant piece of legislation, as it finally gave women the right to vote. It was a hard-won victory for women suffragists, who had been fighting for it for nearly one hundred years.

It was approved in Congress on June 4th, 1919, and adopted into the Constitution on August 26th, 1920. It was the first step toward political equality for women and helped shift the mindset on what a woman's role was supposed to be. The 20th century is when women really started to come into their own, as they started to play a far more active role in American society. The traditional roles evolved, and women began to work outside the home, have careers, receive a formal education, and enter politics, although the changes didn't occur immediately after the Nineteenth Amendment passed. Regardless, this was a hugely historic moment for American women.

Presidents

As we've seen, the government played a more central role during the Progressive Era, as many reforms were pushed by the administrations of the sitting president. Three American presidents were viewed as being more progressive, and they played a significant role in pushing forward progressive reforms. They were Theodore Roosevelt, William Howard Taft, and Woodrow Wilson.

President Theodore Roosevelt

When President William McKinley was inaugurated on March 4th, 1897, he came to the White House with Theodore Roosevelt as his vice president. On September 14th, 1901, he died of gangrene caused by wounds sustained from an assassin's bullet. Roosevelt became president; he was the youngest man to serve as president.

Theodore Roosevelt believed that governments had a role to play when it came to the public's welfare, society's progress, and keeping businesses under control, just like the progressive reformers. And he was keen on implementing some meaningful changes.

For instance, Roosevelt was responsible for the Square Deal, one of the most important and influential policies of the 20th century. The domestic policy was geared toward helping the middle class and had three key goals:

- Protecting the consumer
- Controlling large corporations
- Conserving natural resources

He had a reputation as a "trust-buster," and during his time in office, his administration filed forty-four antitrust actions against some of the biggest corporations in the country. He was strongly supportive of regulating corporations, as he believed it would ultimately benefit the public at large. The regulations he passed ensured that the rights of both the consumer and the business were protected.

The Square Deal led to the establishment of several important acts and policies that continue to influence America today. Some of these include the Pure Food and Drug Act of 1906, the Meat Inspection Act, the National Child Labor Committee, and the Antiquities Act. Each of these acts was designed to safeguard the consumer.

A lover of nature, Roosevelt saw the need to protect and preserve nature. He was the first president who worked to conserve the country's natural resources. He worked hard to cherish and promote the vast, natural beauty of the United States. His preservation efforts included establishing 150 national forests, several national parks, game preserves, and national monuments.

Theodore Roosevelt's legacy continues to live on today.

President William Howard Taft

Once Roosevelt's presidency ended, William Howard Taft, a man whom Roosevelt had handpicked to replace him as the Republican presidential candidate, won the election.

Taft became president in 1909 and continued a lot of the work that Roosevelt had started. He filed nearly ninety antitrust actions and developed the Mann-Elkins Act, which gave the Interstate Commerce Commission (ICC) the authority to regulate phones, telegraphs, and cable companies. The act also put an end to railroad companies giving away free tickets or reduced fares to employees and their families.

Taft was a big supporter of the Sixteenth and Seventeenth Amendments and helped to create the Federal Children's Bureau and the Bureau of Mines, an agency dedicated to setting safety standards for miners.

Through the course of his presidency, Taft began to lose support within his party. Roosevelt considered running again, but ultimately the Republicans stuck with Taft as their candidate. Roosevelt created the Progressive Party with his supporters. Neither man won.

President Woodrow Wilson

The Democrats chose Woodrow Wilson as their nominee for the 1912 presidential election.

President Woodrow Wilson.
https://commons.wikimedia.org/wiki/File:Thomas_Woodrow_Wilson,_Harris_%26_Ewing_bw_photo_portrait,_1919_(cropped).jpg

Because the Republican vote was split between those who supported Taft and those who wanted Roosevelt, Wilson swooped in with the largest electoral majority seen in any presidential elections until that point.

Wilson's presidency was significant for a number of reasons. The last time Democrats had been in power was during the Civil War, and now they suddenly had power in the White House and both houses of Congress.

One of Wilson's campaign promises was around tariff and banking reforms. He put together an economic reform package called the New Freedom. The agenda dealt with issues involving tariffs, labor reforms, and banking. It went through Congress in late 1913.

The New Freedom plan introduced the concept of a federal income tax for the first time and outlined banking regulations, tariff reductions, and antitrust legislation.

But by 1914, Wilson's attention was on other things happening in Europe. The First World War had begun.

Wilson was determined that America's role in the global conflict would be as a peacemaker. He wanted the US to remain neutral and stay out of the war. The neutral position lasted until December 1917, when the US formally declared war on Austria-Hungary. Germany had started to engage in submarine attacks, and the US became the unwitting victim. Wilson felt the US had to enter the war in order to "make the world safe for democracy."[5]

Panama Canal Construction

One of America's goals throughout the 1800s was the construction of a trans-isthmian canal. They recognized that constructing a waterway between the Atlantic and Pacific Oceans would allow them to move ships and goods quickly and efficiently, which would lead to increased business.

In 1880, the man who built the Suez Canal in Egypt, Count Ferdinand de Lesseps, decided to tackle the project that would come to be known as the Panama Canal. The company quickly realized this would not be an easy task. Environmental factors like heavy rains and landslides and illnesses like malaria kept delaying the project. De Lesseps came to the conclusion that building a canal at sea level was too challenging and hard, so the project came to an abrupt end in 1888.

---

[5] "Woodrow Wilson." https://www.whitehouse.gov/about-the-white-house/presidents/woodrow-wilson/.

In 1902, the US, under the guidance of President Theodore Roosevelt, bought the French equipment and resources for $40 million and approached Colombia for the right to build on its territory. Colombia turned the US down, so the US helped the Panamanians with their fight for independence from Colombia. In November 1903, it formally recognized the Republic of Panama.

Following Panama's independence, the American government signed the Hay-Bunau-Varilla Treaty with Panama to get exclusive rights to the canal zone they needed. In exchange, the US gave Panama $10 million. It also agreed to pay an annuity of $250,000, which would start being paid nine years later.

The US formally began work on the canal in the spring of 1904 and almost immediately began to come up against much of the same obstacles faced by the French. The following year, John Stevens, a railroad specialist, was put in charge of the project. He implemented some changes right away, such as finding more efficient ways of doing the work and hiring West Indian people to work on the canal.

The working conditions for the workers building the Panama Canal were horrific and far from ideal. Canal workers made around twenty cents an hour, and their day was filled with hardships. If the backbreaking work wasn't bad enough, they were subjected to racial tensions and abuse. They also lived in constant fear of contracting a life-threatening disease, such as yellow fever or malaria.

They also had to work in a rough environment and deal with the changing weather conditions. Machinery accidents were common. A combination of all these factors resulted in daily deaths. It is estimated that around twenty-five thousand workers were killed during the construction of the canal.

A drawing of the Panama Canal

Stevens also suggested constructing a lock canal as a workaround to the issue of landslides. A lock canal would allow ships to be raised to the level of the oceans before being lowered back down to the sea level.

William Gorga, the chief sanitary officer, also played an important role by systemically wiping out all the mosquitos in the area with crude oil and kerosene. This helped eliminate some of the diseases the workers suffered from.

Construction began in November 1906 and faced a few setbacks, such as Stevens resigning from the project and construction having to cut through mountains, but the obstacles were overcome. The project was completed in 1913.

On August 15th, 1914, the Panama Canal was officially opened. A grand celebration had been planned for the opening to showcase America's exceptional power and ability to do the impossible. However, due to World War I, the celebrations were scaled back.

In the end, the project cost the American government over $350 million and required over forty thousand laborers. Many of them died. The estimated number of deaths is 5,600, but historians believe the actual number is much higher. Thousands more sustained permanent injuries and were left crippled or disabled.

What did the Panama Canal do for America? Well, it made the nation one of the most powerful nations in the world because it had control over where two oceans meet. It also saved American ships a lot of money and time and generated new businesses because ships were able to move more quickly.

The Rise of Industrialists and Bankers

The Progressive Era wouldn't have been what it was without the influence of the industrialists and bankers.

Once the Civil War ended, the US went through the Reconstruction. When the dust settled, the country went through rapid industrial growth. New industries, such as steel manufacturing, petroleum, electricity, and many others, emerged while existing industries expanded and grew. Railroads, especially the transcontinental railway, transformed society.

In this period of enormous growth and expansion, a new social class emerged: industrialists and bankers, who were either very wealthy or lived an upper-middle-class life. The blue-collar class also expanded exponentially; after all, industries could only grow and prosper as a result of the working class. The poorer classes mostly consisted of new immigrants, who arrived in droves.

While there were a number of rising industrialists and bankers, there was a handful who were considered the most prominent and powerful. They left behind an enduring legacy.

John D. Rockefeller

John D. Rockefeller, a Republican, championed many social reforms and was considered to be a very progressive and liberal man. He became wealthy by dominating the oil industry, which also had a profound impact on the Industrial Revolution.

He founded the company Standard Oil and controlled nearly 90 percent of the oil refineries all over America.

John D. Rockefeller.

Rockefeller's refineries turned oil into kerosene, the product used by Americans in their homes. Some people admired him greatly, while others felt he was unethical and immoral.

Rockefeller was often criticized by journalists, reformers, and other people for the way he made his money. He was accused of being greedy and of building his empire by crushing the competition through secret dealings and threats. He also took advantage of other people's failures to enrich himself.

Most businessmen likely engaged in similar tactics to build their wealth, so the criticisms may not be entirely fair. What we do know of Rockefeller is that he treated his workers fairly and well. He praised where praise was due, ensured his workers felt respected, and was even known to occasionally work alongside them.

Whatever one's opinion, there is no doubt that he did a lot for society. He retired in 1896 and spent the rest of his life doing philanthropy. He championed public sanitation and helped with the fight against diseases like yellow fever and malaria. Rockefeller also funded schools and organizations to help the next generation move forward.

His legacy endures to this day, as the Rockefeller Foundation continues to champion causes that affect society.

Andrew Carnegie

Known and revered as one of the most successful businessmen in American history, Andrew Carnegie came from very humble beginnings and went on to become one of the richest men in America. His fortune was built through the steel industry.

Carnegie co-founded a steel company in the early 1870s and spent decades building it into a steel empire. He was innovative and worked hard to bring down the cost of steel and make it more affordable. He purchased iron mines and railroad companies, which allowed him to reduce his own costs, which, in turn, meant he could sell his steel at a reduced cost.

Andrew Carnegie also adopted a new invention that allowed steel to be made from iron in a more efficient manner. His steel mills were incredibly modern and served as a model to be emulated by other companies in the industry.

Thanks to his fight to lower prices, America was able to start building skyscrapers at a reasonable cost. The United States' first skyscraper, the Home Insurance Company Building, began construction in Chicago in 1884 using steel girders.

Carnegie's treatment of his workers was anything but generous and has generated a lot of controversy over the years. His workers worked twelve-hour days, seven days a week. They had no holidays or days off besides the Fourth of July. The working conditions were harsh and dangerous, and the workers' wages were barely enough to get by. Carnegie cut those meager wages further to keep a higher profit.

Work-related deaths were not uncommon. In 1880, an explosion occurred in one of his factories that resulted in several workers dying. Carnegie was more concerned with the material losses incurred than the lives lost, which cast him in a villainous light.

Carnegie's wealth was built on the backs of the mill workers, yet he seemed to care very little about them. It's hard to understand why he would treat his workers in such a way when he had been born and raised in a very humble and hard environment.

However, he was known for being generous and became a great philanthropist in his later years. He donated the bulk of his wealth to charitable causes. Carnegie was a great champion of education and helped to establish schools, colleges, and other nonprofit organizations like public libraries, museums, and even a music hall.

Andrew Carnegie's s contributions to American society cannot be denied, but neither can his treatment of the men and women who built him his empire.

J. P. Morgan

John Pierpont Morgan was one of the most powerful bankers in the Progressive Era. He had a particular talent for bringing stability to a business and making it profitable. He became an extremely powerful railroad magnate by reorganizing and merging several railroad companies and buying stock in those companies.

In 1898, he did something similar with steel and provided financing for the creation of the Federal Steel Company. Morgan later merged several steel companies and created the United States Steel Corporation. Through a number of strategic and bold moves, he amassed a fortune.

When the United States was facing economic crises, it had no way of handling them because the country did not have a central bank. Morgan stepped in to loan over $60 million to the government, helping to rescue the country's gold standard. Aside from helping the federal government with the economy, Morgan also helped Roosevelt bring an end to the Coal Strike of 1902.

Morgan would go on to become the head of the banking firm known as J. P. Morgan & Co. Today, the bank is one of the largest financial institutions in the world.

Like Rockefeller and Carnegie, he contributed a lot to society and donated millions of dollars to educational institutions, museums, and other public institutions.

There are arguments to be made about how much good the rich industrialists and bankers brought to society. They typically used dubious means to acquire their wealth and used their money and influence to impact politics and the government. But it cannot be denied that their philanthropical work helped shape society as we know it today.

SECTION FIVE:
WWI, Great Depression, and WWII (1914–1945)

Thanks in large part to the rapid industrial growth, a surge in global exports, waves of immigration, and a booming economy, the United States was slowly but surely gaining a global reputation as a rising and influential power. But America's handling of the First and Second World Wars would cement its position as a worldwide superpower.

Chapter 18: World War I and the Roaring '20s

US and WWI

For decades, the United States had steadfastly maintained a position of isolationism when it came to world events. It was more concerned with its own expansion and growth.

So, when Austrian Archduke Franz Ferdinand was assassinated by the Black Hand, a Serbian nationalist group, on June 28th, 1914, it wasn't seen as a monumental event in the United States, or at least an event worth getting involved with.

Of course, nobody could have predicted that the assassination would set off a chain of events, ultimately leading to a global conflict between the Allies (France, Russia, Great Britain, Serbia, and eventually the United States) and the Central Powers (Germany, the Ottoman Empire, and Austria-Hungary).

President Woodrow Wilson and WWI

When the war broke out, the United States had no interest and no stakes in the conflict. President Woodrow Wilson openly declared that America would remain neutral. The majority of the American public supported this stance, especially since there were many immigrants in the country whose nations were at war with each other in Europe. Wilson felt it was a delicate issue all around and best to be avoided.

As a neutral country, the US provided raw materials, food, and ammunition to both sides. Banks also provided loans to the countries at war; however, most of these resources and loans went to the Allied countries.

Public sentiment began to shift in May 1915 after the *Lusitania*, a British ship, was sunk by a German U-boat. Approximately 1,200 people died, 128 of them Americans. The war had finally hit close to home, and the diplomatic relationship between the US and Germany became tense.

President Wilson provided a strict warning to Germany but still wanted to stay neutral. Many Americans disagreed with him. Germany torpedoed a French ship in March 1916, and when the US threatened to cut diplomatic ties, Germany promised not to sink any more merchant or passenger ships.

In November 1916, Wilson won a second term as president. By this time, some Americans headed to Europe to help the war effort.

By the end of January 1917, Germany announced that it would resume its submarine warfare. America finally cut off diplomatic ties with the country, and over the next two months, several American merchant ships were attacked and sunk by German U-boats.

The final straw for the American government was the Zimmerman telegram. The telegram outlined an alliance between Germany and Mexico, with Germany pledging to help Mexico regain territories it had lost to America in exchange for support with the war. When the telegram became public knowledge, Americans were beyond outraged. On April 2nd, 1917, President Wilson officially declared war on Germany and entered WWI. Their entry provided a much-needed boost for the war-weary British and French. Through the course of the war, nearly 120,000 American soldiers died.

Wilson and the League of Nations

Once the US entered the war, it was determined to win the conflict. Wilson was horrified by the destruction and brutality of the war and wanted to ensure that such a thing would never occur again. Wilson unveiled his Fourteen Points in early 1918, which were a set of guidelines that he believed would deter another war.

With the Fourteen Points, Wilson outlined his vision of establishing an international organization whose task would be to resolve global disputes before they could get out of hand. He also believed that nations should be open and transparent and that all countries had the right to self-determination.

When the war ended, Allied leaders met in Paris to hash out the terms of peace. Wilson worked hard to make the treaty as fair as he could, given the European countries' intense anger toward Germany. The terms of the treaty put the blame of the entire war on Germany, leaving the country humiliated and in financial ruin. Germany was also forced to demilitarize its forces. The Treaty of Versailles, which ended one world war, would ironically go on to become one of the causes of another world war.

The Paris Peace Conference of 1919 resulted in the Treaty of Versailles, which included a pledge to create the League of Nations. The League of Nations was based largely on Wilson's Fourteen Points and was created to make sure that something like WWI never happened again. The League of Nations had four main goals:

1. To settle disputes and conflicts between countries through peaceful means before they could escalate into anything more serious

2. Improve global welfare

3. Promote collective security

4. Disarmament

Despite Wilson's best efforts to get the United States involved in the League of Nations, Congress was unwilling to consider it. For Congress, American involvement in WWI was a one-time thing. Once it was over, they wanted to go back to their isolationist stance. Congress especially took issue with Article X of the League, which stated that all members of the League had to defend another member country if it faced aggression or in the event of an attack. This was something Congress was not willing to commit to, as they felt the term violated American sovereignty. Due to this opposition, the Treaty of Versailles was not ratified by the Senate, and the US never became part of the League of Nations.

The League was in existence until 1946. Although it failed to prevent WWII, it did negotiate some conflicts peacefully, for instance, Turkey's and Iraq's dispute over Mosul in 1926. Shortly before it was dissolved, the United Nations was created. The UN was based on the same premise and principles as the League of Nations but did not have its weaknesses. The UN also had a lot more support from other countries than the League of Nations did.

By this point, the US felt as if it had a leadership role to play in international politics, so the country was involved with the organization from the very start.

Prohibition

There was a significant revival of religion in the United States in the early 19th century. Some movements called for the abolishment of slavery while also calling for temperance.

In 1838, the state of Massachusetts passed a temperance law. The law only lasted for two years, but it set the wheels in motion for other states to follow suit, like Maine, which passed a stricter law regarding alcohol in 1846.

By the time the Civil War started, many other states had similar laws in place, and temperance societies had become the norm in American society. Women were especially against the consumption of alcohol because they saw the damage it could wreak. Even factory owners were on board with prohibition because they had fewer accidents, and their workers were more efficient and productive.

By 1917, World War I was well under way. America had just joined the Allies when President Woodrow Wilson enacted a wartime prohibition legislation so that grain could be saved for food. Around this time, Congress also submitted the Eighteenth Amendment for ratification.

The amendment was ratified in 1919 and went into effect in 1920. By this time, thirty-three states already had their own prohibition laws. Under the amendment, the sale, transportation, and manufacture of alcoholic beverages became illegal, ushering in the era of Prohibition.

In 1919, Congress put out the National Prohibition Act (commonly referred to as the Volstead Act). This act provided the government with guidelines on how to enforce the legislation. However, even with new legislation and an act in place, it was nearly impossible to enforce Prohibition or eradicate alcohol.

Bootlegging (making, selling, and smuggling alcohol illegally) inevitably led to the rise of organized crime and other illegal operations. It became a dangerous but very lucrative profession. Well-known gangster Al Capone used to make approximately $60 million every year through bootlegging.

This, in turn, led to an increase in gang violence. Businesses, such as restaurants that could no longer sell alcohol, suffered, and many went out of business. Other people died or put their health at risk by drinking homemade liquor like moonshine, which was often tainted. Revenues for the government and the states tumbled.

Prohibition became nearly impossible to control. By the time the 1920s were coming to an end, so was the public's support for Prohibition. By the time the Great Depression hit, the idea of legalizing alcohol again and making money from it was too tempting to resist. When Franklin Delano Roosevelt ran for the presidency in 1932, he promised to repeal the law if elected.

FDR easily beat out Herbert Hoover, and as promised, in February 1933, the Twenty-first Amendment was officially put forward to repeal the Eighteenth Amendment. By December of that year, thirty-six states voted in favor, and it was ratified. Some states continued to hold on to Prohibition. By 1966, none of the states enforced Prohibition anymore.

The Roaring '20s

After the war and the 1918 influenza pandemic, which killed more people than the war did (between fifty and one hundred million), came to an end, Americans entered a new uproarious period of dramatic social and economic changes filled with unrestrained joy and mirth.

Technological progress, industrialization, and the mass production of goods led to the rise of consumerism. As Americans prospered, they began moving away from farms to settle in cities. Employment was at a high, credit was available for cheap, America's GDP more than doubled, and the country saw rapid economic growth. The years of hardship and wartime devastation felt like a story of the past.

All of this led to the emergence of the Roaring '20s or the Jazz Age, a period characterized by growth and change. It would also be the first decade in American history that would be given a nickname.

Before WWI, American culture was still very much following the traditions of the 19th century. But post-WWI, the people were ready to usher in a new era. And it would be a modern, liberating era with dance halls, cinemas, flappers, jazz music, and speakeasies.

Women emerged from their traditional roles to embrace independence and make themselves heard. Flappers courted a lot of controversy with their short bob hairstyle, makeup, scandalous clothes, and a free-spirited lifestyle of smoking and dancing to jazz bands.

An example of a flapper.
https://commons.wikimedia.org/wiki/File:Violet_Romer_in_flapper_dress,_LC-DIG-ggbain-12393_crop.jpg

Fueled by the victory of the Nineteenth Amendment, an ever-increasing number of women began to join the workforce and push for personal freedom.

The Roaring '20s was also a time of artistic expression, new inventions, and industrial growth. The hours for blue-collar workers fell to forty-four hours per week while salaries were increased. Americans suddenly had more money and more time for fun and enjoyable activities like going to the cinema (films had just started to come out), attending dance halls, and watching Babe Ruth play baseball.

Clever marketing linked happiness and success to material goods. Americans bought cars, radios, and other goods, which changed the way they lived and enjoyed life. Technological advancements meant more people had access to electricity, which meant commercial goods like fridges and vacuum cleaners became household necessities for middle-class families, something that was unimaginable at the start of the 1900s.

And then, just as suddenly as it began, the Jazz Age came to a halt as the stock market crashed in October 1929. Prior to the crash, people had invested millions of dollars in the stock market during a period of speculation. When the market crashed, investors lost a combined total of

$26 billion and made paupers out of people overnight.

The economic boom and the Roaring '20s were suddenly over, ushering in the period called the Great Depression.

Chapter 19: The Great Depression and the New Deal

Great Depression (1929-1939)

The Great Depression is typically associated with the collapse of the stock market, and while it was definitely a factor, it wasn't the only reason for the dramatic shift in the country's economy.

To this day, the Great Depression remains one of the worst economic downturns to ever be faced by America and the world at large. Millions of Americans were affected by it. Fortunes disappeared, and people lost their homes and could not afford to eat. Thousands of people lived in shanty towns called Hoovervilles just to have a roof over their heads. The term referenced President Herbert Hoover, who promised that wealth and good times were just around the corner.

For Americans who were receiving very little government assistance or support, comments like this were laughable. Unemployment rose to 25.6 percent at one point, meaning one in four Americans had no source of income and no hope for it either.

When historians look back today on why there was such a change between the 1920s and the 1930s, they look at a few factors that, individually, would have been surmountable but became totally disastrous when combined.

1. The global economy was vulnerable due to high consumer demand and a lack of financial cooperation between nations internationally.

2. The rise of wealth during the Jazz Age made people believe that one could get rich overnight through investments and stocks. People easily fell victim to cons or bad investments. The number of people buying stocks increased dramatically, making prices soar. For a time, this made a lot of people very wealthy, but on Black Thursday—the day the stock market crashed—the bubble finally burst. Within a month, the Dow's value halved, and it kept going down.

3. In the early 1920s, money was plentiful, and interest rates were down, which led to people taking out loans and credit. By the end of the '20s, the Federal Board was concerned about speculation and suddenly raised interest rates, making it harder for people to pay things back or buy new things.

4. When the stock market crashed, investors began to exchange cash for gold, so interest rates were hiked up again as a way of protecting the dollar. But this meant that businesses could no longer afford to take out loans to stay afloat and had to shut down.

5. The Smoot-Hawley Act was a policy that raised US tariffs by approximately 16 percent. When Congress first debated the act in 1929, the economy was still in good shape. But after it was signed in 1930, things started to go badly. Other countries began to add tariffs on goods exported from the US because of the act.

A combination of these factors created a perfect storm for the economy to tumble and usher in a decade of hardship and deprivation. A period of drought also added to the hardships.

The Dust Bowl

A period of intense dust storms damaged and ruined crops in the prairie lands of North America in the 1930s. This terrible time in US history was called the Dust Bowl. Clouds of dust blew continuously for days, falling like snow. The dust even fell through the cracks of people's homes. The storms led to people and livestock dying and crops failing. Entire regions were left decimated and ruined. The dust also impacted people's health, as some people developed chest pains and other health problems.

The dust storms were caused by a combination of poor farming techniques, extremely hot weather, prolonged drought, and severe winds. These factors created the perfect storm for dust bowls to sweep through the states of Texas, Colorado, Kansas, New Mexico, Oklahoma, and Nebraska.

The continuous dust storms, also known as "black blizzards," forced thousands of people to leave their homes and become migrants as they looked for work and a better quality of life. Around two and a half million people left the dust bowl states; it was the largest migration of people in the country.

To help the people, President Franklin Delano Roosevelt provided emergency relief to affected people. Farmers were resettled on different lands that were more productive, and aid was provided to migrant farm workers.

Roosevelt also wanted to solve the environmental problems so that this wouldn't happen again. The government planted over 200 million trees to prevent the soil from blowing over the Great Plains. The trees also helped with the wind. Within five years, the benefits could be seen. By 1938, the efforts had reduced the blowing soil by 65 percent.

For the most part, the Dust Bowl came to an end in 1939 when rain returned to many of the dry areas.

New Deal Programs

During the 1932 presidential election, Franklin D. Roosevelt (FDR for short) defeated Hoover and won the presidency in a landslide. He took office while America was facing its greatest economic crisis in history.

FDR knew he had to do something to solve the crisis. During his inauguration speech on March 4th, 1933, he promised as much to the people. Two days after his speech, FDR shut down all the banks across America for a period of four days so people would stop taking out money from banks that were already unstable. About nine thousand banks had already closed during the Great Depression.

Through Roosevelt's Emergency Banking Act, which was passed on March 9th, the banks that were insolvent were shut down permanently, while the rest were reorganized. Americans were urged to put their money back into the banks, and surprisingly, people began to do so.

This was FDR's first step toward his goal of ending the Great Depression. He swiftly got to work to solve the problems the public was facing and came up with the New Deal. The New Deal was a series of financial reforms, public projects, and other programs and regulations that were established to stabilize the economy and bring financial relief to struggling Americans.

FDR also requested that Congress end Prohibition, which it did by ratifying the Twenty-first Amendment.

The Tennessee Valley Authority Act was signed into law several months later in May. Under this law, the government was allowed to build dams down the Tennessee River to control issues with flooding. Another bill was passed by Congress that paid some farmers not to plant anything on their fields to increase the prices of agricultural products and to end the surpluses.

Workers were given the right to create and be part of unions through the National Industrial Recovery Act, which also led to the creation of the Public Works Administration. This act allowed workers to collectively ask for better wages and working conditions.

In addition to these acts and legislations, FDR passed a dozen other laws, including a banking bill and a Home Owners' Loan Act. All of this was accomplished in his first one hundred days as president!

Second New Deal

Despite FDR's aggressive approach to tackling the Great Depression, the financial crisis continued. Unemployment was still at a high, the economy was still struggling, and most Americans continued to be filled with desperation and anger.

So, FDR launched a second round of federal programs in 1935, which is often referred to as the Second New Deal. One of the first programs to be launched was the Works Progress Administration (WPA). Under this program, unemployed people were given jobs in the public sector to build things like schools, parks, and bridges. The program also created jobs for people in the arts by hiring writers and artists.

The National Labor Relations Board was created in July 1935 to maintain the integrity of union elections and to ensure that employers did not treat their workers poorly or unfairly. The Social Security Act, which was drafted in the same year, provided unemployment insurance. The government also pledged that children and disabled people would be cared for.

While the New Deal helped resolve some issues, it still faced many political setbacks, especially from the conservatives on the Supreme

Court, who pulled back initiatives like the National Recovery Administration, which sought to establish fair workplace practices.

But FDR was not deterred. He refused to allow the Supreme Court to keep changing his programs, so in 1937, he announced that more liberal justices would be added to the Supreme Court so that there could be a better balance. When the justices discovered this, they started to vote in favor of FDR's projects. All the while, the Great Depression dragged on.

Economy and Culture

In 1937, the economy was back in a recession, and Roosevelt was having difficulty pushing forward new programs or policies. Two years later, the New Deal began to fizzle and eventually came to an end. World War II would ultimately bring the US economy back on top.

But the work FDR did on the New Deal programs between 1933 and 1941 greatly improved the lives of people who were struggling during the Depression. It gave them hope in a particularly difficult time. It also changed the political and social landscape of American society by creating the conditions for the emergence of a new political coalition, which suddenly included a more diverse group of Americans, including African Americans and working-class Americans. They were linked together in their common desire to see programs like Social Security succeed.

There was also a huge cultural shift, as more women began working outside the home. Roosevelt facilitated this by increasing the number of administrative and secretarial jobs in the government.

FDR's programs created the foundation for present-day America. Many of the things Americans take for granted today, like welfare and unemployment insurance, stem from the New Deal.

Chapter 20: WWII: America Becomes a Superpower

World War II

After more than a decade of suffering, the Great Depression came to an end when Japan bombed Pearl Harbor.

However, that wasn't the start of the war. When Adolf Hitler broke the terms of the Munich Agreement and invaded Czechoslovakia, the United States stayed out of it, even as it became apparent that war was inevitable. And when war broke out when Hitler invaded Poland in 1939, the US government fell back on its isolationist foreign policy and remained neutral for the first two years of the war.

The Neutrality Act passed by Congress in 1935 specifically prohibited the US from exporting any arms, money, supplies, or ammunition to any countries that were at war. After the Spanish Civil War of 1936–1939, the act was amended to be even more stringent and included greater restrictions.

All of this made it very difficult for FDR to get involved in the war, even though he firmly believed the country should. He had the foresight to see what Hitler's invasion meant for the world, and he knew America had a role to play in stopping him.

So, he found creative ways to bend the rules. For example, pilots flew WWI-era aircraft from the US and left them just a few feet away from the Canadian border. The Canadians took it from there and sent them to Allied forces in Europe.

But when Hitler got bolder and invaded Poland, triggering the start of WWII, it became more difficult to remain neutral and do nothing. Congress was eventually persuaded to amend the act to implement a "cash and carry" policy. Under this, Allied powers fighting Germany could purchase supplies made in America using "cash" and then "carry: it back to Europe on their own ships or planes.

Lend-Lease Policy

This worked well until Germany invaded and then occupied France, leaving Great Britain to battle it out alone against Hitler in western Europe. Newly elected British Prime Minister Winston Churchill reached out to FDR to tell him Britain was running out of money and would soon be unable to pay for supplies.

FDR had won his reelection for his third term as president with the promise to keep America out of the war, but he still wanted to help, so he convinced Americans and Congress that providing help to the Allies was in their best interest.

By the end of 1940, a new policy was introduced, allowing America to lend supplies to Britain for the war. Under this policy, payments wouldn't need to be made in cash and could be in a form acceptable to Roosevelt. The payments would also be deferred. FDR assured the American people that they had a critical role to play as the "great arsenal of democracy."[6]

After months of debate, Congress passed the Lend-Lease Act in March 1941, and FDR began to place orders for supplies, tanks, ships, weapons, and food to send to Great Britain. Within the year, the Lend-Lease program was expanded to include allies like Russia, and it kept being extended. In total, over the course of the war, over thirty countries around the world received $50 billion of aid from the US through the program (equivalent to $690 billion today).

America Joins the War

After staying neutral, the United States was finally forced to join the war when Japan bombed Pearl Harbor in Hawaii on December 7th, 1941. Over 2,400 American troops and nearly seventy civilians died in the attack. Nineteen ships, including eight battleships, were destroyed. Americans were incensed at the carnage.

---

[6] "Lend-Lease Act." https://www.history.com/topics/world-war-ii/lend-lease-act-1.

Within a day, Congress declared war on Japan, prompting the Axis powers to declare war on the US. This would become a turning point for the war, which, so far, seemed to be going better for Hitler and his Axis allies than for the Allied powers.

At home, the war was changing the way society functioned. Women were starting to enter the workforce in droves and enjoyed a newfound sense of purpose and freedom. Concerts, fundraising activities, and victory gardens all created a feeling of patriotism amongst Americans and added to the feeling of unity and standing up for what was right.

The war also created some ugliness at home, as the government created internment camps to house Japanese Americans. Since the Allies were fighting against Japan, there was a natural distrust toward Japan and its people. This spilled over into distrust, dislike, and even hatred of the Japanese people in America, who had previously been neighbors, friends, and co-workers. Through Executive Order 9066, Japanese people were rounded up and sent to camps that were scattered throughout the US.

They would remain incarcerated, living in poor conditions for the duration of the war. Almost two thousand died. Families were displaced and torn apart forever. When the Japanese were eventually released and allowed to return to their lives, they found everything they had worked for was gone. The effects of their incarceration would last for generations.

Meanwhile, American troops took part in dozens of battles and conflicts on numerous fronts, although the US played more of a leadership role in the Pacific theater. We have selected a handful of the most significant battles fought by the US.

Battle of the Coral Sea (May 4th–May 8th, 1942)

The Battle of the Coral Sea was significant because it was the first time that a major Japanese operation had been stopped.

Japanese forces managed to successfully occupy the island of Tulagi, but American troops, who had been expecting the invasion, tried to intercept the Japanese troops. For four days, the two air powers engaged in an intense battle, which resulted in the destruction of sixty-six warplanes on the American side and seventy on the Japanese side.

This battle was interesting because neither country's carriers fired shots at each other. Instead, as the planes took off from the carriers, they battled against each other. This battle and style of warfare was a foreshadowing of how the battles on the Pacific front would play out.

The battle was a tactical victory for Japan, which succeeded in occupying all of the Solomon Islands and destroyed several key Allied ships, including the fleet carrier *Lexington*. However, it came at a great cost since Japan couldn't continue with its planned invasions of Port Moresby and other targets in the South Pacific, which had been its primary objectives.

When Japan met the US again at the Battle of Midway, it was in a much weaker position.

Battle of Midway (June 3rd–June 6th, 1942)

While Hitler's target was Europe, Japan had its sights set firmly on dominating the Pacific. Its first hurdle in its plan was the setback faced at the Battle of the Coral Sea, which forced it to turn away from its other targets.

However, the commander of the Imperial Japanese Navy, Admiral Isoroku Yamamoto, was convinced they could defeat the Americans by replicating another attack similar to Pearl Harbor. He planned to launch another surprise attack against the American troops on Midway Island, which was being used as a naval base for the Allies. Ideally located between the two countries, it was the perfect target for Japan.

Yamamoto meticulously planned a three-pronged attack. There would be an air attack, followed by a naval invasion. Then, once American reinforcements arrived, they would engage in battle. The problem with the plan was that cryptanalysts in the US Navy had been decoding Japan's communication codes since 1942 and knew about Yamamoto's plans. They figured out that Midway was the target.

On June 3rd, an American reconnaissance plane spied what it believed was the majority of the Japanese fleet. Later that afternoon, American bombers struck at the target but were unsuccessful.

A scene from the Battle of Midway.
https://commons.wikimedia.org/wiki/File:SBD-3_Dauntless_bombers_of_VS-8_over_the_burning_Japanese_cruiser_Mikuma_on_6_June_1942.jpg

A second attack from the US took place the following morning, which was again unsuccessful. Japan then sent over one hundred warplanes to Midway and significantly damaged the base. American torpedo bombers carried on the *Hornet* and *Enterprise* began an attack on Japan's ships, but they were all shot down.

A second wave of US bombers arrived an hour later and set fire to the Japanese carriers. Additional US dive bombers continued attacking. By this point, Yamamoto knew that the battle had been lost. He retreated on June 6th, bringing the Battle of Midway to an end.

It was a decisive and critical victory for the Americans, as it put a stop to Japan's plans to expand its empire in the Pacific. The battle started to turn the tide of the war in favor of the Allies.

D-Day (June 6th, 1944)

One of the most significant battles and victories for the Allied powers during the war was the Battle of Normandy, commonly referred to as D-Day and codenamed Operation Overlord. The goal was to take back France from German occupation.

When the US joined the war, the main strategy was "Germany first," meaning the priority was to defeat Germany and Hitler. But the British wanted to focus on campaigns in Italy and North Africa before going after Hitler. The US didn't agree with that approach, but nonetheless, the early waves of American troops were sent to support the British in their other campaigns away from Germany. Operation Overlord was delayed until 1944.

Normandy was chosen as the location of the invasion because it was less defended and not the obvious choice. Allied powers set up decoys to trick the Nazis about the location of the invasion. Hitler fell for the trick and scattered his resources.

Prior to the Allied landings, the beaches were bombed heavily to clear the area. Bridges and roads were destroyed so Germany couldn't easily get reinforcements or leave. After the bombings, paratroopers were dropped behind the beaches to secure the ground in preparation for the land invasion. The beaches were codenamed Utah, Gold, Omaha, Sword, and Juno.

Despite careful planning, things started off rocky. The weather delayed the invasion. Some of the bombers missed key targets that had to be taken out, and many paratroopers landed in the wrong place, often ending up in enemy hands. Some tanks and vital equipment sank before making it to shore.

An iconic image of the landing at Omaha Beach.
https://en.wikipedia.org/wiki/File:Into_the_Jaws_of_Death_23-0455M_edit.jpg

The forces landing from the sea began the invasion on June 6th, 1944, at 6:30 a.m. Gold, Juno, Utah, and Sword were easily captured. However, Omaha faced heavy resistance from German troops, and the Americans suffered more than two thousand casualties.

Through the course of the day, the Allied powers managed to successfully storm the beaches. Within a week, the beaches were completely secured. As more troops and equipment arrived in Normandy, Allied forces were able to push back German troops in France, although the fighting was bloody and intense.

In August, Allied troops arrived at the Seine River, and France was soon liberated. With German troops pushed out of northwestern France and Paris secured, the Battle of Normandy was over.

End of the War

The victory at Normandy turned the tide of the war against Germany. With France no longer under his control, Hitler was unable to build his Western Front as he had planned and thus had no protection against the Soviets when they began to advance.

After France, the Allied powers turned toward Germany and eventually made Hitler fight the war on two fronts.

The Battle of Berlin (April 16th–May 2nd, 1945)

When Russia and the Allies joined forces, they had one common goal: to get rid of Hitler. After Italy's surrender to the Allies on September 8th, 1943, and the liberation of France, it was clear that Germany was losing ground.

By 1945, the Allies were fully focused on defeating Germany. Daytime raids on Berlin by the US air forces became a regular occurrence. Starting in March 1945, British RAF (Royal Air Force) Mosquitos dropped bombs on the city every night for more than a month.

The bombings stopped when Soviet troops marched into Berlin on April 16th, officially starting the Battle of Berlin. Within days, the Soviets, who vastly outnumbered the Germans, had surrounded the city. The fighting between the two sides became violent and fierce.

By the end of the month, the Soviets were close to the center of the city. It was clear to everyone, Hitler included, that defeat was imminent. Knowing the war was lost, Hitler decided to commit suicide on April 30th, 1945.

On May 2nd, the city garrison surrendered, but the fighting only fully stopped on May 8th. Berlin stayed under Russian occupation until Western Allied troops arrived in Berlin two months later and took charge of the occupation.

Liberation of Dachau – April 1945

Ending the war in Europe and getting rid of Hitler and the Nazis also meant the end of the Holocaust and the liberation of the concentration camps.

Dachau was the first concentration camp the Nazis built. Within weeks of Hitler becoming

chancellor, the plans for Dachau were well underway. Originally intended to house political prisoners, the camp would go on to play a crucial role in the Holocaust.

In the camp's first year of existence, around five thousand people, mainly German communists and political opponents, were imprisoned at the camp. Over the next few years, the number of prisoners grew substantially to include Roma people, criminals, gay people, and anyone else that Hitler or the Nazis deemed "undesirable." The prisoners were put to work to construct new additions to the camp.

Starting in 1938, the majority of the prisoners became Jews. When the Holocaust started in earnest, the other concentration camps were closely modeled on Dachau, which became a training center for Hitler's concentration camp guards. Medical experiments using humans also began in Dachau.

Once the Allied forces began to win the war and started to advance into Germany, prisoners from other concentration camps were transferred to Dachau. The march of the mostly Jewish prisoners is often referred to as the "death march." By late April 1945, American troops were already in Germany, and on April 29th, three US Army divisions arrived at Dachau. American soldiers witnessed the horrors of the Holocaust.

A small skirmish with the SS guards followed before the camp was officially liberated, and the

Prisoners were freed. The same day, another group of American troops, the 42nd Rainbow Division, liberated a subcamp of Dachau.

Battle of Okinawa – April 1ˢᵗ–June 22ⁿᵈ, 1945

One of the bloodiest battles of the Second World War was also its last major battle. While Allied troops were advancing into Germany, bringing the war in Europe to an end, the US Navy, the Marine Corps, and the US Army, along with other Allied contingents, were busy pushing the Japanese off the island of Okinawa in the Pacific.

The war in the Pacific theater raged on with one battle after another. American troops had destroyed Japan in the Battle of Iwo Jima, and now they turned to Okinawa. Securing the bases on the island was the final hurdle before they could reach Japan. Okinawa was the perfect place for the Japanese to mount a final defense.

On April 1ˢᵗ, 1945, American troops bombarded the beaches to allow for troop landings, similar to what was done for D-Day. Morale was low, and the Allies expected a strong Japanese resistance. Instead, waves of tanks, supplies, and troops were able to come ashore with virtually no opposition.

Within hours, American soldiers secured the Kadena and Yontan airfields. Unbeknownst to them, they were falling perfectly into the trap set out by Lieutenant General Mitsuru Ushijima, the man leading Japan's 32ⁿᵈ Army. The 130,000 men had been told not to fire on the Americans; instead, they were told to watch as they waited in defensive positions.

As the Americans came farther inland, the battle started in earnest. The fighting was fierce and bloody, and both sides lost a staggering number of people. The Japanese engaged in kamikaze warfare (suicide attacks). The Americans succeeded in pushing the Japanese back toward the southern coast of the island.

On April 7ᵗʰ, a Japanese battleship, *Yamato*, prepared to launch an attack on the US troops, but it was spotted by the Allied powers. The ship was bombed and sunk. A crucial battle on Hacksaw Ridge took place on April 26ᵗʰ. By this point, the soldiers on both sides were engaging in vicious, hand-to-hand combat. The fighting was intense and brutal. Ten days later, on May 6ᵗʰ, the Americans were able to successfully take Hacksaw Ridge. Instead of surrendering, many Japanese soldiers chose to kill themselves, including General Ushijima and his chief of staff.

By June 22ⁿᵈ, most of the Japanese resistance operations had been taken down. The Americans lost 12,520 men, and over 36,000 soldiers were wounded. The Japanese lost around 110,000 soldiers, and it is believed that nearly as many Okinawa citizens died, some of whom committed suicide after Japanese soldiers lied to them about what lay in store if the Americans won the battle.

The Nuclear Era

The Manhattan Project

Despite Germany's surrender, the war was technically not over. Japan was still fighting, and it refused to surrender. With Germany under control, the Allied powers, especially US President Harry Truman, who took over after FDR died on April 12th, 1945, were determined to get Japan to surrender and bring the war to a quick and definite end. Truman's plan to bring the war to a swift end worked, but it would have far-reaching repercussions and consequences for decades to follow.

In 1938, German physicists in Berlin discovered nuclear fission, which opened the door to exploring the creation of nuclear weapons. And that's exactly what happened.

While the war was going on, other countries worried that Germany would develop nuclear weapons to use during the war. Several nations began to try and develop nuclear weapons themselves, including the United States. The project to develop the atomic bomb was officially authorized by FDR on December 28th, 1942, and given the codename the Manhattan Project.

A number of scientists and officials, led by Robert Oppenheimer, began working on the top-secret project in Los Alamos, New Mexico. At one point, 130,000 people were part of the project. Two and a half years after the project began, three atomic bombs were developed by scientists. One of the bombs was tested in a desert in New Mexico on July 16th, 1945. The project was deemed a great success.

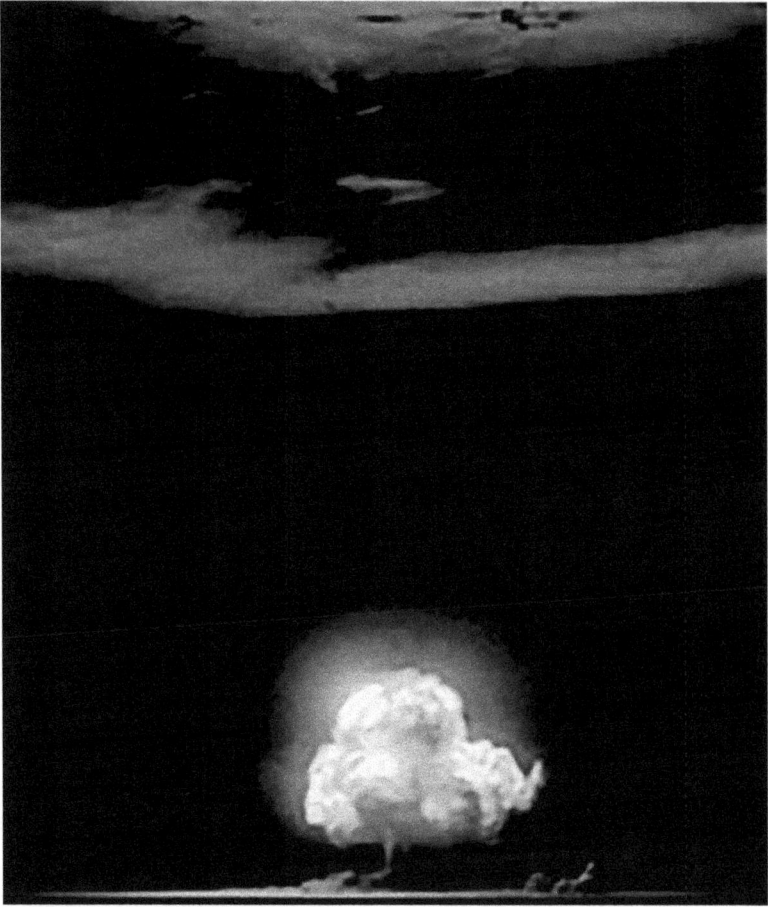

The Trinity Test, the first nuclear test explosion.
https://commons.wikimedia.org/wiki/File:Trinity_shot_color.jpg

The United States had managed to build the first atomic bomb.

Hiroshima and Nagasaki

By the time the bomb was tested, the war in Europe was already over. Germany had surrendered, the fighting had stopped, and peace negotiations were being started.

However, the fighting between Japan and the Allies, namely the United States, continued. Toward the end of July, President Harry Truman announced the Potsdam Declaration, which stated that if Japan refused to surrender, the US would take harsh and destructive action. Japan refused.

After much back and forth, President Truman then made the difficult decision to drop an atomic bomb on the country. The *Enola Gay*, a bomber plane, carried the first bomb, dropping it on Hiroshima on August 6th, 1945, destroying large parts of the city. Between 70,000 and 135,000 people died that same year, while tens of thousands died later from radiation or other bomb-related causes.

Japan still refused to surrender. Perhaps the government believed the US wouldn't use another bomb on them after seeing the devastation or that the US would have used all its bombs at once to get rid of Japan for good.

Whatever the reasoning, three days later, on August 9th, a second bomb was dropped on Nagasaki, leading to between sixty thousand and eighty thousand deaths that same year (it is hard to know exactly how many died instantly, which makes sense due to the lack of manpower to tally such high counts and sift through the wreckage in a reasonable amount of time).

Hiroshima after the bombing.
https://commons.wikimedia.org/wiki/File:Hiroshima_aftermath.jpg

Japanese Emperor Hirohito surrendered six days later. Thus, August 15th became known as VJ Day or "Victory over Japan Day." Some historians believe that the Soviet Union's invasion of Japan would have been enough to make the Japanese surrender. Truman's reasoning behind using the atomic bombs was to save his men, as the Japanese threatened to fight to the very end. However, innocent people were killed. As you can likely tell, the atomic bombings remain a controversial topic to this day.

A formal surrender from Japan took place on September 2nd in Tokyo Bay on the USS *Missouri*. After six long and devastating years, the global conflict was over.

However, the effects of the bombing would last for decades, as people died of leukemia and cancer and suffered from the horrible side effects of nuclear radiation. It is estimated that hundreds of thousands of people died in the two cities because of post-radiation effects, but the actual number may never be known.

Occupation of Japan

When Japan surrendered to the Allies on September 2nd, 1945, it officially ended the Second World War. Between 1945 and 1952, Japan was occupied by the Allied powers. The occupation was mostly overseen by the American forces, who were led by General Douglas MacArthur.

The US had two very specific goals for the occupation. It wanted to eliminate Japan as a possible threat in the future by demilitarizing the country, and it also wanted Japan to become a democratic nation, one closely allied with the Western world.

During the period of occupation, the American government invested $2.2 billion (around $18 billion today) in Japan's reconstruction and helped stabilize the country. Under MacArthur, a new constitution was created, which replaced the Meiji Constitution that had been written in 1889. Power was put in the hands of elected officials and not the emperor, although the monarchy was not abolished. It remained in place as a cultural symbol but did not have any real power. Under the new constitution, new civil liberties were granted to the population, such as freedom of speech.

Today, Japan is considered to be a developed country. Its population is well educated and affluent. Japan also boasts one of the most developed economies in the world. In a nutshell, the American occupation after the war can be seen as a huge success for both Japan and the West.

SECTION SIX:
The Cold War and the Space Race Begin (1945–1969)

Chapter 21: The Truman Years: The Cold War Begins

When the war ended, the US was the only nation that had managed to develop nuclear weapons, but the USSR was busy working. On August 29th, 1949, the Soviets were ready to test their first one. Seeing this, America created a program in 1950 dedicated to the development of nuclear weapons.

By this time, the United States was no longer actively practicing isolationism. Having played an integral role in ending the war, drafting the peace terms, and providing financial aid to the nations ravaged by war, it emerged as a global superpower. The USSR was also determined to assert itself as a superpower, which created conflicts between the two nations and ushered in the Cold War.

President Harry Truman

When FDR died unexpectedly weeks before Germany's surrender, Vice President Harry Truman became the new president. He carried the country through to the final end of the war and made the fateful decision to drop the atomic bombs on Japan.

While the terms of the peace treaty ending the war were being discussed, Truman was also working to improve America's social and economic state. On September 6th, 1945, Truman presented his 21-Point Plan to Congress. Under this plan, he proposed expanding the Social Security program, creating more public housing, and establishing the Fair Employment Practices Act, which FDR had created, as permanent legislation, among other things.

On the international front, one of the most significant policies to be implemented by Truman was the Truman Doctrine.

President Truman.
https://commons.wikimedia.org/wiki/File:Harry_S_Truman_-_NARA_-_530677_(2).jpg

In a bid to increase the reach of communism and its own influence, the Soviet Union looked at Greece and Turkey. The Soviets wanted to topple their governments and establish a communist regime. With this as the end goal, the Soviet Union supported communists within the countries during their civil wars.

During a joint session of Congress on March 12th, 1947, Truman spoke passionately about Greece's and Turkey's plight and asked for $400 million to help the two countries. He said it was imperative that the US help countries that were being threatened with terror by the Soviet Union. He was certain that if the US did not help the two countries, they would fall to communism. He felt America had an obligation to help countries be free and democratic.

This speech became known as the Truman Doctrine and was seen as an official declaration of the Cold War. Two months after the speech, Congress approved his request to send aid.

The doctrine was meant to counter Soviet communism expansion and officially changed America's stance on foreign policy by pledging to help any country that wanted to resist communism. With the Truman Doctrine, the US effectively moved away from its isolationist stance to take a more active role in international conflicts and events.

The argument didn't win over everyone, but it convinced most Americans that the Soviet Union and the spread of communism was a very real and horrifying threat. The Truman Doctrine set the stage for America's relationship with the Soviet Union for the next four decades.

Greek Civil War (1946–1949)

During the Second World War, the Axis powers occupied Greece from 1941 to 1944, leading to over 400,000 deaths and untold horrors. Greece's Jewish population was almost entirely exterminated. A year into the occupation, resistance groups began forming to fight back against the Axis.

The socialist National Liberation Front (EAM) was an alliance of a number of political parties and other organizations that fought for Greece's liberation from its occupation by the Axis. An anti-communist group called the National Republican Greek League (EDES), which received covert support and supplies from the British, fought against EAM. The exiled Greek government did not support EAM, while EDES did not support the exiled government.

The fear that the Soviets would install a communist regime in Greece was very real, and Churchill felt that Britain had to do something.

In September 1944, German troops finally began to leave occupied Greece. EAM sprang into action and, within months, had taken over most of Greece. On December 3rd, 1944, a violent and ferocious civil war erupted in Greece. Fighting between the communists and anti-communists, the latter of whom were supported by British forces, continued throughout the month.

By early January 1945, Britain launched an attack to seize Athens from enemy hands. Approximately 210 British troops died during the offensive, and hundreds more were wounded, but the attack was a success.

However, their victory was short-lived. The communists fought viciously. More than fifteen thousand Greeks and one thousand British civilians were captured by them. Many captives died.

As the war dragged on, Britain eventually pulled out from the fight in early 1947. But in 1948, following the Truman Doctrine, America stepped in and offered support to help the Greeks fight against the communists. This bolstered the Greek army. On October 16th, 1949, the communists declared a ceasefire, ending the civil war.

It was one of the earliest examples of America shifting its foreign policy and a foreshadowing of the types of roles it would continue to play in the future.

Another important policy that impacted America's role in the international world order was the Marshall Plan.

The Marshall Plan

Post-war Europe was left in utter shambles, with food shortages, diseases, and an unstable infrastructure. People were desperate, disheartened, and hungry. It was not outside the realm of possibility that these nations would turn to communism for help. The US realized one of the best ways of preventing it was to ensure European nations had economic stability and democracy.

On the heels of the Truman Doctrine, Secretary of State George Marshall delivered a speech on June 5th, 1947, which became the basis of the Marshall Plan. The plan, also known as the European Recovery Program, was simple: provide financial aid to nations in western Europe whose economies were left crippled by the war. By doing so, the plan's two goals would be achieved:

- The spread of communism across western Europe would be prevented.
- International stability would develop free-market economies and democracy.

The Marshall Plan was implemented in 1948. A total of sixteen nations in Europe received over $13 billion in aid through the plan. The money was not distributed equally. More money was given to industrial powers like Great Britain, which received approximately a quarter of the total aid, and France, which received one-fifth.

Countries like Italy, an ex-Axis power, received less. The one major exception was West Germany. With East Germany under complete Soviet control, it was imperative that West Germany's economy be revitalized and that the region become a democracy.

The Marshall Plan was deemed a resounding success, as it helped rehabilitate the shattered nations. By 1952, the economic growth in the sixteen nations that had received aid from the US exceeded pre-war levels.

For America, the plan also boosted its own economy, as more countries began trading with American companies. American interests in Europe were also firmly cemented, as some of the aid money was given to the Central Intelligence Agency (CIA) to establish businesses in European countries. These served as a front for America to gather information and further its own interests.

In short, a combination of the Truman Doctrine and the Marshall Plan ensured America's position in the world as a superpower.

North Atlantic Treaty Organization (NATO)

The Marshall Plan also acted as a catalyst for the creation of NATO.

While many European nations were in a better economic situation by the late 1940s and early 1950s, they didn't feel completely secure and safe. It became evident that some form of formal military cooperation would need to be established. So, some western European countries banded together and created the Western Union in 1948.

The North Atlantic Treaty Organization (NATO) was created in 1949 to defend the enlisted countries against any foreign threats. It came into existence with twelve founding countries:

- The United States
- The United Kingdom
- Canada
- France
- Belgium
- Denmark
- Italy
- Iceland
- The Netherlands
- Luxembourg
- Portugal
- Norway

The treaty was signed in Washington in early April of 1949, formally establishing Article 5, which essentially stated that if any member country was attacked, it would be seen as an attack on all the member countries. The members of NATO would have to retaliate. The main goal of the treaty was to safeguard NATO members' freedom and security through military and political assistance and to make sure Europe stayed at peace.

So far, Article 5 has only been invoked once, after 9/11. Today, membership in NATO has more than doubled, with thirty active members.

Given the fear of Soviet aggression, there were concerns the Western Union wasn't strong enough, so Truman made a proposal to Congress in 1949 to create the Mutual Defense Assistance Act. It was a military foreign aid legislation and would provide financial assistance to NATO countries. Congress signed off on it in October, and $1.4 billion dollars were set aside for it.

The United Nations

After the end of WWII, the world realized that it needed to develop friendly relationships and stay united to maintain international cooperation and global peace. This had been tried once before with the creation of the League of Nations. But lessons had been learned from the failed League of Nations, and the world was ready to try again.

The foundation of the League of Nations paved the way for the establishment of the United Nations. The United Nations was created after American President Franklin Roosevelt and British Prime Minister Winston Churchill issued a declaration outlining a commitment to maintaining international peace. The declaration was signed by twenty-six countries, which all vowed to do the same. The United Nations was officially founded on October 24th, 1945, and was a reflection of how the US had taken on an international leadership role.

Over the years, the responsibilities of the UN have expanded to include helping developing countries find their footing socially, politically, and economically. Fifty-one nations initially joined the organization, but since then,142 more countries have joined, bringing up the number of member states to 193.

Chapter 22: The Ike Years: Coup d'états and Civil Rights

President Dwight D. Eisenhower

After Truman's second term as president ended, Dwight D. Eisenhower, an important military leader during World War II (he was the Supreme Commander of the Allied Expeditionary Force and a five-star general), won the election and took office. He revised America's national security policy so it would be more balanced, allowing the US to maintain its military commitments for the Cold War while keeping the country's finances in mind.

President Dwight D. Eisenhower.

Eisenhower thought it was important to reduce government spending. Like Truman, Eisenhower also prioritized the elimination of communism and keeping it at bay. However, unlike Truman, Eisenhower was more focused on domestic issues, like the civil rights movement, rather than international relations. Eisenhower gave the CIA a lot of authority, particularly on matters outside of Europe. Two of the CIA's covert operations took down the Iranian and Guatemalan governments.

After becoming president, he ended the Korean War, which had started in June 1950 between North and South Korea.

The Korean War

After Japan surrendered in the Second World War, in August of 1945, Korea was divided in half along the 38th parallel by America and the Soviet Union.

With the Soviet Union rising as a possible power, it was crucial for the Allied powers to stop communism from advancing any further. So, while the Soviet forces set up camp and a communist regime in the north, the United States helped South Korea set up a military government.

Over the next five years, the two sides engaged in simmering tensions, which came to a head on June 25th, 1950, when North Korea invaded South Korea. The threat of the spread of communism was one of the major factors of the war.

North Korea was supported by the Soviet Union, which sent resources and equipment, and by China, which sent troops to fight in the war. Democratic Western nations sided with South Korea, although the bulk of the military assistance, aid, and troops were sent by the United States. During the three-year war, the US spent approximately $67 billion.

The Korean War ended up becoming a war of ideologies, as both sides fought to gain supremacy as the "real" Korea. The US was committed to helping South Korea resist communist expansion by North Korea. Negotiations for peace started in July 1951 and were finalized two years later.

An armistice was signed on July 27th, 1953, which means the war never officially ended (technically, it is still ongoing to this day). Around 2.5 million people died during the war. The war left the country destroyed and in shambles without resolving anything. Under the armistice, a demilitarized zone was established that ran along the length of the 38th

parallel. But the two sides remained firmly divided and continue to be so.

Today, South Korea enjoys a strong economy and has a good support system in the international community with strong ties to democratic Western nations. Its people enjoy greater freedoms and a much better quality of life than the North Koreans.

The communist country has almost no ties with the outside world and continues to be ruled by one family. North Korea's economy is underdeveloped, and the people are cut off from the world and only given access to whatever the ruler wishes for them to have. North Korea's unpredictable behavior and desire to develop nuclear weapons pose a very serious threat to the United States and the world at large.

In some ways, Korea was just another casualty of the Cold War. The Korean War spun out of control, and it's far too late to reel the tensions back.

While Eisenhower didn't hesitate to spend money on defense, he was not keen on having American troops fight overseas, although military actions did take place. Eisenhower was also determined to improve the relationship with the Soviet Union, especially after Joseph Stalin's death on March 5th, 1953, which temporarily resulted in a thaw in the Cold War.

Cold War after Stalin

After Stalin's death, Nikita Khrushchev took over as head of the government and openly denounced Stalin's way of ruling and the crimes he perpetrated. After meeting with President Eisenhower in Geneva, Khrushchev expressed a desire for peace on both sides. The Soviet Union stated it would reduce the size of its military force by getting rid of over 600,000 troops.

His desire to get along is exactly what Eisenhower wanted as well. In September 1959, Khrushchev even visited the United States. But the relationship quickly started to get tense over Cuba.

Nikita Khrushchev

Fidel Castro, who took over in 1959 after finishing the Cuban Revolution, began to take steps that showed he was planning to make Cuba a communist country. This was something the US did not want, especially so close to its doorstep. Tens of thousands of Cubans fled, with many settling in Florida. When Eisenhower approved the overthrow of the Castro regime, Khrushchev warned him that Cuba would be protected by the Soviet Union through the use of nuclear missiles if needed.

After this, the tentative friendly relationship between the two leaders disintegrated, and America formally cut diplomatic ties with Cuba in 1961. Things further deteriorated when an American spy plane was shot down by the Soviet Union in 1960.

At home, Khrushchev's approach was more relaxed and less terrifying than Stalin's. Rules around censorship became more relaxed, the secret police was given less power, political prisoners were released, and the country even started to receive visitors. He launched the first satellite to orbit Earth, Sputnik, in 1957, kicking off the Space Race. In 1959, the Soviets crashed a rocket on the moon.

Khrushchev's approach emboldened eastern Europeans to seek greater freedom, but things went badly when Germans in East Berlin resisted increased working hours for the same wages. Violent riots broke out, leading three million Germans to flee to the West. To prevent any more people from leaving, Khrushchev authorized the building of the Berlin Wall in 1961, demonstrating he could be authoritarian when he wanted to.

The Space Race

At its core, the Cold War was a competition between two of the world's superpowers: the US and the Soviet Union. Each side wanted to prove it was the superior power, whether in politics, military, or technology. Everything was a race.

Like the arms race, space exploration was just another arena for the two competitors. Fueled by their desire to outpace the US, the Soviet Union launched Sputnik on October 4th, 1957. The artificial satellite would become the first manmade object to orbit Earth.

Replica of Sputnik 1.
https://commons.wikimedia.org/wiki/File:Sputnik_asm.jpg

Unsurprisingly, the US was not happy about the launch of Sputnik. The American government felt as if the Soviet Union was overtaking them. Thus, the Space Race began.

The following year, Explorer I, a US satellite, was launched into space. In response to the launch of Sputnik, Eisenhower also signed an order on July 29th, 1958, authorizing the creation of a civilian agency called the National Aeronautics and Space Administration (NASA), which would be entirely dedicated to exploring space. The US and the Soviet Union each achieved some very important milestones, but perhaps the most important one was landing on the moon, which the US achieved in 1969. This will be discussed in further detail in the next chapter.

Rise of the Third World

While the Cold War was going on, there were many countries that chose not to align with either side. Those countries, the ones who were not a part of NATO or a part of the Warsaw Pact, were referred to as "Third World" countries.

On May 9th, 1955, NATO members decided to make West Germany a member and allowed the country to remilitarize. This was an obvious threat to the Soviet Union, which quickly drew up a treaty between itself and seven other European countries. It was signed in Warsaw on May 14th, 1955, and became known as the Warsaw Pact.

It was essentially the Soviet version of NATO's Article 5. Under the terms of the treaty, the countries that signed (Poland, Albania, Hungary, Romania, Czechoslovakia, Bulgaria, East Germany, and the Soviet Union) all agreed to defend each other if any of them was attacked by an enemy. The countries would band together and present a united front. Albania was expelled from the pact in 1962 because it started to question Nikita Khrushchev's policies. The pact remained in place until February 1991, when the Soviet Union started to dissolve.

The "First World" countries were developed Western nations like Canada, the United States, Japan, etc. Communist nations like China, North Korea, the Soviet Union, and Cuba were seen as "Second World" countries.

Most of the "Third World" countries had a colonial past and were struggling to recover from the atrocities committed against them. Over time, Third World became synonymous with countries in Asia, Africa, and Latin America. They were mostly considered to be underdeveloped because of a higher rate of poverty, disease, lower life expectancy, etc.

The terms were used to provide a broad political grouping of the countries around the world. Once the Cold War ended, the use of the term decreased and evolved. Today, we use terms like "developing countries."

American Society during the Cold War

As America embraced its role as a global superpower and exerted its influence on international conflicts and matters, domestically, the country was going through rapid social and economic changes.

Even though the Cold War was not an actual war (the Soviet Union and the US never directly fought each other), it still affected American society. Americans were terrified of communism and naturally distrustful of communists. This gave rise to McCarthyism, a political campaign that was based on the fear of communism in the United States. The campaign was spearheaded by Senator Joseph McCarthy. Many people who were accused or suspected of being communists were treated like the enemy in the US. They lost their jobs and were blacklisted.

The constant fear of a nuclear threat led to the creation of the National Defense Education Act and the interstate highway system. One of the common beliefs is that highways were built so that cities could be evacuated quicker in the event of a nuclear attack.

Defense or not, interstates changed the way Americans lived, ate, and socialized. New towns were built around interstate exits and grew rapidly. Small businesses and shops were replaced by motel chains and fast-food restaurants. The ease of traveling in and out of cities also led to more people moving away from the cities and settling into the suburbs.

Suburban life created a market for housing, grocery store chains, and new schools, parks, and other things. This, in turn, created new opportunities for jobs and industries.

Post-war America saw a huge boom in its economy, as trade with other countries increased dramatically. The production of goods and a strong economy led to the rise of consumer culture. Technological advancements in mass media helped advertise products and goods. Soon, people were recognizing brands and labels.

American society was becoming more modernized and more like the life we know today.

Civil Rights Movement

During the Progressive Era, most of the fight for social justice and reforms didn't really include black people. Even though Congress passed a few amendments, such as giving black men the right to vote, they were still not viewed as equals in society. Laws, like the Jim Crow laws, were established to segregate African Americans and keep them away from white society. However, some of the steps taken during the Progressive Era helped build the bridge toward a bigger movement in the 1950s and 1960s.

One of the catalysts for the civil rights movement was Rosa Parks. Rosa was a black woman who was sitting on a bus in a designated seat at the back of the bus, as per the segregation laws in Alabama. After some white passengers got on the bus and couldn't find a seat, the bus driver asked Parks and other African Americans sitting in her row to give their seats. Three of them moved; Rosa Parks refused.

Rosa Parks.
https://commons.wikimedia.org/wiki/File:Rosaparks.jpg

Because Rosa Parks refused the order, she was promptly arrested, which outraged the African American community and led to the creation of the Montgomery Improvement Association (MIA), which was led by

Rev. Dr. Martin Luther King Jr. The MIA planned a boycott of the bus system, which lasted for over a year and led to the Supreme Court ruling that segregated seating went against the Constitution.

Although Eisenhower was the president when the civil rights movement began, Harry Truman was a great champion of civil rights. For instance, in 1948, he issued Executive Order 9981, which put an end to segregation in the Armed Forces. His views and stance on civil rights also made it easier for President Eisenhower to convince Congress of the need to write new civil rights legislation. The Civil Rights Act of 1957 was signed by Eisenhower, but blatant prejudice against black people continued.

Inspired by Gandhi, nonviolent protests by activists began to crop up around the country to protest against unfair laws like "whites only" lunch counters. As time passed, more radical groups were established, as not much seemed to be accomplished with peaceful protests.

During the 1960s, a group of activists made up of both black and white Americans called the Freedom Riders traveled to the South to protest against unfair segregation laws. They were treated horrifically by the police and white protestors. However, they also gained international attention, which put the world's focus on the civil rights movement in America.

Chapter 23: The Kennedys and the '60s: Dream up a Better World

American Culture in the 1960s

The foundation that was established in the 1950s for civil rights and other demands for social and political reform gained momentum in the 1960s, ushering in a tumultuous decade.

During the 18th and 19th centuries, several critical events, like the American Revolution, the Industrial Revolution, and the transcontinental railway, significantly altered the American landscape. The 1960s were also enormously important and peppered with profound events and movements that completely transformed America.

Some of the most notable events were the rise of the civil rights movement, the anti-war movement, multiple assassinations, and protests demanding reforms for social issues such as poverty, unemployment, and segregation. Feminists also actively fought for and demanded more equality. Society as a whole was moving toward a more liberal mindset, led in large part by baby boomers, who started the hippie movement in the late 1960s and early 1970s.

The name "baby boomers" was given to children born between 1946 and 1964; it was coined sometime in the early 1960s. In the 1960s, teenagers and young adults rejected the morals, values, and beliefs imposed upon them by their parents and society. The rejection of these traditions lay at the core of the hippie movement. People belonging to the movement adopted some distinct characteristics, such as long hair (for men and women), colorful tie-dye shirts, and flower crowns, to name a few.

The movement embraced the concept of free love and turned away from the idea of monogamy, preferring instead to live communally. They experimented sexually and were very open about love and sex, especially compared to the more conservative social mores in place at the time. Institutional religion was also rejected, and there was greater interest in religions like Buddhism. Drugs like LSD and marijuana were also used by many hippies. This type of free-flowing love, laid-back, easy way of living was reflected in the art and music of the decade.

While America was going through this profound social change, an extraordinary man named John F. Kennedy became the thirty-fifth president of America.

President John F. Kennedy

JFK was a remarkable leader who had big dreams for America. His vision of a united America included equal opportunities and human rights for all races, religions, and genders, which was perfectly aligned with the social reforms of the decade.

His time in office was unfortunately cut short, but within that limited time, he championed civil rights and helped the movement make great strides. He handled one of the worst Cold War crises with a cool head and diplomatic aplomb and inspired people to serve their country.

The Moon Landing

In the 1960s, the Space Race was well underway, and competition was heating up, especially with the establishment of NASA. Soon after JFK took office, one of his top priorities was the expansion of NASA and the space program.

In 1961, President Kennedy boldly declared that America would have a man on the moon before the end of the decade. His proclamation came true when, on July 20th, 1969, Apollo 11 landed on the moon. Astronaut Neil Armstrong walked on the moon, saying, "That's one small step for man, one giant leap for mankind."

An image of Buzz Aldrin on the moon.
https://commons.wikimedia.org/wiki/File:Aldrin_Apollo_11_original.jpg

With the moon landing, America emerged as the clear winner of the Space Race with Russia. JFK did not live to see it happen, but he certainly pushed for space exploration while he was alive.

The Bay of Pigs

When it became clear to the United States that Fidel Castro was steering Cuba toward a communist regime, the administration decided it had to take action since his regime would be a threat to American interests.

As soon as Castro came into power in 1959, he started to implement policies that would reduce the amount of influence America had over the country. Industries like sugar, which had been dominated by the US for decades, were nationalized. He introduced land reforms and encouraged other countries in Latin America to become more autonomous and rely less on the US.

In response, the US decided to stop exporting sugar from Cuba, which would have been disastrous for the country's economy since 80 percent of its sugar went to America. To help Cuba out, the Soviet

Union, which had already established diplomatic relations with Cuba, agreed to buy that share. These were things America did not want, so it began to carefully plot Castro's removal. In 1961, the US cut off all diplomatic ties with Cuba.

For the next two years, the CIA and the US State Department tried to remove Castro from power. They even recruited exiled Cubans who were living in Miami as part of their overthrow mission. However, they did not have much success.

With Kennedy's approval, on April 17th, 1961, the CIA and Cubans exiles launched a full-scale attack on Cuba. They were certain the invasion would be the definitive event that would get rid of him for good. But things did not go as planned, as it was a disaster almost from the start. Within a day of fighting, the vastly outnumbered American troops surrendered. Over 100 American troops died, and an additional 1,100 were captured.

Cuba would be the cause of tension once more during the Cuban Missile Crisis the following year.

The Cuban Missile Crisis

In October 1962, the Cold War reached new heights of tension when the US discovered that the Soviet Union had stationed nuclear missiles in Cuba.

After the Soviet Union's pledge to defend Cuba, Khrushchev started to store ballistic missiles in the country. Their proximity to the US was concerning because if they were launched, they had the potential to destroy huge swathes of the country.

The installations were discovered on October 14th, 1962, by a pilot flying an American U-2 spy plane. He took pictures and reported back. The following day, CIA analysts spotted missiles and launchers. Kennedy met advisors following this discovery to decide on the best course of action. An attack or war was out of the question for the president, so he settled on a naval quarantine to buy some time and figure out his next steps.

On October 23rd, Khrushchev replied to JFK's letter. He refused to remove the missiles, saying they were there purely for defensive reasons. Throughout the back and forth between the two leaders, the world held its breath, expecting nuclear weapons to go off at any minute. The threat of a nuclear war was a very real possibility.

War seemed imminent when, on October 27th, an American U-2 plane was shot down over Cuba. The pilot was killed. After some investigating, the US government concluded the order to shoot down the plane did not come from the Soviets. The incident made both sides realize just how dangerous things were becoming. It was clear neither side wanted war.

Thankfully, Khrushchev decided to remove the missiles, but he had some conditions. He wanted JFK to withdraw American missiles from Turkey and to stay out of Cuba. President Kennedy publicly agreed the US would not attack Cuba and also consented to take nuclear weapons out of Turkey.

Americans sighed a breath of relief on October 28th when Khrushchev wrote to JFK, agreeing to dismantle and remove the missiles from Cuba. The crisis and a potentially deadly war had been avoided.

Assassination of JFK

John F. Kennedy was an extraordinary president who ushered in a period of idealism and optimism, especially among the younger generation. As the youngest man to ever be elected president, he was a symbol of vigor and youthfulness and was viewed as "cool." His beautiful and elegant wife, Jackie, only added to his charm. When he was assassinated on November 22nd, 1963, it shocked the nation.

On the day of his assassination, he was driving in an open-top convertible with the governor of Dallas and his wife on a ten-mile motorcade through Dallas, Texas.

JFK motorcade.
https://en.wikipedia.org/wiki/File:JFK_limousine.png

Vice President Lyndon B. Johnson was also in the motorcade; he was several cars behind JFK.

At 12:30 p.m., three shots were fired, hitting President Kennedy and Governor John Connally. JFK died shortly afterward at Parkland Hospital in Dallas. Absolute chaos ensued, and Vice President Johnson was quickly sworn in as the thirty-sixth president on Air Force One.

That afternoon, a man named Lee Harvey Oswald was arrested for the murder of the president. On November 24th, when he was being taken to another county jail, he was swarmed by a crowd of people and killed by Jack Ruby as "revenge" for murdering JFK.

To this day, there are many conspiracy theories surrounding the Kennedy assassination and the real motive behind Ruby killing Oswald. Many believe he was killed to keep the truth about Kennedy's death hidden. Whatever the truth may be, the world and America lost an inspiring leader that day.

On November 25th, Kennedy was buried at Arlington National Cemetery with military honors. An eternal flame was lit by Jackie. It burned at his burial site until 1998 when it was moved to the National Museum of Funeral History.

JFK managed to leave behind a lasting legacy. He led the nation through part of the Cold War, albeit with some missteps. He fought to give Americans equal rights and encouraged people to take social and political action. He inspired an entire generation to do something for their country, their government, and the world by telling them during his inaugural address, "Ask not what your country can do for you—ask what you can do for your country."[7]

Vietnam War

During the Cold War, due to America's new foreign policy focused on containing communism, the US was actively involved in the war in Vietnam.

After the French rule in Vietnam, which began in 1861 with the occupation of Saigon, came to an end on May 7th, 1954, the country was divided. War eventually broke out, lasting for two decades.

The divisive conflict began in 1954 with the Vietnamese movement to get rid of French colonial rule. It eventually evolved into a war between the communist government in North Vietnam against democratic South Vietnam.

American sympathy and support, of course, lay with South Vietnam, which fought against the Viet Cong (Vietnamese communists). The US was worried that if Vietnam fell to communism, other countries nearby would follow suit in a domino effect.

In 1961, Kennedy was advised to provide military, economic, and other aid to the South Vietnamese to help defeat the Viet Cong. While Kennedy increased the amount of aid, he didn't commit to a large military intervention. When the conflict started in 1955, there were less than eight hundred American troops in Vietnam, but by 1962, that number had jumped to nine thousand troops.

As the political instability increased in South Vietnam, President Lyndon B. Johnson, the man who replaced Kennedy after his assassination, agreed to increase military aid and support. By June 1965, eighty-two thousand American troops were in Vietnam.

---

[7] "Ask Not What Your Country Can Do for You."
https://www.jfklibrary.org/learn/education/teachers/curricular-resources/elementary-school-curricular-resources/ask-not-what-your-country-can-do-for-you

American soldiers fought far from ideal conditions. They were fighting in unfamiliar, complicated terrain in a country fraught with political tensions and uncertainty. And worse, the American government didn't seem to have a clear motive or objective for the war, which seemed to drag on endlessly. Those taken as prisoners of war were subjected to psychological and physical abuse.

As the number of American casualties increased, people began to question what the US was actually doing in Vietnam. By the time the war ended, around 58,000 American soldiers had been killed, with another 300,000 wounded.

The media's portrayal of the war also turned public opinion against the fighting. Military personnel began to desert, and anti-war protests swept across the country, leading to violence, riots, and deaths. American involvement came to an end after Nixon became president and started to withdraw troops. The war would only end in the mid-1970s.

Kent State Shooting

The Vietnam War was a source of tension and conflict for the United States. The controversial war had left the country deeply divided. While most people believed the US was doing the right thing, a very vocal part of the US public was against American intervention in Vietnam. And as the war continued, more people turned against it. People took to the streets to protest the war and the military draft.

One of the reasons Nixon won the presidential election of 1968 was his promise to bring the war to an end. But two years later, on April 30th, 1970, instead of calling the troops back, Nixon gave permission to the armed forces to invade Cambodia, which was being used by communist Vietnamese soldiers to launch attacks in the south.

The tension surrounding the war came to a head following this decision. On May 1st, 1970, hundreds of students gathered together at the Kent State University campus and began to protest the invasion. They spoke out against Nixon and the war and clashed with the police.

At 11:00 a.m. on May 4th, approximately three thousand protesters, anti-war activists, and spectators arrived on campus to start a scheduled protest. Around one hundred Ohio National Guardsmen were also there, and they ordered the peaceful protesters to leave and disperse. Things quickly escalated and got out of hand, with the guardsman firing tear gas at the protesters and eventually firing into the crowd.

Four Kent State students were killed, and an additional nine were injured. To this day, it is not clear why the shots were fired or whether it was necessary. During court trials and investigations, the National Guard has maintained a firm stance that it was necessary.

The tragedy of the protest marked a turning point for the war, as it cemented the anti-war sentiments of the public. Some historians believe the Kent State shooting was partially responsible for Nixon's downfall.

Civil Rights Act

Martin Luther King

The civil rights movement, which had taken off in the 1950s, gained momentum in the 1960s. The movement was led by people like Martin Luther King Jr., Malcolm X, James Farmer, and many others. The figure most closely associated with the movement is likely Martin Luther King Jr.

King was the founder of the Southern Christian Leadership Conference (SCLC). He was a Baptist minister and a radical who challenged systemic racism. He was determined to gain equality, not just for African Americans but also for other people who came from disadvantaged backgrounds. He wanted freedom, human rights, and a universal income for all people, as it would enable them to maintain a basic standard of living. He fought for these things through peaceful means.

Martin Luther King Jr.
https://commons.wikimedia.org/wiki/File:Martin_Luther_King,_Jr..jpg

One of the earliest things he organized was the Montgomery bus boycott, which happened after Rosa Parks's arrest. He played a key role in the Memphis sanitation worker's strike, as well as the March on Washington, where he gave his famous "I Have a Dream" speech.

While many civil rights leaders in the 1950s and 1960s emphasized the need for nonviolent protests and passive resistance, protests by the general public were often anything but. There were also radical groups, like the Black Panthers, who believed that peaceful protests were not enough to get changes made at the highest level. Violent clashes and events and peaceful marches and protests dominated most of the decade.

But it wasn't all for nothing. The protests and the conflicts helped bring awareness to the plight of African Americans in the US and the need for equality. The fearless work done by the civil rights movement led to legislation like the Civil Rights Act and the Voting Rights Act.

Congress passed the Civil Rights Act in 1964. It prohibited anyone from being discriminated against because of the color of their skin, their race, their gender, or their religion. It was a huge victory for the civil rights movement since it meant, for the first time in US history, African Americans were treated as equals under the law throughout the country. Segregation was a thing of the past. It didn't get rid of racism, but it was still a big victory.

The Voting Rights Act, which was signed in 1965, was another monumental victory for the civil rights movement. Voting rights had been granted to African Americans in the Fourteenth and Fifteenth Amendments, but they weren't always enforced. Some state governments, especially in the South, made it difficult for minorities to vote. The new act expanded the protections and made it illegal to prevent someone from voting based on the color of their skin.

Why was this so important? Having the ability to vote means having a say in politics, which, in turn, forces political candidates to consider the well-being of all Americans, not just white people. It also allows people to serve on juries and have a say in what happens to one's peers who break the law. Today, the Voting Rights Act is seen as one of the most effective civil rights legislations to ever be produced by the federal government.

King played an instrumental role in some of these key pieces of legislation and was awarded the Nobel Peace Prize in 1964. He is also honored every year through a federal holiday called Martin Luther King Jr. Day.

Assassination of King

King's immense popularity continued in the mid-1960s. There were some African American youths who called for a more radical and confrontational way of forcing change, though. Their views were more aligned with those of Malcolm X, a black nationalist leader who scorned King's nonviolent approaches to the civil rights movement.

In response, King began to speak out publicly on other social issues that concerned all of America, like the war in Vietnam, unemployment, and poverty. As part of his work, King and other members of the SCLC went to Memphis, Tennessee, where sanitation workers were on strike. He gave a speech on the evening of April 3rd. The following evening, while he was standing on a balcony at the Lorraine Motel in Memphis, he was struck and killed by a sniper bullet that pierced his neck. He died in the hospital an hour later. He was just thirty-nine years old.

Shocked by the assassination, people took to the streets to protest. Violent riots erupted throughout the country. President Lyndon Johnson urged for peace. He pressured Congress to pass civil rights legislation, which was scheduled to be discussed by the House of Representatives. The Fair Housing Act, which prohibited any discrimination for buying or renting housing based on sex, race, or religion, was signed a few days later on April 11th.

James Earl Ray, the man suspected of killing Martin Luther King Jr., was caught on June 8th, 1968. He pled guilty, and the following year, on March 10th, 1969, he received a prison sentence of ninety-nine years. There were some doubts back then on whether he actually committed the murder or whether he was framed.

White and black Americans mourned King's death, yet it did not serve to bring them any closer. Instead, it created a greater divide between the two races. Many young blacks also used the assassination to become more radical, and his death led to increased support and participation in movements like the Black Panther Party and the Black Power movement.

Immigration and Nationality Act of 1965

Another significant piece of legislation that is worth mentioning is the Immigration and Nationality Act of 1965. In a deeply symbolic and poignant moment, President Johnson signed the act in front of the Statue of Liberty, which had been given to America as a gift from France as a symbol of America's freedom.

The act did get rid of the national origins quota system that the American government had been using for decades to control the number of immigrants who entered the country and where they came from. This opened up the opportunity for people all around the world to immigrate to America. Over the years, the country would become one of the most multicultural nations in the world.

Lyndon B. Johnson entered office with high ratings, but the violent protests and the Vietnam War made the people view him in a negative light. However, LBJ did a lot for the country. He introduced several major civil rights laws, established programs to aid the poor, created Medicare and Medicaid, and sought peace talks with the Soviet Union.

The Assassination of Bobby Kennedy

Another notable event to take place in the late 1960s was the assassination of Bobby Kennedy.

In 1967, Israel was engaged in a brief but vicious war against Syria, Jordan, and Egypt. Known as the Six-Day War, it was another battle in a string of conflicts between Israel and the Arabs that had started in 1948. The war was won by Israel, and it changed the map of the Middle East and led to tensions that exist to this day.

When Bobby Kennedy, JFK's younger brother, came out in public support of Israel, not everyone agreed with the sentiment or felt happy about it.

On June 5th, 1968, after having won the California presidential primary the day before, Bobby Kennedy was attending a campaign event at the Los Angeles Ambassador Hotel. Just after midnight, he was shot several times in the hotel corridor. The gunman was a young man of Palestinian origin named Sirhan Sirhan. Bobby was quickly rushed to the hospital, where he was pronounced dead the following day, on June 6th. He was forty-two years old.

Bobby Kennedy was devoted to fighting for civil rights and liberties and was widely admired by most of the American population, especially minorities. He was on the cusp of making great strides in politics and would have faced off against Nixon had he lived.

Sirhan was arrested immediately and confessed to shooting Bobby because of his support for Israel, a country that was actively oppressing Palestinians. In April 1969, he was sentenced to death for the assassination. However, he was never executed since the California State Supreme Court invalidated all death penalty sentences in 1972. As of this writing, Sirhan is still alive and is serving a life sentence.

Since Bobby's death, various conspiracy theories have surfaced about what actually happened that night at the Ambassador Hotel. Bobby's own son, Robert F. Kennedy, does not believe Sirhan killed his father. He has spoken out publicly about his belief that there was a second shooter responsible for Bobby's death. Whether this is true or not will likely never be known.

SECTION SEVEN:
Détente and the End of the Cold War (1968–1992)

Chapter 24: The Nixon-Ford Years: Détente and Economic Changes

Nixon-Ford years (1968–1976)

End of the Vietnam War

In 1969, when Republican President Richard Nixon was elected into office, he almost immediately began to withdraw American forces from Vietnam and began entering into negotiations for peace. The US, North Vietnam, and South Vietnam were involved in the negotiations, which stalled out and restarted several times over the course of three years. The Paris Peace Accords was signed on January 27th, 1973, and brought an end to the war in Vietnam.

Under the treaty, the US agreed to withdraw from Vietnam. In exchange, both sides would release their prisoners and would unite as one country peacefully.

Of course, nothing was achieved peacefully. As soon as the Americans left, the communists launched a full-scale attack. Two years later, they were victorious. The country reunified to form a communist regime on July 2nd, 1976. It became the Socialist Republic of Vietnam.

For the US, the war had been catastrophic; it would become the second-longest war the country had ever fought. Billions of dollars had been spent, and approximately sixty thousand lives had been lost, not to mention the decades of time and effort.

By the time the US finally pulled out of the war, over two million troops had served, and it had all been for nothing. Despite the government's best efforts, Vietnam fell to communism. However, the domino effect that the country feared did not happen; Laos is the only other Southeast Asian country today that is communist. As of this writing, Vietnam is one of five communist countries that still exist in the world.

SALT I Treaty

Through all this, the Cold War continued. As part of President Nixon's plan to bring an end to the war, he met with the president of the Soviet Union, Leonid Brezhnev, in Moscow, becoming the first US president to go to Moscow. After more than two years of discussions, the two leaders, who were eager to form a better relationship, signed SALT I (Strategic Arms Limitation Talks) in May 1972.

Under the agreement, both countries agreed to a maximum of two antiballistic missile (ABM) sites. An ABM is a missile that can annihilate an incoming missile. The second point was that they would not expand their inventory of intercontinental ballistic missiles and submarine-launched ballistic missiles to more than what they already had.

Even though there were many things SALT I did not touch or cover, it was seen as the beginning of a better relationship between the two countries.

This more conciliatory foreign policy became known as détente, and the Cold War thawed considerably, with the leaders visiting each other's countries and enjoying a friendlier relationship.

Oil Crisis of 1973

On the heels of the US pulling out of the Vietnam War, the country was faced with another crisis: oil.

The oil crisis of 1973 happened when the Organization of the Petroleum Exporting Countries (OPEC) decided to dramatically raise the price of oil. OPEC also prohibited the exportation of oil to a handful of countries, including those in western Europe and the United States, because they had supported Israel in its war against Egypt and Syria. Additionally, the value of the US dollar had been declining, thus decreasing OPEC's earnings.

The embargo deeply impacted American society. Factories were forced to cut back on hours, businesses placed restrictions on their opening hours, gas stations saw long queues, and the average American scaled back their lifestyle. Smaller cars became more popular, and people became more conscious of waste.

Negotiations between OPEC and the US took place during a summit in Washington. In March 1974, the embargo was officially lifted. But the ripple effects of the crisis would continue to affect the country for the better part of the 1970s.

The Nixon Shock

One of Nixon's objectives was to improve America's economic growth by providing stability in the workforce and the exchange rate of the dollar. He did so by implementing the "Nixon shock," the name given to a set of economic policies established by President Nixon. They were designed to do the following:

- Create better employment opportunities
- Help check the rising cost of living
- Protect the American dollar from international speculators

As part of the plan, Nixon issued Executive Order 11615, which gave tax cuts and put a freeze on any price increases or salaries for a period of three months. The policies were designed to help the American economy but, unfortunately, had the opposite effect. While the order is viewed as a political success, economically, it ended up being the catalyst for the dollar losing a third of its value and the stagflation that characterized the 1970s.

Stagflation is described as a period when economic growth slows or declines while unemployment and inflation rise. This was one of the ripple effects of the oil crisis, and unfortunately, Nixon's policies did not help the situation. Instead, they put an end to the Bretton Woods Agreement.

The Bretton Woods Agreement was established toward the end of the Second World War by the Allied nations to provide stability for international currencies. As part of the agreement, the International Monetary Fund (IMF) and the World Bank were created. The countries who joined the agreement promised to maintain a fixed exchange rate between the US dollar and their own currencies. This meant there was a currency peg to the American dollar that was based on the price of gold.

By establishing this agreement, countries were assured of a stable exchange rate, which was beneficial for post-war global reconstruction. It also created a better environment for fostering international trade.

However, one of the biggest flaws of the system was that in order for it to be successful, all involved countries had to coordinate their policies so the exchange rate would be aligned. After Nixon's policies were implemented, it resulted in the collapse of the Bretton Woods Agreement. However, the two key institutions that were created as part of it, the IMF and the World Bank, left a lasting impact on global currency and continue to play a pivotal role in international finance today.

The main goal of the IMF is to maintain stability in the international monetary system, which influences a country's trade, its investments, and its economy. The purpose of the World Bank is to provide support to underdeveloped countries. One of its main aims is to reduce poverty around the world.

Watergate Scandal

During Nixon's term as president, he accomplished several key things, such as laws to protect the environment, and his administration implemented a handful of important reforms, including *Roe v. Wade* and funding for Planned Parenthood. However, he is most commonly remembered as the only American president to resign because of a political scandal.

When Nixon was running for president again in 1972, there was a lot of tension in the country over the Vietnam War and other social issues. Nixon's advisors felt he needed to run a very aggressive campaign. The tactics soon tipped over into illegal activities, such as wiretapping.

The scandal officially began on June 17th when a few men were caught breaking into the office of the Democratic National Committee's Watergate headquarters to steal documents and fix the wiretaps that were malfunctioning.

A security guard realized something was up and called the police. The intruders were apprehended. Upon their arrest, it was revealed the men were connected to Nixon and his reelection campaign. The shorthand for the campaign was CREEP (Committee to Re-elect the President).

Nixon tried very hard to cover up the crime, including publicly swearing to the American public that his administration had nothing to do with the break-in. Believing in his honesty, the American people once more voted him into office.

But the conspiracy was unearthed by two Washington Post reporters, Bob Woodward and Carl Bernstein, who were given the information anonymously by a source they referred to as Deep Throat. The most damaging piece of information that was revealed was Nixon's involvement and his attempt to bribe the burglars to keep them from talking. It was also revealed that Nixon had tried to convince the CIA to meddle in the FBI's investigation. This was a clear abuse of power.

As more and more of the conspiracy was uncovered and charges were laid out, Nixon's Vice President, Spiro T. Agnew, resigned from office in 1973. He was replaced by Gerald Ford. Less than a year later, on August 9th, 1974, President Nixon resigned. He was never impeached for what he had done, although the process had already begun by the time he resigned.

Upon his resignation, Ford, who was the minority leader of the House of Representatives, succeeded him and took office.

Gerald Ford

When Ford became president, the country was in dire straits. The US was in the middle of one of the worst economic crises seen in nearly half a century. Unemployment and inflation were rising sharply while the recession dragged on. The last time things were that bad in the country was during the Great Depression.

In addition to the economic challenges, the country was also undergoing a domestic energy crisis, which Ford couldn't do much about either.

After Nixon pulled out of Vietnam, North Vietnam's communist influence only grew stronger. Ford wanted to send American troops back into the country to help the South Vietnamese. But this request was flatly denied. So, he instead focused his efforts on reviving the policy of détente, which had been falling apart since the mid-1970s. The US organized the Conference on Security and Cooperation (CSCE) in Helsinki and discussed some critical issues surrounding the arms trade and human rights.

Ford's efforts came to fruition when the Helsinki Accords were signed by Canada, the Soviet Union, America, and all the European countries, with the exception of Albania, after the CSCE. Under the terms of the accord, the countries agreed to decrease tensions between the East and the West. The détente looked to be on the horizon once more.

However, concerns over the violation of human rights in Russia became the cause of dissent, and the policy of détente fell apart for the moment. Russia had been a one-party state with total control over its people since the start of the Cold War. The people of Russia were not afforded the same rights and freedoms as those of democratic nations, which was cause for concern to the West.

Nixon Pardon

Pardoning Nixon was perhaps Ford's most controversial act as president, and it is the thing for which he is most famous. After becoming president, one of the first things Ford did was pardon disgraced former President Richard Nixon for the role he played in the Watergate scandal.

Gerald R. Ford.
https://commons.wikimedia.org/wiki/File:Gerald_Ford_presidential_portrait_(cropped).jpg

The pardon meant Nixon was absolved of all criminal charges. This did not sit well with the American public, who felt the president should have been charged for his crimes and faced justice.

By the time the presidential election of 1976 rolled around, Ford was hugely unpopular, and he lost the election to Democrat Jimmy Carter by a significant margin.

With Ford and the Republicans out of office, the Nixon-Ford years officially came to an end.

Chapter 25: Jimmy Carter: The End of Détente

Carter's Domestic Policies

When Jimmy Carter was campaigning in 1976, one of his promises was changes to American foreign policy. As promised, after he was elected, American foreign policy shifted, with more of an emphasis on human rights.

Carter believed America had an obligation and moral duty to ensure human rights were adhered to and respected. It was an ideological shift for America, but Carter's administration was determined to "speak frankly about injustice, both at home and abroad" and take action as needed.[8]

President Carter believed that every human being had the right to the following:

- Be free from government violation
- Have basic necessities, like shelter, food, and an education
- Have civil and political rights

As such, throughout his political career, he prioritized education, health care, and the well-being of all Americans. While governor of Georgia, a position he held from 1971 to 1975, he pushed forward an

---

[8] "Carter and Human Rights, 1977–1980." https://history.state.gov/milestones/1977-1980/human-rights.

education reform package called the Adequate Program for Education. He wanted to provide a better educational system by reducing the size of classes and ensuring that equal funding was provided to all schools.

Domestically, Carter's administration put a national energy policy in place to help conserve energy. He also encouraged looking into other resources as an alternative to oil.

While in office, he also pushed the Economic Stimulus Appropriations Act in Congress to help resolve the unemployment crisis. He believed the government's role should be to advance the common good, so the policies and acts he implemented were designed with that in mind. He wanted an open, transparent administration but faced a number of significant issues, including a Congress that wasn't entirely supportive of him.

Jimmy Carter was not like most politicians that Congress or Washington was familiar with. He was not happy to participate in back-door dealings or corruption. Carter was a reformer who believed in science and progress, and he had grown up with a strong faith and carried those values and morality with him. When he ran for office, he pledged to be an honest president who would lead the country by example and would never lie to his people. This type of personality was difficult for Congress to deal with, and there was simmering tension between Congress and the president since they had very different approaches to politics.

Carter and the Cold War

In regard to the Cold War, President Carter continued the work the previous presidents had started in trying to establish a better relationship with the Soviet Union.

China's relationship with America also improved greatly, and the two countries formally reestablished diplomatic ties in 1979 through a bilateral trade agreement, which led to significant financial gains for both countries.

In addition, Carter continued to hold additional discussions with the Soviet Union to expand SALT. But these talks fell apart and were put on hold in early 1980 after the Soviet Union invaded Afghanistan in December 1979.

The United States openly condemned the Soviet Union's invasion of Afghanistan. It not only soured the fragile relationship between the two countries, but it also ended the age of détente. President Carter wrote a letter to Brezhnev, making his displeasure clear and stating this aggression was not acceptable. Carter vowed to the American people that Middle East oil would be protected at all costs and would not be allowed to fall into Soviet hands. America put a trade embargo in place.

1980 Summer Olympics

In addition to putting SALT II on hold, President Carter also called for nations to boycott the 1980 Summer Olympics, which were scheduled to take place in Moscow, because of the Soviet invasion of Afghanistan. Following America's example, approximately sixty nations, including Japan, Canada, and most Arab countries, sat out the Olympics. However, some major western European players and American allies, such as France, Italy, and Great Britain, chose not to observe the boycott and sent their athletes to compete.

The Olympics were disastrous, with some countries protesting by refusing to attend ceremonies. Spectators were rowdy and rude, and the officials were clearly biased or even openly cheating.

Therefore, it was not surprising when Russia won a total of 195 medals, 80 of them gold.

Camp David Accords of 1978

One of Jimmy Carter's most astonishing feats as president was the peace agreement between Egypt and Israel, two countries that had waged wars on and off for nearly three decades.

Carter's original goal was to bring peace to the entire Middle East. As such, he wanted to invite countries like Jordan, Syria, and Palestine to the negotiating table. He felt peace in the Middle East would not only help improve America's relationship with the Soviet Union but also give the US a stronger foothold in the Middle East. But when it became clear that Egypt and Israel wanted to deal with just each other, Carter put his goal of a peaceful Middle East aside and focused on bettering the relationship between the two countries instead.

Egyptian President Anwar el-Sadat and Israeli Prime Minister Menachem Begin were keen to stay on friendlier terms since neither country felt very secure and was surrounded by enemies. Egypt was dealing with threats from Libya, while all the Arab countries around Israel refused to acknowledge its existence.

Despite their best intentions, negotiations stalled at multiple points. However, Carter refused to let it all be in vain and insisted on hosting both Sadat and Begin at Camp David. His administration, which was already dealing with an economic crisis and inflation, knew that to fail at this would be catastrophic. A tense two-week period followed, with the three leaders engaged in intense discussions.

The three leaders at Camp David.
https://commons.wikimedia.org/wiki/File:Camp_David,_Menachem_Begin,_Anwar_Sadat,_1978.jpg

Carter drew up a peace proposal and plainly stated that if they could not agree to terms, the US would withdraw aid money and its friendship. During this time, Carter put all his other duties on hold. He finally emerged from the talks on September 17th, 1978, with the news that peace had been agreed upon by Egypt and Israel.

It did not come without growing pains, and absolute peace was never fully achieved, but it was a positive step. To this day, the countries enjoy a cordial relationship. For Jimmy Carter, it was a diplomatic triumph.

Iranian Hostage Crisis (1979)

Within a year after the treaty was signed between Israel and Egypt, Carter faced a new crisis in the Middle East when Iranian students stormed the US Embassy in Tehran. To understand why, we have to go back several years.

Tensions between the US and Iran had been brewing for decades. The two countries often clashed over oil, as the majority of Iran's reserves were controlled by the US and Great Britain. Iranians were also unhappy with what they viewed as too much interference from the US in their domestic affairs.

In 1951, Mohammad Mossadegh was elected as prime minister of Iran. One of Mossadegh's top priorities was to nationalize Iran's oil. This was something America did not want, so the CIA and MI6 (Britain's intelligence service) hatched a plan to remove Mossadegh from power and replace him with someone of their own choosing. By August 1953, Mossadegh had been ousted, and a new government, headed by Mohammed Reza Shah Pahlavi, was established.

As an anti-communist, pro-West, and secular Muslim, Reza Shah was exactly what the Americans wanted. However, he made the Iranians miserable. Reza Shah was a brutal dictator who kept an iron grip on the country through his secret police (SAVAK), which tortured and killed thousands of people.

The Iranians were deeply resentful of the coup and of what the US had done to them. After nearly two decades of Reza Shah's rule, the people had had enough. Led by Ayatollah Khomeini, a radical Muslim, they forced Reza Shah and his government out. The US wisely stayed out of the revolution.

However, in 1979, when Jimmy Carter allowed Reza Shah to come to the US and receive treatment for his cancer, it was the final straw for many Iranians and became the catalyst for the protest in Tehran.

The pro-Ayatollah students forced their way into the embassy on November 4th, 1979, and took sixty-six hostages, many of whom were students, diplomats, and employees. Soon after, thirteen of the hostages were set free, with another being released a few months later. The remaining fifty-two hostages remained captives. While they were never seriously harmed, they lived in constant fear and were subjected to humiliating treatment.

In the meantime, the American government was working hard to set them free, but neither diplomacy nor economic sanctions could sway Ayatollah's stance. Releasing the hostages became a top priority for Carter, but his efforts were all in vain. As a result, he was viewed poorly by the American public.

His reelection campaign suffered greatly because of it. Ronald Reagan, his opponent, played this to his advantage. There were even rumors that Reagan's campaign team had made sure the hostages would stay in captivity until after the election so that Carter couldn't win.

Reagan staunchly denied these rumors and won the election in a landslide. In a curious turn of events, the remaining hostages were released on January 21ˢᵗ, 1981. hours after Regan made his inaugural speech.

Second Oil Crisis of 1979

The Iranian Revolution led to the United States going through a second oil crisis in the 1970s, which is also known as the 1979 Oil Shock.

As a result of the revolution, the global oil supply decreased, which led to the price of crude oil skyrocketing. Just like during the first oil crisis, the dramatic rise in prices led to fuel shortages and people cutting back on necessities.

President Carter encouraged Americans to try and reduce their consumption of energy. He even installed wood-burning stoves and solar panels on the White House roof to reduce energy usage. When Regan moved into the White House, he had them removed.

Things continued to get worse when the Iran-Iraq War began in 1980. Oil production fell sharply, leading to a global economic recession. It would take nearly half a decade for the prices to start going back to normal. Industries that relied heavily on oil began to look at other alternatives and made the switch from oil to other sources of power and energy, such as natural gas. Other countries, like Mexico, Venezuela, and the Soviet Union, began to expand their oil production, making the US less reliant on oil from the Middle East.

Chapter 26: Reagan and Reaganomics

After running a disastrous reelection campaign, Jimmy Carter lost the election to Republican candidate Ronald Reagan by a landslide. A former actor, Ronald Reagan was extremely popular with the public and was in office for two terms, serving from 1981 to 1989.

During his time as president, he achieved a number of significant things, such as getting the economy back on track, bringing an end to the Cold War, and appointing a woman to the US Supreme Court for the first time in history.

Reaganomics

Domestically, one of Reagan's main objectives was to fix the runaway economy. The economic policies implemented by Ronald Reagan are commonly referred to as Reaganomics. It was one of the most ambitious attempts at changing the country's economic policies since the days of the New Deal.

Reagan believed the key to growing the economy lay in reducing the government's growth. His Program for Economic Recovery, unveiled in 1981, was designed to reduce the cost of conducting business. This was achieved through tax cuts and relaxing price controls and regulations. He also aimed to reduce inflation by controlling the supply of money.

Because Reagan's views on government were that it should intervene less, life-saving government-funded programs, like Medicaid, Social Security, education programs, and food stamps, were the first to be cut.

While he cut back on social spending, he increased military spending. By implementing these policies, he expected to reduce inflation and see a rise in investments and savings, which would ensure healthier markets and economic growth.

His policies had both negative and positive effects. Within two years, the economy began to recover. Reaganomics led to a period of prosperity and strong economic growth. For instance, the GDP improved by more than 25 percent, and inflation came down to 4 percent. Unemployment also dropped to 5.5 percent.

Reaganomics helped to reduce poverty, but it also increased social inequality by making the rich richer. His trickle-down economic policy resulted in high earners tripling their income, while low-income families only went up a few percentage points.

The War on Drugs

One of the most important federal legislations to be passed by the Reagan administration involved drugs. In October 1986, the Anti-Drug Abuse Act was passed and signed into law. Under the act, one billion dollars was committed to fighting the war on drugs, while the punishment for drug-related offenses became harsher. For example, if someone was caught with five grams of crack, they could be sentenced to a five-year prison sentence with no possibility of parole.

The act was partially inspired by Nancy Reagan's "Just Say No" campaign on drugs.

Nancy Reagan at a Just Say No rally.
https://commons.wikimedia.org/wiki/File:Photograph_of_Mrs._Reagan_speaking_at_a_%22Just_Say_No%22_Rally_in_Los_Angeles_-_NARA_-_198584.jpg

While the intent of the act and the campaign were done in good faith, there were a lot of negatives. The act did not take into account many socioeconomic factors or that addictions often occurred as a result of prescription medication.

In the long run, many believe Reagan's zero-tolerance policy did more harm than good, as it dramatically increased the number of incarcerations for nonviolent drug offenses, worsened racial inequality, and thrust mostly marginalized people into a cycle of violence and poverty.

Assassination Attempt

Soon after taking office, an attempt was made on President Reagan's life.

A man by the name of John Hinckley shot Reagan on March 30th, 1981, while the president was walking to his limousine after an engagement.

Six shots were fired by Hinckley, who was standing amongst a crowd of reporters. He was apprehended almost immediately. The president, who did not immediately realize he had been shot, was put in the limousine by his security detail and taken to the hospital. The bullet narrowly missed his heart and damaged his left lung instead. He underwent a two-hour surgery and was in stable condition. He even began working from the hospital bed the very next day.

Additional victims also recovered, although some suffered more serious injuries than others. James Brady, the White House press secretary, suffered permanent brain damage. The experience led to him becoming a staunch advocate of gun control.

As for Reagan, the assassination attempt raised his popularity even more.

Reagan and Foreign Affairs

Like his predecessors, Reagan and his administration continued to play a key role in international and foreign affairs, often acting as peacemakers.

When Israel invaded Lebanon in 1982, eight hundred US Marines were sent from the States on a peacekeeping mission to Lebanon. Over two hundred American lives were lost when suicide bombers attacked their barracks in Beirut.

In October 1983, on the heels of the losses in Lebanon, Reagan sent US forces to the island of Grenada after the Marxist government in Grenada launched a coup, killing the prime minister and seizing power. The American government authorized the invasion of Grenada to protect American nationals living on the Caribbean island. Many of these nationals were young medical students.

President Reagan had two thousand American troops sent to the island, and the invasion began on October 25th, 1983. Letting the rebels win would mean another communist government near the US, and Reagan couldn't have that. They met resistance from Grenada's armed forces and Cuban troops, which supported the Marxist government. An additional seven thousand troops were sent from the US. Within four days, the invasion was over, with the Americans coming out as the winners.

The Marxist government was toppled and replaced by one approved by the US. In total, twenty American soldiers were killed, and more than one hundred came back wounded.

Irangate

Reagan's administration did a lot of good for the country and the world; however, they were not entirely free from scandal. One of the biggest political scandals Reagan faced was Irangate or the Iran-Contra affair.

To understand Irangate, we have to go back to 1979 when Iran went through a revolution and overthrew its detested dictator, Reza Shah Pahlavi. Ayatollah Khomeini came to power and quickly created the Islamic Republic of Iran. His dislike for America and its influence on Iran was an open secret.

While Iran was going through its revolution, so was Nicaragua. In Nicaragua, a pro-Soviet group called the Sandinistas took over. Reagan, who was on a mission to eliminate communism, could not have this. He signed a secret order that gave the CIA the authority to provide the Contras—a paramilitary group working against the Sandinistas—money, weapons, equipment, and support. The end goal was to get rid of the Sandinista regime.

However, the money was provided covertly. America was illegally selling weapons and arms to Iran. The profit it made from these sales was secretly funneled to the Contras.

The illegal arms sale was revealed in a Lebanese newspaper while Regan was serving his second term. Reagan denied knowing anything about this but later retracted his words. An investigation, which would last for eight years, was launched.

Reagan was never charged with any crime or wrongdoing, and when his second term ended, Reagan was still very popular and beloved. Even today, his role in Irangate is often overlooked or sidestepped, so his legacy remains intact.

The *Challenger*

One of the more tragic domestic events that took place during Reagan's presidency was the Space Shuttle *Challenger* disaster, which occurred on January 28th, 1986.

Just after 11:30 a.m. that morning, the *Challenger*, which was carrying seven crew members and one civilian, began lift-off. Less than a minute and a half later, the shuttle broke apart and burst into flames. There were no survivors. Millions of students tuned in to watch a teacher ascend into space; instead, they watched as the *Challenger* fell back to earth in pieces.

This was the first major shuttle accident. The government launched an investigation to determine what went wrong. NASA was eventually able to figure out that one of the seals had malfunctioned as a result of the cold. For more than two years, while NASA worked on improving the space shuttles, no more astronauts were sent into space.

Escalation of Cold War

When Reagan became president, he also inherited the Cold War, which had been going on for decades.

After a period of relative stability and even the easing of tensions between the East and the West, things quickly began to deteriorate when the Soviet Union invaded Afghanistan in December 1979. The US strongly denounced this act, which led to an increase in hostilities and an escalation of the Cold War, sometimes referred to as the Second Cold War.

President Carter had placed embargos on Soviet imports, led a boycott of the 1980 Olympic Games, increased military spending, and provided money to Afghani rebels.

When Reagan replaced Carter, he continued in much the same vein, except he was far more aggressive. Reagan openly disliked communism and was determined to eliminate it entirely.

Anti-communist movements and rebels around the world began to receive secret funding from the US to help combat communism. His military spending increased because he invested heavily in troops and weapons as a precaution against the Soviet Union, which he viewed as an "evil empire."

As part of the Reagan Doctrine, financial aid was also provided to African and Latin American movements that rose up against communism.

The Strategic Defense Initiative (SDI) was put in place in 1983. The aim of the SDI was to develop weapons that would be based in space and could be launched at any minute to defend the US and counter any attacks from a Soviet missile.

The Strategic Defense Initiative ended in 1993. By the time President Clinton came into office, the Cold War was coming to an end, and the Soviet Union's nuclear weapons were also getting reduced. As a result, support for the SDI faltered.

In 1993, Clinton's administration ended the program and renamed the agency Ballistic Missile Defense Organization (BMDO). The agency fell under the Department of Defense and was responsible for the country's ballistic missile defense efforts. In 2002, BMDO was renamed the Missile Defense Agency (MDA).

Reagan also strengthened his ties with Western nations, such as the United Kingdom. Margaret Thatcher, the new prime minister of Great Britain, felt just as strongly about communism as Reagan and supported him.

The Second Cold War quickly became financially draining for the Soviet Union. When Mikhail Gorbachev became the leader of the Soviet Union in 1985, he felt the resources that were being poured into Cold War commitments could be better used to help Russia and its people.

Mikhail Gorbachev.

An agreement was signed by both countries in 1987. They agreed to get rid of intermediate-range nuclear missiles. Feeling emboldened by this historic progress, Reagan delivered a speech at the Berlin Wall and challenged Gorbachev to dismantle it.

The Berlin Wall, which had divided East and West Germany for many years, came down nearly two and a half years later on November 9th, 1989. When the Berlin Wall fell, it was viewed by many as a symbolic ending to the Cold War.

Reagan brought back a piece of the Berlin Wall with him to America. Today, it is displayed in Simi Valley, California, at the Ronald Reagan Presidential Library.

Chapter 27: George H. W. Bush: The End of the Cold War

After Ronald Reagan's second term ended, the Republicans stayed in power, with George H. W. Bush taking office as the forty-first president of the country. He was inaugurated on January 20th, 1989, and was the sitting president when the Berlin Wall actually fell.

Reunification of Germany (1990)

The reunification of Germany began on November 9th, 1989, when East Berlin's Communist Party announced that citizens would be free to cross the borders. On the first weekend after this announcement was made, droves of people from East Berlin made their way into West Berlin to celebrate and reunite with friends and family. People soon began to break down pieces of the wall until the whole thing came down.

People stand on top of the fallen Berlin Wall.

The Cold War did not automatically end with the fall of the Berlin Wall, nor did it lead to a unified Germany. The reunification of Germany took months and happened officially on October 3rd, 1990, nearly a year after the Berlin Wall came down.

Malta Summit

While Reagan was president, he started to develop a friendship of sorts with Mikhail Gorbachev, who was also keen on having a better relationship with the West. After Bush took office, he was, at first, hesitant and wary of the Soviet Union, but after some time, he continued the efforts Reagan had made and opened up a dialogue with Gorbachev.

The two leaders decided to meet in Malta to continue their conversations in person. While a formal treaty was not discussed, Bush did allude that US policies toward the Soviet Union might change as their relationship evolved.

The Malta Summit took place on warships that were anchored in the Mediterranean between December 2nd and 3rd, 1989. During the summit, Gorbachev made it clear they were ready to leave the Cold War behind and start fresh.

By this time, a number of communist bloc governments had begun to collapse, including Bulgaria, Poland, and East Germany. The Soviet Union didn't try to resist or intervene in any of these countries. This acceptance was a dramatic change in outlook from four decades ago.

Another shocking shift was the Soviet Union's foreign minister's visit to NATO headquarters. After his visit with NATO Secretary General Manfred Wörner, he stated that he felt the Cold War was over. Gorbachev hoped the East and the West would find a way to end the decades-long confrontation and start building toward cooperation.

START Treaty (1991)

The START Treaty (Strategic Arms Reduction Treaty) had initially been proposed by President Reagan as part of disarmament talks that started in the early 1980s. These discussions continued between President Bush and Soviet leader Gorbachev.

START was signed on July 31ᵗ, 1991, by both leaders. Under the terms of the treaty, both countries were limited to the number of nuclear warheads and Intercontinental Ballistic Missiles (ICBMs) they could have. After the treaty was implemented, approximately 80 percent of the strategic nuclear weapons possessed by the US and the Soviet Union were removed, destroyed, or deactivated.

The START Treaty was ratified in Congress the following year in October. It was one more step toward bringing an end to the Cold War.

Dismantling of the Soviet Union

After decades of iron control, the Soviet Union was beginning to lose the grip it once had on Eastern Europe. The Soviet Bloc began to unravel in 1989 when Poland elected a non-communist government. When the Soviet Union did nothing, other countries began to follow suit like dominoes, clamoring for freedom.

One by one, through peaceful revolutions, communist regimes in Hungary, Czechoslovakia, Romania, Bulgaria, and Albania were all ousted and replaced by non-communist governments. Latvia, Lithuania, and Estonia, the three Baltic states, also declared their independence from the Soviet Union.

End of the Cold War

The Cold War didn't formally end in any type of dramatic way; instead, it was a series of events that started during the 1980s that culminated to a point where there was no more Cold War and no more

Soviet Union.

Gorbachev heavily influenced the last phase of the Cold War, and he is credited with ending it peacefully and without shedding blood. Not an easy feat for a country that saw communism take over in a bloody way. His radical reforms, policies, and redirecting of resources prioritized the growth of the country and the people. The easing of tensions and the more relaxed approach eventually led to the fall of the Berlin Wall and the Soviet Bloc.

By the end of 1991, as more countries moved away from communism, it was clear the Soviet Union was going to collapse. On December 25th, 1991, he resigned, saying, "We're now living in a new world. An end has been put to the Cold War and to the arms race."[9] Boris Yeltsin took over, and on December 26th, 1991, the Soviet Union was officially dissolved.

For his role in helping to end the war, Gorbachev won a Nobel Peace Prize on October 15th, 1990.

First Gulf War (1990–1991)

As the Cold War began to end, another international crisis was looming that would result in American intervention. The leader of Iraq, Saddam Hussein, had been eyeing oil-rich Kuwait for some time. Tensions between the two countries had been brewing for years.

On August 2nd, 1990, Saddam decided to invade the country. He hoped to gain control of the large oil reserves in Kuwait, get out of paying the debt Iraq owed to Kuwait, and expand his power and control in the region.

The Kuwaitis actively resisted and fought back against Iraqi forces, but it did not go well. Over the span of 14 hours, around 4,200 Kuwaitis were killed. Over the next few days, Iraqi forces easily and quickly took over Kuwait City. Members of the royal family of Kuwait and hundreds of thousands of Kuwaitis fled the country and took refuge in nearby Saudi Arabia.

By the end of August, Saddam boldly declared that annexed Kuwait was now a part of Iraq as its nineteenth province. Iraqi troops occupied the country and wreaked a campaign of terror on the Kuwaitis, raping,

---

[9] "Collapse of the Soviet Union." https://www.history.com/topics/european-history/history-of-the-soviet-union

torturing, and killing as they pleased.

Given how protective the West has always been over oil in the Middle East, nations acted swiftly. Within days of the invasion, the United Nations Security Council banned trade with Iraq. In the meantime, American troops were sent to Saudi Arabia.

The Arab League also spoke up and condemned the invasion and supported the UN's resolution. Some Arab countries, like Jordan and Tunisia, were sympathetic to Iraq and took Saddam's side.

In a surprising turn of events, the Soviet Union also came forward to support America. All in all, the invasion was shaping up to be a significant international crisis. It was the first one in a post-Cold War world.

Kuwait was also home to more than 600,000 expats, nearly 10,000 of which were Western nationals. They were all trapped in the country and forbidden from leaving by the Iraqi regime. Westerners soon began to be rounded up by Iraqi troops to be used as shields in case of an attack by the West. Saddam declared that children and women would be allowed to leave, but the situation was too tense and unpredictable. It seemed quite likely he would attempt an invasion of Saudi Arabia next, which would put 40 percent of the world's oil in his control.

America began to plan its overseas deployment, the largest one since WWII. By the end of November 1990, close to half a million US troops were stationed in the Gulf. Additional troops from the UK, Canada, Bangladesh, and France, to name a few nations, also arrived.

All the while, the UN was debating whether the use of force could be sanctioned if Iraq did not comply and leave Kuwait by a specified date (January 15th, 1991). The council decided that it would use "any means necessary" to remove him after that date.

Operation Desert Storm

Saddam, of course, refused to withdraw, and on January 17th, 1991, President Bush gave the go-ahead for American troops to attack Saddam's army. The mission's goal was to get rid of the Iraqi forces that were occupying Kuwait. The campaign consisted of a military coalition of thirty-five countries and began with aerial bombing. The war lasted for forty-two days and consisted of operations on both ground and air.

Oil wells on fire during Operation Desert Storm.
https://commons.wikimedia.org/wiki/File:Operation_Desert_Storm_22.jpg

Saddam's forces were successfully pushed out of Kuwait, and after a heavy bombing campaign on Baghdad, Iraqi troops began to surrender. On February 28th, a ceasefire was declared. Bush had successfully managed to roll back the invasion of Kuwait by Iraq.

NAFTA (1992)

The North American Free Trade Agreement (NAFTA) was established as a way to stimulate trade with participating countries, reduce costs, increase production, create new jobs, and bring prosperity. It was partially inspired by a similar trade agreement that had been created in Europe called the European Economic Community in 1957. The US felt an agreement like this would also help North America gain a more competitive footing globally.

NAFTA was signed in 1992 by American President George H. W. Bush, Mexican President Carlos Salinas de Gortari, and Canadian Prime Minister Brian Mulroney. It was slated to take effect on January 1st, 1994.

With the signing of NAFTA, tariffs on most of the goods produced by the three countries were lifted. In some ways, NAFTA was a positive thing. It did help attract foreign investments and lower the cost of goods, which benefited the consumer. It also increased trade. But in other ways, it had a negative impact on the American economy, as many manufacturing jobs were relocated to Mexico, where labor and the cost of operating a business were cheaper. It affected smaller businesses and farms in Mexico, which couldn't lower their costs enough.

SECTION EIGHT:
From Clinton to Trump
(1992–2021)

Chapter 28: The Clinton Years: The Swift and Scandalous '90s

During the presidential election of 1992, Bush ran for reelection but was defeated by Democratic nominee Bill Clinton.

President Bill Clinton.
https://commons.wikimedia.org/wiki/File:Bill_Clinton.jpg

Clinton would go on to serve two terms in office. His presidency is generally viewed as an easy time for America. International conflicts and events were still taking place, but they were nothing like the tension-filled Cold War years.

By the time the '90s rolled around, America had really found its footing, both at home and globally. It was the decade when the fruits of past labors could be enjoyed. Hard-won freedoms by civil rights activists, women's groups, and other reformers had all allowed for the progressive, modern, diverse, and advanced society that America was in the 1990s.

Clinton's Domestic Policies

When Clinton was campaigning, he promised to tackle important social issues like unemployment, health care, and the economy. During his presidency, he implemented many domestic policies and legislations to help address and advance those issues.

Within his first year in office, Clinton passed an economic package called the Omnibus Budget Reconciliation Act of 1993. Under this act, the federal income tax for the upper class went up from 31 percent to 39.6 percent. The corporate tax rate went up, while government spending was cut by $255 billion over a period of five years. This negatively affected struggling Americans, who relied on many of the programs the government was cutting.

Although it was not popular with Republicans, Clinton's economic policy brought the government's deficit down from $290 billion to $203 billion in a matter of two years. And by the end of the 1990s, the economy was not only booming but also had a surplus of over $120 billion. A combination of low inflation, low interest rates, and low unemployment rates made the American economy one of the strongest and most enviable in the world.

Clinton also fulfilled another campaign promise by passing a sweeping reform bill on welfare assistance. He increased the minimum wage to $5.15 an hour.

At this point in American history, gay men and lesbians were excluded from the military. Clinton vowed to change this. A bitter political fight ensued with conservative individuals in the military. Congress eventually forced Clinton to reach a compromise. He proposed the "don't ask, don't tell" policy. If military personnel didn't ask about someone's sexual orientation, they wouldn't need to discuss it. It wasn't a perfect solution, but it was something.

On February 5th, 1993, Clinton signed the Family Medical Leave Act into law. The law granted workers family and medical leave of up to twelve weeks if the need arose. The leave was unpaid, but the act ensured their jobs would be protected and that their health insurance would be unaffected.

One of the things Clinton failed to do, something that was very close to his heart and important to him, was provide affordable health care for all Americans. While Clinton was running for office, there was a great deal of chatter and interest surrounding health care reform. Today, the US and South Africa are the only developed nations that do not provide universal health care for their people. Back in the 1990s, Clinton wanted to change this. Socially, it would be life-changing for Americans, and politically, it would ensure that the majority of the middle- and working-class population would align themselves with the Democrats.

The Republicans were fiercely determined not to let this happen and strongly objected to a health reform bill.

After Clinton took office, he created a task force to develop a proposal. His wife, Hillary, was put in charge of drafting the bill. The final product, a 1,350-page proposal, was difficult to understand for the average public, and it never got off the ground.

There are a few reasons why the health care reform failed. Firstly, Clinton presented it to the Senate after budget discussions had already been completed instead of beforehand. Thus, it should have been no surprise when the Senate did not approve the proposal. In the Senate's view, it would cost too much money, and the coverage provided to Americans was too extensive.

The administration's unwillingness to compromise on it made matters worse. The general consensus was that the proposal was too radical. By the time a task force did start to look at some compromises, the momentum was lost, and the reform ultimately failed and was shelved.

To this day, universal health care and gun control remain hotly contested and deeply divisive issues in America.

Columbine High School

Around 11:19 a.m., on April 20th, 1999, two teenagers armed with guns went to Columbine High School in the suburbs of Denver and started shooting at students outside the school. Then, they went inside the school and gunned down more students.

By 11:35 a.m., thirteen people had been killed: twelve students and one teacher. An additional twenty-one people were left wounded and injured. Just past noon, the teens killed themselves, bringing an end to their shocking and senseless killing spree.

Although Columbine was not the first school shooting in America, the public was left devastated and outraged that something like this had taken place. It affected Clinton on a deeper level, and the way he handled the tragedy set a precedent for how future presidents should behave and led to the examination of how presidential roles have evolved over time.

After the Columbine shooting, Clinton visited the victims' families. He comforted them, listened to them, and played the role of "Counselor in Chief." It was a break from the often-stoic attitude of past presidents who kept their emotions in check.

Following the shooting, Clinton advocated for stricter gun control but was not successful in getting anywhere. Gun control is a divisive topic in US politics today, and school shootings, as well as other mass shootings, still remain a problem.

Clinton's Foreign Policies

When Clinton became president, he wasn't very experienced in foreign affairs or policy. He came to power at a very interesting time. The Cold War had ended, and the Soviet Union had collapsed; it was almost like a new world.

Clinton swiftly understood the importance of globalization and saw it as a way of developing international relationships, enjoying shared prosperity, and promoting peace. He believed American foreign policy should be designed for the global age and that it must constantly evolve and adapt to keep up with the changing times.

In 1993, he welcomed new members into NATO, allowing it to evolve from Cold War alliances to include new friendships and partnerships. Russia was brought into the G-8, and Russian troops were even used to help NATO missions.

Clinton reduced tensions with North Korea through diplomacy and, in 1994, even managed to negotiate an agreement with the country to dismantle nuclear weapons. He also worked hard to create stronger bonds with South Korea.

In short, he tried to create a more inclusive global environment. We will take a closer look at some of the more notable international events and conflicts that took place during Clinton's presidency, although, like most topics in this book, this only scratches the surface of what happened during his presidency.

War in Bosnia

The Bosnian War began with the break-up of the Socialist Federal Republic of Yugoslavia, which included Croatia, Bosnia-Herzegovina, Serbia, Slovenia, Macedonia, and Montenegro. As the Soviet Bloc began to collapse, the six republics within Yugoslavia began to also divide based on their ethnicity.

In June 1991, Slovenia and Croatia declared independence. Less than a year later, Bosnia-Herzegovina also stated its intention to separate. It officially became independent on March 1ᵗ, 1992, which became the catalyst for the war.

Using the crisis to their advantage, Bosnian Serbs, with the help of Serbia, set out on a campaign to ethnically cleanse the country of Bosniaks or Bosnian Muslims. Their end goal was to wipe out the Muslim population and create a state free of Bosniaks. They began their offensive by bombing and seizing Bosnia's capital, Sarajevo. Bosnian Muslims fled by the thousands.

The genocide in Bosnia took nearly 100,000 civilian lives, most of which were Bosniaks. More than two million people were displaced, and up to fifty thousand women were subjected to rape, violence, and other brutalities. Thousands of others went missing, never to be found again.

At first, the UN and the US refused to intervene until the summer of 1995, when Bosnian Serbs killed eight thousand men and boys in Srebrenica within ten days. Srebrenica had been designated by the UN as a safe refuge. Between twenty-five thousand and thirty thousand women and children were abused and/or forced to move to other Muslim areas. Some of them got on buses and were never seen again.

It was at this point that Clinton decided that something had to be done. He put Operation Deliberate Force in motion. NATO led air strikes, launched an offensive in Croatia, and intervened in the war.

The Clinton administration negotiated the peace treaty. The Dayton Agreement, which was signed by Bosnia, Serbia, and Croatia in 1995, brought the long and bloody war to an end. According to the treaty, Bosnia would remain a single state but have two parts: the Federation of Bosnia and Herzegovina, which was mostly populated by Croat-Bosniaks, and the Republika Srpska, which was mostly populated by Serbians. The capital city, Sarajevo, stayed undivided.

American intervention and the subsequent peace treaty served to showcase America's prowess on the international scene and Clinton's negotiation skills and diplomacy. The agreement still stands today and is used in the governing structure of Bosnia and Herzegovina.

The way Bosnia was handled also provided a precedent for what would happen in Kosovo around four years later.

Kosovo Conflict

Three years after the war in Bosnia ended, ethnic Albanians were fighting against Serbs and the Yugoslavian government in Kosovo. After Slovenia and Croatia declared independence, ethnic Albanians in the Federal Republic of Yugoslavia decided to also separate and create their own republic called Kosovo. The crisis led to another round of ethnic cleansing by Yugoslavia, as Yugoslav soldiers, mainly Serbians, drove Albanians out of the country or had them killed.

Having witnessed the war in Bosnia, this time, the international world was determined not to sit on the sidelines. A national emergency was declared by Clinton on June 9th, 1998, and NATO intervened shortly after launching Operation Allied Force.

NATO and American forces began air strikes, targeting government buildings and other infrastructures in Yugoslavia. After enduring eleven weeks of bombing, Yugoslav forces withdrew from Kosovo.

The Kumanovo Treaty was signed on June 9th, 1999, with the Yugoslavian government agreeing to withdraw after NATO forces did. After the Yugoslavs left, NATO troops came into Kosovo to begin a peace support mission.

In both these examples, we can see how Clinton and America took charge; they decided on a course of action and followed through with it. There was no questioning America's authority or superiority as a global power in the 1990s.

Clinton-Lewinsky Scandal

Finally, no chapter on Clinton can be complete without bringing up his affair with Monica Lewinsky. The political sex scandal rocked the nation and is still widely discussed and talked about today.

During the summer of 1995, recent college graduate Monica Lewinsky started working at the White House as an intern in the office of the chief of staff. A few months later, in the fall, she was moved to the West Wing, along with a few other interns, for basic administrative duties. This brought her into contact with Clinton, who was very taken by the beautiful, young Lewinsky.

Monica and President Bill Clinton.

Monica herself was quite smitten with the president. The two quickly became involved and continued to meet and have sexual encounters, even after Monica took a job in another office. By 1997, they stopped their sexual trysts and mostly kept in touch over the phone.

The affair came to light after Monica confided in a friend and coworker named Linda Tripp, who betrayed Monica by telling the story to a literary agent and secretly recording their phone calls. In the meantime, Kenneth Starr, an independent counsel who was looking into Bill and Hillary's investments in a business venture, stumbled onto the scandal. The story quickly took on a life of its own, and the scandal erupted. Americans were both shocked and fascinated.

At first, Clinton denied the affair, but when a blue dress worn by Monica with semen stains on it came to light, he backtracked. Clinton later admitted to a grand jury that he had, in fact, engaged in inappropriate behavior with Lewinsky. He publicly apologized for his behavior.

In October 1998, the House of Representatives moved to impeach him. At Clinton's trial in February 1999, he was acquitted. Although Clinton had clearly broken the trust of the American public, he finished his term as president while maintaining strong ratings.

The scandal might have shocked the country, but it did not lessen many people's admiration or devotion to Clinton. However, Hillary faced a lot of criticism for standing by his side. Lewinsky was publicly shamed and bullied. The stigma of the affair clung to her for decades. In 2016, when Hillary Clinton ran for president against Donald Trump, the scandal was dredged up again and used against her in smear campaigns.

Despite doing a lot of good and leaving behind quite a legacy, Clinton's presidency will always be marked by the Lewinsky affair.

Chapter 29: The George W. Bush Years: 9/11 and the War on Terror

If Clinton's time in office was easy, smooth, and tension-free, George W. Bush's presidency was the exact opposite. His presidency started badly almost from the very beginning, starting with the election itself.

The race for the presidency between him and Democratic nominee Al Gore had been a tight one. By the time election day was coming to an end on November 7th, 2000, it wasn't really clear who the winner was. The race in some states, such as New Mexico and Oregon, was too close to call and stayed that way for days.

Eventually, Florida became the focus of the presidential election results, with some networks announcing that Al Gore was the projected winner. This was reversed later, with Bush being declared the winner. Al Gore called Bush on November 8th to congratulate him and concede. However, by the next morning, it was discovered that only a few hundred votes separated Bush and Gore, putting the margin of victory at around 0.1 percent. Al Gore called Bush again to rescind his concession.

Legal teams from both parties went to Florida, and a machine recount took place, which put Bush ahead of Gore by just over three hundred votes. But other legal issues and questions continued to plague Bush's win, which continued to be contested. The case was taken all the way to the US Supreme Court, where the decision was made to terminate the recounting process. The twenty-five electoral votes in Florida were given to Bush, cinching his win. Bush was inaugurated as the forty-third president on January 20th, 2001.

When Bush left office, his approval rating hovered somewhere in the twenties. His administration was excessive, and he was not a stellar leader. Therefore, he was woefully underprepared for the events to come.

9/11

About eight months after Bush took office, the United States was attacked by terrorists. On September 11th, 2001, between the hours of 7:59 a.m. to 8:42 a.m., four passenger planes took off. Two planes were from Boston, Massachusetts, one was from Washington, DC, and a fourth took from Newark, New Jersey. The flights were all headed to the same place: California. What none of the passengers could have known was that terrorists with links to al-Qaeda were sitting among them.

The four planes were hijacked. They never made it to their destination. Instead, two of the planes headed for New York City and crashed into the Twin Towers of the World Trade Center. The first plane hit the North Tower at 8:46 a.m.; the second one crashed into the South Tower at 9:03 a.m.

Twin Towers burning.

The third plane crashed into the Pentagon at 9:45 a.m., while the fourth plane, which was likely meant to target the White House or the Capitol, crashed in a field in western Pennsylvania because the passengers fought back.

The attacks are commonly referred to as 9/11. A total of 2,996 people died during the attacks, with thousands of others sustaining injuries. Most of the victims were from the World Trade Center.

Americans were shocked, then grief-stricken, and then enraged by the attacks. All eyes were now on Bush.

Global War on Terrorism

Following 9/11, Bush had one goal in mind: to defeat terrorism. He soon launched a campaign called the Global War on Terror. One of the first things he did was freeze the assets of any groups linked to terrorist activities while demanding that the Taliban stop protecting al-Qaeda members.

By early October, he was planning for military strikes in Afghanistan against al-Qaeda. He planned for the American military to also provide aid to those in need in Afghanistan.

The invasion of Afghanistan by American and Allied troops happened within a month of the 9/11 attacks. Bush saw it as an act of self-defense. His target was the Taliban regime since it had provided a safe haven for al-Qaeda.

During the early days of the war, the US carried out air strikes. After losing some key players, the Taliban regime began to crumble, although it didn't remain that way for long. The Taliban regrouped. For the next two decades, things continued in this fashion, with each side gaining a little and then losing a little.

Afghanistan became the longest war that America had ever fought. When US troops finally left in 2021, it became clear the US had lost the war.

War in Iraq

While trying to root out al-Qaeda, Bush began to put pressure on Saddam Hussein for a number of things, including his ties with terrorists and his weapons of mass destruction. Saddam, of course, refused to cut ties or dismantle the weapons. By March 2003, Bush decided that Saddam had to go, and military operations were put in place for that purpose.

The official reason provided by the Bush administration for the invasion of Iraq was to disarm the country, root out al-Qaeda, and free the Iraqi people from Saddam's tyranny. However, it is a commonly held belief that the invasion had more to do with oil than with freeing people since there was no actual evidence of WMDs in Iraq or evidence that Saddam had any relationship with al-Qaeda. Some believe the US wanted to stabilize the global oil supply and make sure there would be no disruptions in oil coming out of Iraq. Others believe it was Bush's way of asserting American dominance over the world again after the terrorist attacks.

Whatever the real reason, American troops invaded Iraq in March 2003. Some troops from other allied countries also joined in the invasion. By April, most of Baghdad was under American control, and Saddam had gone into hiding. In December, he was captured by the US and convicted and executed three years later in December 2006 by the Iraqi High Tribunal.

However, this did not immediately end the war. Instead, Saddam's removal led to a power vacuum.

The war in Iraq, also called the Second Persian Gulf War, lasted until December 2011, when the US finally withdrew from Iraq after it was unable to negotiate an extension of its stay with the Iraqi government. In November 2011, the Senate voted to end the war, and on December 15th, the war came to a formal end.

Bush's Domestic Policies

While Bush and his administration were busy with the War on Terror, he also had to deal with numerous crises domestically.

The Great Recession

One of the biggest challenges facing Bush at home was the Great Recession. It was viewed as the worst economic crisis the country had seen since the Great Depression.

The recession was caused by three main things:

- The unstable housing market. In the early 2000s, the housing market was booming, and lenders were approving mortgages to poor creditors. Many of the loans defaulted, and the housing market plummeted.
- Bank crisis.

- Dramatic fall of the stock market, which wiped out a large chunk of wealth.

In response to the recession, the American Recovery and Reinvestment Act of 2009 was passed by Congress. The act put aside $800 billion to help with the economy's recovery. Another program called Troubled Asset Relief Program (TARP) also helped the economy grow. Bush also introduced tax relief that helped small businesses.

Health Care

When it came to America's health care, Bush helped to strengthen it by reforming Medicare and adding drug benefits. His policies gave approximately forty million people better access to prescription drugs. His reforms were aimed at making health care more affordable and accessible for Americans.

Bush won a second term as president, partially due to his heightened popularity immediately after 9/11 and his campaign against terrorism. His time in office was marked by a number of really difficult events, but as a president, he was fairly unremarkable.

The legacy he left behind is mainly tied to 9/11 and terrorism and his poor handling of Katrina. Ironically, he has become more respected and popular in his post-presidency years.

Hurricane Katrina

The fall of 2005 was a particularly difficult period in Bush's presidency. In addition to 9/11, which eventually led to the war in Iraq, President Bush also had to deal with the devastating consequences of Hurricane Katrina.

A Category 5 tropical cyclone, Katrina swept over The Bahamas and hit the southeastern United States on August 23rd, 2005. When it made landfall near the Miami and Fort Lauderdale area in Florida, it was a Category 1 hurricane, but over the following days, as it continued to move and circulate, it gained strength. When it finally arrived in New Orleans, it had turned into a Category 5. Southern Louisiana felt the brunt of the hurricane.

With 1,392 fatalities, Katrina would become one of the deadliest hurricanes. It would also become the most expensive hurricane to ever hit the country, causing between $97 and $145.5 billion in damages.

President Bush's response to Katrina was heavily criticized at the time and continues to be viewed in a negative manner to this day. His administration was slow to respond to the disaster and did not act decisively or empathetically. It took days for federal troops to make their way to the area. To make matters worse, while Katrina was pummeling the Gulf coast, Bush was on vacation in Texas and remained there. When he did return to Washington, he flew over New Orleans, viewing the devastation from above. The public perception of this move further damaged his image.

However, once Bush got the ball rolling, 7,200 troops were dispatched to New Orleans. On September 2nd, he signed a $10.5 billion relief package. Over the years, government assistance increased dramatically and is estimated to be somewhere between $126 billion and $140 billion, including tax reliefs. Bush also made sure to visit the area several times and meet with people.

However, the impression etched in people's minds was that he could have and should have done more.

Chapter 30: Barack Obama: The First Black President

During the 1950s and especially in the 1960s, when riots, violence, and protests around the civil rights movement were at their peak, it seemed unimaginable that, one day, America could have a black president.

In 2008, Barack Obama won the presidential election, becoming the forty-fourth president of America. He was the first African American president. It was a monumental and historic event. Suddenly, it felt as if nothing was impossible in America anymore.

President Obama.
https://commons.wikimedia.org/wiki/File:President_Barack_Obama.jpg

After the stressful, angst-filled years under the Bush administration, Obama felt like a fresh start, a hopeful beginning, and the turning of the tide to most of America.

Obama's Domestic Policies

During Obama's two terms as president, he contributed positively and negatively to the country. When he took office, he inherited an America that was going through many challenges. It was struggling to recover from an economic collapse and dealing with the aftermath of several wars, including the War on Terror. American troops were embroiled in a war in Afghanistan, and the future seemed bleak.

While campaigning, Obama promised the American people he would revive the economy, cut the deficit in half, and close the highly controversial US detention center in Guantanamo Bay in Cuba, where prisoners were rumored to be tortured and abused. He promised to bring about change and ensure America's stature globally. They were big promises to make. While Obama certainly left an enduring legacy and did a lot for the country, he wasn't able to keep all his promises.

During Obama's first term, he passed acts on three important issues: the economy, health care, and financial institutions.

One of his economic policies, the American Recovery and Reinvestment Act of 2009, helped to jumpstart the economy and decrease the unemployment rate. Tax reliefs provided a much-needed boost to American incomes and prevented approximately 5.3 million from slipping below the poverty line.

Obama helped restructure the American International Group (the country's largest insurer) to prevent future collapses. He did the same with the financial system to make sure institutions would be able to withstand any economic downturns. Obama's policies also brought stability to the housing crisis and saved the automotive industry.

His biggest legacy might be the signing of the Affordable Care Act. Obama pledged to make health care affordable and equal for all, as he believed that health care was a right and not a privilege. As we've seen in previous sections, health care had been a hotly contested issue during numerous presidencies. The act, commonly referred to as Obamacare, ensured that every American could afford a health insurance plan. The act mandates that all health insurance companies have to provide a certain type of coverage with their plans.

This was life-changing for struggling families that could not even afford to see a doctor. The most impacted families were blacks, minorities, small business owners, and those who fell below the poverty line.

Unfortunately, not everyone was a fan of the act. One of the main reasons people didn't support Obamacare has more to do with partisan politics than the act itself. Some Democrats felt the act didn't do enough and gave insurance companies too much control. They wanted to move toward a health care system that was fully run by the government.

On the other hand, many Republicans felt very strongly that the federal government should stay out of the health care system. They also opposed the tax increases that were necessary to get the act rolling, as well as the higher premiums with insurance companies.

The hike in premiums left some people feeling that health care was costing a lot more than it did in the past. This wasn't helped by the rising costs in health care and cost of living.

Obamacare did not provide the free, universal health care that some have dreamed of, but it was the start of something and changed the lives of millions of Americans.

Obama and the LGBTQ Community

According to LGBTQ advocates, President Obama was the most pro-LGBTQ president. He did a lot to advance their cause. Bush's administration had done nothing for the community; in fact, he set them back by supporting a constitutional amendment that would ban same-sex marriage.

Obama promised to do the opposite. He wanted his administration to work hard to support them. In 2009, the right to same-sex marriage was enshrined in the Constitution. Federal and state governments no longer had the authority to ban same-sex marriages.

A federal hate crime law was also passed that year to protect the rights of LGBTQ people. Clinton's "don't ask, don't tell" policy was repealed in 2010, allowing LGBTQ members of the military to serve without prejudice. In addition to these steps, Obama also signed executive orders to protect the LGBTQ community from being discriminated against by employers.

He was the first president to support marriage equality, as well as the first one to acknowledge the existence of transgender people, even inviting the executive director of the National Center for Transgender

Equality to the White House.

Obama's actions advanced the LGBTQ community's progress by leaps and bounds after remaining stagnant for decades.

Domestic Crises

At home, several disastrous and tragic events unfolded during Obama's presidency, which required him to rally the country and provide emotional support and strength.

One such tragedy was the Sandy Hook Elementary school shooting, which took place on December 14th, 2012. It was the deadliest elementary school shooting in American history, leaving twenty children and six adults dead. The shooter was twenty-year-old Adam Lanza.

After killing his own mother in their home with a rifle she had purchased for him, he gathered his other weapons and drove to the elementary school. He gained entrance into the locked school by shooting a window around 9:30 in the morning. His rampage lasted for less than eleven minutes and ended with him taking his own life.

Later that day, Obama addressed the American public and said tragedies like this had to be brought to an end and that change was necessary. Despite his desire to change gun control laws, by the time he left office, very little progress had been made.

Another notable tragedy was the Boston Marathon bombings. This terrorist attack was perpetrated by two brothers who were Chechen Kyrgyzstani Americans.

While the Boston Marathon was taking place on April 15th, 2013, the two brothers detonated two bombs close to the race's finish line. Three people died, and hundreds of other people were injured, many of whom lost body parts and became permanently disabled.

Obama once again spoke to the American people and paid tribute to the victims and everyone else involved with the rescue efforts. In each of these incidents, he grieved with the nation and comforted the people, much like Bill Clinton had done after the Columbine massacre.

Obama's Foreign Policies

Aside from an economic mess, Obama also inherited two wars in Iraq and Afghanistan that Bush had started during his campaign against terror. One of his campaign promises was that he would withdraw American troops from the wars and establish better relations.

A year into his first term, Obama announced that the number of American troops serving overseas would be scaled down drastically from 160,000 troops to 50,000 within the year. He planned for the rest to be withdrawn by 2011. The process went as planned, and by 2012, there were only 150 American troops still stationed in Iraq.

However, in Afghanistan, Obama agreed to the military's request to send an additional twenty-one thousand troops into the country to keep the Taliban regime in check. He soon decided that a new course of action would be required in Afghanistan since the war had been dragging on for so long. He felt the Afghanistan government needed to be in a position to defeat the Taliban on its own.

One of his greatest achievements in the fight against the Taliban regime was the killing of Osama bin Laden, the leader of al-Qaeda and the mastermind behind 9/11. Navy SEALS killed him in May 2011. American soldiers began to disengage from the region in earnest after this.

Obama also managed to restore America's diplomatic ties with Cuba, which had been severed since the early days of the Cold War.

Obama and ISIS

When ISIS grew in power, Obama, at first, underestimated the threat. Knowing that Americans and the government were feeling "war-weary," he wanted to change the narrative of America perpetually fighting in wars. So, he chose not to launch strikes in Syria or do anything to stop the rebel group. Unchecked, the radicals expanded dramatically into a dangerous, extremist group.

In 2014, Obama spoke to the Americans and stated he would destroy ISIS. Within weeks, he ordered strikes on ISIS targets in Syria. The number of American troops in Iraq was increased to help fight against ISIS. By the time his tenure as president ended, the situation in Iraq and Syria remained unstable and precarious.

Adding to an already complicated situation, Russian leader Vladimir Putin had growing ambitions in the Middle East and Ukraine, where he ordered a military occupation. Sanctions from America and other countries did nothing to change his plans.

Obama's Wars

As a direct or indirect consequence of America's war against ISIS, the Taliban, and al-Qaeda, the US ended up getting involved in a number of other wars. Obama's campaign promise to end American involvement in grueling international conflicts like Iraq and Afghanistan was one he was unable to keep. Obama won the Nobel Peace Prize in 2009 but publicly stated that he felt certain events and circumstances justified a country going to war.

For the entirety of his presidency, American forces remained at war, with military campaigns in at least seven countries: Iraq, Syria, Afghanistan, Libya, Pakistan, Somalia, and Yemen.

Why did he begin these wars? The causes are varied and complicated, but here is a quick breakdown.

- The involvement in Iraq began with humanitarian crises that could have impacted American interests and quickly evolved into a fight against ISIS.

- At first, Obama tried to stay out of Syria, even when Syrian President Bashar al-Assad authorized the use of chemical weapons against the civilian population. However, when ISIS became a serious and viable threat, Obama felt he had no choice but to attack the country.

- Afghanistan was an inherited war that Obama started to put an end to by withdrawing troops when a new president came to power in the country.

- The war in Libya began as part of a UN mission with allied powers to protect Libyan civilians from an oppressive regime. The UN Security Council approved the use of force. After Moammar Gadhafi's death, the air strikes in Libya stopped. However, the situation in Libya is anything but stable today.

- America got involved in Pakistan because of the Taliban.

- Somalia was attacked due to its affiliations with a terrorist network.

- Yemen faced threats from al-Qaeda.

In each situation, Obama felt he had to intervene for American security and interests. However, it doesn't change the fact that when he left office, the country was involved in more wars than when he came in.

One of the crucial things that changed was the way war was fought. Obama moved away from traditional troops battling it out in war zones, preferring to use elite commando units and technology like cyber weapons and armed drones. Obama authorized nearly 550 drone strikes, which killed nearly 4,000 people. Some of these were civilian deaths.

Obama's Legacy

The impact of Obama's legacy and his popularity with the American people cannot be denied. He had his critics. Many people did not agree with his style of governing. He had an average approval rating of 47.9 percent, and when he left office, he did so with an approval rating of 53 percent, just slightly below that of two other enormously popular presidents, Reagan and Clinton.

Obama tried to fix many of the challenges America was facing in the early 2000s and did a lot of good. Unfortunately, he also embroiled America in more international conflicts.

However, the biggest and most enduring legacy he left behind was that a black man of humble origins and a middle-class upbringing could become president. Suddenly, it didn't seem all that impossible to imagine a woman or a minority becoming president. His legacy is one of hope that anything *can* be possible.

Chapter 31: Donald Trump: A Controversial President

As Obama's presidency ended, so did any semblance of normality for America and the world at large. Donald Trump's astonishing win in the 2016 presidential election disrupted the world order and ushered in a period of turbulence and deep instability, both at home and abroad.

But first, let's take a quick look at Trump and how he became the forty-fifth president of the United States.

Donald Trump

Born in a wealthy family to parents of German descent, Trump attended private schools and had a privileged upbringing. He eventually joined his father's business called Trump Management. In the early 1970s, he was made president of the company.

Trump soon renamed the business to Trump Organization and expanded into real estate. Over the years, he created a billion-dollar empire and went on to dabble in a number of different things, including having his own television show, *The Apprentice.*

He also dabbled in different political parties. He was a Republican in 1987. A decade later, he was affiliated with the Reform Party. A few years later, in 2001, he was registered as a Democrat before switching back to Republican in 2009.

On June 16th, 2015, Trump held a campaign rally in New York City at Trump Tower. He came down a golden escalator and announced his intention to run for president. Trump ran against Democratic candidate Hillary Clinton, whose educational background, time in Washington, and accomplishments showed that she was a suitable candidate to run the country. Trump, on the other hand, captivated the people, although he had no real political background, instead focusing on running a business empire.

In a stunning turn of events, Trump won the election.

President Donald Trump.
Gage Skidmore from Peoria, AZ, United States of America, CC BY-SA 2.0 <https://creativecommons.org/licenses/by-sa/2.0>, via Wikimedia Commons https://commons.wikimedia.org/wiki/File:Donald_Trump_(30023082644).jpg

How did Trump do it?

He echoed the message of Ronald Reagan by promising to "make America great again." This simple message meant something to a significant portion of the population. Tired of the wars and tired of feeling that nothing was being done for their country, many people liked the message of the nation becoming great once more and regaining what had been lost.

While Hillary appealed to people's logic, providing cool, thoughtful proposals and promises, Trump appealed to people's emotions. It didn't matter that his promises made no sense or were illogical; he said what people wanted to hear.

Another thing Trump had on his side was the fear of electing a woman as president. A woman had never led the country before, and it seemed many Americans were not prepared for that. Many people (women included) also harbored an intense dislike for Hillary as the woman who supported her husband during his sex scandal. Some viewed her as controlling and "bossy." The email scandal from her time as secretary of state during Obama's presidency also resurfaced and was detrimental to her campaign. The scandal had to do with Hillary using her private email server to handle sensitive and classified information. It led to an FBI probe and investigation. Even though Hillary publicly apologized and took accountability for it, the scandal played a huge role in why people didn't trust her. The FBI eventually determined that none of the documents were marked classified.

Whatever the reasons may be, Trump won the election. Hillary won the popular vote. She had almost three million more votes than Trump, making her loss the largest popular vote margin in US history.

America First

Trump talked a lot about putting "America First," but what did that mean?

The concept of America First wasn't a new one; it dated back to a Republican campaign slogan that was first used as early as the 1880s. It was the notion that American nationalism should come first and that the country should maintain a non-interventionist stance.

Trump's America First policies were highly controversial because it was a complete break from the role the United States had played for many decades. After the end of the two world wars, America emerged as a superpower. The nation often played a peacekeeper role and worked to maintain balance in the international order. America was seen as a diverse, multicultural, democratic nation where human rights, equality, and individual freedoms were prioritized.

Previous presidents strongly felt that America had a moral duty to fulfill a certain role. Trump's stance shifted dramatically away from this. He also unleashed some thoughts and beliefs that many had kept in check for years, with his values giving rise to the notion of white supremacy.

Some key points of the Trump administration's economic policies include the following:

- Tax cuts for individuals and corporations
- Efforts to get rid of and replace Obama's Affordable Care Act

- Restrictions on immigration

His policies had a direct impact on numerous acts and agreements. Let's take a brief look at some notable events and moments from Trump's presidency.

Immigration Policies

For decades, America had been a country where new immigrants flocked to in droves, mostly in search of a better life and the "American Dream."

One of Trump's immediate priorities was to crack down on immigration. He famously talked about erecting a wall between Mexico and the United States to prevent migrants from illegally crossing over.

Some of the things he implemented as part of his immigration policies include the following:

- Phasing out the Deferred Action for Childhood Arrivals (DACA). The name DREAMers (for the Development, Relief, and Education for Alien Minors Act) was given to children who entered the country through illegal means as a child. Under DACA, they did not have the same rights as an American citizen (for instance, they could not vote), but they were allowed to work, have a social security number, and many other things. Trump tried to dismantle the program on numerous occasions. DACA was approved to continue with some minor changes in August 2022.

- Separating family members at the Mexico border. Children were taken away from their parents or guardians. While the adults were prosecuted legally, the children were taken away and put in holding centers. Many families will likely never again be reunited.

- Imposing a travel ban and suspending the arrival of refugees

These are just some of the policies he implemented, essentially ripping apart everything that America has stood for, especially in the eyes of other countries around the world.

Dissolution of NAFTA and the New USMCA Agreement

Trump dissolved NAFTA with Mexico and Canada, which had been in effect since 1994. The agreement allowed for free trade between the three countries and increased trading between them. Every day, approximately $1.4 billion of goods flowed across the border.

In Trump's views, NAFTA was one of the worst deals the US had ever made, and he made it clear during the elections that he was going to get rid of it if he was elected. While it's true NAFTA resulted in the loss of about 800,000 jobs over nearly two decades, over 6 million jobs were dependent on continued trade with Mexico. It also kept the cost of goods low for consumers.

Trump repealed the agreement and replaced it with USMCA (United States-Mexico-Canada Agreement) in 2018. Essentially, the new document was just an update of the old agreement. According to Trump, the updates should create 176,000 new jobs by 2024. It is not yet clear whether the United States is on track to meet this goal.

When Obama became president, an important foreign policy goal for him was to maintain peace and foster a better relationship with Cuba. He did so by removing Cuba from the list of blacklisted countries. Trump's approach to foreign policy has been focused mostly on America first, and as such, he reversed Obama's decision in early 2021. His administration imposed new sanctions on Cuba and redesignated the country as a "state sponsor of terrorism," which includes other countries like North Korea, Syria, and Iran.

Trade with China

Trump was determined to crack down on trade negotiations with China, but this agreement was more unclear. The agreement signed in January 2018 left many things unresolved.

When Trump imposed trade tariffs on China, he was trying to force the country to change what he believed was unfair trading and lower the trade deficit it had with America.

In 2021, a study was conducted to see whether Trump's trade war with China was profitable. Instead of being profitable, his impulsive trade policies cost the American economy around one-quarter million jobs.

Paris Climate Agreement

On December 12th, 2015, 196 countries agreed to an international treaty around climate change called the Paris Agreement. Under the treaty, the participating countries agreed to reduce their greenhouse gas emissions to limit global warming and achieve climate neutrality. This was a landmark treaty because, for the first time in history, most of the world was working together toward a common goal: to combat climate change.

Within a year of taking office, Trump announced his intention to withdraw from the Paris Climate Agreement. Delays with UN regulations meant there was a three-year delay. By the time the withdrawal took effect, a new presidential election was underway.

In 2021, after Biden was elected president, the US rejoined the Paris Climate Agreement.

Abraham Accords

Nearly every president has had a say in the ongoing conflict in the Middle East, and Trump was no different. One of his most notable achievements was the Abraham Accords.

The Abraham Accords was an agreement reached between the United States, the United Arab Emirates, Bahrain, and Israel on August 13th, 2020, to improve the relationship between the countries. It was named Abraham since he is a prophet in both Judaism and Islam.

As the Palestine-Israel conflict continues to escalate, Biden is trying to use the accords to encourage other Arab countries to also normalize their relationships with Israel.

Coronavirus Pandemic

The latter part of Trump's presidency came to a halt as a pandemic swept through the world. The Trump administration was woefully unprepared for the virus, as Trump had disbanded the pandemic response team in 2018.

Utter chaos and confusion followed, with Trump refusing to acknowledge that there was even an issue. He even praised China for handling the virus in an effective manner and assured the American people that the pandemic would not touch them or enter the country, even as he was being advised to the contrary by experts.

Some of Trump's claims during the crisis included denying the virus, saying it would miraculously go away in the spring, that it was nothing more than the flu, that claims of deaths were grossly exaggerated, and that none of this was his fault.

Trump did pass bills that helped Americans with their daily living needs. However, most still believe that Trump did not handle the pandemic in a suitable manner, with detractors saying his administration left Americans to fend for themselves.

Presidential Election of 2020

When the 2020 presidential election rolled around, Trump announced his intention to seek reelection. A significant majority of Americans and the world felt strongly a second term under Trump would be disastrous, yet it seemed quite likely that he would win another term.

Joe Biden, Obama's vice president, who had previously said he would never run for president, became the presidential nominee for the Democratic Party.

An intense period of campaigning followed between the two nominees, and on November 3rd, 2020, Biden won the election. Trump refused to concede defeat and claimed voter fraud had taken place and that he had, in fact, won the election.

He and his supporters continued to spread these ideas, and on January 6th, 2021, when the election results were being certified in the Capitol, Trump supporters attacked the Capitol. The mob was determined to interfere in the transfer of power and claim the presidency for Trump. As rioters stormed toward the Capitol, Trump did nothing to stop them immediately. As of this writing, the Justice Department is winding down its official investigation into Trump's role in the riot.

Despite the rioting, the certification was completed. Joe Biden was officially recognized as president-elect. He was inaugurated on January 20th, 2021, as the forty-sixth president. Since taking office, he has worked hard to overturn many of Trump's policies and reforms. He also prioritized the pandemic by signing a $1.9 trillion relief bill and promised Americans a quick rollout of vaccines. By his 100th day in office, the Biden administration had managed to deliver 200 million vaccines.

Many of Biden's campaign promises centered around bringing America and the presidency back to what it was before Trump. Whether or not that can be managed remains to be seen, as some of Trump's policies have changed the landscape of America, and their effects will last for decades to come.

For instance, Trump nominated three Supreme Court judges (an unheard-of feat) in the modern day. This changed the balance of power in the Supreme Court, which meant many important court rulings could be more easily overturned. This happened on June 24th, 2022, when the Supreme Court overturned Roe v. Wade, a landmark legislation that had made the right and access to abortion a federal right.

The true cost of these decisions will likely be seen and felt in the decades to come.

Conclusion: Looking Forward

The United States is a remarkable nation that was built and created out of almost nothing. A group of people with a dream got together centuries ago and decided they wanted to cut ties with Europe and forge their own paths. And through all of the country's ups and downs, this is the theme that endures: the desire to be independent, to be a leader, and to follow a dream.

Dreams of equality spurred women's movements and civil rights movements. The pursuit of the American dream brings thousands of new immigrants into the country to this day.

There is no doubt the last few years have been turbulent ones for America, both at home and internationally. But this is nothing they haven't lived through before. If we can learn anything from America's history, it's that the United States always finds a way of overcoming the odds and coming out on top.

As the world begins to settle into a new post-pandemic reality under the guidance of a new administration, the hope is that America will once more regain the prestige and influence it used to enjoy and be a beacon of democracy, human rights, and equality.

Part 2: The American Revolution

An Enthralling Overview of the American Revolutionary War and Its Impact on the History of the United States of America

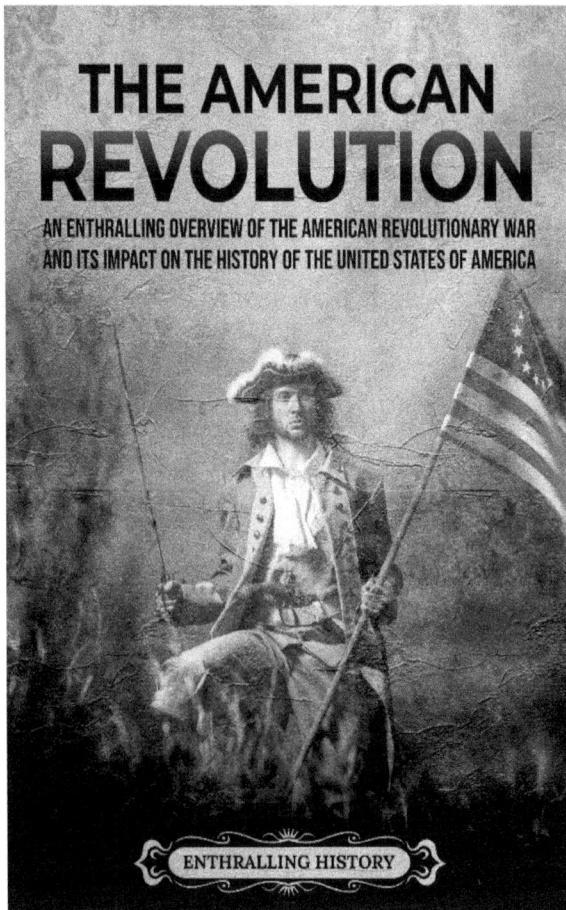

Introduction

The American Revolution is best described as the impossible dream that came true. Before the American Revolution, it was inconceivable that an army primarily made up of farmers and tradesmen could go up against the best navy and army in the world and come out the winner. The story of this American epoch continues to fascinate people to this day.

The American Revolution merits our study and appreciation. After all, the Treaty of Paris in 1783 resulted in what would become one of the largest and most powerful countries in the world: the United States of America. The revolution can also be considered an evolution in society and the rights of man. What this conflict generated inspired others and continues to be a source of reference for political scientists and historians.

We will be looking at the origins, the battles, and the compromises and decisions that led to the American Revolution and the colonists' independence. There will be instances when the reader will become enthused, and there will be times when some depression sets in. Not everything that happened during the American Revolution was sensational or the right thing to do. People made mistakes, but fortunately, they learned from most of those errors.

We want to introduce people to the American Revolution in the hope that it will spark their interest so much that they will continue reading about it. There is so much to know regarding the decisions and the actions that occurred, especially since the results remain with us. The more we understand the American Revolution, the more we will appreciate the consequences that have shaped the country Americans live in today and the world at large.

Chapter 1: Prelude to a Revolt

<u>Colonial Commerce</u>

The Thirteen Colonies in British North America were a rich and diverse basket of activity. They were not reliant on one cash crop, and the regions had distinct economies. These colonies were not centers of gold like Mexico or contained silver caches like Peru, but they were still a source of wealth and opportunity.

Agriculture served as the cornerstone of the colonies' economies, with each region specializing in crops suited to its environment. The New England colonies, whose people grappled with rocky terrain and a harsh climate, primarily engaged in subsistence farming, complemented by fishing, whaling, and timber harvesting. They capitalized on the natural resources at hand. In contrast, the Middle Colonies, which were blessed with fertile soil and a milder climate, emerged as the "breadbasket" of the Thirteen Colonies, producing surpluses of wheat, barley, and oats, feeding not only the local population but also those abroad.

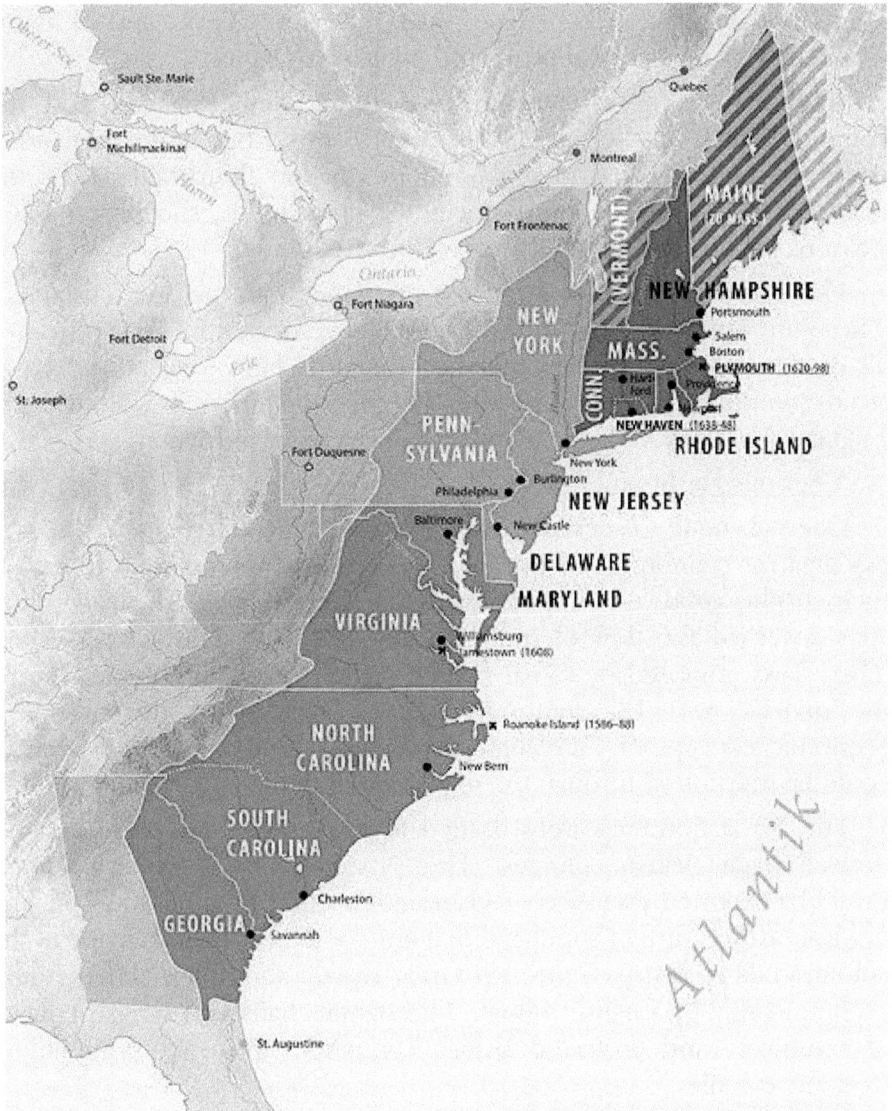

A look at the Thirteen Colonies. The dark red is New England, the red-brown is the Middle Colonies, and the brown is the Southern Colonies.

Richard Zietz, CC BY-SA 3.0 <https://creativecommons.org/licenses/by-sa/3.0>, via Wikimedia Commons; https://commons.wikimedia.org/wiki/File:Thirteencolonies_politics_cropped.jpg

Agriculture was a significant economic sector, but there was also industry. Although most textiles were manufactured in Britain from raw materials imported from the colonies, textiles were produced in

Pennsylvania using flax.[10] Ironworks in New York and Virginia manufactured utensils and processed pig iron for exports.

Shipbuilding was an essential activity in New England, and the colonies built vessels for all kinds of use. Sloops, brigs, and frigates were readily assembled. Artisan and craft production flourished across the colonies, with skilled laborers, including blacksmiths, shoemakers, and weavers, contributing to a burgeoning local economy.

The Thirteen Colonies were less profitable than the "sugar islands." Those tiny specks of land in the Caribbean generated more wealth than all of the colonies on the Atlantic seaboard. However, business was steady, and there was a robust trade between the Thirteen Colonies and England. However, Atlantic commerce was a point of friction.

A Serious Flashpoint

External trade, especially with Europe and the Caribbean, was essential for economic prosperity, as it permitted the colonies to export their surplus goods and import necessary commodities. The Navigation Acts governed the flow of traffic to and from the Thirteen Colonies. These laws, imposed by Great Britain on its American colonies during the mid-17th and 18th centuries, were influenced by the prevailing economic concept of mercantilism, which held that national strength could be maximized through the regulation of trade.

The Navigation Acts were drafted to monopolize the trade benefits derived from British colonies. They asserted that colonial products would be exported exclusively to England or other English colonies. The Navigation Acts further stipulated that any goods sent from Europe to the colonies had to first pass through Great Britain and utilize ships crewed predominantly by English sailors. The statutes tightened British control of commerce and protected British companies from any competition from the colonies.[11]

Economically, the Navigation Acts were a problem for the colonies. They guaranteed a British market for certain colonial goods, such as tobacco and sugar. However, the laws also severely limited the colonies' ability to engage in international trade freely with countries that might have more competitive prices for goods and services. The requirement

---

[10] Hurst, N. T. (2020, March 17). Made in American. Retrieved from Colonialwilliamsburg.org: https://www.colonialwilliamsburg.org/trend-tradition-magazine/spring-2018/made-american/.
[11] Wigington, P. (2018, November 29). What Were the Navigation Acts? Retrieved from Thoughtco.com: https://www.thoughtco.com/navigation-acts-4177756.

that all European goods be shipped via England increased the cost of these goods in the colonies and throttled economic growth.

Opposition in the Colonies

Initially, some colonists accepted these trade restrictions as part of their contribution to the empire's broader economic strategy. Great Britain practiced a policy of salutary neglect in the 17th century and most of the 18th century. Salutary neglect was Britain's laissez-faire attitude about enacting laws in the colonies. In other words, the American colonists had a higher amount of freedom than other British colonies.

The Seven Years' War broke out in 1756. Conflict actually broke out in North America the year prior; that theater of the Seven Years' War is known as the French and Indian War. The war created financial hardship for Great Britain, and there was a perceived need for Parliament to tighten economic control by actively enforcing the laws that had been created. The strict enforcement of the Navigation Acts created opposition in the American colonies. The people believed the laws were creating economic constraints and saw the British monarch as an overbearing imperial ruler who exploited colonial resources without offering fair political representation or economic freedom.[12] The opposition was especially vocal in New England, where maritime trade was a cornerstone of the economy.

The Navigation Acts were more than just trade regulations. They were rules that shaped the economic landscape of the American colonies. By 1770, the effects of these acts had laid bare the contradictions between the colonies' economic aspirations and the realities of British mercantilist policy. The resentment and resistance they engendered among colonists contributed significantly to the breakdown of British colonial authority.

Enforcement led to widespread smuggling as a form of economic resistance and a political statement against the acts. The laws also fostered a political awakening among the colonists, who began questioning the legitimacy of British rule. Many began to envision an independent economic and political future.

The Source of the Problem

The Seven Years' War (1756–1763) was at the heart of the soured relations. It was a global conflict that spanned continents. Although Great

---

[12] American History Central. (2024, February 4). The Navigation Acts. Retrieved from Americanhistorycentral.com: https://www.americanhistorycentral.com/entries/navigation-acts/.

Britain and her allies won, the victory was expensive.

Britain's national debt after the war was more than 130 million pounds. This debt was exacerbated by the price of maintaining and defending new territorial acquisitions. The British Parliament sought to address the financial crisis by redistributing the fiscal burdens across the empire. The American colonies, who had benefited from the successes of the British army, were expected to pay their fair share. This time, the policy of salutary neglect would not be used. Payments from the colonies were to be extracted by a series of revenue-generating laws.

Parliament enacted several legislative measures to increase revenue from the colonies and pay off the debt. A series of tax bills were passed; the most notable were the Sugar Act of 1764 and the Stamp Act of 1765. These firmly proclaimed Parliament's right to tax British overseas possessions.

The Sugar Act was not a major piece of legislation. It imposed a lower tax on sugar and molasses imports in the hopes that the tax would actually be paid (the earlier tax was mostly ignored by the colonists). The act also revised the current customs regulations to administer stricter controls on the smuggling of sugar and molasses, thereby increasing revenue and reducing obvious criminal activity. It was repealed in 1766.

The Stamp Act, however, was a more direct form of taxation. It required that a wide array of documents, newspapers, and even playing cards in the colonies be produced on stamped paper, signifying the payment of the tax. The Stamp Act imposed a cost, no matter how slight, on items that were once less expensive and, in some cases, were even free.[13]

There was a serious disconnect between the British government and the colonies. Americans were accustomed to local government and having a voice in decisions that affected them. There was no colonial representation when these taxes were imposed, so the colonists felt insulted. The Stamp Act was especially onerous and vigorously protested.

The British government's failure to anticipate the intensity of the colonies' response was a grave mistake. Parliament underestimated the colonies' political experience, which had been nurtured through decades of relative autonomy and self-governance. Some members of the British

---

[13] Triber, J. E. (2024, February 4). Britain Begins Taxing the Colonies: The Sugar & Stamp Acts. Retrieved from Nos.gov: https://www.nps.gov/articles/000/sugar-and-stamp-acts.htm.

Parliament recognized the risks of angering the American colonists and argued for their right to tax themselves. However, the prevailing sentiment of Parliament was that the American colonies needed to pay their fair share. These members underestimated the colonies' resolve and unity, leading to unanticipated problems.

"No taxation without representation" became a rallying cry in the colonies. The subsequent boycott of British goods and harassment of stamp distributors demonstrated the American colonists' resolve to have a voice in the policies that affected them.

The Stamp Act Congress

The opposition to the Stamp Act was so widespread that a formal response was considered necessary. A gathering of delegates from nine of the Thirteen Colonies met in New York City in October 1765 for that purpose. The final product of what would later be called the Stamp Act Congress was the adoption of the Declaration of Rights and Grievances. The Stamp Act Congress produced a bold statement that declared only the colonial legislatures had the legal authority to tax the American colonies. It was radical because this was a statement of colonial rights and the rejection of parliamentary interference in colonial matters.

Petitions were sent to King George III and Parliament demanding the repeal of the Stamp Act. The petitions stressed colonial loyalty to the British Crown and Parliament. The British government was shocked when they received the petitions, and there was pressure from British business leaders to do something to end the boycott of British products. The Stamp Act was formally repealed In February 1766. The American colonies had achieved a victory.[14]

The Stamp Act Congress was a significant event in American history. It was the first major action taken by the colonies in opposition to British policy and showed a sense of colonial unity that had not been seen before.

The Stamp Act Congress introduced several influential statesmen to colonial politics: James Otis of Massachusetts, who led the movement for the Stamp Act Congress to meet; John Dickinson of Pennsylvania, who played an essential role in drafting the petitions and other documents;

---

[14] Zielinski, A. E. (2021, November 17). What Was the Stamp Act Congress and Why Did It Matter. Retrieved from Ameicanbattlefields.org: https://www.battlefields.org/learn/articles/what-was-stamp-act-congress.

Stamp Act Congress chairman Timothy Ruggles of Massachusetts; and John Rutledge of South Carolina, who would later be a signatory of the United States Constitution. They would perform greater services to the American cause later.

Parliament's Dirty Little Secret

The American colonies won this battle, but the war was going to continue. On the same day the British Parliament repealed the Stamp Act, it passed the Declaratory Act. This legislation stated Parliament unequivocally had the power to bind or legislate the colonies. John Adams warned others that Parliament would use this power to attempt to tax the colonies once again.[15]

The concept of "no taxation without representation" caused controversy among members of Parliament. This argument exposed the existence of "rotten boroughs,"constituencies with small electorates controlled by wealthy landowners. These boroughs allowed the landed gentry to manipulate elections in favor of their preferred candidates despite having only a handful of eligible voters. Despite their small size, rotten boroughs were able to send members of Parliament to the House of Commons.

Old Sarum, an ancient hill fort near Salisbury, was a striking example of a rotten borough. Old Sarum had no residents, yet it continued to send two members to Parliament. Meanwhile, places like Manchester that had populations numbering in the thousands had no representation in the British Parliament. The outcry from the American colonies was no doubt raising the eyebrows of those who were concerned about corruption in the British government.

In Summary

The Seven Years' War marked a significant shift in British colonial policy and set the stage for the American Revolution. The war's cost prompted Great Britain to reassess its relationship with the American colonies. Parliament responded by taxing the colonies to alleviate the national debt burden, which sparked widespread protest and resistance. The British government's inability to understand the extent of American discontent with these new laws was a crucial mistake that would be repeated again. Britain's stubborn approach to dealing with the American

---

[15] Zeidan, A. (2024, February 4). Stamp Act Congress. Retrieved from Britannica.com: https://www.britannica.com/topic/Stamp-Act-Congress.

colonies led to consequences that likely could have been avoided.

Over time, the conflict between Great Britain and its American colonies transformed into more than just a dispute over taxation. The issues of rights, representation, and national identity became prominent, highlighting the difficulties of governing an empire and the struggle to balance the need for revenue with the desire for freedom and self-governance.

The colonies faced their own economic challenges, such as income inequality and debt burden. These local issues, combined with British demands for taxes and trade restrictions, set the stage for the colonies to eventually unite in their quest for independence and the right to control their destiny.

Chapter 2: Growing Discontent

Despite the anger created by the Stamp Act, American colonists considered themselves loyal subjects of the British Crown. They just wanted a voice in how they were taxed and preferred to govern themselves with as little interference as possible. The Americans were going to be disappointed on both counts.

The years following the repeal of the Stamp Act were critical in the evolving relationship between Great Britain and the American colonies. There was increasing tension over taxation, representation, and how Great Britain would govern its extensive North American empire. Parliament enacted a series of measures intended to assert its authority over the colonies, and those legislative measures sparked strong emotions within Great Britain and America.

The Mood of the Chamber

The immediate passing of the Declaratory Act after the repeal of the Stamp Act showed Parliament's prevailing sentiment of authority and control, proclaiming Great Britain had the right and authority to legislate for the colonies "in all cases whatsoever." That was a phrase with broad meaning that could stir up trouble. Nevertheless, Parliament was determined to uphold the British government's sovereignty and ensure the colonies' financial contribution to the empire's maintenance and defense.

The members of Parliament thought that was only fair. The economic burdens of the French and Indian War had forced Great Britain to stabilize its finances, and the colonies were seen as a critical revenue source. Besides, the Thirteen Colonies had benefited from the war and were now safe from any French incursions. They should be able to help pay for the expenses incurred for protecting them.

Parliament had energetic debates regarding the appropriate response to the colonies' growing discontent and the principles at stake. The Thirteen Colonies were not without friends in the chamber.

Support for the Americans

Despite the prevailing mood of authority and control, there were members of the British Parliament who spoke up for a more nuanced approach toward the American colonies. These figures stressed the principles of liberty, the rights of Englishmen, and the dangers of escalating conflict through heavy-handed actions. They sought to prevent matters from getting worse.

Edmund Burke, a prominent Whig politician and philosopher, emerged as a vocal advocate for understanding and reconciliation with the American colonies. Burke warned about the counterproductive nature of any punitive measures, and he championed the unique character and rights of the American colonies within the empire.[16]

William Pitt, Earl of Chatham and a respected member of Parliament, supported a more conciliatory approach. Criticizing the government's policies as shortsighted, Pitt consistently called for respecting the colonies' grievances and fostering mutual respect. He believed that such empathy was not a sign of weakness. Instead, he stressed a reasonable approach to the differences that would strengthen, not diminish, the bonds of the empire.[17]

Charles James Fox, a prominent Whig parliamentarian, regularly opposed the government's disciplinary measures against the American colonies and supported the cause of American liberty. His position was grounded in a wide-ranging vision of the non-codified British constitution and the universal rights of Englishmen, which included those subjects of

[16] Oxford Learning Link. (2024, February 11). Document-Edmund Burke, Excerpts from "Conciliation with the Colonies." Retrieved from Learnnglink.oup.com: https://learninglink.oup.com/access/content/schaller-3e-dashboard-resources/document-edmund-burke-excerpts-from-conciliation-with-the-colonies-1775.

[17] Colonial Williamsburg. (2024, February 11). William Pitt's Defense of the American Colonies. Retrieved from Slaveryandrembrance.org: https://www.slaveryandremembrance.org/Almanack/life/politics/pitt.cfm.

the Crown who resided in the colonies.[18]

Collectively, these members of Parliament recognized the legitimacy of the colonies' grievances and the potential for a more harmonious resolution. Their advocacy for dialog and mutual respect displayed the complex interplay of interests and ideologies that defined the pre-revolutionary relationship between Britain and the American colonies. There were also colonial agents like Benjamin Franklin and Arthur Lee who lobbied Parliament and worked behind the scenes.

Parliamentary Obstinacy

Though there were vigorous defenses of colonial rights, most members of Parliament still wished to assert control and ensure financial contributions from the colonies to the empire's coffers. The years preceding the American Revolution were noteworthy for legislative measures that sought to reinforce parliamentary authority, often at the expense of colonial autonomy and rights.

A series of laws enacted by the British Parliament became the fulcrum around which the colonial resistance leveraged its arguments for independence. These laws, passed between 1765 and 1774, were increasingly harsh measures to raise tax revenue and impose restrictions on the American colonies.

The Laws of Parliament and the Crown

- The Declaratory Act (1766)

As mentioned above, this law affirmed Parliament's right "to bind the colonies and people of America ... in all cases whatsoever." It did not impose a tax. The Declaratory Act represented a symbolic assertion of Britain's undiminished authority over the colonies, including the right to tax them. This legislation highlighted the fundamental conflict at the heart of the colonial dispute: the question of whether Parliament had the legitimate authority to govern the colonies without their representation.

- The Townshend Acts (1767)

The Townshend Acts of 1767 introduced a new series of taxes on imports to the colonies, including glass, lead, paint, paper, and tea. Unlike the Stamp Act, which was a direct tax, the Townshend duties

---

[18] Powell, J. (1996, September 1). Charles James Fox, Valiant Voice for Liberty. Retrieved from Foundation for Economic Freedom: https://fee.org/articles/charles-james-fox-valiant-voice-for-liberty/.

were indirect taxes on imports, but the distinction did little to appease the American colonists. The revenues collected were earmarked to pay the salaries of colonial governors and judges, further eroding the autonomy of local colonial governments. The Townshend Acts reignited the flames of resistance, leading to boycotts of British goods and the emergence of organized protest movements.[19]

- The Tea Act (1773)

The Tea Act was an 18th-century corporate bailout. The British East India Company was running into financial trouble. The British Parliament, whose members included prominent company shareholders, passed the Tea Act in 1773, which allowed the British East India Company to sell surplus tea directly to the colonies, effectively bypassing colonial merchants and undercutting their business.

While the Tea Act actually lowered the price of tea, it reinforced the notion that the colonists were not in control of their own governance. The colonists viewed this act as a cunning attempt by Britain to make them consent to the idea of parliamentary taxation.[20]

Colonial dissent grew gradually more vocal, and the opposition became destructive with the Boston Tea Party. The British Parliament responded severely.

- The Coercive Acts (1774)

Also referred to as the Intolerable Acts, the Coercive Acts were a set of statutes intended to penalize the people of Massachusetts for the Boston Tea Party and to deter further acts of resistance. These acts closed Boston Harbor until the destroyed tea was paid for, altered the Massachusetts Charter to increase royal authority, and allowed royal bureaucrats accused of crimes in the colonies to be tried in Britain.

The passage of the Coercive Acts did not keep the colonists in line. British politicians had massively miscalculated where American sentiments lay. Rather than being cowed by disciplinary measures, the Coercive Acts unified the colonies, leading to the formation of the First Continental Congress and marking a decisive step toward

---

[19] History.com Editors. (2009, June 13). Townshend Acts. Retrieved from History.com: https://www.history.com/topics/american-revolution/townshend-acts.
[20] History.com Editors. (2024, February 11). British Parliament Passes Unpopular Tea Act. Retrieved from History.com: https://www.history.com/this-day-in-history/parliament-passes-the-tea-act.

independence.[21]

Each piece of legislation chipped away at the loyalty of the American colonists to the British Crown and highlighted the untenable nature of a relationship defined by unilateral governance and economic exploitation. These acts did more than impose taxes; they challenged the identity and rights of the colonists as Englishmen.

The colonial response, characterized by intellectual arguments against taxation without representation, economic boycotts, and direct action like the Boston Tea Party, reflected a growing belief in self-governance and the inherent rights of individuals. The statutes reshaped the political landscape, fostered a sense of American identity, and sowed the seeds of a revolution that Parliament might have avoided had its members applied common sense.

The Coercive Acts and the Boston Tea Party allowed two colonial leaders to introduce themselves to the public in a big way. These men were the "influencers" of their day.

The Adams Family

It is trite to think of the American Revolution as a family affair, but one Massachusetts clan had two members who were well-known advocates of independence. Samuel (Sam) and John Adams were second cousins. Each had a different temperament, but both had a common goal.

- Sam Adams

Sam Adams stands tall in the history of the American Revolution. His name conjures up images of a firebrand orator or perhaps a shadowy figure plotting a rebellion in Boston's taverns. He was a little more complex than that, and his role in the American Revolution is fascinating.

Samuel Adams was born in Boston, Massachusetts, on September 27th, 1722. He came from a family with a solid religious backbone and possessed a puritanical sense of moral purpose that would later influence his political career. Although he began as a businessman, his growing

---

[21] Mount Vernon. (2024, February 11). The Coercive (Intolerable) Acts of 1774. Retrieved from Mountvernon.org: https://www.mountvernon.org/library/digitalhistory/digital-encyclopedia/article/the-coercive-intolerable-acts-of-1774/#:~:text=The%20Coercive%20Acts%20were%20meant,particular%20aspect%20of%20colonial%20life.

disgust for British tax laws made him increasingly more political. Sam Adams soon became a vocal member of the Massachusetts Assembly and a well-known public figure. He was blessed with profound oratory skills and had a flair for writing influential pieces promoting colonial rights.

Adams was at center stage in organizing opposition to the Stamp Act of 1765 and the Townshend Acts. His persuasive essays helped unite colonists from different regions, igniting conversations about self-determination.

In 1768, Adams composed the Massachusetts Circular Letter, urging colonies to resist British impositions, establishing a reputation for himself as a radical willing to challenge the current situation. He would be pivotal in organizing the Boston Tea Party in 1773 (more on that later).

Sam Adams had a knack for organizing groups for public action. He helped create the Sons of Liberty, an underground group opposed to the Crown's policies. Adams instigated various boycotts and protests. He had an unmatched ability to harness the energy of discontented colonists.[22]

• John Adams

John Adams was not as overtly passionate as his cousin, but he was just as dedicated to the cause of American independence as his hot-headed kin.

John Adams came into this world on October 30th, 1735, in Braintree (now Quincy), Massachusetts. His father was a deacon and a farmer, and he had also served in the militia. John attended Harvard and, upon graduation, began a career in law. His legal practice in Suffolk County gave him a front-row seat to the growing political friction between the colonies and Great Britain.

John Adams's erudition and gift of the written word became his most potent weapons in the prelude to the war. His abilities as an influential, persuasive writer were showcased in his political essays and responses to the tyranny perceived in British policies, such as the Stamp Act and the Townshend Acts. Essays such as "A Dissertation on the Canon and Feudal Law" (1765) passionately defended colonial rights and governance while deconstructing British arguments. These works

[22] Boston National Historical Park. (2024, February 10). Samuel Adams: Boston's Radical Revolutionary. Retrieved from Nps.gov: https://www.nps.gov/articles/000/samuel-adams-boston-revolutionary.htm.

solidified John's status as a radical voice and bolstered his credibility among colonial leaders.[23]

Both cousins would be focal points in two of the most dramatic events of the American colonies.

The Boston Massacre

To understand the events leading up to the Boston Massacre, one must consider the socioeconomic tensions that had been brewing for years. The Townshend Acts were passed into law by the British Parliament in 1767, imposing taxes on various essential goods, including paper, paint, and tea, leading to widespread protests and boycotts among colonists. The British Crown responded to these acts of defiance by deploying troops to Boston. This military occupation agitated the already resentful citizens, setting up a volatile atmosphere. The events of the Boston Massacre unfolded against the backdrop of such seething colonial anger.

On the night of March 5th, 1770, as snow blanketed the ground and tensions clouded the air, a simple dispute between a wigmaker's apprentice and a British private rapidly escalated as rowdy onlookers joined, hurling snowballs, icicles, and insults at British soldiers. The crowd continued to grow, and the British sentry called for reinforcements, which came almost immediately. The confrontation reached its climax when a soldier, hit by a club, discharged his musket, triggering a domino effect of gunfire from the other redcoats. By the time the guns went silent, three colonists lay dead, with two more dying afterward from their wounds. Blood stained the snow, and cries of anguish resounded throughout the city.

Public reaction was swift and furious. News of the bloody encounter spread like wildfire, galvanizing the already strong anti-British sentiment. Leading patriots like Samuel Adams and Paul Revere harnessed the incident's power, branding it as a "massacre" and fueling the flames of revolution through sensationalized accounts and engravings.

[23] Ellis, J. J. (2024, February 4). John Adams. Retrieved from Britannica.com: https://www.britannica.com/biography/John-Adams-president-of-United-States.

An engraving of the Boston Massacre by Paul Revere.
Paul Revere, CC0, via Wikimedia Commons;
https://commons.wikimedia.org/wiki/File:The_Boston_Massacre_MET_DT2086.jpg

In a time when facts were not as readily verifiable as they are today, such portrayals were the accepted narrative for many, cementing the notion of British tyranny in the hearts and minds of colonists.

The soldiers were not lynched, but they were required to stand trial. It would take considerable courage for any lawyer to defend them, but a brave man did step forward.

<u>In Defense of Fair Justice</u>

The British soldiers found an unlikely defender in John Adams. Although a fervent patriot, Adams believed strongly in the right to a fair trial and the rule of law.

Accepting the case posed significant risks to Adams's reputation and law practice. His potential alienation from patriotic groups, personal danger, and the suspicion of being a loyalist sympathizer meant Adams was walking a legal and social tightrope. His sense of duty to justice, however, surmounted these risks.

The crux of Adams's defense lay in proving that the soldiers acted in self-defense against a mob with violent intentions. He dissected eyewitness accounts and highlighted inconsistencies in their testimonies. Adams skillfully argued, "Facts are stubborn things; and whatever may be our wishes, our inclinations, or the dictates of our passion, they cannot alter the state of facts and evidence."

His ability to remain dispassionate, his insistence on separating fact from inflammatory fiction, and his articulation of the complexities of the law to the jury won him the case. Most of the soldiers were acquitted. The two who were proven to have fired directly into the crowd were found guilty of manslaughter and branded on the thumb as a first offense.

The acquittal of the British soldiers was a triumph for the principle of due process. Adams's successful defense highlighted his formidable skills as a lawyer and his profound belief in justice. His participation in the trial did not hamper his career; instead, it bolstered his reputation as an honest and fair man. Years later, Adams reflected on his involvement, considering it one of the best services he had rendered to America.

A painting of John Adams in 1766.
https://commons.wikimedia.org/wiki/File;John_Adams_(1766).jpg

Worthy of a Mad Hatter

The acquittal verdict did not soothe the tensions between the Thirteen Colonies and Great Britain. Other incidents occurred that highlighted the conflict between the two entities. None of them are as memorable as the Boston Tea Party.

The British government still wished to exert control and the power of taxation over its American subjects. With the Tea Act of 1773, the British government granted the struggling East India Company a monopoly over the tea trade in the colonies, effectively undercutting local merchants. It was a classic example of taxation without representation, and the act infuriated the colonists. The apparent anger of the Americans was a potent opportunity for a notorious colonial instigator named Sam Adams.[24]

Stirring the Pot

As an influential leader in the Massachusetts legislature and the clandestine Sons of Liberty, Sam Adams played a spirited role in organizing opposition to the Tea Act of 1773. Adams used his exceptional oratory skills and political network to inflame and unite the public. He guided the resistance movement that planned a bold act of defiance.

On the evening of December 16th, 1773, members of the Sons of Liberty, disguised as Mohawk Indians, boarded three British ships moored in Boston Harbor. The ships were laden with chests of tea. In a few hours, 342 chests of tea had been thrown overboard into the harbor water. The loss of this tea was significant; the Sons of Liberty destroyed around $1.7 million dollars' worth of tea in today's money.

Sam Adams was not there dumping tea into the harbor with the protestors. However, there is no doubt that he rallied the Sons of Liberty to execute such a brazen act.

Stern Consequences

As mentioned, the Boston Tea Party had immediate and momentous repercussions. In the eyes of the British government, the destruction of the tea was an unacceptable act that demanded a swift and harsh response. However, the British government's severe retaliatory measures did not force the colonists into submission. Instead, it galvanized the

---

[24] History.com Editors. (2009, October 27). Boston Tea Party. Retrieved from History.com: https://www.history.com/topics/american-revolution/boston-tea-party.

Thirteen Colonies to form a more cohesive unit of resistance to what they considered tyranny.

The clouds over the relationship between Great Britain and its American subjects were getting darker.

of independence by stripping away self-determination. Instead, they forged a crucible for revolutionary fervor. Every tightening of the noose reaffirmed for many the necessity of open resistance. Socially, requiring colonial legislatures to pay for and provide accommodations for British soldiers fueled resentment and added to the growing tensions.

The British government was tired of colonial defiance and took its anger out on individuals and colonies. The most notable person who endured the British government's wrath was Benjamin Franklin.

Franklin was perhaps the most well-known American of his time. Franklin lived in London as a colonial agent for Pennsylvania (and later for Massachusetts, Georgia, and New Jersey). His role was to represent the interests of the colonies to the British government, advocating for fair treatment and liberation from oppressive legislation. Regrettably, this distinguished man was caught up in the conflict and was singled out for abuse before the King's Privy Council.

The humiliation stemmed from a stack of letters. Franklin had obtained a pile of correspondence written by Thomas Hutchinson, who was the royal governor of Massachusetts, and other officials, which he then sent back to America. These letters called for an abridgment of the rights and freedoms of the colonists, suggesting they were too liberty-minded. When the letters were eventually leaked and published by the *Boston Gazette*, they caused an uproar amongst the colonists since they were seen as a direct threat to their liberties. Hutchinson and his supporters were outraged and demanded retribution. The Crown was only too happy to oblige.

On January 29th, 1774, Franklin was called before the Privy Council in the Whitehall Palace's "Cockpit" to address the leak of the letters. He stood to defend his actions but was instead subjected to harsh public censuring. Solicitor General Alexander Wedderburn unleashed a torrent of verbal abuse upon Franklin, attacking his character and reputation. Franklin was accused of being a thief and a spy and portrayed as embodying the colonies' ingratitude.

In a hall filled with spectators, Franklin was humiliated and ridiculed without the opportunity for a proper defense. He stood in stoic silence, absorbing the mockery and jeers, powerless against the assaults of Wedderburn's words. Franklin would later compare the episode to bull-baiting. The man was thoroughly disgraced.[26]

Franklin's feelings after the Privy Council meeting are best summarized in a letter he wrote but did not send to William Strahan, an English printer and publisher:

"You are a Member of Parliament, and one of that Majority which has doomed my Country to Destruction. You have begun to burn our Towns, and murder our People. Look upon your hands! They are stained with the Blood of your Relations! You and I were long Friends; You are now my Enemy, and I am, Yours."[27]

The incident was pivotal in changing Franklin's view of the British Empire and its leaders. He had once worked tirelessly for reconciliation between America and Britain, but by the time he returned home, he had become disenchanted and aligned with those advocating for complete independence. Benjamin Franklin would soon prove how potent an enemy he was.

Colonial Defiance in the Face of Adversity

Despite these challenges, Boston's response was emblematic of the times. Far from breaking under pressure, the city became a beacon of rebellion. Massachusetts, the focal point of British punishment, quickly became a hub for colonial defiance.

The patriots in Massachusetts coordinated a series of underground meetings, which culminated in the formation of shadow governments known as Provincial Congresses. These groups, authorized by the people, met in secret and began taking over the functions of local governance.

Support for Massachusetts resonated throughout the other colonies. In what became known as the Suffolk Resolves, the colonies were urged not to obey the Intolerable Acts, and the residents of Massachusetts were asked to appoint militia officers and arm themselves. The Suffolk Resolves also called for economic sanctions against Great Britain.[28]

Colonies rallied to this common cause. Virginia's House of Burgesses

---

[26] Founders Online. (2024, February 10). The Final Hearing. Retrieved from Founders Online: https://founders.archives.gov/documents/Franklin/01-21-02-0018.
[27] Franklin, Benjamin. (2024, February 10). Benjamin Franklin in His Own Words. Retrieved from Loc.gov: https://www.loc.gov/exhibits/franklin/franklin-break.html.
[28] American History Central. (2024, February 10). The Suffolk Resolves. Americanhistorycentral.com. Retrieved from Suffolk Resolves Summary 1774: https://www.americanhistorycentral.com/entries/suffolk-resolves/.

declared a "Day of Fasting and Prayer," showing solidarity with Massachusetts and challenging the legitimacy of the British Parliament. South Carolina created a Committee of Correspondence, which facilitated communication and coordination among the colonies, creating a united front against British influence. Eleven colonies would eventually have their own committees.

Public demonstrations were held in New York and Pennsylvania to educate the local populations about the unjust nature of the Intolerable Acts and their implications for colonial liberty. A network of committees, the rise of the Provincial Congresses, and the support expressed through aid to Boston all provided evidence that the colonists would not buckle under the weight of oppressive legislation.

The response to the Intolerable Acts demonstrated a level of political maturity and unity that had not been seen before in the colonies. These collective acts of defiance and the resultant convening of the First Continental Congress provided the organizational framework necessary to mount a successful challenge to British rule.

Parliament's refusal to see reason was a tremendous opportunity for colonial radicals and rabble-rousers. The Coercive Acts were an inspiration for these 18th-century influencers. Samuel Adams made sure to take advantage. He was a very busy man in 1774.

Sam Adams worked tirelessly to promote the Suffolk Resolves, which called for outright resistance to the Intolerable Acts, rejecting their legitimacy and asserting colonial rights. His ability to navigate and negotiate with other delegates led to the endorsement of the Suffolk Resolves by the First Continental Congress.[29]

The Meeting of a Congress

The embers of unrest found their flames fanned by the Intolerable Acts. These laws would be the catalyst for the First Continental Congress. Adams knew then that the time for talk was nearing its end and that the time for unified action was upon them.

In an atmosphere of escalating tensions, the First Continental Congress was convened on September 5th, 1774, in Carpenters' Hall in

---

[29] Boston National Historical Park. (2024, February 10). Samuel Adams: Boston's Radical Revolutionary. Retrieved from Nps.gov: https://www.nps.gov/articles/000/samuel-adams-boston-revolutionary.htm.

Philadelphia. The assembly was born from a collective colonial need to address grievances against the British Crown and to form a unified front. The Congress brought together representatives from twelve of the thirteen colonies, with Georgia being the exception.[30]

The First Continental Congress laid the groundwork for American unity in the face of British oppression. It displayed intercolonial cooperation and political solidarity. It was hoped that a strong message to the royal government would prevent further infringements on what the American colonists perceived were their rights.

Carpenters' Hall in Philadelphia.
https://commons.wikimedia.org/wiki/File:CarpentersHall00.jpg

---

[30] Horan, Katherine. (2024, February 10). First Continental Congress. Retrieved from Mountvernon.org: https://www.mountvernon.org/library/digitalhistory/digital-encyclopedia/article/first-continental-congress/#:~:text=One%20of%20the%20Congress%27s%20first,and%20to%20raise%20a%20militia.

The Leaders

Those who attended were not drawn from the common folk, but the leadership was still diverse. There were wealthy landowners, lawyers, and merchants, each of whom promoted their colony's wants and needs. Principal assembly members included Samuel Adams and John Adams from Massachusetts, John Jay from New York, and George Washington from Virginia.

Sam Adams understood the cultural significance of the First Continental Congress. It was not merely a gathering of representatives; it was also the embodiment of an American identity separate and distinct from the British. His push for unity and his argument that the fight against the Crown was everyone's fight helped forge a nationalistic spirit that transcended boundaries.

In essence, Sam Adams did more than shape opinions about the Continental Congress; he used it as a platform to bind the colonies together for a shared purpose, creating momentum for independence.

John Adams entered the First Continental Congress, aware of the colony's burgeoning civil unrest. Fueled by his fiery commitment to colonial rights and legal acumen, Adams became a central figure in advocating for resistance against onerous British policies.

Adams tackled the complex legal and philosophical underpinnings of colonial rights. His talent for persuasion and tireless work ethic helped to draft resolutions that underscored the legitimacy of the Congress's cause. Adams strived to bridge provincial conflicts that threatened unity, understanding that a collective front was the only viable path against British dominion.

John Jay was less famous than other attendees, but he quickly distinguished himself through his pragmatic approach to diplomacy. A conservative by nature, Jay was not an immediate advocate for outright rebellion; instead, he favored moderate policies and strategic discourse with the Crown.

Jay's meticulous nature shone through in his role during the Congress. He contributed to the drafting of the "Address to the People of Great Britain," in which he articulated the colonists' grievances and desires in a firm yet conciliatory manner, reflecting his foresight and desire for a peaceful resolution.

George Washington brought his stately presence and a sense of steadfastness and resolve to the First Continental Congress. His military experience and leadership during the French and Indian War gave him a reputation of unwavering dedication to the colonial cause.

While Washington was not as vocal as some of his colleagues, his contributions came through his composure and the respect he commanded from fellow delegates. His presence alone was a testament to the seriousness of the First Continental Congress's intent, and when he spoke, it was with the clarity and conviction of a leader fully aware of the gravity of their situation.

Many other men attended the Congress, and most showcased facets of leadership, be it through enthusiastic advocacy, strategic negotiation, or stoic unity, inspiring others to take action.

The Debate and the Results

Since the delegates came from different colonies, they had varied attitudes toward rebellion. Some sought reconciliation with Great Britain, while others, like Samuel Adams, believed independence was the only viable path forward. The delegates debated passionately. By the time the First Continental Congress adjourned, several resolutions and recommendations had been determined.

The First Continental Congress endorsed the Suffolk Resolves, which rejected the Massachusetts Government Act. Instead, they would prepare for armed resistance against the British. The Congress created a Declaration of Rights and Grievances, establishing the colonies' entitlement to participation in government as extensions of the Crown and cataloging the perceived infringements and abuses by Britain. This asserted a political identity separate from Great Britain despite still claiming allegiance to the British Crown.

The most significant outcome was the Continental Association. It set forth a system of non-importation, non-exportation, and non-consumption to boycott British goods. This economic weapon aimed to pressure Britain into repealing burdensome legislation.

A thread of loyalty to the Crown persisted in the First Continental Congress. The delegates chiefly sought to address specific injustices rather than pursue outright separation. However, as events unfolded, the people's alignment with Britain slowly disintegrated.

Parliament's Reaction

The First Continental Congress was a gathering that signaled the colonial resolve against what they saw as oppressive British policies. But what was the reaction across the ocean. How did politicians respond within the hallowed halls of the British Parliament?

Parliament's reaction was mixed and highlighted vast differences in opinion between members. Some foresaw the danger of escalation and advocated for reconciliation. Others, however, interpreted the Congress's actions as outright defiance, warranting a firm response to maintain British authority. The dominating sentiment was that concessions would only encourage the rebellious spirit.

The debates within Parliament were tense and fraught with emotion, reflecting the gravity of the situation. There were those, such as Lord North, who felt the colonies' actions could not go unchecked. Others, like Edmund Burke and William Pitt the Elder, argued the American colonists were entitled to certain rights as Englishmen and that Parliament should aim to mend the relationship, not deepen the chasm. In various speeches and proposals, they urged their peers to recognize the legitimate concerns of the colonies stemming from legislation like the Stamp Act and the Tea Act.

The colonies represented significant commercial interests, and their cooperation was essential for the mercantile system's smooth functioning. Despite this, Parliament chose to prioritize asserting authority over securing these economic ties. The opposition argued the principle of parliamentary sovereignty was at stake. To many British lawmakers, conceding to colonial demands would be tantamount to admitting that Parliament did not hold ultimate legislative authority over the colonies. Conceding to the North American colonies might mean conceding to the colonists living on the profitable Caribbean islands.

Ultimately, the Crown viewed the First Continental Congress as an illegal assembly and rendered any of its decisions null.

At the heart of Parliament's reaction was a fundamental misunderstanding: the British saw the First Continental Congress as a challenge to their authority rather than a response to policies that the colonists considered unjust. The reaction of the British Parliament stemmed from the inherent conflict between the need to control a vast empire and the growing desire of the colonies for self-determination.

In Summary

The First Continental Congress was a precursor to the Declaration of Independence and the eventual American Revolutionary War. Its legacy is enshrined not just in the outcomes and correspondence that originated from it but also in the unity and resolve it fostered among diverse colonies that had different interests and cultures. At the time, however, the changes the First Continental Congress hoped for did not happen. Parliament underestimated the colonists' resolve, leading to a hardened stance that aggravated tensions. The British response served only to alienate the colonies further, paving the way for actions with drastic consequences.

There was a mutual disagreement that no longer permitted calm debate or reasonable resolution. Both sides were moving toward a point where bullets were more appealing than words. The final decision about the future would not happen in London or Philadelphia; it would be made on the village green of two small towns.

Chapter 4: The Shot

The year 1775 was a pivotal one for the Thirteen Colonies. A series of cultural, economic, political, and social events stirred the pot of revolution, leading to the fateful encounters in Lexington and Concord.

These events did not occur in isolation; instead, they culminated in rising tensions and grievances that had been festering for years. Parliament's reaction to the First Continental Congress shattered attempts at reasonable reconciliation with Great Britain.

Amidst the backdrop of legislative acts was the silent, steadfast preparation for conflict. The Minutemen—colonial part-time militiamen—began drilling more frequently. Gunpowder and arms were stockpiled, and colonial leaders, including Samuel Adams and John Hancock, roused support through the Committees of Correspondence. Some Americans hoped for a peaceful resolution, but many were less sanguine. Patrick Henry appeared to sum up the popular mood when he said, "The war is inevitable—and let it come! I repeat it, sir, let it come."[31] People were starting to prepare for war.

The Power of Communication

Communication in the face of oppression took a formalized shape through the Committees of Correspondence. This system was the Facebook of its time—a revolutionary fiber-optic network minus the

---

[31] Wirt, William (ed. 1973). Give Me Liberty or Give Me Death. Retrieved from Colonial Williamsburg: https://www.colonialwilliamsburg.org/learn/deep-dives/give-me-liberty-or-give-me-death/.

optics and fibers. These committees served as the information highways among the Thirteen Colonies, spreading news, coordinating responses to British policies, and sowing the seeds of unity for colonial resistance.

By 1775, the Committees of Correspondence had evolved into powerful tools of diplomacy and advocacy. They did not stand still; instead, they morphed into dynamic bodies advocating resistance and alignment against the overreach of imperial governance. These committees worked tirelessly to coordinate stances regarding British policies, nurtured intercolonial partnerships, and rallied support for the burgeoning cause of independence.

These instruments of colonial communication excelled in a few pivotal roles:

- Dissemination of information: Acting like a colonial "pony express," these committees rapidly spread the news of British actions along with interpretations that boosted the patriotic cause.
- Unity: The committees fortified a sense of solidarity and collective resolve among the colonists, encouraging shared ideals and goals.
- Local leadership: Serving as local and intercolonial governing bodies, the committees heavily influenced colonial policies and local governance.
- Event chronicling: They meticulously documented events and British policy outcomes, creating a written record that served as potent propaganda and historical documentation.

The committees' incessant efforts empowered individuals, instilled a collective consciousness among the American people, and ignited the flame of self-determination. They kept the fires of resistance burning brightly.[32]

Radicals kept colonists alert to what was happening and stirred public opinion. Understanding who the radicals were in the months leading up to the American Revolution in 1775 is crucial. These weren't mindless rebels without a cause; they were strategic, driven, and embraced revolutionary sentiments that would realign the trajectory of an entire

---

[32] Longley, R. (2020, October 14). Committees of Correspondence: Definition and History. Retrieved from Thoughtco.com: https://www.thoughtco.com/committees-of-correspondence-definition-and-history-5082089.

nation.

These leaders did not work in isolation; they spearheaded a network of like-minded revolutionaries, navigating through British constraints to orchestrate a full-scale movement toward revolution. They weren't necessarily middle-class businessmen. Among these firebrands was one man who happened to be one of the wealthiest men in the colonies.

John Hancock: Plutocrat and Patriot

In the story of the American Revolution, John Hancock is a man whose name has become synonymous with bold signatures, but his deeds reached far beyond the flourish of a quill. The year 1775 found John Hancock at the epicenter of colonial resistance. His financial support and leadership through various colonial committees marked him as a target for British authorities. His proximity to pivotal figures like Samuel Adams and Paul Revere linked him irrevocably to the cause for American independence.

Born on January 23rd, 1737, in Braintree, Massachusetts, Hancock inherited a substantial fortune from his uncle, Thomas Hancock, which granted him both affluence and influence in the Massachusetts colony. As a merchant, Hancock's involvement in trade introduced him to the harsh realities of British colonial policies and the simmering discontent of the colonies. Given his considerable wealth, he ought to have been a loyalist, but he was not.

He sympathized with the radicals, and he might have been one of those behind the scenes who organized the Boson Tea Party. The British suspected him of being a smuggler, but John Adams was able to help Hancock escape being convicted of smuggling charges.[33]

John Hancock's statute rose when he was elected president of the Second Continental Congress in 1775. This significant role placed him at the helm of colonial affairs during critical moments. Hancock bore the responsibility of uniting disparate colonies, galvanizing military efforts, and facilitating the dialog that would eventually draft the Declaration of Independence.

The British Commander

In the history of the American Revolution, few British figures are as simultaneously prominent and controversial as Lieutenant General

---

[33] NCC Staff. (2021, May 24). 10 Fascinating Facts About John Hancock. Retrieved from Constitutioncenter.org: https://constitutioncenter.org/blog/10-fascinating-facts-about-john-hancock

Thomas Gage. He played a pivotal role as a British commander during the early stages of the American Revolution. Gage served as the governor of Massachusetts Bay and the commander in chief of the British forces in North America. His tenure in this volatile environment was marked by increasing tensions between the American colonies and the British Crown.

Thomas Gage's relationship with North America was long-standing. He first arrived on the continent as a lieutenant colonel in 1754 to partake in the French and Indian War. After various military appointments and a brief return to England, Gage came back to the colonies in 1763 as the commander of all British forces in North America. His profound familiarity with the land and its people spanned over two decades.

During his years on the continent, Gage had the opportunity to develop his opinions about the American colonies and their inhabitants. These perceptions would influence his strategies and policies in the years leading up to the revolution.

Gage's responsibilities were extensive and multifaceted. As the military governor, he was tasked with implementing and enforcing the increasingly unpopular acts passed by the British Parliament. His duties included maintaining order, overseeing the colonial administration, and commanding the British troops stationed across North America. He was the linchpin in Britain's efforts to sustain colonial obedience, an unenviable position amid the rising tide of revolutionary spirit.

Thomas Gage.
John Singleton Copley, CC0, via Wikimedia Commons;
https://commons.wikimedia.org/wiki/File:Thomas_Gage_John_Singleton_Copley.jpeg

While Gage recognized the resourcefulness and resolve of the colonists, which he gleaned from their performance in past conflicts, he also harbored a certain disdain for their rebellious streak. In correspondence with his superiors, Gage frequently expressed a belief that American agitators were a minority, though a loud one, and that many colonists remained loyal to the Crown.

However, as the agitation grew and the whisper of revolution became a clamor, Gage faced mounting challenges. His attempts to constrain the patriots, such as the enforcement of the Coercive Acts and his actions leading up to the Battles of Lexington and Concord, reveal a man who underestimated the resolve and capabilities of a populace inching closer to war.

Gage's stance on the rebels hardened over time. With reports of undisciplined colonial militias and the chaos of mob actions, Gage's dispatches to London became increasingly critical of the American colonies. Under pressure, he advocated for more troops and stricter measures, which only fanned the flames of rebellion.

Training in Secret: Colonial Militias

On the cusp of revolutionary outbreak, militias were quintessential to the defensive and, at times, offensive strategies of the colonies. While British soldiers were stationed in Boston, militias were rallied throughout the rural regions of Massachusetts and beyond. The militias were composed of local men, from farmers to tradespeople, ready to defend their rights and homes. They trained persistently, their drills shrouded in secrecy to avoid punitive actions by the British.

It was within this crucible of unrest that the militia system began to transform. Leaders like Samuel Adams and John Hancock in Massachusetts, amongst other colonial firebrands, started to view these local forces as defenders and instruments of potential insurrection.

Militias engaged in secret assemblies and drills. These were not the regular, somewhat leisurely musterings that characterized peacetime training. They were intense and frequent and were held under the guise of normalcy. By day, the militia members were tradesmen, farmers, and artisans; by evening, they were soldiers in training.

Books, such as *A Plan of Discipline, Composed for the Use of the Militia of the County of Norfolk,* penned by William Windham and George Townshend in 1759, found their way across the Atlantic, providing a framework for military exercises. Inspired by such manuals, the militias were drilled with a newfound sense of urgency, learning to maneuver, fire, reload, and respond to commands efficiently. The colonists had one strategy that came from personal experience for many. They had fought the Native Americans throughout the years and learned the value of ambush and the use of the woods for defense.

Understanding the necessity of being well equipped for an impending conflict, militias began stockpiling weapons and gunpowder. This was no simple task under the watchful eyes of British officials.

Each community had committees of safety, which played a pivotal role in the collection and distribution of arms and munitions. For instance, in Salem and Marblehead, Massachusetts, secret stashes of gunpowder were amassed, which would later become vital to the cause. All these preparations suggest that the British army would not be facing a mob but groups of colonists who had an idea of how to wage war.

The Days Before

An encounter that heavily foreshadowed the Battles of Lexington and Concord was the Lexington Powder Alarm in September 1774. British troops moved to seize colonial gunpowder, leading to widespread alarm and the formation of militia units. Though this event ended without bloodshed, it served as a rehearsal for the battles to come.[34]

Communication between colonies was essential, and a clandestine network of spies and messengers was established to share intelligence about British troop movements and garrison strengths. The famous "Midnight Ride" of Paul Revere was only one of many critical information relay operations enacted during the months leading up to the clashes in April 1775.

In the weeks leading up to April 19th, 1775, the tension between the British troops in Boston and the Massachusetts colonists was palpable. General Gage was acutely aware of the restive mood of rebellion. He had orders to disarm the rebels and arrest their leaders.

Yet, the colonial militia, or Minutemen, were ominous shadows sliding through the towns and countryside, readying muskets and munitions. Intelligence of such activities was well known to Gage, who had dispatched spies throughout the region. In response, he planned a

---

[34] Rust, R. (2023, April 14). The Powder Alarm of Massachusetts in 1774. Retrieved from Americanhistorycentral.com: https://www.americanhistorycentral.com/entries/powder-alarm-1774-massachusetts/.

tactical strike designed to seize colonial arms stored at Concord and to capture revolutionary leaders like John Hancock and Samuel Adams, who were rumored to be staying near Lexington.

On the other side were the colonial leaders. Foreseeing conflict, they strategically spread out their stockpiles of weapons and ammunition across various rural locations. The atmosphere was one of silent resolve; conversations were held in hushed tones as plans were meticulously laid out for the anticipated call to arms.

The colonial leaders also established intricate networks of messengers and signals to alert the countryside of any British advances. The night before the skirmishes at Lexington and Concord, Gage sent seven hundred troops to destroy the colonials' weapons cache. Paul Revere and William Dawes embarked on their famous midnight ride to warn Adams and Hancock and rouse the Minutemen.

The Midnight Ride

"LISTEN, my children, and you shall hear

Of the midnight ride of Paul Revere,

On April 18, in Seventy-five;

Hardly a man is now alive

Who remembers that famous day and year."

People are thrilled by the cadence of that famous poem by Henry Wadsworth Longfellow. It is exciting to read and fun to imagine that ride through the night to warn people of the British march. Longfellow told a great story, but he used considerable poetic license. What happened that evening was quite different from what he wrote.

The ride was not spontaneous; it was a carefully coordinated alarm through lantern signals and a relay of riders. Paul Revere, along with William Dawes and later joined by Dr. Samuel Prescott, raced against time to warn communities and urge Hancock and Adams to go into hiding. Revere was captured before reaching Concord, and it was Prescott who successfully carried the news to the men. Because of Henry Wadsworth Longfellow's famous poem, Revere's role is fixed in the American spirit as the herald of revolution.[35]

---

[35] The Paul Revere House. (2024, February 14). *The Real Story of Paul Revere's Ride.* Retrieved from Paulreverehouse.org: https://www.paulreverehouse.org/the-real-story/.

Battles Fought

Just before dawn on April 19ᵗʰ, 1775, the militias were called upon to challenge the British march toward Concord. Those months of secretive preparations had paid dividends. As dawn approached on that fateful April day, British forces under Lieutenant Colonel Francis Smith and Major John Pitcairn arrived in Lexington. They encountered a ragtag band of American militiamen, led by Captain John Parker, lined upon the common. Confusion ensued, a shot rang out—the legendary "shot heard round the world"—and eight colonists lay dead in the aftermath. Historians still debate who fired the first shot, but its impact was nevertheless unmistakable.

The British column then moved to Concord, where they were stymied by the absence of most of the munitions they had come to destroy, cleverly hidden by the foresighted colonists. As they searched the town, colonial reinforcements swelled, leading to a confrontation at Concord's North Bridge. A more organized battle ensued, and the British were forced to retreat.

The retreat damaged the British column. The colonists used a strategy they learned long ago from the Native Americans. The Minutemen did not openly confront their red-coated adversary; they picked away at the retreating British by firing from behind trees or underbrush and then vanishing into the landscape before the British could respond. As the British neared Boston, their ranks were thinned, exhaustion had set in, and morale had plummeted.

By the time the column reached the safety of Boston, the British had suffered 19 officers and 250 regulars killed or wounded. American casualties were less than one hundred. The Americans considered this a strategic victory that proved they could stand up against one of the world's most powerful armies.[36]

The Aftermath of the Fight

The Battles of Concord and Lexington were not isolated events but rather the result of a complex interplay between sociopolitical movements and stealthy military preparations. These confrontations set the stage for a war that would challenge the might of the British Empire

---

[36] BritishBattles.com. (2024, February 14). Battle of Lexington and Concord. Retrieved from Britishbattles.com: https://www.britishbattles.com/war-of-the-revolution-1775-to-1783/battle-of-lexington-and-concord/.

and raise the banner of independence for the nascent United States of America.

What happened that April morning was more than a mere military engagement; symbolically, it marked the decisive step from peaceful protest to armed resistance in the colonies. Ralph Waldo Emerson later termed the conflict at North Bridge as "the shot heard round the world," encapsulating the global significance of America's fight for independence.

The ripples of Lexington and Concord expanded far beyond Massachusetts. The colonies quickly became a hive of revolutionary activity. The First Continental Congress had adjourned with the understanding that another one could be called for in the future if things did not improve. Given the events at Lexington and Concord, the Second Continental Congress was assembled on May 10th, 1775, at Independence Hall in Philadelphia.

A Revolutionary Congress

The delegates gathered at this second historic Continental Congress represented a cross-section of the revolution's leaders. There was John Adams, who pushed for independence from the outset, and there were moderate figures like John Dickinson who sought reconciliation with the Crown. These men played a significant role in defining the American cause and shaping the revolution's trajectory.

On June 14th, 1775, the Second Continental Congress voted to create a Continental Army from the militia units gathered outside Boston. The Congress went further and drafted a statement explaining the colonies' reasons for taking up arms. The Declaration of the Causes and Necessity of Taking Up Arms, issued on July 6th, 1775, outlined the grievances the colonies had with the British government and their commitment to defending their rights and liberties. The Second Continental Congress was not yet ready to declare full separation from the British Crown, though. The Olive Branch Petition, an attempt at securing peace with the Crown, was signed by the delegates on July 8th.

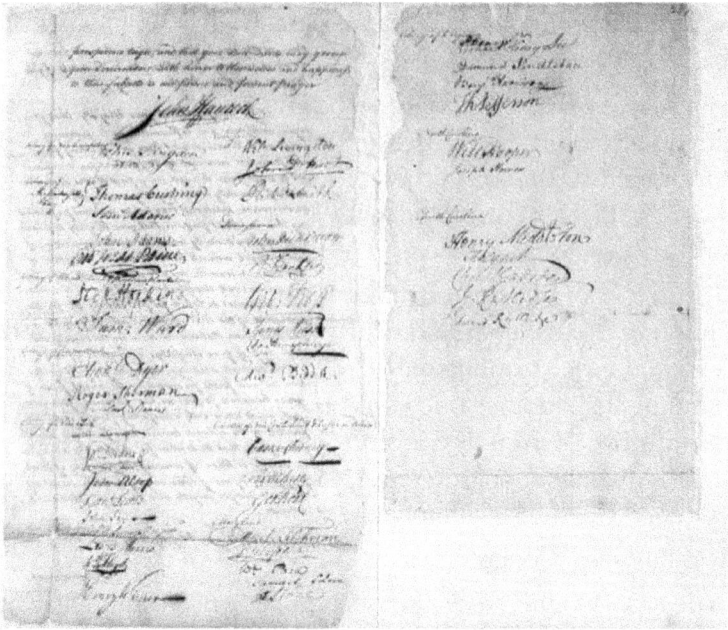

The Olive Branch Petition. You can see John Hancock's signature at the top of the left page
https://commons.wikimedia.org/wiki/File:Olive_petition_petition_big.jpg

In Summary

The years of debate and attempts to find some means of compromise were over. The efforts to persuade the British Crown that there were alternatives for addressing colonial concerns and that colonial representation in Parliament was necessary failed. The Second Continental Congress's resolutions proved that words were no longer sufficient.

The British Parliament bears responsibility for what happened in the spring and summer of 1775. If its members had listened to Burke and other colonial sympathizers, there might have been a way to raise the needed money without harsh measures. Unfortunately, Parliament was obstinate and fixed in its resolve to be the only judge of what needed to be done. What happened next would be eight years of war that pitted the greatest army and navy of Europe against thirteen colonies whose armed forces were primarily composed of civilians.

Chapter 5: Early Successes

At the dawn of war, George Washington was a leader weighed down by the enormity of the task before him. Appointed as the commander in chief of what would become the Continental Army on June 15th, 1775, his mantle was one of responsibility and expectation. He is a fascinating study in leadership. He possessed a stoic, unyielding presence that inspired confidence and loyalty.

Portrait of George Washington.
https://commons.wikimedia.org/wiki/File:Gilbert_Stuart_Williamstown_Portrait_of_George_Wa shington.jpg

Washington was faced with a confluence of challenges. The Continental Army was in its infancy and comprised a disparate collection of militias. More organized training, equipment, and, crucially, experience in fighting as a unified force were needed. Succeeding in battles was critical to establishing the legitimacy of the American cause and persuading wavering colonists to support the rebellion.

Creating a Military Force

Washington's primary objective was to transform the ragtag colonial forces into a disciplined army capable of confronting the professional British military.

In the early stages of the war, the Continental Army was an unorganized and untrained mix of volunteers lacking discipline and experience. Washington recognized the need for a complete overhaul to turn these civilians into effective fighters. The first step was establishing a regular army distinct from the state militias. The Continentals could operate as a unified force rather than disparate state units by unifying command and streamlining logistics.[37]

Under Washington's guidance, uniformity in discipline and dress became required. Each day, troops participated in military drills that were focused on mastering essential maneuvers. By drilling the concepts of formation, movement, and firepower, Washington instilled a sense of order and control that was essential in battle. Moreover, implementing a standard uniform and regulations for wear cultivated a sense of unity and belonging among soldiers, inspiring collective identity and purpose.[38]

Training was paramount. Soldiers needed to learn not just how to march in formation but also how to load and fire their weapons efficiently, maneuver on the battlefield, and, most importantly, withstand the rigors of war. Regular training exercises and mock battles simulated real-world conditions, honing the skills of the troops and preparing them for actual combat.

Morale was both the fuel and the result of these undertakings. Promotions were based on merit rather than birth, instilling a sense of a meritocracy that could inspire ambition among the enlisted men and

[37] William P. Kladky, P. (2024, February 15). Continental Army. Retrieved from Mountvernon.org: https://www.mountvernon.org/library/digitalhistory/digital-encyclopedia/article/continental-army/.
[38] Battlefields.org. (2024, January 23). 10 Facts: The Continental Army. Retrieved from Battlefields.org: https://www.battlefields.org/learn/articles/10-facts-continental-army.

promote loyalty to their superiors.

Beyond that, Washington also recognized the significance of non-combat skills. Camp followers, responsible for cooking, cleaning, and other support roles, were integral to maintaining the army. These civilians, often women and children, contributed to the communal spirit and practical functioning of the military, playing a silent but influential role in the war effort.

The transformation of the Continental Army from civilians to soldiers is a saga replete with heroism and sacrifice, but it is also one that illustrates the vital importance of cohesive leadership, strategic foresight, and dedicated preparation.

The Trials of Thomas Gage

On the British side stood General Thomas Gage, who was caught in a conundrum with no easy solution. The British commander was required to face challenges, make decisions, and direct strategies that would determine the direction of the British Empire in North America.

Gage was not facing a small band of discontents. The American colonists were no ordinary insurgents; they were spirited, intimately familiar with the terrain, and motivated by a just, if not desperate, cause. The challenges they presented to Gage were manifold. How does one quell a rebellion amongst one's own, especially when the lines of loyalty are so blurred? Gage had to wrestle with preconceived notions of colonial obedience and British superiority that now seemed obsolete in the face of American resolve. The military force Gage had at his disposal was sufficient to garrison British territory but hardly enough to deal with a revolt that stretched down the Atlantic seaboard. His Boston garrison was no match for a fledgling revolution that was spreading.

The colonists were arming themselves, but where were their depots, and how many men did the colonies? These were more than military questions; they were also political questions that had serious consequences. Failure to act upon gathered intelligence or, worse, engage in a mistaken action that would be deemed overly aggressive by local populations could lead to a damning loss of trust and fidelity. On the other hand, underestimating the colonists' firepower could have equally dire consequences for Gage's own forces.

General Gage also faced a logistical nightmare. The American colonies covered huge areas. Maintaining and sustaining an orderly campaign in the vast expanses of America was almost impossible.

Supplies, reinforcements, and communication lines would be long and vulnerable.

The harshness of winter, disease, and the fierce independence of the American colonies were going to be constant adversaries. Gage's decisions had to weigh strategic value against the very tangible limitations of space and means.

The immediate problem for the British commander was Boston and the appearance of a hostile force on the outskirts of town. Gage received 4,500 reinforcements under the command of Major General William Howe in June 1775. He would have to endure a siege or attempt a breakout.[39]

The Siege of Boston

An initial objective of the Continental Army was to take Boston back from the British. Taking Boston would serve to secure the New England region, which was a hotbed of revolutionary fervor. Thousands of colonial militiamen encamped on the outskirts of the city. The hills surrounding Boston provided an advantageous position from which artillery could command the town and harbor below.

Recognizing this, colonial leaders appointed a commander to oversee the siege of Boston. General Artemas Ward was a respected militia officer with experience in the French and Indian War. He was placed in command. One of his officers, Colonel William Prescott, led some of the soldiers onto the peninsula and built an earthen redoubt on Breed's Hill.

The fortifications constructed on that elevation worried General Gage because it tightened the colonial siege of Boston. He decided that a show of force might break the siege and show British military superiority.

On June 17th, 1775, Gage ordered an assault. Approximately 2,300 British regulars under William Howe's command attacked the redoubt. Although popular legend calls this engagement the Battle of Bunker Hill, most of the actual fighting took place on Breed's Hill.

The battle's outset was marked by the colonists' determination and British underestimation of their opponent. As the British advanced, the famous command attributed to a colonial officer rang out: "Don't fire until you see the whites of their eyes!" This directive aimed to maximize

---

[39] Hickman, K. (2019, June 13). American Revolution: General Thomas Gage. Retrieved from Thoughtco.com: https://www.thoughtco.com/general-thomas-gage-2360620.

the impact of the limited ammunition available to the colonial militia. It required three attempts, but the British eventually captured the hill.[40]

However, it was a Pyrrhic victory. The British suffered more than one thousand dead or wounded in taking Breed's Hill, including many officers. Furthermore, it was a morale booster for the colonists. The battle revealed the firm resolve of the colonial forces and demonstrated that untrained American militias could stand up to British regulars in battle. The heavy losses sustained by the British army also served as a notice to Great Britain that suppressing the rebellion would only come with significant cost.

General Gage was finished. He was recalled home in October, and Howe was placed in temporary command. There was a change of command on the colonial side as well, as George Washington arrived to take over the siege operations.

Washington aimed to establish a network of fortifications around Boston. This would not only serve as a defensive perimeter but also as a training ground for the Continental Army. Fortifying the city was an opportunity to educate his troops in the arts of war while simultaneously containing the British forces in a strategic stalemate.

Washington was faced with a significant challenge. The Continental Army surrounding Boston was low on ammunition and artillery. Washington needed both to conclude the siege successfully. He got what he needed thanks to a ragtag group of Vermont militiamen.

The Taking of Fort Ticonderoga

Fort Ticonderoga was situated on the shores of Lake Champlain in upstate New York and served as a cornerstone in the strategic waterway connecting Canada to the Hudson River Valley. Originally named Fort Carillon by the French, who constructed it in 1755, it was designed as a bulwark against British forces during the French and Indian War. In 1775, the British were using the fort as a central munitions depot. As tensions between the American colonies and the British Crown escalated, Fort Ticonderoga became vitally important due to its large artillery stores. Capturing the fort would give Washinton what he desperately needed.

---

[40] American Battlefield Trust. (2024, February 15). Bunker Hill. Retrieved from Battlefields.org: https://www.battlefields.org/learn/revolutionary-war/battles/bunker-hill.

Only fifty soldiers guarded the fort. A large force was not necessary, but the attackers had to be familiar with the territory and able to approach the fortification undetected. The assault fell to the Green Mountain Boys, who lived in the area.

The Green Mountain Boys were a group of amateur soldiers from the present-day state of Vermont, then known as the New Hampshire Grants (land grants given by New Hampshire). Led by the charismatic Ethan Allen, the Green Mountain Boys were fighting to maintain control of their lands against New York settlers. When the opportunity arose to join the American Revolution, their motivations became aligned with the broader colonial cause. Their expedition included a controversial figure of the American Revolution.

Benedict Arnold was, at the time, an ambitious officer. Arnold was appointed a colonel by the Massachusetts Committee of Safety and assigned the task of seizing Fort Ticonderoga. Upon learning of the Green Mountain Boys' similar mission, Arnold joined forces with Ethan Allen instead of arguing about who would be in command. He accepted his role as Allen's chief subordinate.

On the dawn of May 10th, 1775, Benedict Arnold and the Green Mountain Boys approached the slumbering fort with stealth and decisiveness. They caught the garrison by surprise, capturing the fort without loss of life. The fort's cache of artillery and munitions was enormous. From Fort Ticonderoga and Crown Point (which was captured later), the Americans seized seventy-eight cannons, six mortars, three howitzers, approximately eighteen thousand pounds of musket balls, and thirty thousand flints. The prize was more than Washington needed.[41]

Hauling It to Boston

Capturing the fort was just the beginning. The greater challenge lay in the fact that Boston was nearly three hundred miles away from Ticonderoga. The mighty task of moving massive artillery through unforgiving terrain fell to Colonel Henry Knox, the newly appointed chief of artillery for the Continental Army.

---

[41] American Battlefield Trust. (2024, February 15). Fort Ticonderoga, May 10, 1775. Retrieved from American Battlefield Trust: https://www.battlefields.org/learn/maps/fort-ticonderoga-may-10-1775.

Henry Knox, a twenty-five-year-old with no formal military training, convinced General George Washington that he could transport the sixty tons of artillery to Boston. Washington, impressed by the younger man's confidence and understanding of artillery's impact on warfare, gave Knox his blessing. With that, Knox set off on his daunting journey. He reached Fort Ticonderoga on December 5th, 1775, and the march to Boston started on December 17th.

The journey was fraught with challenges right from the start. Winter had set in, and Knox's convoy had to navigate not just roads but also bodies of water that, despite the cold, had yet to freeze over entirely. They traversed icy rivers, snowy forests, and the Berkshire Mountains with enormous sleds, oxen, and sheer grit. The condition of the roads was calamitous. Knox and his team often had to shore up bridges or dismantle the cannons and carry them piece by piece over particularly rough patches. The great weight of the cannons often caused the sleds to break through the ice. Many cannons had to be retrieved from the icy waters.

The route from Ticonderoga wound southeast to the headwaters of the Hudson River, through Albany, and across Massachusetts. The Knox Trail, as it later came to be known, is a testament to the physical and mental fortitude of those who, despite the harsh winter, pushed forward with relentless determination.

Surprisingly, the rivers served not as barriers but as aids to transport goods. Knox used boats when possible and leveraged the ice as a platform when the waters froze enough to bear the artillery's substantial weight.

After an arduous journey that lasted nearly two months, Knox's expedition reached Cambridge, Massachusetts, on January 24th, 1776, with the cannons intact. The arrival of sophisticated armaments, including cannons, mortars, and howitzers, was a significant boost to American morale and strategy. Washington now possessed the firepower to position guns on Dorchester Heights. The artillery supply train included more than fifty pieces of captured ordnance.[42]

---

[42] massmoments.org. (2024, February 15). Henry Knox Brings Cannon to Boston. Retrieved from massmoments.org: https://www.massmoments.org/moment-details/henry-knox-brings-cannon-to-boston.html.

Fortifying Dorchester Heights

Washington now had the artillery required to bring an end to the siege of Boston. The colonial commander in chief decided to place the cannons on Dorchester Heights.

Fortifying Dorchester Heights stands out as a masterstroke by George Washington and his army. This military operation demonstrated the ingenuity and resolve of the Continental Army and significantly altered the course of the war. Situated at a strategic military location because of its elevation, Dorchester Heights offered commanding views over the city of Boston and its harbor. Any force holding this ground could threaten ships and troop movements, a fact not lost on either side of the conflict. Understanding its significance, George Washington, who wanted to end the siege once and for all, hatched a plan to fortify this location and tighten the noose around British-occupied Boston.

Under cover of darkness, on the night of March 4th, 1776, a force of 1,200 men, including troops, laborers, and even teams of oxen, silently began the laborious task of constructing fortifications. Armed with over three hundred wagons of fascines, gabions, and prefabricated fortifications, they worked through the night under the direction of Colonel Rufus Putnam, who had proved himself an engineer of considerable talent.

Under constant threat of discovery, the American forces managed to transport and assemble artillery and build a formidable position that had been a bare hill before. Large cannons, recently transported overland from Fort Ticonderoga, were also positioned, ready to unleash their power on British-controlled areas.

The men worked with an urgency dictated by their desperation for a decisive move against the British. Their labor in the biting cold, breaking ground that was still frozen and constructing barriers destined to change the momentum of the war, was a testament to their dedication and the brilliance of Washington's calculated risk.

Their movements were so stealthy that the British sentries in Boston remained oblivious to the activities taking place just a few hundred yards away. By the dawn's light, to the shock of the British forces, Dorchester Heights bristled with fortifications.

On the morning of March 5th, British General William Howe woke to an astonishing and disheartening sight. Dorchester Heights, which had been clear the previous day, now presented an imposing military installation overlooking his positions. Reportedly, he said, "The rebels have done more in one night than my whole army would have done in a month." He quickly realized the precariousness of his situation. The newly installed American artillery had the range to inflict severe damage on his ships in the harbor and make the British hold on Boston untenable.[43]

Unable to dislodge the Americans from their newfound stronghold and unwilling to subject his forces and the loyalist population in Boston to bombardment, General Howe had little choice but to evacuate. Washington's strategic placement of forces on Dorchester Heights led directly to the British departure on March 17th, a day still remembered in Boston as Evacuation Day. On that day, the people of Boston witnessed the retreat of British troops, symbolically ending the occupancy that had started nearly eight years before with the Townshend Acts.

The successful siege effectively ended British authority in Massachusetts and set the stage for the Declaration of Independence. However, the departure of British troops did not bring immediate peace or stability to Boston. Despite the victory, the city was left in a state of economic fragility. The blockade had severely impacted trade, a cornerstone of Boston's economy.

Furthermore, a sizeable loyalist population, integrally woven into the local society and economy, had fled, leaving behind homes, shops, and an uncertain future. It took years for commerce to recover. Politically, the departure of the royal governor and his administration allowed for a new, patriot-led government to take control. The Massachusetts Provincial Congress took on greater authority, directing the war effort locally and participating in continental governance.

Boston would face challenges, but the British were gone and would not come back. Boston was now the symbol and center of the patriot cause. It swelled with an energy that fueled the spirit of independence. Washington and the Continental Army had achieved a victory that seemed impossible a few weeks before. It marked the first major military victory for the colonists.

---

[43] Boston National Historical Park. (2024, February 15). Dorchester Heights. Retrieved from Nps.org: https://www.nps.gov/places/dorchester-heights.htm.

In Summary

In retrospect, the year 1775 established the cornerstone of American military tradition. Washington's strategic patience and his willingness to employ unconventional tactics laid the foundation for future successes against the British. The Continental Army emerged from 1775 not only battle-hardened but also imbued with a sense of national identity and purpose that transcended the colonial divide. The year 1775 was only the beginning.

However, the success of the first year did not chase away the dark clouds that were forming on the horizon. The Continental Army had been victorious against a rump force used for garrison duty. Other British regiments were better and standing at the ready. Washington and his officers might have celebrated with the others on that day, but the general and his staff knew a terrible truth. The might of the British Empire had yet to be brought to bear on the Thirteen Colonies. Parliament and the British Crown would not go quietly into the night. They would draw on the considerable military resources Great Britain had and respond in force. A terrible reality would soon sail westward from the mother country.

Chapter 6: A Declaration and Invasions

A subtle push toward independence came from the British government. The Olive Branch Petition, a final effort to convince the British Crown to negotiate a reasonable resolution of differences, was firmly rejected by Parliament in August 1775. King George III refused to read it. The Thirteen Colonies declared they were in rebellion via the Proclamation of Rebellion on August 23rd, 1775.

It Was Common Sense

During the colonial period, many leaders held a philosophical view that was heavily influenced by the Enlightenment. The ideas of reason, natural rights, and people's sovereignty gave weight to the concept of independence. Colonial intellectuals drew inspiration from the works of Jean-Jacques Rousseau's *The Social Contract* and John Locke's belief in the right to life, liberty, and property. These thinkers and their writings encouraged leaders to envision a government that reflected the will of the governed, which was a radical departure from the traditional monarchy. Even ordinary citizens were beginning to desire an independent nation.

Before 1776, the concept of total independence was considered radical by many colonists, who still clung to the hope of reconciliation with the British Crown. Thomas Paine, an English-born philosopher, political activist, and revolutionary, recognized the potential of the written word to unify the colonists and how it could shift their perspective toward outright independence.

A portrait of Thomas Paine.

Common Sense, published anonymously in January 1776, was a timely and strategic masterstroke penned by Paine that crystallized the need for liberty and the immediate severance from Britain. It was direct, easily understood, and unapologetically bold. Arguing against monarchies and hereditary succession, Paine's pamphlet spoke a simple yet powerful truth to common folk, which resonated across the Thirteen Colonies.[44]

Starting with general reflections on government and religion, Paine proceeded to discuss the English constitution, the challenges of monarchial rule, and the machinations of the British monarchy toward the colonies. However, the crux of his argument lay in the notion that independence was feasible and imperative for the growth, prosperity, and preservation of the colonies' rights. Paine facilitated a robust public discourse that shifted the colonists' mindset toward a shared identity and

---

[44] Kiger, P. J. (2023, July 11). How Thomas Paine's "Common Sense" Helped Inspire the American Revolution. Retrieved from History.com: https://www.history.com/news/thomas-paine-common-sense-revolution.

purpose by laying simple truths out in the open.[45]

A Petition Put Forward

The petition for independence was not a hurried document. While the first rumors of independence circulated after the Battles of Lexington and Concord, it wasn't until June 7th, 1776, that Richard Henry Lee of Virginia presented a formal resolution that "these United Colonies are, and of right ought to be, free and independent States."[46]

Thomas Jefferson, who was a Virginia delegate to the Second Continental Congress, was tasked with the momentous duty of drafting the declaration. His command of language and his standing as an ardent advocate for colonial rights made him a natural choice to author the document.

It would be a difficult task. Jefferson faced the challenge of capturing the essence of the American Revolution and the nuances of political theory that were developing during that time. Jefferson patiently wrote and revised the text, distilling the shared will of all Americans into words that still reverberate today. The final draft is still considered a masterpiece.[47]

The Declaration of Independence states clearly that "all men are created equal," not just a privileged few, and all of them are "endowed by their Creator with certain unalienable rights," boldly asserting that the purpose of government is to protect these rights and that the people have the right to alter or abolish said government should it become destructive. The Declaration of Independence's ideological heft was crucial in transmuting the war for colonial rights into a global statement of human rights. Its impact would be felt around the world, inspiring future independence movements.

The Ensuing Floor Debate

The draft of the Declaration of Independence was examined and reviewed by the Second Continental Congress with a critical eye. There

---

[45] Paine, T. (2024, February 17). Thomas Paine, Common Sense, 1776. Retrieved from Billofrightsinstitute.org: https://billofrightsinstitute.org/activities/thomas-paine-common-sense-1776.

[46] Lee Resolution (2022, February 8). Lee Resolution. Retrieved from National Archives: https://www.archives.gov/milestone-documents/lee-resolution.

[47] Bill of Rights Institute. (2024, February 17). Thomas Jefferson and the Declaration of Independence. Retrieved from Billofrightsinstitute.org: https://billofrightsinstitute.org/essays/thomas-jefferson-and-the-declaration-of-independence.

were debates about including the concept of inalienable rights, which was a novel idea at the time. The Declaration of Independence's statement of "life, liberty, and the pursuit of happiness" had to defend its place in democratic discourse.

The discussions were not mere semantics; they were serious debates about the over-empowerment of the executive branch over the legislative and judicial branches. There was also significant debate about the legality of the slave trade.

It is essential to reflect on these debates because they reveal the cautious approach of the Congress and the diverse philosophical currents that underpinned the American Revolution. Ultimately, the argument for independence prevailed, branding King George a tyrant and asserting colonial sovereignty. However, the approval of the Declaration of Independence took time and effort. Because of John Adams's, Benjamin Franklin's diplomacy, and the spirit of those who dared to envision a new republic, the obstacles of indecision and internal strife were overcome, one deliberative step at a time.

Following a final revision and a vote for independence, the Declaration of Independence was formally adopted on July 4th, 1776, but not without controversy. Some delegates hesitated, and others withheld their signatures. There was the lingering belief that the rift with Britain could be mended. The final act of signing the Declaration of Independence on August 2nd, 1776, was not merely ceremonial; it symbolized a crossing of the Rubicon into the unsettling yet undeniably exhilarating frontier of nationhood.[48]

The delegates were aware of the risks. The British had shown in the past, notably during the Jacobite rising of 1745, how they would deal with rebels and their families. The delegates signed, knowing they might all hang separately or together.

The Declaration of Independence is a document that has spurred civil rights movements, guided global ideologues, and set the template for national aspirations. Its words have echoed across diverse landscapes, acting as a beacon for the oppressed and a challenge to the status quo.

---

[48] National Geographic. (2024, February 17). Signing of the Declaration of Independence. Retrieved from Education.nationalgeographic.org: https://education.nationalgeographic.org/resource/signing-declaration-independence/.

However, the story of its creation is a tale of ideological clashes and the evolution of political thought. The Declaration of Independence is more than just a piece of paper; it is the collective thoughts of a nation being born, and its legacy continues to guide us.

The Musings of the Stagirite

A sad irony about the Declaration of Independence is that it speaks of liberty, but there were delegates of the Second Continental Congress who were slaveholders. There appears to be a conflict between beliefs that advocate freedom but consider bondage acceptable.

We know that the Founding Fathers were influenced by Locke's and Rousseau's writings on liberty. Still, there was another philosopher, considered one of the greatest, whose opinions were held in high esteem and whose thoughts were probably considered. His name was Aristotle.

Aristotle's teachings laid the foundation for many disciplines and had a significant impact on the understanding of polis or the city-state and its governance. Aristotle defends the idea of slavery in his work, *Politics*.[49]

For Aristotle, slavery (*doulos* in Greek) was a natural institution. He believed that some individuals were "slaves by nature," attributing this status to those who lacked the ability to reason and govern themselves. In his view, the polis was the highest form of community, with governance reflecting familial dynamics. A master's rule over his slave mimics a ruler's dominion over his subjects. To Aristotle, a just polis would entail a just relationship between masters and those who were slaves. He further believed that slavery was a natural condition and that there were those who were born as natural slaves, likening them to "living tools" or domestic animals. He was not alone in his musings. Plato thought that those who were better had the right to rule over the inferior.

Aristotle's influence on the American Revolution might not have been dominant, but his writings are part of the Western canon. Even though people like Thomas Jefferson, who proclaimed that "all men are created equal," were influenced by Enlightenment thought, they were also products of an environment steeped in the Aristotelian tradition.[50]

---

[49] UKessays.com. (2024, February 17). Aristotle's Views on Slavery. Retrieved from UKessays.com: https://www.ukessays.com/essays/politics/slavery.php.
[50] BBC.com. (2024, February 17). Philosophers Justifying Slavery. Retrieved from Ethics guide: https://www.bbc.co.uk/ethics/slavery/ethics/philosophers_1.shtml.

Attacking North

The invasion of Canada did not happen in isolation, and it was not a spontaneous event. It was part of a strategy that would spread the American Revolutionary War beyond the borders of the Thirteen Colonies. The Province of Quebec was a British stronghold, and the Continental Army believed that by seizing Canada, they could safeguard the northern flank of the colonies and persuade their northern neighbors to join the fight against the British. Success would require the British to spread their armed forces and limit military action against the Thirteen Colonies.

The offensive began in September 1775. Major General Richard Montgomery launched the campaign from Fort Ticonderoga with approximately 1,700 men (the American force would eventually grow to more than 10,000 soldiers). Meanwhile, Benedict Arnold led 1,100 Continental troops from Massachusetts through the state of Maine. Montgomery marched toward Montreal, and Arnold headed toward Quebec City. The overall plan was ambitious: enter Quebec, convince Canadians to support the revolution, and neutralize British influence in the region.

Early Success

In November, Montgomery successfully reached Fort St. Jean, located outside Montreal. This achievement convinced Sir Guy Carleton, the royal governor, to retreat to Quebec, leading to the evacuation of Montreal. The Americans took control of Montreal on November 28th. Meanwhile, Benedict Arnold had made his way through the forests of Maine and had arrived outside Quebec. In December, Montgomery joined Arnold, who then passed his command to the senior officer.

The Americans assaulted Quebec's fortifications on December 31st during a snowstorm but were eventually pushed back. General Montgomery was killed in the attack. Benedict Arnold tried to continue the siege, but in the spring, British reinforcements under General John Burgoyne arrived. The Americans finally left Montreal on May 9th, 1776, and eventually made it back to New York. The dream of a fourteenth colony with Canada joining the fight for independence from British rule faded into the background. The Continental Army refocused its efforts on battles to the south.[51]

---

[51] Sprague, D. (2023, January 24). American Revolution and Canada. Retrieved from

The Death of General Montgomery in the Attack on Quebec, December 31, 1775, by John Trumbull.

https://en.wikipedia.org/wiki/File:The_Death_of_General_Montgomery_in_the_Attack_on_Quebec_December_31_1775.jpeg

While the invasion did not succeed in its ultimate goals, it still played a significant part in the broader theatrics of the American Revolutionary War. It highlighted the tactical and logistical challenges of wartime operations and exemplified the unpredictability of alliances and colonial relationships.

For Americans, it highlighted the limitations of their military might and the necessity for strategic diplomacy. For Canadians, it fostered a sense of unity and reinforced their allegiance to the British Crown, a sentiment that would shape Canada's national identity for years to come.

The British Have Come

The Continental Army returned from the Canadian fiasco but had little time to lick its wounds. An event of devastating proportions was about to happen in New York City. The British returned, and they came in full force. The British invasion of New York in 1776 stands as a pivotal moment in the American Revolutionary War, marking both an escalation in the young conflict and a crucial test for the Continental Army under General George Washington.

Thecanadianencyclopedia.ca: https://www.thecanadianencyclopedia.ca/en/article/american-revolution.

The British invasion of New York was born out of strategic necessity. With New York's harbors offering strategic naval advantages and the city serving as a nexus of commerce and communication, the British command recognized the immense value of controlling it. Control over New York would sever the line of communication between the northern and southern colonies, thus hindering the unity and effectiveness of the colonial resistance.

It was an 18th-century exercise in shock and awe. On June 29th, 1776, witnesses reported seeing hundreds of British ships crowding the horizon, a stark premonition of the vast military force that sought to crush the burgeoning rebellion. The fleet itself consisted of hundreds of ships, among them warships that far outclassed any naval firepower held by the Continental forces. The army component of the invasion was somewhere between thirty thousand and forty-five thousand troops, including Hessian mercenaries hired from the German states.

The high command was a family affair. Sir William Howe returned as the army commander, no doubt anxious to make up for his embarrassment at Boston. The impressive British armada was captained by his brother, Admiral Richard Howe, who was not only a seasoned naval commander but also an appointed peace commissioner by the Crown. He had a dual mandate to both quell the rebellion and negotiate with its leaders.

It would take some time for the massive force to gather, but the British were not worried about an attack from an American fleet. Admiral Howe's fleet arrived at Staten Island on July 12th and began to unload troops and supplies. Another British fleet showed up on August 12th, and a third arrived on August 15th. The British eventually had thirty-two thousand soldiers and ten thousand sailors on Staten Island. This was the largest amphibious assault in European history up to that time.[52]

The American Defense

General George Washington was not caught unawares. Anticipating the move, he had already begun fortifying defenses around New York City, particularly on Brooklyn Heights, which offered a commanding position over the East River. Washington's strategy hinged on the defense of strategic points like Fort Washington on Manhattan Island

[52] Revolutionary-war-and-beyond.com. (2024, February 24). Admiral Howe's Fleet Arrives at Staten Island. Retrieved from Revolutionary-war-and-beyond.com: https://www.revolutionary-war-and-beyond.com/admiral-howes-fleet-arrives-staten-island.html.

and Fort Lee across the river in New Jersey. However, Washington's defensive resources were considerably stretched, and his forces lacked the experience of their British counterparts.

There were also lingering doubts about the loyalties of the city's inhabitants, many of whom were divided in their sentiments toward the patriot cause. Washington was confronted with the possibility of a group supplying intelligence to the Howe brothers.

The Battle of Long Island

Howe wasted no time in preparing his troops for battle against the Continental Army. The two armies faced each other on August 22nd, 1776, in what is known as the Battle of Long Island or the Battle of Brooklyn. The British army had a significant advantage in men and naval power, with approximately twenty thousand well-trained and equipped soldiers supported by a powerful fleet. In contrast, the American forces comprised roughly ten thousand soldiers from the Continental Army and local militias with varying levels of experience and equipment. Washington's troops were spread thin across defensive positions in Brooklyn and Manhattan.

The British executed a well-planned attack, circumventing American fortifications by marching through the Jamaica Pass to attack the Continental Army from the rear, which caught the Americans off-guard. Fierce fighting ensued, particularly around Gowanus Road and Guan Heights. Despite brave resistance, the American forces were outmaneuvered and in danger of being encircled. As casualties mounted, the situation grew dire.

The battle culminated in a decisive British victory. While the exact number of casualties remains debated, estimates suggest that the Americans suffered significant losses, with hundreds killed and up to a thousand captured. The British, while victorious, incurred lighter casualties.

However, the Continental Army was not destroyed. In the face of overwhelming odds, General Washington's leadership shone through. Under cover of darkness and with the aid of some lucky fog, he ordered a strategic retreat. The evacuation across the East River to Manhattan was executed with such secrecy and efficiency that it preserved the core of the Continental Army. It would live to fight another day.[53]

---

[53] Mark, H. W. (2024, January 25). Battle of Long Island. Retrieved from Worldhistory.com:

The Fight for Manhattan

After the Continental Army's evacuation from Long Island, General Washington knew Manhattan would be the next target for the British forces. The Continental Army fortified positions on the island, yet Washington was apprehensive about the defense of the city due to its geographical vulnerabilities.

There was still some hope for a peaceful resolution. Notably, during this period, a peace conference was held on September 11th, 1776, with the Staten Island Peace Conference. However, these attempts failed, as the American delegates, including Benjamin Franklin and John Adams, rejected the British demand for unconditional loyalty to the British Crown.

With peace negotiations at an impasse, combat became inevitable. The following engagements happened in the following weeks:

- **The Landing at Kip's Bay** (September 15th): A British force commanded by General William Howe landed unopposed, forcing an American retreat.
- **The Harlem Heights Encounter** (September 16th): The Continental Army engaged with British forces in a skirmish that, while minor in scale, boosted the morale of American forces.
- **The Battle of White Plains** (October 28th): This engagement saw Washington's troops holding their lines against a superior force until they withdrew.

The military situation changed dramatically on October 18th when four thousand British troops landed at Pelham to outflank the Continental Army. Washington decided to evacuate Manhattan, but he was persuaded by General Nathanael Greene to keep a garrison at Fort Washington, located at the northern tip of Manhattan. Those remaining troops would prevent the British from following Washington as the Continental Army escaped. Washington agreed and left Colonel Robert Magaw with three thousand men.

The Defense of Fort Washington

Fort Washington was a crucial location due to its position. It had a commanding view of the Hudson River, which allowed it to control the

---

vital waterway alongside its twin fortress, Fort Lee, situated across the river in New Jersey. The Continental Army fought bravely to defend Fort Washington, but it ended in a tragic outcome. The fort was surrounded and overwhelmed by a larger British force that was equipped with artillery. As a result, the fort fell on November 16th, 1776, leading to the capture of nearly three thousand American troops. However, although unsuccessful, the tenacious defense by the colonial forces demonstrated that they would not surrender easily, defying British expectations of a quick end to the rebellion.

The British now had complete control of New York City and would remain there until the end of the war. General William Howe technically won the campaign to take the city, but he made some tactical errors. On Staten Island, Howe missed a critical opportunity to destroy Washington's army before it could solidify its position in Manhattan. Howe's hesitation allowed Washington to evacuate his troops and regroup, a decision that some historians assert prolonged the war.

Once in Manhattan, Howe again demonstrated his cautious nature by not aggressively pursuing the retreating American forces after their defeat at Fort Washington. His failure to capitalize on his victories gave Washington the chance to retreat and fight another day. Howe beat the Continental Army, but he did not destroy it.[54]

Winter Weather

Undoubtedly, the British in New York City must have chuckled about the Declaration of Independence. Their army had been the winner on the battlefield. The Continental Army was in disarray, and its soldiers were running for their lives across New York and New Jersey. The final capitulation of the rebels would happen in a couple of weeks.

Meanwhile, snowy weather was coming, and the British soldiers and officers were settling into their winter quarters and looking forward to a welcome vacation of a few months. There would be parties, balls, dinners, and other festive occasions. There were so many delightful things to occupy the minds of the British generals.

Washington and his ragged band of ruffians were about to spring a surprise on the unsuspecting British.

---

[54] Mark, H. W. (2024, February 1). New York and New Jersey Campaign. Retrieved from Worldhistory.com: https://www.worldhistory.org/article/2364/new-york-and-new-jersey-campaign/.

Chapter 7: The Miracles of Trenton and Saratoga

Major General Charles Cornwallis (First Marquess Cornwallis) was sent in pursuit of the fleeing Continental Army after the Americans left New York City. Claiming that he would catch Washington the way a hunter catches a fox, Cornwallis marched with a column of ten thousand soldiers across the wintery countryside. Thanks to the stubborn resistance of Fort Washington, the Continental Army had a head start. George Washington was able to stay one step ahead of the hounds.

He did this with an army whose ranks were depleted by disease and desertion. Washington knew a pitched battle with the pursuing British would be suicide. The American commander adopted a Fabian strategy: he would keep evading the British until time and circumstances allowed him to fight on better terms. This meant he would continue to retreat until the right moment arrived for him to fight. Others criticized his decision, but it allowed Washington to preserve his forces and position them opportunistically for future engagements.

A few weeks passed, and then an opportunity arose. Washington had the Delaware River between him and the British.

Cornwallis stopped his pursuit and placed his men in winter quarters. It was a military custom practiced by European armies, and the British would not fight unless necessary. Washington knew he could launch a surprise attack, so he went after the Hessians encamped at Trenton, New

Jersey.[55]

Hessian Mercenaries

The Hessians were German soldiers hired by the British as mercenaries. This practice provided various small German states with much-needed funds and military activity for their surplus soldiers. Hessians were predominantly recruited from the Hesse-Kassel state but included individuals from other German principalities. Recruitment into Hessian service was not always voluntary. Many of these soldiers were "spirited away"—a euphemism for involuntary drafting. Their journey across the Atlantic was not just a voyage toward war but also a bitter separation from their homeland.

They were tough, disciplined soldiers with a reputation for ferocious fighting. Striking them was not without serious risk, and they had to be taken by surprise. Washington had that in mind as he prepared to recross the Delaware River in the early hours of December 26th, 1776.

The Crossing

Washington's master plan brewed over weeks, a careful concoction of intelligence gathering, troop management, and the hope that the winter weather could keep his strategy veiled from the overly confident British.

The Americans secured all available watercraft on the Delaware River. These included Durham cargo boats, which had shallow drafts and were forty to sixty feet long. The Durham boats would ferry across the soldiers while flat-bottomed ferries would bring across the artillery and horses. New Englanders from Marblehead, Massachusetts, provided the labor to row the boats across the Delaware. The crossing commenced the night of December 25th.[56]

Washington led his weary but resolute soldiers in a treacherous crossing. The elements were as much a foe as the British, but the inclement weather also played a hand in Washington's favor. The driving snow and freezing conditions kept the Hessian garrison in Trenton numb with cold and complacent in their security.

---

[55] Mark, H. W. (2024, February 1). New York and New Jersey Campaign. Retrieved from Worldhistory.com: https://www.worldhistory.org/article/2364/new-york-and-new-jersey-campaign/.
[56] Mountvernon.org. (2024, February 21). 10 Facts About Washington's Crossing of the Delaware River. Retrieved from George Washington's Mount Vernon: https://www.mountvernon.org/george-washington/the-revolutionary-war/washingtons-revolutionary-war-battles/the-trenton-princeton-campaign/10-facts-about-washingtons-crossing-of-the-delaware-river/.

The crossing was a tactical marvel. The where, the when, and the how were all perfectly executed. Once across, the Continental Army had to march ten miles to Trenton. They reached Trenton by 8:00 a.m. and advanced in two columns. Fortunately, the Hessians had been carousing the night before. None of them expected to be attacked.

The Hessians never saw it coming. Within ninety minutes, Washington and his men had secured Trenton. Several hundred Hessians escaped, but almost one thousand of the mercenaries were captured. Four Americans were killed in what was a total victory.[57]

Inspired Leadership

The victory was the result of a combination of discipline and professionalism. Washington's move was not just strategic but also tactical. His careful planning included ensuring the discipline of his forces in the aftermath of the battle. It would have been easy for him to lose self-control, but Washington knew that showing restraint and order would amplify the respect for the new American army and their cause. It was a tremendous morale boost, and Washington desperately needed that.

After the Battle of Trenton, Washington addressed the troops whose enlistments would expire on December 31st at the stroke of midnight. Washington begged them to stay at least one more month. His request resulted in two hundred men volunteering to reenlist at that moment.

Princeton

Washington was not finished with the British that winter. He made the strategic decision to press on, aiming to attack and rout a British garrison at nearby Princeton, further unnerving the British forces and solidifying patriot gains. By using bold, deceptive tactics and precisely timing his movements, Washington caught a brigade of British regulars off-guard.

On the morning of January 3rd, 1777, Washington's army, which now numbered over five thousand with reenlistments and new volunteers, faced off against approximately eight thousand British regulars. As the armies met, a dense fog settled over the battlefield, providing cover for Washington's men as they clashed with the British. The engagement was fierce, with both sides fighting tenaciously. Under the command of

---

[57] History.com. (2024, February 21). George Washington Crosses the Delaware. Retrieved from History.com: https://www.history.com/this-day-in-history/washington-crosses-the-delaware.

Generals Hugh Mercer and John Cadwalader, the Americans managed to blunt assaults by British regulars and Hessian mercenaries.

The turning point came when Washington led a charge against British forces from the rear, a brash and bold move. The British, believing they had the upper hand, were taken by surprise and soon outmaneuvered. They found themselves in a retreat as Washington's troops gained the field.

The American victory at Princeton was a strategic success that vastly outstripped the Continental Army's original objectives. The Continental Army had managed to outmaneuver and outfight the British, an army considered to be the best in the world. The casualties were relatively light, but the impact was immeasurable.[58]

The Aftermath of Victories

The Battles of Trenton and Princeton sent shockwaves through the British and Hessian commands. They were forced to reassess the American forces, recognizing that they were not simply rebels but a cunning and determined adversary. These shocks rippled through the British grand strategy, impacting their tactics and the overconfidence that had plagued them in the early stages of the war. The British decision to hunker down in New York after their defeats rather than pursue further conflicts demonstrated the resounding impact these battles had on the revolution's broader dynamics.

The morale within the Continental Army, once on the cusp of collapse, now surged with life. The news of the victory resonated throughout the Thirteen Colonies, attracting additional volunteers to the Continental Army.

The ripple effect of these two victories was felt in the hearts and minds of the American people, forging a determination to see the war through to its conclusion. Trenton and Princeton were not just military victories; they were triumphs of the underdog, a validation of the American cause, and a turning point in the conflict.

Trenton and Princeton embodied the spirit of the American Revolution–the tenacity to fight for one's beliefs, to innovate in the face of overwhelming odds, and to seize opportunities where none seemingly exist. The lessons of flexibility, audacity, and strategic vision that emerged

---

[58] Rosenfield, R. (2024, February 21). Princeton. Retrieved from Battlefields.org: https://www.battlefields.org/learn/articles/princeton.

from these two engagements serve as inspirations for generations of American leaders and military tacticians.

There was more to come in the new year. The year 1777 was the scene of the most decisive battle of the American Revolution.

Gentleman Johnny's Strategy

John Burgoyne was an aristocrat stuck in the American backwoods. He was more familiar with the corridors of power back in London than the wilds of the North American continent. Famous for his wit and charm, Burgoyne was a frequent figure in the social circles of England. He was equally at home composing plays as he was plotting campaigns.

In 1777, Burgoyne was placed in command of a scheme that, if successful, would split the new American nation.

A portrait of John Burgoyne.
https://commons.wikimedia.org/wiki/File:BurgoyneByReynolds.jpg

Saratoga Campaign

It was an innovative idea. Burgoyne's strategy was to divide the rebel colonies and isolate New England geographically. His campaign was bold—advance south from Canada, link forces with British troops in New York City, and split the colonies in half.

The plan looked great on paper. Burgoyne proposed a three-pronged pincer move, expecting support from British forces moving northward and up the Hudson River from New York City. His immediate goal was to capture Albany, a key colonial city, and secure a portion of upstate New York, which was known for its divisiveness and potential loyalist support.

The campaign had several key goals:

- Securing the allegiance of Native American tribes.
- Ensuring supply lines to British-controlled North America.
- Leveraging Canadian loyalists to form a substantial fighting force.

The Hudson Valley was an appealing route. Control of the Hudson River meant control of a vital artery for the movement of arms and supplies, as well as a means to effectively divide and manage the colonies, which was a desired goal of British military planners.

For Burgoyne, the Hudson represented the promised land, replete with the spoils of war and the glory of conquest. Gentleman Johnny, as he was known, forgot some key elements, though. In pursuing his goals, he failed to fully comprehend the difficulties of the terrain and the determination of the colonial forces defending it.

<u>An Elaborate Pincer Move</u>

The Saratoga Campaign had three movements coming from separate starting points. General Burgoyne commanded the northern pincer and was the central assault force. Burgoyne commanded a force of approximately eight thousand soldiers, some freshly transported from England, others drawn from those already stationed in North America. Burgoyne's army started south in June 1777. Its first objective was Fort Ticonderoga.

The western pincer was under the command of Lieutenant Colonel Matthew "Barry" St. Leger. His 1,600 troops were a mix of British regulars, Hessians, Native Americans, Canadians, and loyalists. St. Leger would move through the Mohawk Valley from Lake Ontario and act as a diversion before joining with Burgoyne in Albany. A force from the south under General William Howe would advance from New York City to meet Burgoyne in Albany. Everything looked great on paper, but things gradually fell apart.[59]

[59] Bill, R. (2021, August 4). The Northern Campaign of 1777. Retrieved from Nps.gov: https://www.nps.gov/fost/blogs/the-northern-campaign-of-1777.htm.

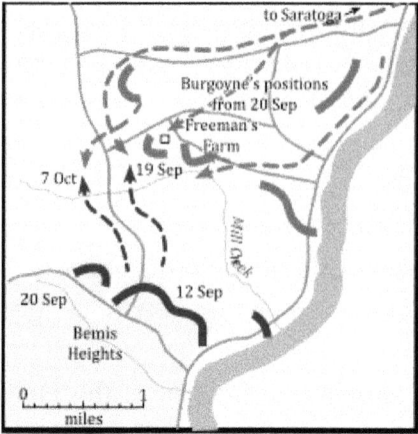

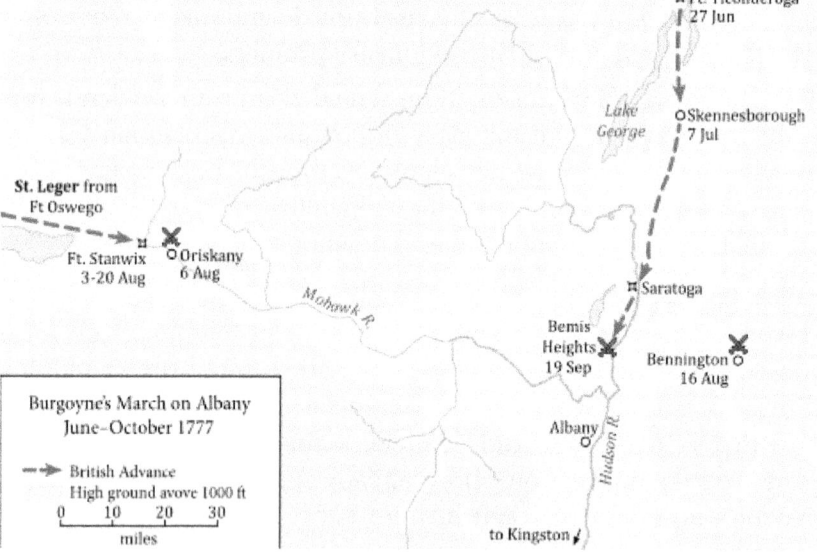

Burgoyne's march on Albany.

Logistical Problems

Burgoyne quickly captured Fort Ticonderoga, and his troops were steadily moving south in August. St. Leger besieged Fort Stanwix. Everything looked promising. That is about the time when things started to go wrong.

Burgoyne assumed a much larger populace of loyalists on the path from Ticonderoga to Albany, a mistake that led to insufficient intelligence about enemy dispositions and support. He expected a wave of support from local loyalists that never materialized, depriving him of crucial local knowledge and aid. Burgoyne's progress required extensive supply lines over rugged terrain, and logistics were not given the same attention as the grand strategic strokes of his campaign.

In the 18th century, the Hudson Valley was a rugged, inhospitable landscape dotted with thick forests, swamps, and treacherous mountains. The lack of infrastructure and the terrain's intimidating nature magnified the campaign's challenges. The British logistical system was designed for European warfare, where supply was less of an issue. In the American wilderness, however, the system struggled to keep pace, leading to shortages of food and ammunition. Wagons and draught animals, vital for mobility and life support, were lost at a worrying rate to the harsh conditions and enemy attacks.

Burgoyne's supply lines from Canada were tenuous at best, and his army was forced to rely heavily on foraging and requisitioning local provisions. This approach alienated the local population, sapped the army's strength, and made deterring Native American scalping parties a pressing concern. As Burgoyne's forces moved farther from their base, they became increasingly isolated and vulnerable. The worst challenge the flamboyant British commander faced was an opponent who refused to back down from British military might.

The American Resistance

The Americans did not follow a European plan. They learned from the Native Americans about how to use the land to their advantage. As the British moved south, the Americans put a strategy of attrition to work. They destroyed crops, burned bridges, and harassed the British flanks. This constant pressure disrupted the supply chain and sowed seeds of discontent among British soldiers already enduring exhausting conditions.

Marauding bands led by statesmen and soldiers like Seth Warner and John Stark encapsulated the spirit of defiance. Utilizing their intimate knowledge of the local terrain, they engaged in hit-and-run tactics, keeping the British on their toes and creating a sense of insecurity within their ranks.

There were instances where the Americans stood and fought. The Battle of Hubbardton pitted the Continental troops against British forces. The Americans were tactically outmaneuvered but managed a successful withdrawal. The British suffered a delayed advance and significant casualties.

American Commanders

The Continental Army was led by highly competent commanders who guided their troops with skill and ingenuity during this campaign.

General Philip Schuyler was the original commander tasked with fortifying the Hudson River against the British. A respected leader both on the battlefield and in the political arena, Schuyler's character was marked by his unyielding commitment to the cause of American independence. His leadership was characterized by a deep sense of duty and an unwavering dedication to safeguarding the principles of the revolution. Horatio Gates replaced him.

A portrait of Horatio Gates.

A veteran of the British army before joining the Continental Army, General Horatio Gates's command style was marked by meticulous planning and caution. His character was the exact opposite of Benedict Arnold, his mercurial subordinate. Benedict Arnold's primary role was assembling the forces to halt Burgoyne's advance. Though ultimately controversial, Arnold's unorthodox tactics and sheer audacity demonstrated the value of thinking outside the conventional military playbook.

The American commanders' ability to be adaptable and creative in their approach contributed significantly to the efforts made to frustrate the British.

The Demise of St. Leger

The first sign that the Saratoga Campaign would be a British failure was at Fort Stanwix. St. Leger began the siege on August 2nd, but contrary to expectations, the garrison refused to surrender and stubbornly resisted. St. Leger received false information that Benedict Arnold was coming with three thousand men to relieve the fort (Arnold only had seven hundred men with him). St. Leger believed the report and, on August 22nd, abandoned the siege of Fort Stanwix. That permitted the Americans to concentrate more on destroying Burgoyne's advance.

The Advance to Disaster

Burgoyne's column continued to push through the natural obstacles and enemy attacks. The British endured a defeat at the Battle of Bennington on August 16th but were still moving south toward Albany. General Gates moved north on September 7th to oppose the British and created fortifications at Bemis Heights.

General Howe's Choice

William Howe was an intriguing figure. There were times when his tactical prowess achieved great success, such as the Battle of Long Island, but there were times when his cautious behavior created serious problems. A decision he made during the Saratoga Campaign would effectively doom John Burgoyne. Howe chose to launch a major assault against Philadelphia. He advised Burgoyne of this decision on July 17th in a secret dispatch. Howe's decision isolated Burgoyne, but the latter pressed on in hopes of still making it to Albany. That forward progress was stopped fifty miles away from New York's future capital.[60]

Saratoga, The Final Act

Burgoyne's army was demoralized, but it was still a professional fighting force. He had lost most of his Native American allies and had almost no field intelligence to work with. The Americans were blocking the road, and Burgoyne had no alternative but to engage his enemy and

---

[60] Howe, W. (2024, February 1). William Howe Goes His Own Way. Retrieved from Clements.umoich.edu: https://clements.umich.edu/exhibit/spy-letters-of-the-american-revolution/stories-of-spies/howe-goes-his-own-way/

hope for the best.

The Battles of Saratoga represent a poignant chapter in the story of the United States. The Saratoga region of New York was a formidable battleground. The densely forested area, broken by occasional clearings and twisting waterways, presented challenges and opportunities for both sides. Control of terrain and the high ground, in particular, would prove vital to the outcome of the conflict.

The first encounter was at Freeman's Farm on September 19th. As the British attempted to flank the American positions, an engagement ensued. The two armies clashed with ferocity, each side exchanging volleys and bayonets. It was technically a British victory, but the Americans were able to stop the British advance. The next battle would be the decisive one.[61]

Bemis Heights

The terrain at Bemis Heights was rugged, a challenge that the American forces under General Horatio Gates and his subordinate, General Benedict Arnold, would use to their advantage. What happened at Bemis Heights was a lesson in strategic warfare that saw the Americans use the landscape and innovative tactics to secure a critical victory.

The British, led by the resolute but increasingly embattled Burgoyne, sought to break through the American lines with a direct assault up the slopes of Bemis Heights. The heart of the American defense was a redoubt known as Balcarres Redoubt, a strategic strongpoint that would bear the brunt of the British assaults. As the redcoats charged the heavily fortified position, they were met with firepower that all but broke their resolve. The tactical maneuvers on both sides, including feints and envelopments, ultimately swung the advantage in favor of the Americans. General Simon Fraser, Burgoyne's best field officer, was killed by American sharpshooters. Throughout the battle, General Benedict Arnold emerged as a catalyst for the American cause, his brilliant leadership and personal courage inspiring his troops to superlative feats of arms.

The outcome of the Battle of Bemis Heights was the strategic withdrawal of General Burgoyne's forces to Saratoga, where they found

[61] Maloy, M. (2024, February 21). The Battle of Freeman's Farm: September 19, 1777. Retrieved from Battlefields.org: https://www.battlefields.org/learn/articles/battle-freemans-farm-september-19-1777.

themselves surrounded. Burgoyne knew the fight was over. After several days of negotiations, General Burgoyne surrendered on October 17th. His army of over six thousand men and forty-two artillery pieces were placed in American custody. The campaign effectively ended Burgoyne's military career and cast a long shadow over his reputation.

The surrender at Saratoga was a devastating blow to British morale and a turning point in the war. It convinced France to formally enter the conflict on the side of the Americans, a decision that would have profound implications for the war's outcome. America was about to gain some valuable allies.

Chapter 8: Allies and Adversaries

The story of France and the American Revolution is filled with political maneuvering, strategic alliances, and the hope for a new world order. From initial covert assistance to a full-fledged partnership, the journey France undertook to support the fledgling United States was fraught with risks and had some benefits for both countries.

France watched the growing conflict with a mix of interest and caution. The causes of the American rebellion echoed the burgeoning calls for reform and revolution in France. Yet, initial French involvement was minimal, mainly consisting of covert aid in the form of munitions and funds provided by private citizens, most notably from the Marquis de Lafayette and the polymathic researcher Pierre Beaumarchais.

<u>Brothers to the Rebels</u>

The Marquis de Lafayette is a central figure in the early relationship between France and the United States. Driven by his own ambitions for military glory and a genuine belief in the American cause, Lafayette's private lobbying of French leaders became instrumental in securing French support.

Beaumarchais, a skilled political operative who counted playwriting and inventing among his many talents, orchestrated clandestine arms deals that funneled French support to American revolutionaries. His most significant scheme, conducted under the Comte de Vergennes, involved the creation of a fictitious company, Roderigue Hortalez and Company, which provided the colonies with the crucial resources they needed to sustain their war effort. Yet, despite these individual efforts, the French government maintained an official stance of neutrality; it was wary of provoking its perennial adversary, Great Britain.

The Marquis de Lafayette wearing the uniform of an American general.

The Efforts of Ben Franklin

The victory at Saratoga transformed French hesitancy into a resounding yes to send aid. The American delegation, led by Benjamin Franklin, managed to secure the Treaty of Alliance with France in 1778. As a seasoned diplomat, Franklin's negotiations were instrumental in securing French support. His skillful navigation of French politics, such as leveraging the country's own motivations for weakening the British Empire, demonstrated the careful art of diplomatic finesse. The Treaty of Alliance pledged military support and financial and diplomatic backing that would prove vital to the American cause.

Settling a Few Scores

French intervention in the American Revolution was not entirely based on idealism or kind feelings for the Americans. France had a barely concealed agenda.

Few rivalries have been as brooding and long-standing as the Franco-British feud. From the Hundred Years' War to the later Napoleonic Wars, these two mighty nations seemed fated to clash time and time again. Even today, echoes of their rivalry reverberate through international relations.

The 18th century brought about colonial expansion and the rise of the global British Empire, casting a long shadow over France's imperial ambitions. As France sought to reassert its dominance and recoup its losses, it was at odds with the burgeoning power across the English Channel.

The American Revolution marked a pivotal moment in the Franco-British feud. For France, the conflict was not solely about supporting the American cause for independence; it was also an opportunity to undermine the British Empire. Unwittingly, the American colonies became a battleground for two of the most formidable military forces of the time. France did not want to weaken Great Britain, but it did want to redress the balance of power in Europe and secure its own interests.

France's entry into the American Revolution was not without its costs. France's internal economic strains from decades of royal excess were exacerbated by financial support for the American Revolution, contributing to the economic crisis that ultimately led to the overthrow of King Louis XVI and the fall of the ancien régime. It also created an alliance between France and the United States that continues to this day.[62]

Spanish Involvement

While France's contribution to the United States' struggle for independence is well documented, it is equally important to recognize the support of other allies. Spain's role tends to be overshadowed, cloaked in the shadows of the more glory-laden French alliance. However, Spain's assistance to America was pivotal, if indirect.

Spain was a major colonial power with vast territories in the Americas, including the Caribbean, Louisiana, and Florida, and possessed strategic interests in North America. Internationally, Spain was recovering from economic woes and was intent on regaining its footing as a formidable global empire.

---

[62] McGee, S. (2023, August 25). 5 Ways the French Helped Win the American Revolution. Retrieved from History.com: https://www.history.com/news/american-revolution-french-role-help.

Spain initially maintained a stance of neutrality in the conflict between the American colonies and Great Britain, but as the war progressed, it saw an opportunity to weaken its old adversary. Under the leadership of King Charles III, Spain secretly but systematically supported the American forces, sending arms, ammunition, and financial aid. Furthermore, Spain's diplomats, such as Diego de Gardoqui, were instrumental in forging an alliance to guarantee Spanish assistance to the revolutionaries. This diplomatic coup fortified the Second Continental Congress's resolve and maneuvered Spain into a more influential position on the world stage.

Under Admiral Luis de Córdova y Córdova, the Spanish fleet played a pivotal role in critical naval engagements supporting the American cause. Spanish troops, led by Bernardo de Gálvez, undertook successful military campaigns against the British, securing important victories in the Gulf Coast and the Mississippi Valley. Gálvez's efforts were noteworthy, as his forces helped ward off British advances and facilitated coordination between Spanish, French, and American troops.

The post-war negotiations bore the fruit of Spain's calculated support for the American colonies during the war. The Treaty of Paris, signed in 1783, secured territorial gains for Spain, including control over Florida and the Mississippi River, which opened up new opportunities for Spanish expansion in North America. This was a defining moment for Spain, marking both a diplomatic triumph and an expansion of its imperial reach.[63]

The Dutch Presence

There is an unsung hero in the tale of American revolutionary support: the Netherlands, or the Dutch Republic as it was known in the 18th century. This maritime nation played a little-known but crucial role in the American War of Independence.

In the 1770s, the Dutch Republic was a fading titan in European power politics. Its navy had once been the envy of the world, and its trade, especially with its vast East India and West India companies, had made its merchants astoundingly wealthy. However, by the time of the American Revolution, the Dutch Republic was navigating treacherous diplomatic waters. It was a relatively small, strategically located nation

---

[63] Museum of the American Revolution. (2024, February 18). Spain and the American Revolution. Retrieved from Amrevmuseum.org: https://www.amrevmuseum.org/spain-and-the-american-revolution.

surrounded by larger, more aggressive powers.

The Dutch had historic ties with America since the days of the New Amsterdam colony (modern-day New York). When the American colonies rebelled against British rule, the Dutch found themselves in a difficult position. Their economy benefited from trade with the British, and they were wary of provoking a conflict that their military might be ill-prepared for. Yet, there was a potent undercurrent of Dutch sympathizers who saw America's struggle echo their own fight for independence from Spain in the 16ᵗʰ century.

The Dutch Republic excelled in financing wars, something it had done for centuries with the strategic use of bonds and loans. When the American colonies sought financial backing for their war effort, they turned to the Dutch and found willing lenders. The Dutch financiers saw a potentially profitable investment in the colonies with potentially high returns if America emerged successful.[64]

While officially neutral, Dutch merchants proved critical in smuggling goods to American revolutionaries. The port city of Amsterdam, in particular, became a hotspot for a variety of contraband, from weapons to tobacco. Dutch officials were often complicit, as were those in other European nations who had a vested interest in the success of the American rebels. The Dutch Republic's quiet support for America's quest for freedom illustrates how the actions of even the most minor players can have an impact.

British International Arrogance

British diplomacy during the 18ᵗʰ century was a delicate web of alliances and betrayals. The heart of the matter lay in the simmering dissatisfaction among the French, Spanish, and Dutch elite against the British Empire and its ambitions to redraw colonial boundaries. Armed with a powerful navy and burgeoning imperial reach, Great Britain often wielded a domineering hand.

Historians speculate why Great Britain's diplomacy became a mixture of arrogance and hubris. Some suggest that British actions resulted from overconfidence and a belief in its invincibility. This viewpoint suggests that neglecting to engage with potential allies diplomatically and underestimating the resolve of colonial dissent was born from hubris.

[64] Jstor.org. (2024, February 18). Foreign Intervention ... in the American Revolution. Retrieved from Jstor.org: https://daily.jstor.org/intervention-american-revolution/.

Other scholars argue that Britain's aggressive stance was a calculated risk, part of a larger realpolitik strategy to quash potential rivals and consolidate power within key colonial holdings. Whatever the reasons, Great Britain cooked a stew of international resentment it was ultimately forced to eat.

The American allies required Great Britain to fight a war it did not want. The French alliance, forged in the crucible of mutual contempt for British domination, resulted in crucial military support for the American forces. With Spain's entry into the conflict, the theater of war expanded to the Mediterranean and the Spanish Main (the parts of the Spanish Empire in the Americas). The Dutch Republic's financial support and its nuanced approach to sustaining the American cause meant that Great Britain faced not just a military juggernaut but also a formidable financial adversary. Matters got progressively worse.

The Native Americans

In studies of the American Revolution, something that often escapes the limelight is the involvement of various Native American tribes. Their allegiances and actions paint complex patterns that influenced the trajectory of this historic conflict.

The indigenous landscape was a checkerboard of allegiances. The Oneida and Tuscarora stood with the fledgling United States, while the Mohawk, Seneca, Cayuga, and Onondaga sided with the British. Likewise, the Muscogee Nation and the Cherokee sided with the British, aiming to check American expansion into their lands.

British promises of honoring native land claims and preserving their way of life were not just rhetoric. Proclamations and treaties sought to secure Native American loyalty with perceived guarantees, although these promises often went unfulfilled. The line between genuine support and strategic manipulation by the British was thin, with Native Americans bearing the brunt of a revolution not of their making.

The Indian Confederacy, a union of various Native American nations, proved to be a malleable yet formidable supplement to British military efforts. Envisioned by British Superintendent of Indian Affairs Sir Guy Johnson and Mohawk leader Joseph Brant, the coalition was a shrewd diplomatic move that sidestepped the burgeoning movement for native sovereignty by leveraging inter-tribal tensions.

The alliance presented an opportunity for both parties. The British, by and large, saw in the confederacy a disruptive force to American expansion and a dependable military ally. For the Native Americans, it was a buffer against encroachment on their lands and a chance to reclaim territories and rights.[65]

Fracturing the Iroquois Nation

Once a powerful and unified confederacy, the American Revolution brought fissures within the Iroquois. Thayendanegea, also known as Joseph Brant, saw an opportune moment to harness British strength to help the Iroquois, leading many of his people to fight for the Crown. His sister, Molly Brant, worked parallel channels, securing Mohawk aid for the British cause.

As a statesman, warrior, and visionary, Brant was a formidable figure. He led devastating raids against American settlements, with his guerilla tactics earning him the moniker "Monster Brant" in American folklore. Brant was not without his detractors within the Mohawk community, and his decision to side with the British left a lingering legacy of resentment and displacement. He was a man of ambition, intent on securing the Mohawks' future in an ever-changing world.

The decision to side with the Americans was strategic and ideological for the Oneida and the Tuscarora. Led by Han Yerry, known as the Cherry Valley leader, these two tribes remained steadfast in their support.

The resulting split within the Iroquois Confederacy was more than just a rift; it was a fracture that would leave lasting scars, as brother fought brother in a bitter civil war.

Cherry Valley Massacre

The Cherry Valley massacre stands as an unforgettable testament to the confluence of agendas that converged to fuel the revolutionary era. Occurring on November 11th, 1778, in a small settlement in New York, the onslaught orchestrated by loyalist and indigenous forces sent shockwaves through the colonies.

The attack was a strategic endeavor to disrupt American expansion and cast doubt on the allure of independence. The brutality of the assault—a storm of flames and bullets that consumed the lives of patriots and civilians alike—served as a linchpin for the British strategy that saw in

---

[65] Makos, I. (2021, April 13). Roles of Native Americans during the American Revolution. Retrieved from Battlefields.org: https://www.battlefields.org/learn/articles/roles-native-americans-during-revolution.

the Native Americans a potent weapon to counter the nascent Republic.

A campaign of retribution led by Generals James Clinton and John Sullivan followed. The mission was two-fold: to quench the Native American resistance and to displace them from lands they perceived as strategic barriers to American westward expansion.

The Clinton-Sullivan campaign, which commenced in 1779, sowed the seeds of a bitter harvest. As the American forces carved a path of destruction through the heart of Iroquois territory, they executed a scorched earth policy, decimating villages, crops, and resources vital for the sustenance and economic viability of the Native American nations. The campaign, therefore, was not simply a military expedition but also an act of aggression. The deliberate destruction of homesteads fractured social structures and uprooted the fabric of daily life. The Clinton-Sullivan campaign was a disaster from which the Iroquois Confederacy never fully recovered.[66]

The Tory Fifth Column

While battles were raging in the countryside, a civil war was waged within America that pitted the patriots, supporters of the evolution, against the Tories, supporters of the British Crown.

Tories, also known as loyalists, were American colonists loyal to the British monarchy during the revolutionary era. Their numbers, and therefore their impact, were significant. It is estimated that between 15 and 20 percent of the white population identified as loyalists—a substantial portion of colonial society. They included many prominent figures like the Anglican Church clergy and wealthy merchants with ties to Britain. Crown supporters included notable people, such as William Franklin, the royal governor of New Jersey and Benjamin Franklin's son. Their motivations ranged from a sense of patriotism for Britain to a fear of the unknown surrounding the patriot cause.

Tory numbers varied across the Thirteen Colonies, but they were mainly concentrated in the Middle Colonies, especially New York and Pennsylvania, which accounted for nearly half of the population. Other areas with large loyalist populations included the southern backcountry and coastal cities, such as Charleston and Wilmington.

---

[66] National Park Service. (2024, February 18). The Clinton-Sullivan Campaign of 1779. Retrieved from Nps.gov: https://www.nps.gov/articles/000/the-clinton-sullivan-campaign-of-1779.htm.

Their allegiance to Britain was more than a simple proclamation; it also resulted in active service in British military units against the patriots, passive resistance, and outright sabotage of the revolution's cause. Tories were involved in some of the most infamous acts of the war, including the hanging of patriot prisoners, acting as guides for British forces during campaigns, and, in some cases, participating in atrocities, such as the Cherry Valley massacre, which saw the slaughter and displacement of patriot families.

Many Tories could not envision a world order without the British Empire at its center, believing firmly in the monarchy system. Some saw the rebellion as an affront to the social order and a step toward anarchy. Others feared the economic ramifications of severing ties with the British trade network.

For many loyalists who had built lives and identities rooted in their devotion to Great Britain, the prospect of an independent America threatened their sense of self and stability. They foresaw the complexities of creating a new government and were distrustful or skeptical of the promises and capabilities of the patriot leadership. Moreover, loyalists contended with the personal implications of losing their status, relationships, and livelihoods should the Crown fail to maintain control. Their resistance to independence was not born solely out of loyalty to the monarchy but also from a place of deep concern for the future of their families.

The loyalists were the subject of reprisals by the patriots, leading to a vicious cycle of violence and retribution that afflicted civilians on both sides of the conflict. These acts of violence against loyalists were part of a deliberate campaign to intimidate them from supporting the British.

African American Tories

The narrative of African Americans' involvement in this pivotal era often takes a backseat in historical accounts. Most are familiar with the story of Crispus Attucks and his role in the Boston Massacre.[67] What is less commonly shared but just as profound in its impact is the tale of the African American Tories. They were as much a part of the conflict as those who helped the patriots.

---

[67] For those who are not familiar with his story, Attucks was a sailor of mixed African and indigenous ancestry. He is regarded as the first person to die in the Boston Massacre. Some see him as the first American to be killed during the American Revolution.

The Earl of Dunmore's Proclamation of 1775 represented a turning point for enslaved African Americans in the colonies. This controversial document promised freedom to any slave of a patriot who left their master and fought on the side of the British. What is not commonly known is that the earl of Dunmore owned slaves and that any runaways who were owned by loyalists were returned to their masters. The proclamation was not an emancipation but a reasonably successful recruiting scheme.

Approximately twenty thousand African Americans fought for the British in the American Revolution. Fighting units were created from the runaways. The Ethiopian Regiment, also known as Lord Dunmore's Ethiopian Regiment, was comprised of black slaves who joined the British. Other African Americans served in various units of the British army, including the Black Pioneers.

There were more than six hundred African Americans in the British ranks during the siege of Savannah in 1779. Dozens more served in support roles as cooks, guides, and laborers.[68]

It is estimated that five thousand African Americans fought for the patriot cause, notably the 1st Rhode Island Regiment.

It is essential to think about the motives and experiences of those who fought on either side. Patriotism or loyalty to the Crown were probably less important to these soldiers. Personal liberty and the chance to lead a better life would have been their primary motivations.

Saratoga was a turning point in the war, but it didn't mean the conflict would soon end. British command changed hands in 1778, and new British strategies were developed. The most brutal fighting of the American Revolution was in the years ahead.

---

[68] Mobley, C. (2006, September 24). Hundreds of African-Americans Campaigned for the King during 1779 Struggle for Savannah. Retrieved from Savannahnow.com: https://www.savannahnow.com/story/news/2006/09/25/hundreds-african-americans-campaigned-king-during-1779-struggle-savannah/13826035007/.

Chapter 9: Trying Times

John Burgoyne accused William Howe of sabotaging the Saratoga Campaign by not moving aggressively north to Albany. There might have been some personal animosity between the two, but Howe had a bigger prize in mind that, if won, would eclipse any success of Burgoyne.

The prize to be seized was Philadelphia, the rebel capital. Howe would lead an army of eighteen thousand men up the Chesapeake Bay, outflanking General George Washington's force that was in the rebel capital. Howe's capture of Philadelphia could be the masterstroke that would end the revolt. If Burgoyne successfully took Albany, that would be the icing on Howe's cake.

General Howe began his southern drive from New York City in late June. With an army of eighteen thousand men, Howe decided against a direct assault on Washington's entrenched forces and launched a maritime campaign to capture Philadelphia instead. His first objective was to navigate around Washington's army and cross New Jersey to reach the head of the Chesapeake Bay.

Washington's Preparations

George Washington was not idle; he was preparing for the arrival of the British. However, military preparations in the face of Howe's impending campaign were an immense task. Washington, whose army was still a fledgling force compared to the seasoned redcoats, sought to gather his troops and augment their numbers. Washington's meticulous preparation involved amassing men and morale; he was aware that the strength of his army lay not just in numbers but also in the tenacity and spirit of its individuals.

One of the most storied aspects of Washington's preparations was the fortification of the Delaware River, a strategic bulwark against Howe's anticipated advance. The construction of Fort Mifflin, a formidable structure on the river's edge, and the lesser-known works at Red Bank provide a glimpse into the labor-intensive enterprise aimed at stalling the British onslaught.

Engagement at Brandywine

Howe deftly employed flanking maneuvers, amphibious assaults, and practical subterfuge to outwit Washington's less disciplined troops. The rolling hills and dense forests provided ample cover for both the attackers and defenders. It also hindered communication and coordination—a dual-edged sword that would cut both ways.

The British advance was methodical, but it was contested. American resistance, guerrilla tactics, and a strategic decision not to engage in pitched battles unduly stretched the British supply lines and resolve. General Howe's route to Philadelphia might have been sprinkled with tactical victories, but it also bred strategic indecision that foreshadowed future repercussions.

The two armies met at Brandywine Creek on September 11th, 1777, each having fifteen thousand soldiers. Howe ordered General Wilhelm von Knyphausen to demonstrate against the Americans at Chadds Ford to distract them. At the same time, the main British force crossed the creek upstream. Howe's forces appeared on Washington's right flank, and von Knyphausen stuck hard.

The ferocity of the battle was only eclipsed by its scale. British soldiers, whose discipline was sharpened by the empire's many military campaigns, advanced with a precision that cut through the Continental lines. The Americans, with their characteristic bravery, fought fiercely. Washington's line eventually broke, but the Continental Army retreated in good order thanks to the rearguard defense of troops under Nathanael Greene. The road was open to Philadelphia for the British.[69]

In the face of the British advance, Washington faced the daunting prospect of defending a city against an enemy with naval superiority. He had to consider tactical maneuvers and the larger strategic picture. The

---

[69] Battlefields.org. (2024, February 21). Brandywine. Retrieved from Batlefields.org: https://www.battlefields.org/learn/revolutionary-war/battles/brandywine.

American commander decided to evacuate the capital, and the British entered Philadelphia on September 26ᵗʰ, 1777.

Washington's decision to abandon the city did not come lightly. It was a calculated move weighed against the prospect of a protracted and potentially debilitating siege. He was under no illusion about the symbolic and material loss of the colonial capital. His overarching concern was to preserve the Continental Army and, by extension, the revolution itself.

Battle of Germantown

General Howe wanted to capture the American fortifications on the Delaware River. He stationed nine thousand men under Generals James Grant and von Knyphausen in Germantown to protect Philadelphia. Desperate to regain the initiative, Washington gambled and attacked Germantown, hoping to score a success similar to the one gained at Trenton. He divided his forces between General John Sullivan and General Nathanael Greene and attacked the British on October 4ᵗʰ. A combination of the two groups being separated and Sullivan's men running out of ammunition created confusion and an opportunity for the British. The Americans were eventually forced to retreat.[70]

The engagement might have been a strategic loss since it did not impede the British occupation of Philadelphia. However, the significance of Germantown lies in its portrayal of American resolve. It showed that despite setbacks and inexperience, the colonists were willing and able to engage the British forces on their own terms.

Geopolitics Takes Center Stage

The autumn of 1777 should have been a splendid season for General William Howe. His campaign against Washington had been a great success, and the rebel capital was taken. Everything seemed wonderful, but disaster struck on October 17ᵗʰ when General Burgoyne surrendered his army.

The diplomatic fallout of Saratoga was no less severe. The surrender of Burgoyne's army was a significant victory for the American cause, reverberating across the Atlantic and shifting people's opinions in Europe. Most notably, the French, who had been covertly aiding the Americans, now openly sided with their cause, dramatically altering the

---

[70] Battlefields.org. (2024, February 21). Germantown. Retrieved from Battlefields.org: https://www.battlefields.org/learn/revolutionary-war/battles/germantown.

conflict's nature.

Moreover, the French were impressed with the colonists' conduct at Brandywine and Germantown. The Continental Army, though suffering defeats, remained resolute, showing adaptability and a commitment to the fight. Meanwhile, the British forces, though overwhelmingly powerful, struggled to translate that power into gaining a strategic advantage. The Americans were beaten but retreated in good order; they were not a disorganized mob.

Analysis of the Philadelphia Campaign

The failure of the British to deliver a knockout blow in the Philadelphia campaign had consequences that echoed far beyond the battlefield. The British victory did not bring a swift end to the rebellion. Washington's army remained intact and continued to harass Howe's army in a series of hit-and-run skirmishes, demonstrating the tenacity and determination of the American forces. Additionally, the British were now extended deep into hostile territory, which exposed their supply lines to constant attacks from colonial militias.

The inability of the British to maintain control over the newly captured territory left them increasingly isolated in Philadelphia. This isolation, combined with the demonstrated resolve of the American forces, began to sow seeds of doubt among the British leadership about the wisdom of continuing the war.

The decision to march on Philadelphia can be seen as a high-stakes gamble that failed to pay dividends for the British. Although they eventually captured the city, the cost of time and resources was significant. Their failure to fully capitalize on this victory and the subsequent strategic miscalculations that followed set the stage for the ultimate failure of British efforts in the American Revolution.

The Miracle of Valley Forge

The campaigning season ended, and the Continental Army moved to Valley Forge to quarter for the winter. They had been beaten by the British, but the Americans were still a fighting force. The Continental Army entered Valley Forge on December 17th, 1777, with approximately twelve thousand soldiers.

The winter at Valley Forge has since emerged as a potent symbol of endurance, suffering, and, ultimately, triumph in the annals of the American Revolutionary War. Narratives of resilience and sacrifice color this pivotal chapter in American history, as General George Washington and his Continental Army endured a brutal winter of disease, starvation, and harsh living conditions. The conventional tale of Valley Forge conjures images of ragged soldiers, frostbitten feet, and a beleaguered commander in chief grappling with a struggle against the British Empire.

The Continental Army arrived at Valley Forge following several defeats and retreats. The soldiers wore ragged clothing and suffered from widespread hunger. Many did not even have shoes to protect them from the snow. The winter claimed the lives of nearly 2,500 soldiers due to various hardships, but the suffering extended beyond mere physical deprivation.

The army was demoralized, and discipline was waning. The men faced an enemy that had occupied the capital and a hostile winter landscape. Washington's challenge was to keep his men alive, sustain the revolutionary fervor, and command an effective fighting force against the superior British military might come spring. The logistics of supplying and supporting his forces seemed impossible; it was a test of both his leadership and the will to win.

<u>The First Days</u>

The topography of Valley Forge and the harsh winter provided a natural challenge, but a lack of provisions and poor planning exacerbated the situation. Troops were exposed to the elements with inadequate clothing, shelter, and food. Frostbite was widespread, and many went hungry. Disease, particularly smallpox, was rampant in the close quarters of the encampment. It seemed as if the suffering was ceaseless. The very survival of the Continental Army was in question.[71]

---

[71] Keesling, D. K. (2024, February 21). Valley Forge: A Place of Transformation for the Continental Army. Retrieved from Thepursuitofhistory.org: https://thepursuitofhistory.org/2022/10/24/valley-forge-a-place-of-transformation-for-the-continental-army/.

Soldiers' quarters at Valley Forge.

Thomas Paine's *The American Crisis*, a series of pamphlets published throughout the war, provided the intellectual ammunition for the soldiers' morale. His words, "These are the times that try men's souls," served as a clarion call for perseverance and resistance.[72] Paine's works transcended the written page, becoming a rallying cry that resonated within the hearts of every soldier at Valley Forge.

Washington had more to worry about than just his troops' physical distress and morale. His leadership was being seriously questioned.

The Conway Cabal

The problems started before the troops arrived at Valley Forge. The Conway Cabal was a conspiracy of ambitious people who were highly critical of George Washington and wanted him removed as commander of the Continental Army. The primary conspirator was Thomas Conway, an Irish-French soldier known for his intelligence and gallantry. Conway was also fiercely critical of Washington's military leadership, and he was not alone. Horatio Gates, the hero of Saratoga, aligned with Conway to

---

[72] Paine, T. (1776). The American Crisis. Retrieved from Library of Congress: https://www.loc.gov/resource/cph.3b06889/.

question Washington's position. Congressman Thomas Mifflin and, allegedly, Benjamin Rush also disapproved of Washington's leadership. Their grievances against the commander in chief ranged from handling military campaigns to personal disagreements.

A flurry of correspondence with questions about Washington's competence ensued. Washington was informed about it and received Conway, who was promoted to inspector general by the Continental Congress, with cold courtesy when Conway visited Valley Forge in late December. Washington's professional demeanor caused Conway to back down, and he wrote a letter of apology to Washington. The plot fizzled as more about the conspiracy became public. Attempts to orchestrate a "no confidence" vote in Washington were fiercely disputed in Congress. The final consequence of the Conway Cabal was that it consolidated Washington's standing as a unifying symbol of American resilience and resolve.[73]

The Drill Officer

General Washington's leadership during this time was crucial. The soldiers needed to become more professional to have a chance against the British in the coming year. At Washington's request, officers taught the soldiers European military tactics and instilled discipline, marking a turning point in the Continental Army's professionalism. The arrival in the camp of a unique individual enhanced their training.

This man's name was Friedrich Wilhelm von Steuben, and he claimed to be a baron and a former lieutenant general of the Prussian Army (Washington later discovered that von Steuben was no more than a captain who was born a commoner). Von Steuben was highly recommended by Benjamin Franklin and proved to be a superior military trainer.

---

[73] Scythes, J. (2024, February 21). Conway Cabal. Retrieved from Mountvernon.org: https://www.mountvernon.org/library/digitalhistory/digital-encyclopedia/article/conway-cabal/#:~:text=The%20Conway%20Cabal%20refers%20to,with%20Major%20General%20Horatio%20Gates.

Portrait of von Steuben.

Von Steuben's purpose was simple yet profound: he was to instill discipline and tactics in the Continental Army, which were hitherto nonexistent, transforming it from a loose coalition of militias into a unified fighting force. His approach was rigorous and methodical. He drilled the soldiers in the art of war, from basic maneuvers to complex formations that would be essential on the battlefield. His "Blue Book," a training manual that would become the cornerstone of American military education, standardized the army's techniques and military protocol.

Von Steuben's contributions transcended the tactical; he reformed the army's administrative systems, established rigorous standards of hygiene and health management, and integrated training for soldiers of all ethnicities and languages in an act of profound inclusivity. The unity forged in the fires of adversity kindled a new spirit among the troops.[74]

His efforts generated results. The soldiers emerged from Valley Forge as a cohesive unit and as seasoned combatants. The transformation was remarkable; what was once a dispirited band was now a source of pride, a force bedecked with a newfound sense of discipline and confidence. Von

---

[74] Mary Stockwell, P. (2024, February 21). Baron Von Steuben. Retrieved from Mountvernon.org: https://www.mountvernon.org/library/digitalhistory/digital-encyclopedia/article/baron-von-steuben/.

Steuben's training had forged soldiers and stewards of a new nation's future. Washington was ready to take on the British and fight on a level playing field.

At the heart of the Valley Forge narrative is the leadership of George Washington.

Washington's advocacy for his soldiers, his willingness to share their suffering, and his unyielding belief in their ability to triumph against all odds forged a bond of trust between leader and army. This trust and the resilience nurtured within the encampment formed the backbone of the American military ethos.

1778 Military Strategy

Washington and his advisors devised a multi-faceted campaign to cement alliances with European powers while maintaining pressure on British troops. The campaign's goals included the following:

- **Consolidating military presence:** Expanding control over crucial areas to enhance the Continental Army's strategic position.

- **International diplomacy:** Leveraging military successes to garner support from France and other potential European allies.

- **Domestic morale boost:** Building on earlier victories to reinforce the the revolutionary spirit among the populace and the troops.

These objectives underpinned a series of maneuvers that combined military prowess with a statesman's eye for global politics.

One of the most significant facets of the campaign of 1778 was the successful negotiation of the Franco-American alliance, which was formalized on February 6th, 1778. French support was a game changer, as the French brought a formidable naval force that could challenge British maritime dominance. The Treaty of Alliance solidified the collaboration, which promised mutual military assistance against the British.[75]

Sir Henry Clinton

William Howe resigned as the commander in chief of the British army in North America when he learned of Burgoyne's defeat. He remained in Philadelphia until May 24th, 1778, and was replaced by Sir Henry Clinton.

---

[75] Encyclopedia.com. (2024, January 30). Franco-American Alliance. Retrieved from Britannica.com: https://www.britannica.com/event/Franco-American-Alliance

Machiavelli's political treatise, *The Prince*, advocates for practicality over ethics, a philosophy that often shapes the approach of political and military leaders. Clinton embodied this pragmatism in his strategic decisions as he sought a path to victory filled with tactical caution and calculated risks. His mission was to wage war and win it by any means necessary.

Clinton believed the British army needed a place and some time to regroup and reorganize to succeed. He decided New York was the place to do both. To him, Philadelphia had no strategic value. Consequently, on June 18th, 1778, Clinton and fifteen thousand British troops evacuated Philadelphia, leaving the loyalists behind in panic for their lives.[76]

<u>Battle of Monmouth</u>

General George Washington led the Continental Army to strike a blow against the British forces retreating from Philadelphia. The campaign was marked by tactical retreats, scorched earth policies, and the cloak-and-dagger strategies of spying and intelligence gathering.

The Battle of Monmouth, fought on June 28th, 1778, was significant for several reasons. It was one of the most extensive engagements of the war, involving over twenty-six thousand soldiers. The intense heat of the day and a lack of proper decision-making—most notably, the controversial performance of Major General Charles Lee, who ordered a retreat that enabled a British counterattack—contributed to a battle that culminated in a draw. The British ultimately moved on to New York City but not without suffering heavy casualties.

The resolve and resilience displayed by the soldiers who braved the blistering heat and the chaos of the battle instilled a newfound confidence within the ranks. The stories of men's courage and sacrifice spread, kindling the embers of hope and determination. Monmouth demonstrated the growing proficiency of the Continental Army. This performance galvanized public opinion in favor of the patriot cause and dispelled any lingering doubts about the viability of the American forces.

The new British commander in chief was in a peculiar position. Great Britain had overwhelming military might, better funding, and a robust navy controlling critical waterways. However, an extended supply chain and a growing aversion to the war within Britain demanded an expedited

---

[76] Editors, H. (2024, February 21). British Abandon Philadelphia. Retrieved from History.com: https://www.history.com/this-day-in-history/british-abandon-philadelphia.

resolution. Moreover, the Continental Army was proving resilient. Henry Clinton decided on a change of direction.[77]

His solution was in the South, a theater of war that was less populated and less defended. His strategy centered on a belief that by securing the South, British control over the colonies might crumble the rebellion. This Southern Campaign, as it was dubbed, was a concerted effort to exploit divisions within the American leadership and populace. The bloodiest days of the American Revolution were about to begin.

---

[77] National Park Service. (2024, February 21). Henry Clinton. Retrieved from Nps.gov: https://www.nps.gov/people/henry-clinton.htm#:~:text=Sir%20Henry%20Clinton%20replaced%20Sir,to%20face%20the%20rebellio us%20American .

Chapter 10: The Southern Campaign

The more well-known conflicts in the North often overshadow the battles of the Southern Campaign. Yet, these engagements were vital in the larger strategy of both the Continental Army and the British forces. Here, the loyalists, colloquially referred to as Tories, formed a significant force that defended British interests and shaped the course of the American Revolutionary War. The decision to remain loyal was often complex, influenced by socioeconomic status, cultural ties, and the belief that British governance offered greater stability. Thomas Brown, Patrick Ferguson, and David Fanning were instrumental in leading loyalist militia units. These leaders were skilled tacticians and adept at cultivating support from local loyalists, often by suppressing patriot activities.

Loyalists saw the conflict through the lens of law and order, with a deep distrust of what they viewed as the anarchy inherent in the patriot movement. Their loyalty was often rooted in a conservative worldview that prized stability and tradition over the revolutionary fervor gripping the patriots.

The Reliance on Loyalists

The loyalist population in the south was sizeable but less uniform in its support for the British than the British thought. Amidst the conflicting loyalties and complex social dynamics, many aspired to remain neutral, forsaking the British and the colonial militias. These allegiances were often fluid, influenced by immediate circumstances and the local progress of the war.

The military presence of the British and their loyalist allies emboldened some to declare their support openly, igniting a bitter civil war within the revolutionary movement. It is estimated that around 20 percent of white southern colonists were Tory loyalists, with a notable concentration in South Carolina and Georgia. The British sought to utilize this population to create a political and military base.

The Georgia Phase

The Southern Campaign began with a foray into the most southern colony, Georgia. This was the last American colony settled by Great Britain, so Clinton assumed the Georgians would welcome the presence of British soldiers to defend the civilians against Native Americans.

On November 26th, 1778, Clinton sent nearly three thousand soldiers under Lieutenant Colonel Archibald Campbell to Savannah with instructions to take the city. Savannah's defenses included swampy land that the patriots believed would prevent a British advance. However, a slave pointed out an undefended trail that led to the Continental Army's barracks. A strong detachment of British soldiers followed that path and effectively flanked the Americans.

Savannah fell on December 29th, 1778. A significant number of American soldiers were taken prisoner. Loyalists aided the British in taking Savannah, and that was the start of an alliance that would be highly successful in the coming months.

Savannah was now a base of operations for the British. Augusta would later fall as British and Tory forces began raiding into South Carolina. Georgia would formally receive a royal governor in July 1779. A later effort to retake the city by a combined American and French force resulted in a failed siege that lasted from September 16th to October 20th, 1779.[78]

There were American victories at Port Royal Island, South Carolina, and at Kettle Creek, Georgia. The backcountry of Georgia was still in American hands, but the situation became dramatically worse in late December 1779. Sir Henry Clinton sailed from New York City with fourteen thousand men to Charleston, South Carolina, to besiege that significant southern port.

---

[78] Battlefields.org. (2024, February 20). Siege of Savannah. Retrieved from Battlefields.org: https://www.battlefields.org/learn/revolutionary-war/battles/savannah.

The Fall of Charleston

The siege of Charleston began in earnest on April 1st, 1780. It lasted until May 12th, when ill-equipped American forces commanded by General Benjamin Lincoln surrendered Charleston to British troops under General Sir Henry Clinton. The swift and decisive blow dealt to the patriot forces spelled the largest surrender of American troops until World War II, with over 5,500 soldiers laying down their arms.

The siege was a flagrant display of British military might. In the broader narrative, one can infer the beginning of the end for the revolutionary cause in the southern theater. The loyalists in Charleston benefited tremendously from this British victory.

A depiction of the siege of Charleston.
https://commons.wikimedia.org/wiki/File:Sullivans-island-1050x777.jpg

The Loyalist Opposition

The population of Charleston was significantly divided. While patriots fervently rallied for independence, a distinct and substantial segment of the population remained loyalist, with notables such as Rawlins Lowndes staunchly advocating for the Crown.

The political and cultural divisions were most pronounced in the South Carolinian socioeconomic elite. Due to longstanding trade connections and familial ties to England, these individuals became a bridge—albeit a delicate one—between the burgeoning American identity and European heritage.

The siege of Charleston cast a long shadow. For the loyalists, the British capture of Charleston was a moment of victory and presented them with a terrible risk. Their fortunes and their lives depended on British success. Failure would leave the loyalists in the hands of a patriot faction looking for revenge.

The Collapse of South Carolina

Following the capture of Charleston, the British military embarked on a series of armed conflicts designed to assert their supremacy and discourage rebellion. Some of the most prominent among these clashes were the Battle of Waxhaws and the Battle of Camden.

The Battle of Waxhaws pitted the Americans under Abraham Buford against Banastre Tarleton on May 29th, 1780. This was a small battle, but the aftermath was shocking. Americans who were trying to surrender were massacred by British soldiers surging through the broken American lines, generating the phrase "Tarleton's quarter" as a description of British barbarity. By the summer of 1780, the American revolutionaries had begun to feel the weight of British resurgence under the command of General Charles Cornwallis.

The Battle of Camden happened on August 16th, 1780. The British were commanded by General Cornwallis. Horatio Gates, the hero of Saratoga, led the Americans. The nature of the battle was asymmetrical, with the well-drilled ranks of the British pitted against the Americans. The British numbered around 2,200, while the American force tallied approximately 3,700. Strategies from both sides aimed to exploit each other's weaknesses, with Cornwallis seeking to assert British dominance in the South through a swift and decisive victory and Gates hoping to bolster American morale with a successful defense.[79]

The Battle of Camden was a disaster for the Americans. In the face of a relentless British advance, the American lines crumbled, and the troops from Virginia fled, leaving the Continental Army exposed. Troops under Johann de Kalb stayed on the field as other Americans ran for their lives. The casualty count was devasting, and de Kalb was killed. The reputation of General Gates was destroyed, as the American commander fled the

---

[79] Battlefields.org. (2024, February 20). Waxhaws. Retrieved from Battlefields.org: https://www.battlefields.org/learn/revolutionary-war/battles/waxhaws.

field and did not stop running until he had covered more than 150 miles.[80]

Organized American resistance was eliminated at Camden. Only disorganized militiamen and guerrillas were left to fight the British troops and their Tory allies. It would take an aggressive commander to save the revolutionary cause in the South. That miracle worker was a Quaker from Rhode Island.

<u>Nathanael Greene and His Strategy</u>

Nathanael Greene was one of the most capable and audacious generals of the American Revolutionary War. He was born into a devout Quaker family in Rhode Island in 1742. Unlike the dogmatic pacifism of his upbringing, Greene was drawn to the intellectual ferment that gave rise to the revolutionary cause. His military acumen quickly elevated him through the ranks when the conflict erupted.

He was one of the most innovative and strategic minds of his time, known for his tactical flexibility, logistical acumen, and ability to inspire troops. Greene's strategic vision considered the constraints of massive distances, poor roads, and the growing state of the Continental Army. His approach to warfare was innovative at a time when the conventional wisdom of European military orthodoxy held sway.

In 1780, Greene was appointed as commander of the Southern Department, facing an almost impossible situation. The British had just captured Charleston, and British General Cornwallis seemed unstoppable. Greene, however, refused to accept defeat. His strategy was to relentlessly harry the British, wearing down their forces through attrition and quick, carefully chosen battles that capitalized on American advantages.

---

[80] Battlefields.org. (2024, February 20). Camden. Retrieved from Batlefields.org: https://www.battlefields.org/learn/revolutionary-war/battles/camden.

Portrait of Nathanael Greene.
https://commons.wikimedia.org/wiki/File:Nathanael_Greene_by_John_Trumbull_1792.jpeg

Greene's Plan for Victory

Morale among American forces had plummeted, and the economic and social fabric of the South was in dire straits. Greene faced a deceptively simple yet daunting task: to rally a demoralized army and turn the tide of war against the formidable British presence.

With compassion and a sharp understanding of human nature, Greene embarked on a twofold mission to rejuvenate his forces. He recognized that victory on the battlefield was but one facet of the war; resilience and resolve were equally crucial. Greene restored confidence through relentless training, instilling discipline and fostering unity among the disparate militia groups that comprised the southern army. His leadership style eschewed authoritarianism in favor of a participatory approach, earning him the respect and loyalty of his men.

Aware that conventional tactics would fail to redress the imbalance, Greene embraced unorthodox methods to outmaneuver the superior British forces. He repeatedly withdrew his army, utilizing the South's expansive geography to his advantage. His knowledge of the local terrain allowed him to play to the strengths of irregular warfare, leveraging the speed and stealth of his forces to harry the British without committing to head-on confrontations.

Moreover, Greene recognized the importance of maintaining the local population's support. He forbade his troops from engaging in the wanton destruction that often accompanied war, instead appealing to the southern civility ingrained in social structures. By winning over the hearts and minds of the people, Greene developed a network of intelligence and a continuous flow of recruits that sustained the patriot effort.

Fabian Strategy, Southern Style

What Greene was doing was similar to Washington's plan of action after the fall of New York City, but there was a difference. Greene's strategy was one of attrition, in which the goal was not to defeat the British outright but to wear down their will and resources. He effectively stretched the British supply lines through his tactical retreats, forcing them to overextend and weaken their grip on the southern territory. This relentless pressure, coupled with the irregular engagements that disproportionately taxed British forces, hastened the erosion of British strength.

At this time, a highly effective guerrilla leader was Francis Marion, who was also known as the "Swamp Fox." Operating in the swamps of South Carolina, Marion's irregular tactics became a thorn in the side of the British forces. His leadership of small bands of militia allowed for sudden strikes and rapid disappearances into the familiar marshlands, disrupting enemy communications, supply chains, and fortifications.

Francis Marion's unconventional warfare dovetailed with Greene's approach of avoiding large-scale engagements in favor of a war of attrition. He could strike swiftly and without warning, sapping British morale and helping regain control of the South Carolina backcountry. His actions not only weakened the British but also provided Greene with vital intelligence and preserved the fighting spirit of the patriot cause in the South.

Overmountain Men

In the frontier lands of Virginia, the Carolinas, and Tennessee, a group of rugged settlers known as the Overmountain Men began coalescing. These frontiersmen, primarily of Scottish-Irish descent, were fiercely independent. They had migrated to escape the authority of the coastal elites and carved out an existence in the wilderness. When the call to arms echoed through the mountains, the Overmountain Men saw an opportunity to strike a blow against the loyalists they despised. Despite the challenging obstacles of distance and terrain, they united under the command of several leaders, most notably Benjamin Cleveland, John Sevier, and William Campbell. They set out on a dangerous march to the Piedmont region of South Carolina to fight.

Major Patrick Ferguson, a British officer in command of the loyalist militia, opposed them. Known for his sharpshooting and discipline, Ferguson set his sights on hunting down patriots in the southern backcountry. His proclamation that he would " hang their leaders and lay their country waste "spurred the patriots into action. Ferguson's overconfidence and contempt for the patriots, whom he thought a "rabble" not worth pursuing, proved to be a fatal miscalculation.

A Fight on a Mountainside

The battle occurred on October 7th, 1780, at Kings Mountain, South Carolina. It began as an encirclement. The Overmountain Men, who had been preparing for combat during their march, used their knowledge of the mountainous terrain to their advantage. They attacked from all sides, moving in small groups, covering under the brush, and shouting, "Remember Waxhaws!" The loyalists, unprepared for this style of warfare, quickly found themselves surrounded and outflanked, their morale broken and their force divided.

In a heated and brutal fight that lasted barely an hour, the tide turned decisively in favor of the patriots. Ferguson was slain, and the loyalists, leaderless and outnumbered, suffered heavy casualties. The patriots secured a resounding victory, capturing more than a thousand prisoners, although the number is still a topic of historical debate and was initially exaggerated.

The Tory prisoners faced frontier justice. On October 14th, drumhead courts-martial were held, and thirty-six loyalists were convicted of various offenses. Nine were hanged before the proceedings were stopped. The remaining prisoners escaped or were paroled.[81]

The victory at Kings Mountain altered the trajectory of the war in the Carolinas. It marked the high point in patriot morale for a conflict that had, until that moment, been a series of setbacks and retreats. Kings

---

[81] Revolutionarywar.us. (2024, February 21). The Battle of Kings Mountain. Retrieved from Revolutionarywar.us: https://revolutionarywar.us/year-1780/battle-kings-mountain/.

Mountain energized the revolutionary cause in the South, ending the British presence in the western Carolinas.

The victory came at an opportune time. Nathanael Greene's troops were ready to engage the enemy.

<u>Greene's Offensive</u>

General Greene divided his forces, luring Cornwallis deeper into the hostile interior of the Carolinas. Greene's soldiers steadily chipped away at the British by leveraging local knowledge and utilizing hit-and-run tactics. His decision to avoid an open battle against a superior enemy was among the most challenging, but it ultimately paid off. The colonial forces, comprised of regulars and militia, gradually gained confidence as they inflicted casualties and captured supplies. The year 1781 witnessed several significant battles as the British and Americans fought to control the Carolinas.

• Cowpens

The Battle of Cowpens took place on January 17th, 1781. This battle stands out as a masterstroke of military strategy and demonstrated the effective use of coordinated ranks and militia forces under American commanders Brigadier General Daniel Morgan and Colonel Andrew Pickens.

On the rolling fields of the South Carolina upcountry, Morgan employed a tactical double envelopment that integrated the use of Continental Army regulars, militia fighters, and cavalry in a sophisticated retreat-and-counterattack maneuver. The American forces effectively lured the British into a false sense of victory as the frontline militia performed a planned retreat, only for the British to be met by a staunch line of Continental Army regulars who withstood the British charge and fought back with ferocity. The British forces, led by Banastre Tarleton, were decisively defeated, suffering heavy casualties. The British loss significantly contributed to the weakening of British military operations in the southern colonies.

• Guilford Court House

On March 15th, the American and British forces met in the fields around Guilford Courthouse, North Carolina. The outcome was a tactical victory for the British, who held the field at the end of the day. Yet, it was a Pyrrhic victory. While Cornwallis technically won the battle, his forces were severely depleted. On the other hand, Americans held their ground and did not suffer the catastrophic losses of Camden. Greene and his men withdrew, leaving the British in control of the battlefield but without the tactical advantage they had gained from previous encounters. Cornwallis retreated to Wilmington, North Carolina, for reinforcements and supplies.

- Siege of Ninety-Six

The siege of Ninety-six took place ninety-six miles from the nearest Cherokee village; the town was a major crossroads in western South Carolina. Greene laid siege to the Star Fort located there and its loyalist garrison from May 22nd to June 18th. He broke the siege when he learned a relief force was coming from Charleston.

<u>Cornwallis Abandons the Carolinas</u>

Cornwallis's struggle to assert British control in the Carolinas brought him face to face with the realities of the southern conflict: a lack of popular support, logistical difficulties, and an adaptable, if not always conventional, American response. The Southern Campaign was costly in terms of lives and resources, which the delicate British supply lines struggled to maintain. The specter of French and Spanish intervention in the war loomed over military decision-making, already complicating matters elsewhere.

The global context of the war meant that, for the British, maintaining a presence in the already secured southern territories had to be weighed against opportunities and threats elsewhere. Virginia, as one of the wealthier and more populous colonies, offered strategic advantages in recruiting loyalist fighters and supplies, and it represented a central location from which to launch operations in other theaters of the war.

Cornwallis recognized that Greene was being supplied from Virginia. The British general hoped to cut off the supply lines to Greene and proposed to Lord George Germain, Secretary of State for the Colonies, that he, Cornwallis, should invade Virginia. Germain ignored the chain of command, which would have meant that Sir Henry Clinton would be involved in the decision-making, and agreed to Cornwallis's idea. Cornwallis then left Wilmington and headed north to Virginia with his army.[82]

---

[82] Revolutionarywar.us. (2024, February 21). Southern Theater. Retrieved from Revolutionarywar.us: https://revolutionarywar.us/campaigns/1775-1782-southern-theater/.

Greene continued a mop-up campaign in the Carolinas, driving what was left of the British to Charleston and Wilmington. The Battle of Eutaw Springs on September 8th, 1781, was the last major battle in the Carolinas. The British were no longer able to stop Nathanael Greene.

Nathanael Greene's stewardship of the Southern Department was integral to the patriots' victory in the American Revolutionary War. Greene's legacy exemplifies how the underdog can prevail through cunning, adaptability, and courage.

Benedict Arnold's Treason

The story of Benedict Arnold is often cited as the ultimate tale of betrayal in American history. Once a celebrated and courageous military leader for the fledgling United States, Arnold's legacy was forever stained by his decision to become a turncoat and offer the strategic fort of West Point to the British during the American Revolutionary War. His name, once synonymous with selfless patriotism, metamorphosed into a benchmark for disloyalty. However, the motivations behind Arnold's betrayal and the intricate events leading up to his plan paint a complex picture of a man and a nation at the crossroads of history.

Before he became America's villain, Benedict Arnold was an ardent and courageous supporter of the American cause. He was renowned for his bravery during the Battles of Saratoga in 1777, where his tactical brilliance helped secure a critical victory for the Continental Army. Despite his achievements, Arnold felt a profound sense of betrayal by the government he had served so faithfully.

Disillusioned by the lack of recognition, compensation, and the promotion of other officers ahead of him, Arnold's disenchantment simmered. Simultaneously, personal slights and accusations of misconduct tarnished his reputation in the eyes of the American leadership. These grievances laid the groundwork for Arnold's eventual turn to the enemy.

Unbeknownst to Washington and other senior officers, Benedict Arnold was communicating secretly with Sir Henry Clinton. The American general knew he was being considered for the command of West Point. On July 12th, 1780, he sent a coded message to Clinton, offering to surrender West Point to the British once he was placed in command. The price for the treason was £20,000.

Situated on the Hudson River north of New York City, West Point carried immense military importance during the American Revolutionary

War. Its control divided the northern and southern states, ensuring a critical line of defense against British advancement. West Point provided a secure base for the Continental Army to store arms and munitions. Arnold's plot to surrender West Point to the British was a potential coup that could have altered the war's course. His actions would have not only delivered a devastating blow to the Continental Army but also provided a morale boost for the British, who had been unable to make inroads in the face of colonial resistance.

Benedict Arnold became commander of West Point on August 3rd, 1780. He received a coded message from Clinton on August 15th, accepting Arnold's price for the fort. West Point would be a British outpost in a few days.

The Plot Revealed

Everything was going according to plan. However, Arnold's plot started to fall apart when his British contact, Major John André, was caught by the Americans on September 23rd. Papers containing incriminating evidence were found on the British officer, detailing the financial offers to Arnold for turning traitor and providing tangible proof of his collusion.

With the discovery of John André and the damning evidence in his possession, Arnold hastily fled West Point on September 24th. In the early morning hours, he boarded a waiting barge and insisted under the pretense of security that the crew row him down the Hudson River to the HMS *Vulture*, a British sloop of war. Through this daring escape, Arnold avoided capture by mere hours. George Washington arrived at West Point to find his disgraced general already gone.

Portrait of Benedict Arnold.

Upon joining the British ranks, he was commissioned as a brigadier general but received a lukewarm reception from his new peers, who viewed him with suspicion and never fully accepted him. Arnold led British forces in several raids, including an attack on New London, Connecticut, which was considered by many as a ruthless act against his compatriots. Despite these efforts, the rewards and recognition he had hoped to gain from the British were modest at best.

The discovery of Arnold's scheme was perhaps equally if not more critical than the intended treachery. Preventing the British occupation of West Point preserved the stronghold as a linchpin of American defense and bolstered the resolve and trust in each other within the revolutionary leadership. Benedict Arnold received lasting fame, but he is remembered as an infamous traitor, not a devoted patriot.

Chapter 11: Yorktown

<u>War on the Frontier</u>

One area we haven't looked at yet is the west. The land west of the Appalachians was fiercely contested. The vast lands comprising modern-day Ohio, Indiana, Illinois, Michigan, and Wisconsin were the battleground where small bands of patriots, Shawnee and Delaware warriors, and French settlers fought to repel British and loyalist incursions. The American Revolution on the frontier was a struggle for land and identity, and the tenuous alliance between settlers and indigenous peoples reshaped conflict dynamics.

The vast resources of the northwest—primarily furs, timber, and highly fertile land—made it an economic prize for any power that could secure it. The British created a formidable barrier to American westward expansion by controlling the fur trade and the Ohio River.

The establishment and conquest of forts were pivotal in controlling the vast territory west of the Appalachians. Fort Vincennes, Fort Kaskaskia, and other strongholds shifted several times between British and American hands, as both sides vied to control these strategic positions. Each skirmish was a calculated risk that would either extend the boundaries of American influence or reinforce British occupation.

<u>The Inhabitants</u>

The French presence in the northwest added a layer of complexity to the conflict. While French settlers had enjoyed relative autonomy and were wary of American expansion, they were equally discontent with British rule. Myriad loyalties and an overarching desire for self-governance characterized their role in the American Revolution.

American settlers played a pivotal role during the war. These frontiersmen carved out settlements in hostile landscapes, creating homes and communities in the face of untold hardships. Many settlers joined local militias or the Continental Army during the conflict, providing manpower in critical battles and campaigns. Their intimate knowledge of the frontier's rivers, forests, and mountains proved invaluable in countering British strategies, and their resilience in the face of adversity added a crucial layer to the colonial war effort.

Indigenous tribes were central figures in the western theater. They played a complex and often decisive role in the unfolding conflict. Native American nations like the Shawnee, Delaware, and Miami found themselves in a precarious position as they faced pressure from American colonists and British forces. While some tribes sought to remain neutral, others entered into alliances that they hoped would preserve their territories and way of life. As allies to the British, they contributed significantly to the defense of territories, using their knowledge of the land, guerrilla tactics, and strategic insight to stem the tide of American expansion.[83]

<u>British Western Strategy</u>

In the aftermath of the French and Indian War, the Royal Proclamation of 1763 was announced. To mitigate potential tensions with indigenous peoples and their alliances, the proclamation drew a demarcation line along the crest of the Appalachian Mountains, effectively preventing colonial expansion westward.

In theory, the proclamation sought to foster peaceful coexistence with the indigenous nations, who were now to be managed under the Crown's direct authority. The British were adept at the art of treaty-making and alliance-building, using a combination of coercion and promises to maintain a patchwork of alliances among the indigenous nations. They built a series of fortresses to secure their western territory.

These fortresses weren't just physical bulwarks; they were also a testament to Britain's commitment to holding the line against any potential colonial insurgency. Forts like Fort Niagara, Fort Toronto, and

---

[83] Orrison, R. (2024, January 3). Native American Impact on British War Strategy in Southern Campaign. Retrieved from Battlefields.org: https://www.battlefields.org/learn/articles/native-american-impact-british-war-strategy-southern-campaign.

Fort Detroit were built to assert British dominance, control strategic points, and keep indigenous nations on the side of the Crown. They also served as outposts for the fur trade.

American Goals and Objectives

The frontier represented an opportunity for untapped economic potential, with natural resources in abundance and land offering a fresh start. The motivation to venture west was a heady mix of economic opportunity, the pursuit of freedom, and a deep-rooted sense of Manifest Destiny.

The American patriots viewed the British presence in the western frontier as a barrier to their expansionist aspirations and a threat to their burgeoning national identity. British forts in the west served as a reminder of Britain's dominance, and British alliances with Native American tribes were seen as strategic moves to limit access to these lands and to stir up resistance against settler encroachment. Such actions by the British only fueled the colonists' resolve to push the frontier westward.

Military Campaigns on the Western Frontier

In 1779, Major General Frederick Haldimand, the commanding officer in the British Province of Quebec, directed a formidable expedition under Lieutenant Colonel Henry Bird. Bird's forces, composed of British regulars, loyalists, and Native American allies, conducted swift and devastating attacks on American settlements in the western frontiers of Virginia and Pennsylvania. The British sought to resurrect the dispirit of the loyalist citizenry while safeguarding the lucrative fur trade against American encroachments.

An equal measure of resilience and adaptability marked the American response to British incursions in the west. Leaders such as George Rogers Clark and Brigadier General Daniel Brodhead would become synonymous with the American campaign in the hinterland. Clark, a daring and resourceful frontiersman, embarked on a campaign that was instrumental in securing the vast expanse of the Illinois Country for the American cause. His audacious march from the falls of the Ohio River to the strategic outposts of Kaskaskia and Cahokia showcased the reach of the patriots' territorial ambitions.

With a contingent of disciplined militiamen and frontiersmen, Clark captured British-held Fort Vincennes in a February 1779 siege. This strategic victory at Vincennes was pivotal; it weakened British influence in the region and delivered a profound psychological blow to their military posture. He demonstrated the capability of the irregular American forces to conduct significant operations in hostile territory.

The British redoubled their efforts to regain the upper hand, dispatching more troops and resources to fortify their remaining strongholds and repel the American advances. Lieutenant Governor Henry Hamilton, a key British figure in the region known as the "Hair Buyer" for reportedly incentivizing the scalping of rebels, was quick to act, reclaiming Fort Sackville at Vincennes.

Clark refused to accept this defeat. Instead, he mounted a counter-offensive in the winter of 1779. In an unexpected turn, he led a lean force of frontiersmen through the flooded plains of the Wabash River, laying siege once again to Fort Sackville. Clark's forces successfully recaptured the fort and took Hamilton prisoner in what would be remembered as one of the most audacious operations of the American Revolutionary War.[84]

A Continuing Stalemate

During the years 1780 and 1781, the military situation in the western frontier of the American Revolution became a complex stalemate characterized by sporadic skirmishes and strategic maneuvers rather than large-scale battles. The British forces maintained their presence in key strongholds, but their domination in the region was contested by American troops, who were well accustomed to the rigors of wilderness fighting.

In this period, the American forces aimed to solidify their hold on the Illinois Country, counteract British efforts to fortify their positions, and incite Native American aggression. A notable event came in August 1780 when Clark led the Kentucky militia in a retaliatory attack known as the August Expedition against the Shawnee towns along the Mad River, a response to Native Americans allied with the British.

Strained by extended supply lines and facing an enemy familiar with the territory, British forces struggled to execute a successful strategy. American troops, although fewer in number, utilized guerrilla tactics and their intimate knowledge of the terrain to significant effect. The region became an arena of small but intense engagements. The final outcome of

---

[84] Hallowed Ground Magazine. (2018, December 18). Revolution on the Frontier. Retrieved from Battlefields.org: https://www.battlefields.org/learn/articles/revolution-frontier.

operations by both sides in the western frontier was decided by the Treaty of Paris in 1783.

The Road to Yorktown

But before the treaty was signed, there was a pivotal battle in Yorktown. Cornwallis intended to strengthen British control in Virginia. His strategic vision, influenced by the idea of maintaining a southern base for the British forces, led him to choose Yorktown. This coastal town provided a secure port for the British Royal Navy and a defensive position against the threat of French naval interference.

Cornwallis's focus on Virginia was both a response to the shifting dynamics of the war and to perceived weaknesses in the American forces. His strategy was to alter the face of the conflict by bringing the fight to less secure colonial territories, capitalizing on potential loyalist support and drawing the French away from their fleet.

Cornwallis's move to Virginia was risky. It meant a shift from a mobile war that primarily involved raiding and engagements designed to destabilize the American effort to a more static form of warfare. Building a base at Yorktown meant committing troops to a fixed location and inevitably turning it into a target for the combined Franco-American forces. Furthermore, it relied heavily upon the Royal Navy for supplies and evacuation, making the British forces vulnerable to French naval superiority. It would later expose a critical flaw in their strategy once the French fleet took control of Chesapeake Bay.

Washington's Countermove

General George Washington received intelligence of Cornwallis's march to Yorktown in the summer of 1781. Recognizing the strategic implications of this British maneuver, Washington saw an opportunity to strike a decisive blow. In coordination with French General Rochambeau, Washington shifted his focus from the planned attack on New York City to a rapid march toward Virginia. This audacious move, with exceptional secrecy and haste, positioned the Franco-American forces for a surprise assault against Cornwallis's stronghold, effectively trapping the British between their encroaching adversaries and the sea.[85]

The French fleet, commanded by Admiral François de Grasse, was stationed in the West Indies during that summer. De Grasse received

---

[85] History.com Editors. (2023, June 21). Battle of Yorktown. Retrieved from History.com: https://www.history.com/topics/american-revolution/siege-of-yorktown.

dispatches from Washington requesting his urgent arrival to Chesapeake Bay to assist in trapping the British. Understanding the potential impact of his ships, de Grasse promptly set sail for Chesapeake Bay, reaching the Virginian coast by the end of August.

The British navy moved to respond to de Grasse with a fleet of nineteen ships of the line commanded by Admiral Thomas Graves. The French and British fleets fought a pivotal naval engagement on September 5th near the entrance of Chesapeake Bay, now referred to as the **Battle of the Capes**. The French won the two-hour battle, and the British retreated to New York City.

The French Navy, reinforced by a fleet under the command of Admiral Louis de Barras, now had control of Chesapeake Bay, preventing the British from reinforcing or evacuating Cornwallis's army at Yorktown. Cornwallis was trapped on land without naval support. The British general solidified his defenses by constructing redoubts with artillery support connected by trenches.[86]

Washington's Arrival

Washington and Comte de Rochambeau, the commander of the French troops, arrived in Williamsburg, Virginia, by the middle of September. Their combined force eventually reached over nineteen thousand men. Nine thousand British soldiers opposed them. The siege of Yorktown formally began on September 28th, 1781.[87]

The Siege

The combined American and French forces conducted the siege with methodical precision. The allies dug parallel trenches, bringing artillery and men steadily closer to the British defensive line. Artillery barrages commenced on October 9th, and French cannons pounded British defenses.

The American attack on Redoubt No. 10 was a memorable action during the siege. Under the command of Lieutenant Colonel Alexander Hamilton, a French and American force overran the redoubt on October 14th and secured a crucial foothold in Yorktown's defenses.[88]

---

[86] NPS.gov. (2021, January 25). Battle of the Capes. Retrieved from Yorktown Battlefield: https://www.nps.gov/york/learn/historyculture/battle-of-the-capes.htm.

[87] Battlefields.org. (2024, February 25). Siege of Yorktown. Retrieved from Battlefields.org: https://www.battlefields.org/learn/revolutionary-war/battles/yorktown.

[88] Battlefields.org. (2024, February 25). Siege of Yorktown. Retrieved from Battlefields.org:

Cornwallis tried to evacuate his troops across the York River on October 16th, but the effort failed. The relief force General Clinton promised him failed to arrive, and the situation was hopeless. A drummer appeared on the British ramparts the morning of October 17th, accompanied by an officer waving a white handkerchief. Lord Cornwallis was ready to negotiate for a surrender.

The Final Surrender

On October 19th, 1781, the siege of Yorktown reached its dramatic conclusion with the formal surrender of General Cornwallis's British forces. The ceremony itself was charged with solemnity and formality. The defeated British soldiers marched out from their positions, laying down their arms in a field cleared for the event. Notably, General Cornwallis claimed illness and sent his second in command, General Charles O'Hara, to offer the British surrender to the American and French commanders.

General Washington remembered the humiliation the Americans were forced to endure at the surrender of Charleston, and he decided to return the favor. He refused a request for a traditional honors of war ceremony and required the defeated to march with flags furled and muskets shouldered. He declined to accept the surrender from O'Hara. Instead, he designated his second in command, General Benjamin Lincoln, who was the defeated American commander at Charleston, to receive the British general's sword. The British surrendered 8,000 men, 214 artillery pieces, and thousands of muskets at Yorktown.

https://www.battlefields.org/learn/revolutionary-war/battles/yorktown.

Surrender of Lord Cornwallis by John Trumbull.

British Reaction to the Surrender

When news of the defeat at Yorktown reached London, it resounded throughout Parliament and the wider British public. People were shocked, dismayed, and in disbelief. Prime Minister Lord North famously exclaimed, "Oh God! It is all over," as he paced in his room, articulating the sense of finality the loss represented for Britain's efforts to retain control over the American colonies. The political ramifications were immediate, with calls for ending the war and for North's government to resign. The public, weary of the protracted conflict and its economic burdens, began to press for peace. The defeat at Yorktown ended the last vestiges of popular and political support for the war in Great Britain.

The victory at Yorktown effectively ended major combat operations in North America, setting the stage for the negotiation of the Treaty of Paris and the formal recognition of the United States' independence by the British Crown. The Americans had done the improbable and achieved the impossible.

Chapter 12: The Final Days

The surrender at Yorktown was not the end of the American Revolution, but it was the beginning of the end. What happened in the following months created the blueprint for the United States of America. The most significant work was done thousands of miles from the North American battlefields.

The Treaty of Paris

The negotiations that led to the Treaty of Paris began with the appointment of a special commission from the United States. Benjamin Franklin, John Adams, and John Jay were charged with representing American interests in talks with the British. (The original group included Thomas Jefferson and Henry Laurens. Jefferson was unable to leave America, and Laurens was a prisoner in the Tower of London.) They arrived in Europe amidst the endgame of a war that both sides wanted to be over and done with.

The earl of Shelburne, who led British negotiations, was a politician known for his forward-thinking stance on colonial autonomy. Assisting him were Richard Oswald, a businessman who understood transatlantic business affairs, and Henry Strachey, an experienced secretary who would become instrumental in articulating the treaty's details. Together, the British trio engaged with their American counterparts in complex discussions that navigated various diplomatic challenges to ultimately define the peace terms between the two nations.

The commissioners found themselves navigating a treacherous sea of European politics. Britain, smarting from the loss of the American colonies, was not the only player at this table. France, a critical ally in the American Revolution, had its own agenda. France sought to weaken its rival, Great Britain, while ensuring the repayment of debts owed by America and maintaining its territorial holdings in the Caribbean. On the other hand, Spain was focused on securing control over Florida, which it had captured from Britain during the war, and protecting its colonies in Central and South America from future American expansion. The American commissioners participated in a delicate dance to ensure that the treaty negotiated with the British did not compromise their relations with the French, Spanish, or other European powers.[89]

The meetings began in the spring of 1782 and were held in Paris. Significant issues that dominated the Treaty of Paris discussions were the recognition of the United States as an independent sovereign free from British rule and the possession of territories, boundaries, and fisheries. Although Great Britain would have to swallow its pride, formal recognition of America as an independent country was a non-negotiable.

A Question of Boundaries

The war on the western frontier was a primary factor in the boundary issues. Hostilities between American frontier settlers and Native American tribes, backed at times by British forces, had become an integral part of the conflict. The United States sought to establish secure and recognized boundaries that would allow for westward expansion and the development of new states. The British held a series of forts in the Great Lakes region, which they were reluctant to abandon. They hoped to maintain a buffer zone to protect their fur trade interests and relations with various Native American tribes. The American commissioners pushed the British to relinquish their forts and any claims to territory east of the Mississippi River, ensuring a clear path for America's growth.[90]

Bargaining over Seafood

Discussions over fisheries may appear trivial to modern society, but these patches of watery real estate held immense economic and strategic importance. The abundant fishing grounds along the coast of Newfoundland and in the Gulf of Saint Lawrence were a vital source of livelihood for many American fishermen and a cornerstone of

---

[89] History.com. (2023, June 21). Treaty of Paris. Retrieved from History.com: https://www.history.com/topics/american-revolution/treaty-of-paris.
[90] Ruppert, B. (2016, August 4). How Article 7 Freed 3000 Slaves. Retrieved from Allthingsliberty.com: https://allthingsliberty.com/2016/08/how-article-7-freed-3000-slaves/.

commerce for the northeast. British recognition of American fishing rights was a non-negotiable element for the American delegates, as it would secure a prosperous and strategically valuable industry for the newly independent nation.[91]

What to Do with the Loyalists

For the British, offering protection to the loyalists was an obligation of honor to those who had supported Great Britain's cause and a reflection of its commitment to its subjects. Assurances for their safety and compensation for their losses were vital in maintaining the British Crown's honor and forestalling future insurrections within the rest of the empire.

The Final Copy

Through skillful negotiation and strategic maneuvering, the commissioners crafted a treaty that would shape the future of their respective nations. The recognition of American independence was a watershed moment, laying to rest any lingering doubts about the permanence of the new nation. The delineation of boundaries, most notably the extension of the United States to the Mississippi River, set the stage for westward expansion and the acquisition of vast territories.

The treaty also provided for the British evacuation of their forces from the United States, marking the end of a military occupation that had long outstayed its welcome. In return, the Americans agreed to ensure property restitution to loyalists and take steps to prevent further seizure or harm.

Great Britain dealt with the American allies in separate agreements. France regained territories in the Caribbean occupied by the British, fortifying its foothold in the region. Spain regained Florida, which it had lost to the British during the Seven Years' War, and it also secured the expansion of its territory in North America, including control over the strategically important port of New Orleans. These gains were critical to Spain's objective of reinforcing its colonial empire and securing a buffer against future American expansion.[92]

---

[91] Cronin, A. (2015, April 3). Untangling North Atlantic Fishing, 1764-1910 Part 2: Anglo-American Treaties Regarding the Fishery, 1783-1818. Retrieved from Masshist.org: https://www.masshist.org/beehiveblog/2015/04/untangling-north-atlantic-fishing-1764-1910-part-2-anglo-american-treaties-regarding-the-fishery-1783-1818/.
[92] Famguardian.org. (2024, February 26). The Definitive Treaty of Paris 1783. Retrieved from Fanguardian.org:

The Treaty of Paris was signed by the American and British delegates on September 3rd, 1783, and formally ended the American Revolutionary War. The Continental Congress ratified it on January 14th, 1784, and Great Britain did the same on April 9th, 1784.

The Last Days: The Newburgh Conspiracy

There were still hostilities as the Treaty of Paris was being negotiated. The fighting between the Americans and the Native Americans on the western frontier was intense. However, the fighting was winding down since everyone knew peace was being ironed out. Nobody wanted to be the last person to die in the war.

There was a mutiny of Continental soldiers in Pennsylvania because of back pay issues. It was put down quickly by a contingent of 1,500 soldiers sent by Washington. A noteworthy dissent was the Newburgh Conspiracy. Once again, back pay was an issue.

Many officers of the Continental Army were on the cusp of open revolt. Their discontent stemmed from Congress's indecision on whether to honor its promise to pay the war veterans and the belief that their sacrifices for the cause of independence were being disregarded. Those stationed at Newburgh, New York, were deeply worried that the Continental Congress would not honor its obligations, including pensions, to those who had risked their lives for the new nation. A memorandum composed of officers led by Henry Knox was sent to Congress in December 1782, expressing frustration over the issues of back pay in arrears and pensions. The Continental Congress discussed the issue, but the primary problem was that there was no money to fund the demands. That admission only made things worse.

A letter reportedly written by Major John Armstrong circulated in the Newburgh camp, stating that the army should disband before the peace treaty was signed unless their demands were met. The possibility of a military coup d'état was implicit in the letter. Despite Washington's opposition, a meeting of all officers was called for on March 11th, 1783. Washington asked the officers to wait four days before they met to allow tempers to cool. The officers' meeting was held on March 15th. To everyone's surprise, General Washington entered the room and asked to be allowed to speak. The commander in chief knew that a full-scale

https://famguardian.org/PublishedAuthors/Govt/USTreaties/DefinitiveTreatyOfPeace1783.pdf.

mutiny could happen and made the most of his time.[93]

Washington appealed to their sense of honor, patriotism, and shared struggle, urging them to give the government time to make good on its promises. Washington's words were a heartfelt call to the ideals and values upon which the nation was being founded. He emphasized that the very essence of the republic for which they fought hinged on subordination to civilian authority and denounced any actions that would undermine the fragile roots of American democracy. Washington's address was a masterful blend of persuasion and leadership, dissuading his officers from taking a path that could irrevocably alter the course of the young republic.[94]

George Washington was a father figure to these officers. His emotional pleas stirred these men who had watched the general share their sufferings and bear the burden of command for years. Many wept. The officers resolved to respect the wishes of their commander. The bond that Washington had worked to build with his officers made the difference.

Final Days: The New York Evacuation

The departure of thirty thousand British soldiers from New York City was not merely a military maneuver; it set off a chain reaction that reshaped the political, social, and economic fabric of the fledgling United States. On November 25th, 1783, the British began their evacuation. With hundreds of ships, the British ferried their men, equipment, and loyalist supporters out of the city to the waiting vessels in the harbor.

The process was not without its complications; disputes over the protection of loyalists and the logistics of the withdrawal posed significant challenges. Yet, the retreat was mostly peaceful, and the transition of power to the newly independent United States was underway.

Integral to the complexity of the evacuation was the fate of the loyalists. It was a topic of heated debate during the peace negotiations and remained a point of contention until the last moment of the

---

[93] Hattem, M. (2024, February 26). Newburgh Conspiracy. Retrieved from Mountvernon.org: https://www.mountvernon.org/library/digitalhistory/digital-encyclopedia/article/newburgh-conspiracy/.

[94] Washington, G. (2024, February 26). Newburgh Address: George Washington to Officers of the Army, March 15, 1783. Retrieved from MountVernon.org: https://www.mountvernon.org/education/primary-source-collections/primary-source-collections/article/newburgh-address-george-washington-to-officers-of-the-army-march-15-1783/.

withdrawal. The British assured safe passage to loyalists who chose to leave with them. Those who did not leave faced an uncertain and often hostile reception from their former countrymen.

Estimates suggest that thousands of loyalists were evacuated from New York City alongside the British troops. Their departure led them to various destinations, primarily other parts of the British Empire, where they sought safety and the chance to rebuild their lives. Many sailed to the Canadian provinces of Nova Scotia and New Brunswick, which the British government had prepared to receive them. Others found refuge in Quebec, Ontario, and Prince Edward Island, while many others relocated to Britain or other British colonies in the West Indies. This large-scale migration forged new communities and impacted the demographics and cultures of the areas where loyalists settled.

The Departure of African Americans

On the docks of New York City at the time of the evacuation, there were chaotic scenes similar to what happened at the fall of Saigon in 1975 and the evacuation of Kabaul in 2021. A palpable sense of urgency gripped the African American population in New York City, particularly those who had escaped slavery and fought for the Crown. The promise of freedom was within reach, yet the chaos and uncertainty of the evacuation sparked fear of recapture and re-enslavement by American forces. They had reason to be concerned.

The Treaty of Paris included an unprecedented article in international law: Article 7. This provision, championed by the American negotiators, stipulated that the British would return any slaves belonging to Americans "in whatever part of the world British forces might occupy." This meant that those who were once slaves and had escaped to the British lines might be returned to their former owners.[95]

The British military commanders, recognizing the dedication and contributions of these individuals to their cause, felt an obligation to honor the promise of freedom that was given in exchange for service.

To facilitate the safe passage of those former slaves who had served the Crown, the British meticulously documented their names in the "Book of Negroes," a ledger that served as a form of protection and legitimacy for their evacuation. This level of record-keeping provided a

---

[95] Ruppert, B. (2016, August 4). How Article 7 Freed 3000 Slaves. Retrieved from Allthingsliberty.com: https://allthingsliberty.com/2016/08/how-article-7-freed-3000-slaves/.

loophole, allowing the British to argue that these individuals had earned their freedom through service rather than being considered property that needed to be returned to American slaveholders. The information allowed the runaway slaves to be evacuated alongside British forces as they were transported to British territories. It is believed around nine thousand African Americans left with the British.[96]

The question of slavery could not be swept under the carpet forever. It eventually resulted in a war that would kill hundreds of thousands.

The evacuation of New York City marked the dawn of a new era for the United States. Americans were no longer the subjects of the British Crown. They were now part of a new nation that had unique challenges and obstacles to overcome.

---

[96] Tsaltas-Ottomanelli, L. G. (2023, November 15). Black Loyalists in the Evacuation of New York City, 1783. Retrieved from Gothamcenter.org: https://www.gothamcenter.org/blog/black-loyalists-evaculation-zy4la.

Conclusion

The American Revolution shook the world and introduced a period of change that lasted well into the 19th century. No one expected the Americans to take on the British and win, but it happened.

Some history lessons learned from the American Revolution are worth considering today. The Fabian battle strategy worked. Washington and Greene avoided an enemy with superior numbers and fought another day numerous times. They sometimes lost, but they often inflicted serious damage on the British anyway, so any victory was expensive. Interestingly, many British officers were very familiar with classical history. The generals overlooked a strategy that permitted the Romans to defeat Hannibal.

Arrogance and pride do come before the fall. The British Parliament had many opportunities to be reasonable and negotiate with the dissatisfied colonists. The Americans were willing to stay a part of the British Empire until the Olive Branch Petition failed. Consequently, they decided they had no choice but to declare independence and go their separate ways. The British government was too proud to admit it was wrong on occasions when Parliament was taking the wrong path. Parliament should have listened to people like Edmund Burke but didn't. The British paid dearly for not listening to wise counsel.

Courage wins battles, but persistence wins wars. The American Continental Army could have disbanded after several battles, but it did not. Instead, the patriots stuck together and stayed the course. Valley Forge is a striking example of perseverance under enormous hardship.

The Americans believed in a cause and were prepared to continue the struggle.

The United States of America continues to be a positive example to other nations. Liberty is a cause worth fighting for, and Americans in the American Revolutionary War put their lives on the line for the right to be free. That struggle and the common people's fight for their rights is something that all Americans can justifiably be proud of.

Part 3: The American Civil War

An Enthralling Overview of the War Between States

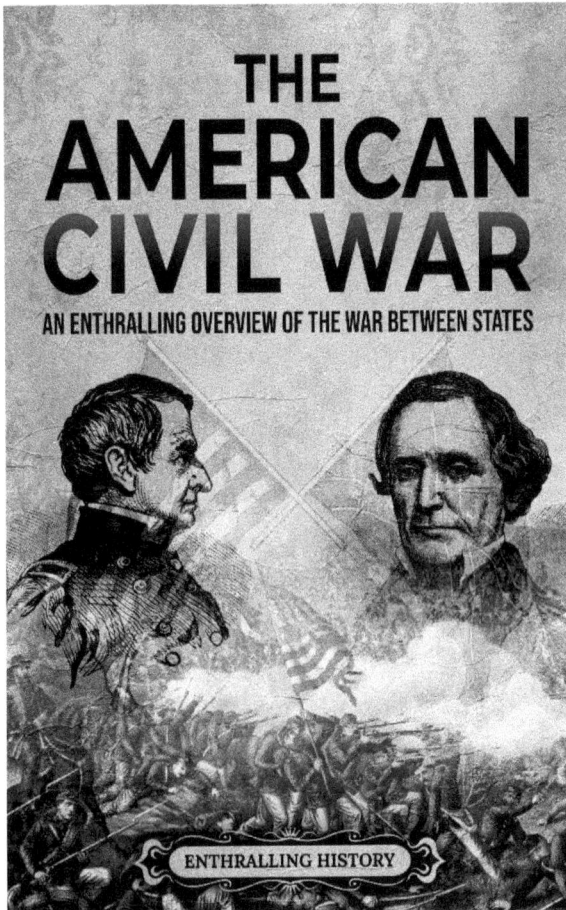

THE

AMERICAN
CIVIL WAR

AN ENTHRALLING OVERVIEW OF THE WAR BETWEEN STATES

ENTHRALLING HISTORY

Introduction

The American Civil War has become one of the most defining moments in US history. Not a century had passed since the Declaration of Independence, which was adopted in July 1776. Since gaining independence and existing as a sovereign nation, complex social, political, and economic issues had been quietly growing in the United States. Instead of addressing them, the country was distracted by different priorities, mainly acquiring new territories and becoming a regional superpower. However, by the 1860s, the divide within American society reached its peak. The nation disintegrated into four years of bloody conflicts and instability, which cost the lives of more than one million Americans.

Compared to other major US conflicts, the Civil War holds a special place in the hearts of Americans. The war was a pivotal point in the 19th century and completely changed the course of the country. The consequences of the Civil War can still be felt today, as the country is perhaps the most polarized it has been for a very long time. Some compare it to the infamous North-South divide. Despite the immense importance of the war for the US and, to a large extent, world history, many people outside the US are unfamiliar with what happened almost 160 years ago.

This book wishes to cover the extremely interesting history of the American Civil War and explain the events that took place. Not only will the book provide an overview of the main events that shaped the American Civil War, but it will also explore many details that are often left out when discussing the conflict.

The first part of the book will be devoted to the situation that existed in the United States before the start of the war in 1861. It will cover the events that led to the extreme socio-political turmoil of the country by the end of the 1850s and talk about some of the main differences between the Northern and Southern states. It will also discuss the extremely important concept of Manifest Destiny and how it impacted the growth of America for the first part of the 19th century. Then, we will turn our attention to the Mexican-American War, the Texas question, and the effects these events had on slavery. Finally, we will talk about the political processes in the 1850s, which escalated the tensions between the Northern and the Southern states, and explore the severity of the divide within the country.

The middle part of the book covers the actual conflict itself. Explore the chronological account of the war, and learn about the figures who made a name for themselves. The book will also cover all of the theaters of the war in great detail, starting from the Eastern and Western Fronts in the heart of the United States to the Trans-Mississippi, Pacific, and Lower Seaboard theaters near the Gulf of Mexico. The American Civil War remains the largest conflict fought in the US. Diving into details about the campaigns is pivotal in understanding how the war unfolded over the years.

Finally, the book will talk about the outcome of the war and its end. We will explain the circumstances that led to the North's victory over the South and the final stages of the conflict. Then, discover the immediate and long-term consequences of the Civil War. We will also mention the international reaction that followed the end of the conflict. Examining these effects is crucial in understanding the influence the war had on the US and the rest of the free world.

The American Civil War is perceived to be a conflict where the side that fought for the values of freedom, democracy, and social equality managed to emerge victorious. Besides being a pivotal point in US history, it also is one of the most popular ideological clashes in the 19th century. To some degree, the war was inevitable—one could see the tensions between the two sides from a mile away—but this factor, coupled with many other reasons, is why this war holds a special place in the hearts of Americans. So, let's dive into the American Civil War, one of the most instantly recognizable conflicts in history.

Chapter 1: 19th-Century America

Let's take a look at some of the existing issues in the American socio-political landscape, from the early 19th century all the way to the 1850s—the decade that preceded the American Civil War. We will focus mainly on the ideological struggle present in the country at the beginning of the 1800s, as well as describe the general economic structure of the US. Historians often disagree on which of these issues is the true "cause" of the Civil War. However, instead of focusing on individual issues, it is better to provide a general overview of the situation that existed prior to the start of the war.

The Land of the Free and the Different

As many historians have recognized, the United States in the 19th century was differently organized than other countries in the world, something that was even noticed by the European contemporaries who visited the States back then. Europe had essentially given birth to America and American society, but the US was not modeled after the European states. The pro-democratic movements in the late-18th-century US started a wave of nationalist revolutions throughout Europe, which characterized the continent for the whole of the 19th century.

This weird symbiotic relationship existed between the Old and New World, but it was only present in the US and not in other colonial or post-colonial European societies like, for example, Canada and Mexico. The United States was still being forged, both culturally and socially, by the time the Civil War began in the 1860s. It was also making developments in its unique political structures that largely defined the country since it gained independence in 1776. American society borrowed a lot from European societies, but whatever it borrowed, it tried to change in its own way.

In the 19th century, the country was still trying to find its footing in the world. The United States had been born under special circumstances. After centuries of colonization and outside rule, anti-imperialism was innate in the hearts of the average American. Their hatred toward Great Britain and King George united the American public, for the most part, during the Revolutionary War.

This anti-imperialist sentiment led to the promotion of freedom and liberty. However, it became clear that anti-imperialism could not be the only factor that glued American society together. Thus, most of the early 19th century was devoted to forging a new, unique American identity that would take the liberal democratic principles that the country had been founded upon and mix them with core European values to create something distinctive. Thanks to an array of factors, including rapid technological improvements, the age of industrialization, and geographic isolation, the Americans were able to get to work.

Practically every inch of Europe had been explored in great detail. The same could not be said about North America. Although the lands of the continent had been divided between the French, the Spanish, and the British, by the late 1810s, only the latter had any ambition, let alone the resources, to put up a challenge for North America. Europe had been swept up in a universal uproar due to Napoleon's conquests, which meant that both France and Spain had to mobilize the majority of their resources domestically, leaving their overseas possessions unattended. In turn, this caused the French to sell their North American territories— more than 828,000 square miles of land—in the famous Louisiana Purchase of 1807 to the ambitious United States. The Mexican Revolution effectively kicked the Spanish out of continental America by 1820.

The weakening of America's direct rivals meant there was an opening for the United States to sweep the continent and claim whatever it could for itself. The dream of stretching the American lands from the East Coast of the Atlantic to the West Coast of the Pacific was born. This idea became a defining characteristic of 19th-century American foreign policy. Manifest Destiny was imprinted into the minds of the Americans. It was a belief that the United States was destined by God to spread American ideals from the east to the west.

Inspired by this "righteous" idea, the American settlers swarmed the continent to try and expand American territories as far as they could, first colonizing the center of the continent before reaching the distant rich lands of California and Oregon. The settlers were resilient in their divine mission of spreading American ideas of liberty, democracy, and prosperity while claiming an immense chunk of land for themselves at the same time. They persisted despite the resistance they found, forcibly displacing natives. They were even ready to challenge the British over what they believed was rightfully theirs.

American Progress, a painting depicting the concept of Manifest Destiny.
https://commons.wikimedia.org/wiki/File:American_Progress_(John_Gast_painting).jpg

Thus, the idea of Manifest Destiny, in a way, was a diversion from anti-imperialism. Arguably, it was one of the earliest signs of American imperialism, as it displayed the qualities found in all empires of the 19th century, such as forced colonization and the spread of ideas. However, for the United States, Manifest Destiny was merely the fulfillment of its destiny, so its morality was rarely questioned. Most people paid attention to the spread of liberal, democratic principles instead of the ugly stuff.

Anti-imperialism was replaced by a form of anti-Europeanism, which is most clearly identified in the famous Monroe Doctrine of 1823. This was a policy by US President James Monroe that stated the United States would oppose the formation of any future European colonies in the Western Hemisphere. In exchange, it would remain neutral in European matters. The Monroe Doctrine fused with the concept of Manifest Destiny: the latter was a belief that the US was destined to colonize the rest of the continent by itself, while the former guaranteed that the US would be the only one that could do it. Both reflected the public sentiment of the time relatively well and promised a bright future. In addition, they also underlined the fact that the United States, although still a relatively new country, was ambitious and ready to stand up for itself, something that put it on the radar of the bigger European powers.

Even before the concepts of Manifest Destiny and the Monroe Doctrine became official, the country made an impressive effort to establish itself as a regional power. The War of 1812 was the first sign that signaled the United States was a force to be reckoned with, as the Americans withstood the mighty British forces and diminished Spain's influence in Spanish Florida. Although the Americans were not officially victorious in the war, they had clearly demonstrated they were powerful. After that, the United States was not afraid to challenge Britain over territorial disputes. Even though their rivalry never resulted in a war, the US managed to achieve several favorable outcomes.

One of the best examples of 19th-century American expansionism is the Mexican-American War, which ended in a decisive US victory. Mexico was forced to give up immense territorial concessions—about one-third of its territory. The war started over the issue of Texas, a province that had seceded from Mexico and wished to join the United States as a new state. The Americans easily overpowered the newly formed Mexican republic, which was plagued with domestic issues and an inferior military. As a result, the United States gained almost all of the modern Southwest, including the rich territories of California and Texas. By the end of the war, the United States had, in a way, fulfilled its destiny, as it occupied the heart of the North American continent from the East Coast all the way to the Pacific Ocean.

Thus, the first part of the 19th century was a productive period for US foreign policy. Since the early 1800s, the United States had developed its national identity around the ideas of continental expansion and anti-Europeanism. Let's look at how its assets allowed the US to cement its position as a regional powerhouse.

The 19th-century US Economy

As the decades passed after gaining independence, it became clearer that America's isolated geographic position was paying off. Its advantageous location, far away from the power centers of major European countries, meant the United States was relatively secure from external threats. The people's efforts and resources did not have to be used on countries challenging its growing power and influence. Thus, it should come as no surprise that the US economy, at least in the first part of the 19th century, grew far quicker than some may have predicted. The security provided by geographic isolation, paired with a motivated population to explore and colonize the unknown wilderness of the American continent, meant there was much for the taking with very little resistance from Europe.

Naturally, with such a massive landscape to claim, an important economic aspect showed itself early in the 19th century: the profit that could be made from deforestation. This was seen as a sort of win-win situation for the American settlers. They needed lands to settle on and set up agricultural or industrial bases, so huge chunks of land had to be deforested to make room for expansion. This meant that the country, in addition to its already vast coal and iron reserves, had a huge abundance of wood and timber—materials that could be used for energy, manufacturing, and an array of other useful things. Contrary to Europe, where wood was slowly starting to become a luxury due to increased levels of deforestation (a natural consequence of industrialization), the United States had the ability to not only freely use the timber it produced domestically but also have a significant amount left for export.

America's natural resources promised a bright future for the economy. At the beginning of the 1800s, the US still depended on the Old World, mainly Britain, which remained America's largest trading partner for decades. However, this factor could have been attributed to Britain starting the Industrial Revolution, as it gave the empire a natural head-start compared to its rivals. Industrialization in America followed soon after, despite the fact that the majority of the population lived in rural areas—something that was a consequence of dwelling in a largely unexplored continent. In the southern part of the country, the rural population outnumbered those who lived in urban areas. On the other hand, this meant cities easily sprung up in the new territories. Meanwhile, on the East Coast, New York, Philadelphia, and Boston dominated the scene. The American Midwest soon started to rise into prominence, with cities like Chicago and Cincinnati growing almost exponentially before the start of the Civil War.

A population boom further boosted economic growth. This boom was partially caused by a large number of immigrants who arrived in the US from Europe. They sought a new life, one that promised significant improvements from their old one. The country's population reached about twenty-five million in the 1850s; there had been only five million people at the start of the century. This was a promising improvement. All sorts of people were welcome to the country despite their age or profession. Many aspects of life were still in development, and everybody could do whatever fit them best.

An influx of people meant that it was very cheap to buy land, which was in abundance. The government had correctly recognized that the public lands in its possession would be put to better use in the hands of the American people. They sold an acre for $2 to not only the citizens of the country but also the immigrants. This was one of the biggest motivating factors for people to venture out west and settle there permanently. Although Native Americans already lived on the land, the open frontier was likely a somewhat welcome relief to the cramped conditions in the east. By the 1860s, the US government had sold about eighty million acres of land. The people who moved west were happy to develop their possessions as they liked with little regulations. The American Midwest rapidly grew in this period.

In short, the American economy never stopped growing after it achieved independence in 1776. Thanks to an array of factors, such as an abundance of land and resources, a sizeable workforce, and favorable conditions, the US economy quickly picked up the pace and started to catch up with its competitors in Europe. However, there is one vital detail we have not yet talked about: the role of slavery.

The Economics of Slavery

Slaves were pivotal not only to the structure of the American economy in the 19th century but also to many socio-political matters. We shall now look at the economic implications of slavery.

Since the age of colonization, slavery greatly helped the European colonizers in developing and maintaining their newly acquired territories. It was innate that with a blend of cultures, ethnicities, and religions, new hierarchical structures would form. In the colonies, slavery was just one part of the hierarchy, but it was not unknown to the dwellers of the Old World. After all, slaves had always been the lowest strata in every civilized society. They were often not even considered as people or citizens but rather as possessions or property. In the New World, slaves were seen in a similar light. They were used in agriculture, mining, industries, construction, and many other forms of labor.

A family of slaves in Georgia.
https://commons.wikimedia.org/wiki/File:Family_of_slaves_in_Georgia,_circa_1850.jpg

It is sometimes difficult to grasp the extent to which slavery existed in the US, as it was considered old-fashioned in other countries by the time the Civil War broke out. Because slavery was such an efficient way of generating income, it was considered one of the pillars of the American economy. This was more apparent in the Southern part of the country, which was far more dependent on slavery than the North. The Southern states thrived on agriculture, and they made a lot of money from their vast plantations, which were operated by the very slaves they owned. As the early 1800s started, it was clearer than ever that slave ownership was perhaps the most important aspect of the Southerners' lifestyle. It not only determined the wealth of the owners but also their status in society. The more slaves one owned, the more power one had.

The slaves lived in terrible conditions. They were abused and separated from their families time and time again. However, slaves dominated the population of some Southern states. Along the Mississippi

River, in Alabama and Mississippi, as well as in South Carolina and parts of Virginia, they made up most of the population, making up about half of the whole population of the South. Thus, it should come as no surprise that the South was very reliant on slaves. Owning more slaves meant working more land, which, in turn, meant more direct income. Most of the country's agriculture, both domestically and in terms of foreign exports, originated in the South. With these funds, the Southern slave owners would try to expand their wealth by investing more. They would buy new territories and acquire new slaves to work their property.

It was a vicious cycle and a profitable endeavor with a great return on investment. It is important to keep in mind that with the concept of Manifest Destiny becoming more and more prevalent, Southern slave owners were more adamant about claiming new lands for themselves. Not only that, but rich slave owners, those who owned about a hundred slaves or more, lived probably the most lavishly in the whole country. Their properties spanned tens of acres. They had luxurious mansions, diverse plantations and farms, and nothing in the world to worry about. In turn, this motivated farmers who did not enjoy the same privileges to strive to attain the same lifestyle.

In the early 19th century, the South's prosperous slave economy put it in competition with the North, which was slowly abandoning slave ownership and its reliance on agriculture as a whole. Instead, its focus was on other industries, such as textile or machinery manufacturing. By the 1850s, the Southern slave owners had reached the peak of their wealth. In addition to making fortunes by selling and buying slaves, the market price of their products, especially cotton, increased almost exponentially during that period. The southerners, at least the ones at the top of the social stratum, could yield amazing results on their capital investments. They then spent their money on more luxurious and foreign products.

The Southern countryside was an impressive sight, with massive territories owned by single families and tens of slaves working their lands. Interestingly, many Southern planters became so rich from their endeavors that they no longer needed to live on their properties. Instead, they could move to more urban areas, which were popping up all over the country. They could move to the newly acquired lands out west or even leave America to enjoy lavish lives in Europe.

These were only some of the main characteristics of the early 19th-century United States. Since the beginning of the century, a new national identity based on expansion had gained a lot of traction. Supported by an anti-imperialist (or rather an anti-European) foreign policy, the United States saw itself as the sole "protector" of the Western Hemisphere from the old systems of the tyrannical Europeans. All of this generated a drive in the public to acquire and modernize more territories, which, according to Manifest Destiny, the Americans were always destined to liberate. With a motivated population largely united under the same goal, it is no surprise that the American economy boomed in the first half of the 19th century. The American Industrial Revolution soon followed the European one, borrowing the best of its characteristics and fusing them with its newly acquired national identity.

Although America's economic growth was supported by a population boom and some prosperous decades, the creation and development of new industries and societies slowly started to split the country in half. This divide would prove to be fatal for America's future. The cracks started to form within the American public, and it was based not only on geography but also on societal and political differences.

Chapter 2: The North and the South

In the previous chapter, we briefly touched on the North-South divide, which started to make itself apparent in the 19th century. The differences that emerged between the Northern and Southern states spread to almost all fields of life, and their severity increased to all-time highs. The American public became highly polarized and was divided on crucial social, political, and economic issues. In a way, the US abandoned the optimistic spirit that it had upheld since gaining independence.

This chapter will focus on the problems that caused a massive divide in the American public and depict the distinctions in the ordinary lives of Northern and Southern citizens of the country. These problems would cause the Civil War to break out in 1861.

The Mason-Dixon Line

Before we start examining the clear-cut distinctions between the North and the South, it is first vital to understand where the North and South actually began and ended. The border between the two sides was clear at the time of the Civil War, but the exact geography of the conflict cannot fully be considered as "Northern states versus Southern states." For example, California, although located in the west of the country, was considered a Northern state. The divide between the North and the South has implications that reach far beyond simple geography.

The Mason-Dixon Line was once a demarcation line that separated the American states of Pennsylvania, Maryland, Delaware, and Virginia. It gained a sort of symbolical significance decades after its creation in 1767 as a separation line between the Southern and Northern states. Roughly speaking, everything north of this line was considered a Northern state, sharing the same socio-political ideas. The states south of the Mason-Dixon Line were the Southern states, which often held opposing political ideas to the North.

The Mason-Dixon Line.
https://commons.wikimedia.org/wiki/File:Mason-dixon-line.gif

Along this line, the differences between the two sides started to show. Of the original Thirteen Colonies, seven of them—New Hampshire, Massachusetts, Rhode Island, New York, Connecticut, New Jersey, and Pennsylvania—were in the North, while the remaining six—Virginia, Delaware, Maryland, North and South Carolina, and Georgia—were in the South. However, this does not accurately reflect the positions of the states during the outbreak of the Civil War. For example, Delaware and Maryland sided with the North, despite being south of the original Mason-Dixon Line. Still, it is a nice starting point to have when drawing an imaginary line between the two sides.

The country's rapid industrialization and its expansionist efforts in the west slowly started driving a wedge between the Northern and Southern societies. The industrialization process was largely focused in the North instead of the South. States like Pennsylvania and New York were the forerunners in adopting and developing new industries. Their economic systems were almost entirely dependent on them. The vast river and canal systems of the North allowed for faster transportation of manufactured goods, which made the area naturally superior to the vaster and loosely connected South. Connecticut became a hub for America's manufacturing industries. It was located at the crossroads of all the Northern states and had access to the inland rivers and the ocean.

With the introduction of new machinery—one of the most important characteristics of the Industrial Revolution—many jobs that were previously done by hand were quickly being replaced, accelerating not only the production of refined goods from raw materials but also the general growth of different industries. The introduction of these new technologies transformed the American economy, just as had been the case in Europe decades earlier. Crucially, new farming devices, such as binders and reaping machines, were adopted to greatly increase efficiency, making up for the shortage of labor that plagued the country. In addition, the revolutionary invention of the cotton gin in the 1790s made the cotton-picking process easier, as it reduced the time needed to pick a pound of cotton from hours to minutes.

The South, on the other hand, had largely remained rural and based on agriculture. In fact, despite being rich in raw materials, Southern states had to send whatever they produced to the North for it to be refined and manufactured as goods. They would then buy the goods back for higher prices. The South was not really losing money during this process because of extremely high returns on agriculture and slave ownership, but its dependence on Northern industry was becoming more evident as the 19th century progressed.

As we have already mentioned, the very rich in the South had built such luxurious lives for themselves that the majority of the South was motivated to follow in their footsteps, thus causing a general slowdown in the urbanization process. The majority of the Southerners worked as farmers, and the products they grew they consumed or sold locally. Only the ones at the very top could export their materials in large quantities to other states. In the North, the citizens slowly started to move to the cities en masse and work for wages. Meanwhile, the Southerners were hesitant to give up their life's work and just abandon the holdings of which they had grown so proud.

This last factor proved to be a serious problem. Despite the fact that the Southerners aspired to become rich slave owners and enjoy lavish lives on their plantations, the majority of them never reached the same levels as the ones on the top. The wealth distribution in the South was extremely unequal, with only a minority being planters—slave owners with more than a hundred slaves. There were only about fifty thousand people in total out of an estimated five million people. Per capita, the Southern citizens were wealthier than their Northern counterparts. Despite not all of the Southerners enjoying similar privileges and riches as the slave owners, the majority who owned land made great yearly profits and had enough to live comfortably.

Land ownership was crucial for the Southerners, who grew different crops. Cotton—the crop most associated with slavery—was not the most common among slave owners, although it was arguably the most valuable material. Due to the particular conditions required to grow cotton in large numbers, it was only harvested in what's called the Lower South: Georgia, the Carolinas, and Texas, albeit to a smaller degree. Other Southern states grew tobacco, like Virginia. Along the Mississippi, the most common crop cultivated by slaves was sugar.

When comparing the more urban areas of the South with the North, the differences are just as evident. Despite the fact that Southern citizens were just as, if not comparatively, wealthier than their Northern counterparts, most of them lived in rural areas. The economy of the South was so reliant on the citizens' agrarian lifestyle that the urbanization process was greatly halted. Most of the Southerners refused to move their lives to newer towns and cities. Meanwhile, in the North, big cities like New York and Philadelphia were quickly growing, both in size and in population. For example, two of the largest cities of Virginia—Richmond and Petersburg—only had up to about sixty thousand people by the time the war broke out. Chicago, St. Louis, and Cincinnati, which were relatively newer cities, each contained a population of more than 100,000.

When it came to urban areas, most people in the South lived in New Orleans, a city that has nowadays become synonymous with African American culture. Back in the 18th century, it was one of the largest slave ports. The truth is that the South simply could not keep up with the North's growth. The North experienced rapid industrialization, but the South over-glorified and over-relied on the agrarian lifestyle. This had spill-over effects in areas of life, such as the general education level. By the 1860s, a fifth of the Southern citizens were illiterate, not taking into consideration the slaves who made up nearly half of the South's population. Comparatively, about 95 percent of Northerners had at least some type of education. As for the youth, only a third of the Southern children went to school in comparison to the three-quarters in New England and the Midwest.

The Slavery Question

The population boom of the early 19th century did not only include the white citizens of the United States, whose ranks were reinforced by the influx of immigrants who arrived in the country in search of new, prosperous lives. The slave population also increased dramatically in the first few decades of the 1800s but only in the South. While the North was becoming wearier of slavery as a practice and was abandoning the old agrarian lifestyle to pursue new opportunities in cities, the Southerners were happy to continue acquiring more land and expanding their properties. This meant that more slaves were needed to work those lands, and in many cases, they were transported from the Northern states that now had little use for them.

Over time, the planters with the most slaves competed with each other, comparing who provided the best and worse conditions for their slaves—something that is a complete exaggeration since the slaves lived under terrible circumstances no matter what their masters thought.

Christianity had an immense influence on the cultural lives of the slaves. The slaves didn't lose their culture; instead, it evolved, borrowing from the American lifestyle and from long-lasting African traditions to create a unique, rich culture. By the early 19th century, the slave population was predominantly Christian, a consequence of the God-fearing South.

However, as the oppressed blacks increasingly converted to Christianity, the churches found it difficult to accommodate them due to their status as slaves. In reality, the whole slavery ordeal was a pretty unchristian matter, and ignoring that fact was very difficult at times. Black Christianity became a cultural phenomenon, incorporating traditional African elements, such as passionate choir singing and dancing, into Christian rituals. In such a religiously diverse place like the United States, where Christianity had multiple variations and separate churches, not everyone welcomed blacks in their ranks. Some, like the Baptists, were more indifferent about blacks taking part in sermons or regular Christian activities. Black Christians even found themselves as preachers in the churches that welcomed them.

Finding joy and freedom in religion was crucial since it signaled that the oppressed black population had a place to experience true happiness despite living such miserable lives. Religion also somewhat boosted the literacy of the slave population. Although some slaves, mainly those who had day-to-day contact with their owners, were taught by their masters to read and write, most of the slaves who were literate came about as a result of Christians who genuinely wanted the oppressed to learn more about God's deeds.

Another side effect of a growing slave population that was becoming more literate was the creation of special groups of white men called patrols. Interestingly, as the decades passed, slave rights somewhat increased, despite the fact they were still being very much oppressed. For instance, slaves could practice their religion in certain white churches. Over time, slaves were sometimes permitted to leave their master's property. They typically had to have a written pass signed by their owner permitting them to leave for a given time. Patrols were hired by larger slave owners who wished to control the activities of their slaves when they went off their property. The patrols would check the passes of the roaming slaves to see whether or not they had been permitted to leave. If the slaves did not have a permit, the patrollers would violently beat them to teach a lesson. It was yet another measure to try and monitor the slave population as effectively as possible. Recent developments had aroused some suspicion in the slave owners, who feared a large enough slave rebellion might overthrow them from power.

Slave rebellions were nothing new at the time. The famous Haitian Revolution is perhaps the most obvious example in which a predominantly black population gained control through an armed revolt. South America had also seen a couple of instigations in Brazil and Guiana. In the US, the most alarming slave revolt took place in 1831 in Southampton County, Virginia. Led by an enslaved young man by the name of Nat Turner, the Southampton Insurrection was ultimately unsuccessful at undermining the slaves' oppression. It cost the lives of about two hundred blacks and one hundred whites. The rebellion was violently crushed and started a new wave of legislation that sought to further limit the rights of the slave population.

The rebellion of 1831 was perhaps the first time the Southern slave owners were terrified. Their society was dominated by blacks, the majority of which were young men who theoretically could seize control if they managed to achieve high levels of mobilization. To avoid the worst possible scenario from developing, the Southern slave owners spread pro-slavery propaganda. For example, they claimed that slavery was the natural condition of the blacks, something that had been decided by God when he was creating whites as the "natural superiors." Still, the Southampton Insurrection lit a spark in the United States, which quickly spread like wildfire in the following decades.

First Signs of Abolitionism

After the Southampton Insurrection, the anti-slavery movement took off around the nation, especially in the North. Although the movement did not see much success at first, during the 1830s, more people started vocalizing their opinions, believing that the government should eventually do something to prohibit slavery once and for all. Many stated that it was the "right thing to do" or that it had worked in the Old World. Before the insurrection, a common opinion was that slavery would eventually die off. For example, the new machines that had been invented during the Industrial Revolution would eventually replace the human labor that was performed by slaves.

There were no talks of completely freeing the enslaved black population, let alone giving them sufficient rights, but more people slowly recognized the terrible things slavery stood for and how it impacted the social and political development of the country. The most optimistic citizens trusted the US government to implement new policies that would be along the same lines as the abolition of the slave trade, which had been passed in 1808.

It has to be mentioned that, despite having abolished the importation of slaves to the country in 1808, Congress also made decisions that pleased the Southerners. For instance, in 1820, an act known as the Missouri Compromise permitted Missouri to enter the Union as a slave state. Maine would be admitted as a free state, and slavery would be banned from the rest of the lands acquired from the Louisiana Purchase that fell north of the 36° 30' parallel. Before its enactment, the issue of slavery had risen in importance. The legislation was a way of immediately dealing with the matter, but it was by no means a long-term solution to the problem.

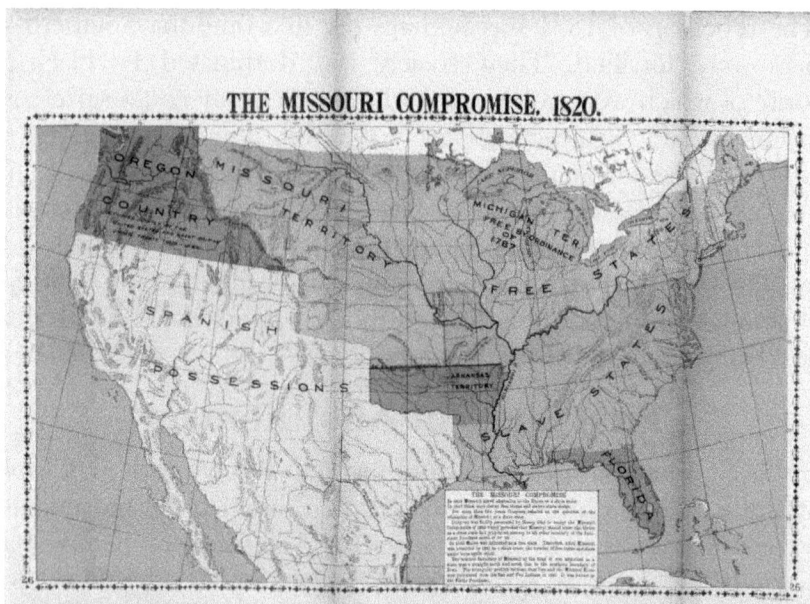

The Missouri Compromise.
https://commons.wikimedia.org/wiki/File:Map_of_the_Missouri_Compromise,_1820.jpg

The Missouri Compromise established some rules regarding the future admission of US states, with both the free North and the slave-owning South agreeing that upsetting the balance between the free and slave states would be detrimental to the country. After 1820, the balance was supposed to be kept equal, and for a time, it was: there were twelve free states in the North and twelve slave states in the South. But the compromise affected the future expansion of the US. As states were added to the Union, the number of slave states would grow just as much as the number of free states. At the time, nobody cared enough to address the matter permanently, and the Missouri Compromise was the law of the land for over a decade.

However, in the 1830s, the socio-political climate had almost completely changed. The advocates for abolitionism became more organized and started publicly voicing their opinions. For example, in 1831, a journalist named William Lloyd Garrison founded a newspaper by the name of *The Liberator* in Boston. It was one of the first publications that were clearly anti-slavery, and it started a snowball effect in the North. Intellectuals, politicians, and regular citizens who believed in the cause concentrated on attacking the practice of slavery. In 1833, three years before two new states were inaugurated into the Union

(Arkansas in the South and Michigan in the North), William Lloyd Garrison helped establish the American Anti-slavery Society in New York. It was a public space intended to discuss abolitionism as a whole and provide an avenue for abolitionists to voice their opinions. It promoted anti-slavery practices in the North and was pretty successful, quickly gaining followers in the big Northern states.

Slowly but surely, a sizeable anti-slavery movement gained traction in the nation, something that alarmed the Southerners who relied so much on the slaves they owned. What boosted public sentiment against slavery were the reports of fugitive slave cases. Slaves who escaped were called fugitives, and if they were caught, they would be returned to their owners. The First Fugitive Slave Act of 1793 permitted local governments to capture and return escaped slaves to their previous owners and punish those who were involved in their flight in any way. Reports of slaves, who had escaped years before, being captured, brutally treated, and then transported back to the plantations against their will continued to shock the abolitionist North and fueled the anti-slavery movement.

What is interesting is that by the time the Civil War broke out in 1861, the issue of slavery had, in a way, transformed into something more than just the North advocating for abolition and the South protecting the practice. As the two sides' opinions on the matter matured over the decades, a pattern started to develop, especially in the higher societies in the North. Most Northerners did not support giving blacks the same rights they held, as it was a way of still distinguishing themselves as superior. Thus, a sense of racism certainly characterized Northern society.

Despite this, the North was ashamed of the fact that the United States claimed to be a bulwark in the free, Western world but still practiced slavery to a large extent. They wanted to abolish the institution and change the Constitution but were not keen on pushing the anti-slavery movement further than that.

As for the South, we have already mentioned that the image that has become associated with a typical 19th-century American Southerner—a rich planter with a large mansion and acres of land worked by slaves—only represented a minority of all slave owners. One could argue that many Southerners were hopelessly trapped in a vicious cycle. They wished to live the same lavish lifestyles as the ones on the very top, but they were largely unsuccessful. However, once they got involved with the slave business, it was very hard to stop. Slavery was a demanding practice; it demanded constant time, energy, and resources to maintain and expand the "business." The slave owners' attention, no matter their social status or the number of slaves they owned, was almost totally focused on controlling their properties. Personally attending to the management of their slaves was a truly tiresome experience and a burden to many. The system that had been established in the United States by the 1860s required slave owners to be careful of every decision they made since it might affect the way their slave business would develop in the future.

When the Civil War broke out in 1861, it became clear that, despite all the negatives that came with being a slave owner, the Southerners were still ready to defend what they considered was their right.

Chapter 3: Rising Tensions

The divide between the North and the South continued to expand, and it became clear by the 1850s that the two parts of the country were almost completely different in nearly all regards. The North was highly urbanized and educated, with more people choosing to work wage-paying jobs. The North was more modernized, not only economically and technologically but also socially. The Northerners developed new social groups and advocated for pursuing principles that had been described as the main pillars of the United States. The South, on the other hand, was hesitant to give up the agrarian lifestyle it had developed for decades. The Southerners continued to be reliant on land and slave ownership. The tensions between the two sides had long existed and showed themselves time and time again, sometimes by citizens but mostly in Congress, where representatives from Southern and Northern states clashed with each other on practically every issue.

With this background in mind, get ready to explore the decade leading up to the breakout of the Civil War.

A Brief Recap of the Mexican-American War

Before we discuss the laws that played a major role in shaping the United States in the 1850s, we must first take a look at an event that greatly influenced the country. The Mexican-American War was waged from April 1846 to February 1848. It was perhaps the single biggest occurrence that indirectly caused the Civil War. The Mexican-American War had both short- and long-term consequences that shook up the socio-political and economic lives of average Americans.

The war between Mexico and the United States ended in a US victory. It was fought over the issue of Texas, a Mexican region that became increasingly inhabited by American immigrants during the first part of the 19ᵗʰ century. The proximity of Texas to the South, coupled with the richness and vastness of its lands, meant that it was quite easy and, in some sense, even desirable for the average American to venture there and settle down. Mexico even encouraged immigration to some extent, although it might be better to say Mexico did not have enough time or energy to properly address the situation since it was caught up in constant conflicts throughout the first decades of the 1800s. Mexico first fought to gain independence from Spain, and then the Mexicans struggled throughout the 1820s and 1830s since the country could not settle on what kind of rule was best. Texas was one of the biggest provinces of the country back then by pure land size. It was so far away from the heart of Mexico that it was largely unpopulated, which was yet another factor that allowed the American settlers to move freely into the territory and start new lives.

The Americans were barely monitored by the Mexican government. Over time, any attempt to enforce some sort of regulating legislation was simply ignored by those who had immigrated. By the mid-1830s, it had become clear there was nothing left in Texas that could be considered purely Mexican. The Americans dominated the province and constituted the majority of the population. In addition, they were mostly Protestant. Mexico, on the other hand, was one of the most Catholic nations in the world by that time. Mainly, there was the ever-so-relevant question of slavery. Slavery was technically banned in Mexico, but the Americans who lived in Texas still practiced it without any real limitations.

Eventually, after a constant back and forth between the two sides, Texas rebelled against the Mexican regime in October 1835. The rebellion was ultimately successful. The Texans fought fiercely. They were led by Sam Houston and reinforced by some American volunteers who aided their co-nationals in their virtuous cause. Texas managed to gain independence, organizing the short-lived Republic of Texas in March 1836.

The formation of the Republic of Texas was devastating for Mexico. Mexico's internal struggles multiplied after the loss of such a large territory. The high command under General Santa Anna tried to hide the news of the defeat but was unsuccessful in doing so. The country did not have the resources to retaliate, and constant domestic troubles made it impossible for Mexico to focus on recapturing the lost territory. However, it never officially recognized Texan independence.

Regardless, the Texans rejoiced. They modeled their country, legislation, and general political system after the US. They even had their own congress and senate. As the days passed, it became clear that the majority of the population wanted to officially become part of the United States. It made sense. Most Texans were American-born, believed and lived by American principles, and lived right next to the American people. In addition, the United States had been seen as a natural ally to Texas, especially since many Americans had fought side-by-side with the people of Texas in its revolutionary war as volunteers. The US was also the first country to formally recognize Texan independence.

However, the situation was not that simple in the US, despite the fact that the majority of the public advocated for the annexation of the territory and its inauguration as a state. After all, it was the age of Manifest Destiny and American expansionism. But annexing Texas would mean that a new slave state would enter the Union, which would upset the balance that had been agreed upon in the Missouri Compromise in 1820. It would greatly displease the North, which no longer supported slavery. Although another northern state could have been theoretically formed from the Indiana Territory, Texas was far more organized and developed, giving a natural edge to the South.

Eventually, thanks to the efforts of newly elected President James K. Polk, Congress would be swayed to annex Texas as a new state in 1845. Polk was enthusiastic about US westward expansion and a firm advocator of Manifest Destiny. His whole presidential campaign had been based on the annexation of Texas. What served as the dealbreaker was the matter of Oregon, another US territory at the time whose ownership was being disputed with Great Britain, which bordered it to the north. Through negotiations, Polk was able to secure Oregon. It officially became a territory in 1848, but he convinced Congress to sign an annexation act in late 1844.

The Texans ratified the treaty with overwhelming public support in early 1845 and officially entered the Union in February of the next year. But naturally, this process did not go unnoticed by Mexico. The Mexican government, desperate for any sort of successful showing, vehemently opposed the annexation of Texas by the US. The country even made several threats to the US, signaling that it believed the annexation of the province to be unjust. There was also the issue of the border that separated Mexico from Texas, which had technically been agreed upon by the two sides after the revolution in 1836. However, it was not respected by either side. Texans claimed they controlled the territory up to the Rio Grande, despite the fact that the farthest Texan settlement was not far from the Nueces River, which Mexico claimed to have been the boundary.

The situation escalated when President Polk sent troops to the disputed area to reinforce the border, suspecting a potential Mexican attack. This was seen as a complete humiliation to the Mexican people, who thought that war was inevitable. In the end, a Mexican scouting vanguard attacked the US patrol on the disputed border in an encounter known as the Thornton Skirmish in April 1846. The two sides went to war.

It was clear from the very beginning that the United States would eventually triumph—and triumph it certainly did. By attacking multiple fronts and stretching the Mexican resources thin, the US forces attained a relatively easy and quick victory against the Mexicans, who neither had the heart nor the necessary resources to resist adequately.

While a portion of fighting was going on at the Texan border, the US fleet and Western Expeditionary Forces also swept into California and the Santa Fe Trail, undermining Mexican defenses and exposing the left flank. Under General Winfield Scott, the main US force landed in eastern Mexico and made its way to Mexico City, rolling over the Mexican troops in the process. The Mexicans finally surrendered about two years later. They signed the devastating Treaty of Guadalupe-Hidalgo, which ended the war and gave the US total control of the territories it had occupied in the conflict. The United States agreed to pay $15 million in physical damages—an amount that meant nothing compared to what the country had gained.

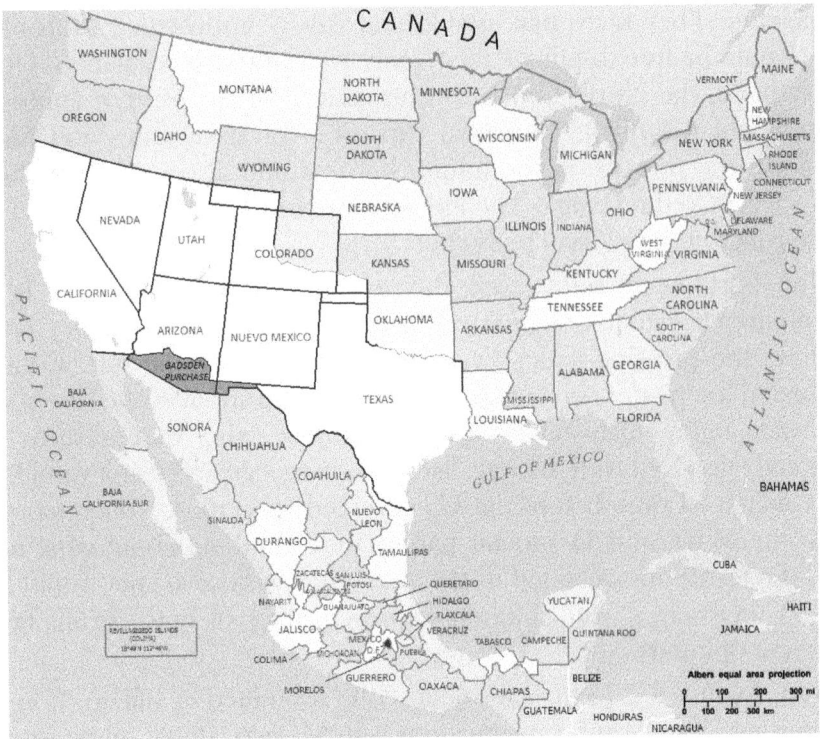

Mexican cession.

Implications of the War

The Mexican-American War was, for the most part, an easy victory for the United States. According to the Treaty of Guadalupe-Hidalgo, the United States assumed possession of about one-third of all Mexican territories. Basically all of the modern Southwest was seized by the Union, including the states of New Mexico, California, Nevada, Utah, and Colorado. It was a massive victory for Manifest Destiny and US expansionism. The American "dream" of connecting the East Coast and the West Coast by land had come true.

However, the country found itself in a dilemma. These new territories meant they would eventually be inaugurated into the Union as states. It was a massive deal for both the North and the South since an expansion of this magnitude could give a significant advantage to one of them. The Southern slave owners wanted more slave states. They would have more room to expand in the west, which meant more opportunities for land, which, in turn, meant more income through agriculture and slave ownership. They knew that establishing slavery in unsettled lands meant they would be free to pursue their goals without much regulation. On the other hand, the North hoped to gain control of the western lands. Not only would it limit the potential expansion of slave states and further diminish the practice in the future, but it would also cut off the South from access to the Pacific. The industrialist North wanted to have reliable trade routes to new Asian markets.

In short, both sides eyed the territories for themselves. It was becoming clear that Congress could not stall much longer; they had to address the pressing issue. Even before the end of the war, Congress discussed the matter. In August 1846, about four months after the start of the war, many high-society members, those who were directly and indirectly involved with the war, had already recognized that it would only be a matter of time before the US emerged victorious. Congressmen in both the Whig and Democrat parties were thinking about what to do with the territories obtained in the war. They were also split within their parties themselves, with different representatives of both parties having different opinions.

On August 8th, 1846, President Polk submitted a bill to Congress requesting $2 million for negotiations with Mexico. Polk's administration thought that it was apparent, even in the first four months of the war, that the US would win, so they wished to please the anti-war opposition by quickly resolving the matter through negotiations. In hindsight, they greatly overestimated the matter, as the Mexicans, despite being at a significant disadvantage, lasted for another year and a half.

Still, before Congress voted on whether or not it would satisfy the president's request, a group of Democrats, led by David Wilmot of Pennsylvania, hurried to add a very important point. Wilmot, who was a sympathizer of Polk's administration, and a group of like-minded congressmen proposed to add an amendment that would prohibit the practice of slavery in all lands that would be acquired from Mexico. The Wilmot Proviso, as the amendment came to be known, was modeled after the Northwest Ordinance of 1787, when Congress adopted a similar law regarding the territories of what is now the Midwest (those that would later be organized into Ohio, Indiana, Illinois, Michigan, Wisconsin, and Minnesota). Wilmot and his supporters wanted the proposal to be added to President Polk's bill so the matter could be voted on.

At first, some Democrats proposed that instead of the no-slavery point applying to the territories, the Missouri Compromise line should simply extend along the 36°30' latitude all the way west to the Pacific, with all territories north of the line remaining slavery-free. However, this proposal was voted down by the House. The House passed the vote to add the Wilmot Proviso to the president's bill, which was successful. The passing of the bill could have major implications on the future of slavery in the US, so the Southern congressmen attempted to kill the bill by postponing or "tabling" it. They failed. The passing of the bill, including the proviso, was put up to vote in the House, and it passed, although just barely, with eighty-five votes for and eighty against. All that was left was for the Senate to ratify it.

However, despite being passed in the House, the Senate never passed the bill containing the Wilmot Proviso. In fact, they never passed any amendment that would prohibit the practice of slavery in the newly acquired territories from Mexico. Vehemently opposed by pro-slavery Whigs and Democrats, the senators for the proviso were always outnumbered, and the votes never fell along party lines. The bill reappeared at the end of the year during the president's renewed request for funds, but the proviso never saw success in both the House and the Senate. Some argued that deciding what to do with the territories prior to actually acquiring them was useless and created more confusion. Some returned to the proposal of simply extending the Missouri Compromise line, but the Southerners did not agree. They realized that about two-thirds of the country would fall north of the line and saw it as a defeat.

The United States entered the 1850s with a highly polarized political climate and a considerable chunk of new territories. The country could barely keep the balance of slave and free states, and now there was great uncertainty regarding the acquired lands. It seemed as if the future of the country would be decided upon in the coming years.

Addressing Post-war Issues

Although the Wilmot Proviso failed to pass, it provides an example of how anti-slavery sentiments had significantly grown in the past years, something that can partially be attributed to the establishment of new abolitionist groups, newspapers, and clubs in the North. The proviso also symbolized the tragic resistance to the matter of ending slavery in newly acquired territories. Still, the Northerners had significant grounds to believe their efforts of fighting against slavery could finally come true.

In 1848, Whig candidate Zachary Taylor narrowly squeezed out a victory in the presidential election. The problem with his candidacy was that the country had not figured out what to do with the territory acquired in the war, and Taylor didn't support a certain camp. His careful campaign pleased both the pro-slavery Southerners, with Taylor promising to take into consideration their economic interests of creating slave states out of the new territories, as well as abolitionist Northerners, who were swayed by Taylor's promises to leave the slavery question largely up to the populations of the newly acquired territories.

Several crucial developments in the late 1840s determined how the congressional debate over the new lands would go in the following years, such as the discovery of gold in California. Before Taylor took office in late 1848, gold was discovered in the region, quickly transforming California from a distant "promise land," where only the bravest dared to venture to start new lives, to the hottest commodity in the country. The discovery of gold started the famous California Gold Rush, which saw hundreds of thousands of people swarm to the west to gain access to the region's riches. This raised the importance of California to the top of the agenda, making it stand out among the other newly acquired lands from the Mexican-American War.

The problem, however, lay in the fact that since California still did not have an official territorial government, despite President Polk's efforts in his last months in office, there were no real laws regulating the collection of its valuable resources. California, like most of the US Southwest acquired in the war, was still under the control of the military, which could only do so much in terms of official legislation. There was an urgent need to set up an official governmental body, either in the form of granting California the status of an organized US territory or skipping that stage and making it a state. The California Constitutional Convention of 1849 further demonstrated public support for this claim. More crucially, the people wanted to outlaw slavery in all of California, disregarding the Missouri Compromise, which would have split the state into two.

There was also the Texas question, or rather a question of its ever-so-problematic borders. Mexico had agreed to recognize the border along the Rio Grande, but that part was not the problem. Texas still claimed a large chunk of land in the north and northwest, which New Mexico disputed. This claim was largely baseless since Texan control never really spread to the lands it claimed. In addition, many New Mexicans were upset about being included with the Texans due to ideological differences. It was no surprise that the two sides were not on good terms with each other, with their differences going back to the Santa Fe Expedition of 1841 when a Texan force unsuccessfully journeyed northward to secure the disputed territories of the valuable Santa Fe Trail. Also, New Mexico, being largely populated by people of Hispanic origin, did not allow slavery, unlike Texas, which was one of the largest US slave states at that time.

Although the territorial issues of California and Texas were higher up on the agenda, they were not the only ones that required the government's immediate attention. The growth of the anti-slavery movement had caused a rising dissatisfaction toward the practice of slavery in the country's capital: Washington, DC. Located right on the historic Mason-Dixon Line, Washington held immense symbolic importance. For the North, the fact that the practice of slavery was permitted in the capital was humiliating for the country's international image. The South, on the other hand, saw great pride in it, believing Washington to be "on its side."

Concerning slavery, there was another matter that required settling. After the rising anti-slavery sentiment, the number of slaves who escaped from their masters in search of freedom greatly increased. They would head north, hoping to reach the free states and start new lives. The North was becoming so unsympathetic toward slavery in general that, in many cases, even if escaped slaves were found in the North, people would not send them back to their previous owners, defying the Fugitive Slave Act. The Northerners passed personal liberty laws, which diminished the power of the Fugitive Slave Act of 1793. They had the legal right to act however they wished when coming across a fugitive slave. This upset the Southerners a great deal, and many representatives of the slave states pushed for new legislation to fix the matter. The prices of slaves were at an all-time high, and the North was constantly pressuring the practice however it could, so losing a single slave could make quite a dent in the pockets of the Southern planters.

The Compromise of 1850

As you can see, President Taylor and his administration had quite a lot on their plate, with different influential congressmen proposing different solutions to the problems. Out of these issues, the one that seemed the most inevitable was California's inauguration into the Union. The Californians had already expressed their desire to join the Union, so the

Taylor administration had something to work with there.

But it would be three men—John C. Calhoun, Henry Clay, and Daniel Webster—who would lead one of the most influential debates on the issues in Congress. The trio, along with some other great politicians of early 19th-century America like John Quincy Adams, are considered to be the torch carriers of the Founding Fathers, a "Great Triumvirate" of politicians. They advocated for the development and promotion of the principles that shaped the lives of everyday Americans in that period.

Henry Clay.
https://commons.wikimedia.org/wiki/File:Henry_Clay.JPG

After rigorous negotiations behind the scenes, Congress had a general idea of what to expect. Henry Clay, a charismatic Whig from Kentucky who had matured in political debate during his time acting as secretary of state, presented eight bills on the floor of Congress in late January 1850. Clay had an infamous reputation among politicians of his caliber. He notoriously owned slaves and resided in a slave state; however, he believed that the future of the country lay in a slave-free society and was for gradual emancipation. He was quite different from many other representatives from Southern states but was still respected a great deal in both the North and the South. His past involvement in politics had earned him the nickname of the "Great Compromiser."

Thus, when he stood before the House to present his eight-part bill that addressed all the problems Clay saw relevant for the future of the country, he did what he did best—offered a compromise. Clay proposed admitting California to the Union as a free state, the establishment of the territories of New Mexico and Utah, debt relief for Texas in return for the state giving up its claims on the disputed borders, and, perhaps most importantly, suppression of the slave trade in the capital in return for a revisiting and implementation of stricter laws concerning fugitive slaves. Clay's bill hoped to please both sides, as usual, and it did to some extent. However, in the end, it fell through, opposed by some Northern Whigs and Southern Democrats.

The debate unfolded completely differently than how some might have imagined, and it lasted for seven months. At that time, both President Taylor and John C. Calhoun passed away, neither one seeing the final form of one of the most historic bills in US history. Taylor was replaced by Vice President Millard Fillmore, while Calhoun's emotional and influential speech shortly before his death was delivered to his colleagues by Senator James M. Mason. Calhoun was one of the firmest supporters of slavery and devoted much of his political career to defending and justifying it as a whole. It can be argued that his speech and the influence he had on his colleagues dragged out the debate for another couple of months.

President Fillmore sympathized with Clay's proposal: a new compromise to try and solve all the problems for both the North and the South while not taking a side. Clay had to leave Congress due to tuberculosis, and he was succeeded by Senator Stephen A. Douglas. Together, Fillmore and Douglas were able to convince the Texan representatives to give up some claims regarding the disputed borders with New Mexico, claiming that it was the responsibility of the United States to protect the rights of New Mexicans. In exchange for debt relief, Sam Houston of Texas and his supporters agreed to adjust the borders. The Senate passed the bill with support from both the Whigs and the Democrats; the only opposition came mainly from the South. Clay's proposal had finally seen the light.

The rest of the bills turned out to be far easier to gain support for. The organization of New Mexico and Utah as two new formal territories was not really opposed by either side, and the South agreed to the admission of California and the restriction of slavery in Washington in exchange for a stricter law on fugitive slaves. That was the whole point of the compromise in the first place. The Northerners got a new free state, limited the expansion of slavery to the Pacific Coast, and limited slavery-related activities in Washington. The Southerners got laws that made it easier for them to get hold of escaped slaves and settled the matter of Texas. In the end, both sides were not fully satisfied.

In September 1850, a historic package of five laws was passed as one bill. It became known as the Compromise of 1850, and it hoped to adequately address the two main concerns that had shaped the 19th-century United States: territorial expansion and slavery. Despite the fact that the "compromise" had been achieved, the extent to which it covered all the problems turned out not to be sufficient.

The admission of California as a free state was perhaps the clearest cut of the five points. There were no more questions left about the future state, and the matter was resolved pretty unanimously. However, the same cannot be said about other territorial issues. For instance, the bill and, to a larger extent, those who passed it had not yet decided what to do with the newly organized territories of Utah and New Mexico, mainly whether the two territories should be allowed to practice slavery. When the time came to split Utah and New Mexico into new states, it was known the debate on slavery would polarize the country even more. Still, this issue was largely ignored and postponed for future generations to decide.

The most attention was paid to redrawing the disputed borders between Texas and New Mexico—a matter that was arguably not nearly as important as the new restrictions regarding the slave trade in Washington, DC, or the expansion of the Fugitive Slave Act. According to new laws, buying and selling slaves were prohibited in Washington, DC, but owning slaves was still permitted. This did not make much sense, considering the inhabitants of the capital could simply take a short journey to the Southern states, buy their slaves, and then return home. The law was not beneficial to either side and was ultimately unsuccessful. The South was furious with the limitations put on Washington, while the North believed the only just way was the complete prohibition of slavery in every form.

As for the Fugitive Slave Act, the laws included in the Compromise of 1850 were blatantly pro-slavery. Upset and disappointed by the growing sentiment against the Fugitive Slave Act of 1783, the Southern slave owners demanded stricter control and monitoring of the fugitive slaves under the new legislation. They were perhaps more successful than what they might have hoped for initially. Under the new act, which went into effect in September 1850, fugitive slaves were prohibited from testifying on their own behalf—something that went against the democratic principles upon which the country had been based. Revoking the basic judiciary rights of escaped slaves was not as devastating as some of the other points. For instance, under new laws, people, regardless of their status or skin color, who were suspected of helping fugitive slaves escape from their owners were to be severely punished. Law enforcers all around the country, not only in the Southern states, were entitled to arrest fugitive slaves on just the basis of the claimant's sworn testimony, and they were required to assist the slave owners in finding their escaped slaves.

The new Fugitive Slave Act was undoubtedly the most shocking bill included in the Compromise of 1850, yet it got the least attention. It completely restricted whatever rights fugitive slaves had in the first place and was blatantly biased to please the planters of the slave states, who had grown distressed by the growing abolitionist movement. The act significantly swung the balance of power in their favor by changing the basic principles of the judiciary branch. For example, judges would be paid double if they found the fugitive slave guilty and returned them to their owners. It was totally undemocratic, but the legislators were so swept up in deciding the future of the newly acquired territories that they simply ignored what an immense implication this would have. However, the Compromise of 1850 achieved the opposite of what the Southerners had hoped. Instead of installing fear in the minds of the slaves, it exponentially increased the support of the abolitionist movement, prompting numerous Northern states to pass laws that would protect the individual liberties underlined in the act.

The Compromise of 1850 was perhaps the most important piece of legislation in antebellum America. Fresh out of a successful war against Mexico, Congress was once again unable to find a long-term solution to the most pressing issue in the country: the slavery divide. Instead, the compromise paid more attention to settling the individual squabbles between Texas and New Mexico and rushed the inauguration of California to the Union as a free state. On the other hand, the new Fugitive Slave Act and restrictions on the slave trade in Washington, DC, did not achieve their intended results. They simply increased polarization on the subject. The two groups were becoming increasingly hostile toward each other, accusing the other of limiting their liberties and stagnating the country's development. For all these reasons, the Compromise of 1850 is often considered to be the beginning of the end for antebellum America.

The Kansas-Nebraska Act

The Compromise of 1850, despite its destructive consequences, was not regarded as destructive after its enactment. Instead of realizing that the public would be more divided on slavery after enforcing stricter laws on it, Congress believed that it had addressed the issue. This sentiment was shared and cemented by the next president, Franklin Pierce, whose 1853 inaugural address mentioned that the matter of slavery in the current and future territories of the United States was settled once and for all. Ironically, the following year would see Congress return to the issue of slavery once again. It was forced to implement new vital legislation in the unorganized territories of the country, something that was part of a larger deal, which was concerned with the further industrialization of the country through the construction of a crucial transcontinental railroad.

The debate on building a transcontinental railroad had been around since the early 1840s. All of Congress, both the Whigs and the Democrats, recognized the immense importance of this infrastructural project. The railroad was the future of transportation and the perfect way to travel long distances. There was no doubt that the country needed a railroad that would connect the east to the west, especially after the victory in the Mexican-American War brought new territories. However, as always, Congress could not come to terms with the exact details of the railroad's construction, such as where it would run and which states it would include. The North and the South both advocated for different routes, each excluding the involvement of the other states in the project. The only thing that was agreed upon was that the railroad should be financed by public land grants.

An important factor that played a big role in the debates over the construction of the railroad was the unorganized territory in the central part of the country, the territory that the United States had acquired through the Louisiana Purchase. In the 1850s, the leftover land that was still unorganized from the purchase was commonly referred to as "Nebraska." As new settlers found their way to the unexplored territory, there was a growing concern about implementing some kind of legislation. The matter of Nebraska should have been explored in congressional hearings, but nobody really had time for it. During most of the 1840s, the country's legislators were busy deciding what to do with the lands annexed from Mexico. Stephen A. Douglas, a Democratic senator from Illinois, had previously proposed organizing Nebraska into an official US territory and had tied in the construction of the railroad in his bill, but the bill never saw the light of day due to the issue of slavery. Most of the territory left over from the Louisiana Purchase fell north of the Missouri Compromise line, meaning that slavery would have been prohibited in those territories/states. The Southern legislators were no longer content with what had been agreed upon in 1820. In 1845, when Douglas first presented the bill, Southern politicians tabled it, urging Congress to divert its attention to more immediate issues.

After the Compromise of 1850, the issue of Nebraska became popular once again, with the House passing a bill in the spring of 1853 to organize it as a territory. The bill was then handed to the Senate. It seemed as if Douglas would finally be able to complete the organization of Nebraska. But it turned out that the Southern senators were not willing to let the matter just slide through. Realizing that the bill did not mention the future of slavery in the new territory west of Iowa and Missouri, they all united in voting against it. There was no mention of the allowance of slavery in Nebraska, which made it obvious that the authors of the bill had envisioned it to be a slave-free state since most of it lay north of the Missouri Compromise line. Led by Missouri Senator David Atchison, the Southerner senators united against the bill, and it was once again tabled. The Senate adjourned its activities, and both sides retreated to work on their strategies.

Once the Senate convened again in December, it was clear that Atchison and his supporters were not open to negotiating the terms of the deal. The South unanimously stood against the organization of Nebraska as a territory as proposed in the bill. This was mainly due to the fact that Nebraska and the railroad issue were increasingly connected with each other, and the Northerners would not let one pass without the other. Atchison and others were prepared to let the organization of Nebraska fall through, even if it was done at the cost of the transcontinental railroad.

The pressure was high on both sides. For the Southerners, the establishment of another territory (and eventually a state) north of the Missouri Compromise line would mean that their hopes of expanding slave territories were basically done for. On the other hand, the Northern senators, especially Douglas, placed more emphasis on the construction of the railroad, which would have given the North massive economic benefits since the railroad would start in Illinois. They also had a legislative edge over their opposition thanks to the Missouri Compromise.

In the end, what determined the fate of Nebraska, the transcontinental railroad, and the matter of slavery in the new territories was a point borrowed from the Compromise of 1850, which stated that the inhabitants of New Mexico and Utah would choose whether or not they would allow the practice of slavery by themselves. However, the two territories, although technically falling on both sides of the Missouri Compromise line, were never a part of the Louisiana Purchase, so whether or not slavery would be allowed there was not subject to the Missouri Compromise. Regardless, a new bill was proposed by Douglas in January 1854 that stated the same principle of popular sovereignty would apply to the Nebraska territory—those living in the vast area that spanned from modern-day Kansas to the US-Canadian border. But this created confusion in the Senate, with many believing that the deal would not be beneficial for the slave owners since it did not fully overturn the Missouri Compromise. Some Southerners thought that problems might arise in the future if they tried to expand their practices on such a vast chunk of land.

Kansas-Nebraska Act.
https://commons.wikimedia.org/wiki/File:McConnell%27s_historical_map_Kansas-Nebraska_Act,_1854.jpg

After another round of meetings between the two sides, which now also involved President Pierce, another version of the bill was proposed to the floor in late January. This time, it explicitly stated a complete repeal of the Missouri Compromise line and divided the original unorganized territory into two parts: Nebraska and Kansas. The justification of the first point was that the Compromise of 1850 had already, in a way, repealed the Missouri Compromise, so there was no need to keep enforcing it (although New Mexico and Utah had never been envisioned to be included by the legislation of 1820). The debate on the matter lasted for about four months and was not limited to Congress. Those in the North who believed in abolitionism took to the streets, organizing protests against the bill. The opposition to the bill, known as the Anti-Nebraska movement, believed that it was clearly pro-slavery and unconstitutional.

Despite harsh opposition, the Senate passed the bill with thirty-seven votes for and fourteen against, with fourteen senators from the free states voting in favor of it. It became clear once the House started its debate on the bill that it had become a sectional issue and that congressmen were no longer acting along party lines. All forty-five Northern Whigs opposed the bill, while the votes among the Northern Democrats were split forty-five in favor and forty-two against. The South was more one-sided, with sixty-nine votes for and nine votes against. On May 30th, 1854, President Pierce signed the Kansas-Nebraska Act into law.

Bleeding Kansas

The signing of the Kansas-Nebraska Act started a chain of events that led to more destabilization in the newly established territories, something that was further amplified by the divides between the Whigs and the Democrats. The act was a clear victory for the Southern slave owners. They believed they had a chance to do, thanks to the popular sovereignty clause that stated the inhabitants of the new territories were entitled to choose their slavery status. As immigrants from both camps started to flood Kansas and Nebraska, it became clear that instead of dealing with the pressing issue of slavery, Congress had once again avoided it, allowing the local population to decide for themselves. Although popular sovereignty sounded just at the moment (after all, the people who lived in the territory would be affected by the decision the most), the events that unfolded proved just how polarized the two sides were and to what extent they were ready to push their beliefs.

However, there never really was a "fair fight" on the rights of slavery when it came to Kansas. The majority of the new inhabitants were pro-slavery, organizing the town of Atchison in honor of the senator who had fought for the expansion of slavery during the debates on the act. Soon, Southern slave owners started to pour into Kansas en masse, trying to sway the upcoming vote in their favor and cement the territory's right to slavery. In a way, it was an organized effort by the Southern slave owners, who migrated from the nearby slave state of Missouri to fight for slavery. These men, who were often armed, were referred to as Border Ruffians. Their only motivation was to help Kansas become pro-slavery. Border Ruffians often raided and intimidated the population, forcing them to pledge allegiance to their cause and to vote against the prohibition of slavery in Kansas. It was a well-organized movement, but whether or not it had any real ties to the pro-slavery governments of the South is not known.

On the other hand, the abolitionists who settled in Kansas were just as resilient and focused. There were far fewer Northern immigrants, but they had settled in Kansas for the cause of abolitionism. The first abolitionist immigrants were praised by Northern media and politicians for their efforts, as they made the Kansas issue a matter of national significance. The abolitionists, often called Free Soilers, founded the towns of Topeka and Lawrence and posed a somewhat firm resistance to the Border Ruffians, despite being outnumbered.

The tensions between the two sides in Kansas escalated during the first election of its territorial legislature in March 1855. This election would be crucial in determining whether or not slavery would be allowed. The election, which took place on March 30th, was heavily influenced by the Border Ruffians, who arrived in large numbers from Missouri to take part in the vote and swing it in favor of pro-slavery candidates. Only two out of thirty-nine seats were won by abolitionist candidates. The Free Soilers protested the results and managed to convince the territorial governor to hold another election in May. They did see improvements but still lost the overall election, with nineteen seats going to the pro-slavery candidates.

In July, the pro-slavery legislature met in the town of Pawnee and drew up legislation, which was largely modeled on the bordering state of Missouri and allowed for the practice of slavery. On the other hand, the Free Soilers, who believed that the election was still fraudulent, convened in Topeka, creating their own version of the legislation and claiming it to be legitimate. By the end of the summer of 1855, there were two highly polarized camps in the Kansas Territory. Both sides handed their legislature to Congress to review and accept, but due to the support of pro-slavery President Pierce, the Free Soilers had no chance. The debate on the matter was postponed, and Congress appointed a special three-man committee to arrive in Kansas and assess the situation. A year later, after conducting a series of investigations and reviewing documents, the committee came to the conclusion that the original election of 1855 had been heavily influenced by non-resident Southern immigrants, who had only crossed the border into Kansas to vote for pro-slavery candidates. The committee declared that the pro-slavery legislation that had been drawn up was fraudulent and did not reflect the opinion of the majority of the Kansas residents.

However, the committee's decision did not change the highly polarized situation in Kansas. The two camps were still going strong, each believing to have been legitimate and now creating their own versions of a constitution to submit to the Senate. The divide soon transformed into an all-out armed confrontation between the Free Soilers and the pro-slavery Southerners.

After a Free Soiler was murdered by a pro-slavery Kansas resident in November 1855 (in a personal matter not related to politics), a series of armed confrontations erupted between the two sides. The pro-slavery Kansas militia, armed with stolen guns and a cannon, encamped near the Free Soiler town of Lawrence. Luckily, the governor of Lawrence managed to negotiate with the militia and avoided further escalation of the conflict.

At the same time, the Senate was busy reviewing the different constitutions of Kansas that had been submitted. The Topeka Constitution, drawn up by the abolitionists of Topeka, was rejected in early 1856, thanks to President Pierce, who said the Free Soiler government of Kansas was illegitimate (something that was partially disproved by the committee's findings). The Lecompton Constitution, which was pro-slavery, was next up, but the Free Soilers refused to show up to vote. The document was still presented to Congress for approval, but Congress sent it back, noting that it did not reflect the opinion of the majority of Kansas voters.

The third document to be reviewed by Congress was the Leavenworth Constitution, drawn up and passed by the Free Soilers. However, the

Senate quickly killed the document since it was not only radically anti-slavery but also demanded voting rights for all male citizens, including blacks. The Wyandotte Constitution, another Free Soiler document, was drafted and sent to Congress for review in 1859. A popular representative referendum in Kansas miraculously approved the passing of the document in October 1859, but the Senate, still dominated by pro-slavery senators, tabled the bill.

As the debates in the Senate continued, so did the efforts of pro-slavery parties to eliminate and undermine abolitionist resistance in Kansas. In the infamous Sack of Lawrence, which took place in May 1856, hundreds of armed pro-slavery inhabitants from Missouri openly invaded Kansas and sacked the abolitionist city of Lawrence. It was a brutal act of aggression—perhaps the first known armed conflict between the pro- and anti-slavery forces in the country. The situation did not die down. In the Senate, the abolitionists brought up the matter more and more. The debates became so heated that South Carolina Congressman Preston Brooks attacked Senator Charles Sumner from Massachusetts, nearly beating him to death. Although his actions were quickly condemned, it became clear that the issue of slavery in Kansas had penetrated into the mainstream and widened the divide between the North and the South.

The struggle for dominance between the Free Soilers and pro-slavery forces in Kansas continued until 1861, which was when Kansas was finally admitted to the Union as a free state. This followed the election of Abraham Lincoln as president and the secession of the Southern states from the Union. The six-year period of instability and high levels of polarization in Kansas is often referred to as "Bleeding Kansas." The events of Bleeding Kansas perhaps best describe the political situation in the country in the 1850s, a decade when pivotal decisions, such as the signing of the Compromise of 1850 and the Kansas-Nebraska Act, led to the start of the war between the North and the South.

Chapter 4: The Republican Party

The signing of the Kansas-Nebraska Act was the final nail in the coffin for the sectional divides within the Democrats and the Whigs. Eventually, this divide caused the creation of the Republican Party, which managed to gain a lot of traction and has become one of the two most dominant political actors in the US today.

The Founding of the Party

In hindsight, when looking at the political climate of the United States after the Mexican-American War, it is clear that both the Whigs and the Democrats had significant problems within their parties. Due to the extreme divide over slavery, the views of the Whigs and Democrats were often not based on their party alignment but rather on where they were from. During the congressional debates, Northern and Southern Democrats and Whigs would often take similar stances on different issues rather than organizing their opinions based on their party's platform. It was very confusing and, to some extent, even unfair to the average voter.

The Whigs were so polarized that they could not reach any type of consensus when it came to slavery. The Southern wing of the Whigs was very conservative and had pro-slavery views, while the members of the newer anti-slavery wing increased in numbers throughout the 1850s. This divide had shown itself during the 1852 presidential election when the Whig candidate, Winfield Scott, a former general during the Mexican-American War, was crushed by Franklin Pierce, the Democratic nominee. A large portion of the Whigs had opposed Scott's nomination in the first place, something that became a pivotal factor in his ineffective campaign and eventual defeat.

After the passing of the Kansas-Nebraska Act, the divides within the Whig Party became more relevant than ever. Viewing the new bill as overwhelmingly pro-slavery, several anti-slavery Whigs, referred to as Conscience Whigs, decided to abandon their party and pursue their efforts independently. A new party was about to be founded in the United States that would quickly transform the political landscape of the country forever. A businessman and leader of the radical abolitionist wing of the party, Zachariah Chandler, and Salmon P. Chase and former President Martin Van Buren, leaders of the Free Soil Party, led the charge.

These like-minded individuals bonded together in the Anti-Nebraska movement, criticizing the passage of the pro-slavery act and urging others to join their cause. At the Anti-Nebraska meetings in Ripon, Wisconsin, in May 1854 and then in Jackson, Michigan, in July, they proposed officially forming a new party, one that would strive to oppose slavery in the territories. They called themselves the Republicans, borrowing perhaps from Thomas Jefferson when he first established the Democratic-Republican Party in 1792; it eventually dropped the second part of its name.

Free Soil, Free Labor, Free Men

The principles on which the newly created Republican Party stood for were a conglomeration of different ideas and values. Obviously, the opposition to the expansion of slavery was the central idea, one that attracted all of the members. However, it was not the only one. The Republicans envisioned a completely free United States, where slavery would be abolished in all the states, despite their history or economic reliance on the practice. To replace such a vast part of the country's economy, the Republicans advocated for the modernization of the US by, for example, building more factories and railroads and implementing a new banking system that would provide new opportunities for average citizens by giving them more flexible terms on loans. In addition, the Republicans also wanted to expand the country's agricultural sphere by gifting the undeveloped western lands to the farmers instead of selling them to already rich slave owners. The Republicans claimed well-functioning, capitalist free-market labor was the foundation and future of the United States. They pledged to do everything in their power to swing the country back to this long-abandoned course. The idea of "Free Soil, Free Labor, Free Men" was born and gave the Republican Party a unique set of values that differentiated it from the Whigs and the Democrats, who were still largely split on major issues.

Amidst the Bleeding Kansas events, the Republican Party organized its first national convention in Pittsburgh, Pennsylvania, in February 1856. There, the members of the party once again revisited and clearly defined their goals, which centered around the cause of fighting against the future expansion of slavery. It also clearly demonstrated their position of defending the Free Soilers of Kansas, who were under direct physical threat by their Southern opposition. The party also criticized President Pierce's overwhelmingly pro-slavery administration, condemning its reckless and hateful activities in the country.

In June of the same year, the Republican Party nominated its first presidential candidate: John C. Frémont. The former major of the US Army during the Mexican-American War, Frémont had played a big role in the Californian campaign and had made quite a name for himself after the end of the war by becoming rich from the California Gold Rush. Although Frémont did not manage to win the presidential election of 1856, he carried eleven states in total, all of which were in the North. He fell short to Democrat James Buchanan, whose campaign was ambiguous on the matter of slavery. The Whig candidate, Millard Fillmore, suffered a crushing defeat, only carrying one state and falling victim to the political chaos that had been established among the Whigs after the party's break-up.

Despite the defeat of the Republicans in the 1856 election, the party's future seemed promising. After all, in their very first election, they gained about a third of the popular vote. The party's success was largely attributed to its clear stance. Many people were drawn to the ideals of "Free Soil, Free Labor, Free Men" and knew exactly what they were choosing when they circled the Republicans on the ballot. Over the next few years, more politicians decided to join the Republican Party from both the Whigs and the Democrats, further contributing to its rise before the pivotal 1860 election.

Chapter 5: The 1860 Presidential Election

The year 1856 was the last time a Whig candidate ran for election in a presidential race. Following the disintegration of the party, the Republicans became the second-largest political entity in the country. The next four years, up until the 1860 presidential election, were characterized by even more polarization between the pro- and anti-slavery camps. The 1860 presidential election had huge implications that forever changed the course of the country and directly led to the outbreak of the Civil War.

This chapter will briefly cover the most important events in the four-year period preceding the 1860 election, explore the election itself, and talk about some of the most immediate consequences of the election.

Dred Scott Decision

Democrat James Buchanan won the presidential election in 1856 with just over 45 percent of the popular vote. However, things were not looking good for his party or the Whigs. The latter had suffered a substantial split, with a number of its most influential members leaving the party to join the growing ranks of the Republicans. The Democrats still had no distinctive course to offer its voters. The issue of slavery was more relevant than ever, as the Bleeding Kansas events were happening concurrent to the election. But unlike former President Pierce, who had at least shown his support for the expansion of slavery in the Kansas

Territory, Buchanan's administration was rather silent on the matter.

The slavery issue was further amplified by the famous Dred Scott case, which gained a lot of national attention in the 1850s. The final verdict was ruled just two days after Buchanan's inauguration. In short, Dred Scott was an African American man born in slavery in Virginia. He lived with his owner first in Alabama and later in Missouri. Eventually, Dr. John Emerson, an army surgeon, purchased Dred Scott from slavery in 1832 and took him first to Illinois—a free state—and then to Wisconsin—a slave-free territory according to the Missouri Compromise. Emerson traveled a lot but eventually returned to Missouri.

After the death of Emerson, Scott and his wife, Harriet Robinson, who was also a slave, tried to buy their freedom from Emerson's wife, Irene Sandford, who became their owner after the death of her husband. Irene rejected their bids, forcing them to file two separate lawsuits against her in April 1846 in Missouri, where they resided. The Missouri statutes at the time allowed African Americans to sue for wrongful enslavement. After a slave's arrival in a free territory, they automatically became free and should not be re-enslaved after reentering territories where slavery was legal. Missouri's famous motto was "once free, always free," and Scott and his wife hoped it would help them gain their freedom.

A photograph of Dred Scott.
https://commons.wikimedia.org/wiki/File:Dred_Scott_photograph_(circa_1857).jpg

However, in June 1847, the court ruled against them. In a retrial three years later, they managed to win their freedom. Irene Sandford was devastated by her loss and decided to appeal the case to the Missouri Supreme Court, combining the two separate lawsuits of Dred Scott and Harriet Robinson into one. She convinced the court to overturn the previous decision and reclaimed the ownership of Scott and Harriet in 1852. It was a spectacle and was swiftly followed by an appeal from Scott to the US Circuit Court in Missouri in December 1854, which he lost.

By that time, the case had gained the attention of many abolitionists, who helped Scott financially and provided legal services to him. With their support, Scott once again appealed the case, this time in the United States Supreme Court, the highest judiciary system in the country.

Despite fully believing that he was not in the wrong and despite all of the support from different abolitionist politicians and civil society figures, the Supreme Court denied Scott the right to his freedom on March 6th, 1857. The decision shocked the country and drove yet another wedge between the Northern abolitionists and the slave-owning Southerners. The case gained popularity due to the Supreme Court's justification. Led by Chief Justice Roger Taney, a Southerner, the Supreme Court made its decision based on two very debatable points. First, all people of African descent, regardless of whether or not they were a slave, were not citizens of the United States and thus were not entitled to sue anyone in federal court. Second, the Supreme Court found the Missouri Compromise of 1820, a piece of legislation that had determined the future of American expansion for over fifty years, unconstitutional. The Supreme Court not only rejected Scott's arguments but also basically said that Congress had no constitutional right to determine the expansion of slavery in the new territories.

The Dred Scott decision was a fatal ruling for antebellum America. It not only overturned a five-decade-long historic act, but it also managed to anger a significant portion of Americans. Northern abolitionists, white and black alike, protested the Supreme Court's decision, calling it unjust. They claimed (and not wrongfully) that the Supreme Court's final decision was not American in any sense and did not take into consideration the democratic principles on which the country was founded.

Thus, just two days after entering office, President Buchanan found himself and the whole country in a blazing fire that had been caused by the issue of slavery. The fate of Kansas was on the docket, and the Dred Scott decision greatly upset the abolitionists; it seems that Buchanan's term was doomed from the beginning. The North and South hated each other. It was a full-blown political crisis, with neither party willing to give an inch. It is not surprising that in the years following his inauguration, Buchanan and his administration were unable to introduce any effective measures to address the situation.

The Feud in the Democrats

The creation of the Republican Party was not only destructive for the Whigs. It was almost equally as bad for the Democrats, who had long been struggling among themselves and were perhaps the most polarized out of the two big parties in the country. The sectional divides in the Democrats were largely caused by the extreme pro-slavery wing of the party called the Fire-Eaters. Not only were these Southern Democrats the biggest advocates of slavery and its expansion in the US territories, but they also advocated for the secession of the Southern states from the Union. They believed that the differences between the North and the South had become unfixable and that the damage had already been done. The Fire-Eaters constituted only a minority of the party at the start of the 1850s but slowly grew in numbers as the Democrats gained more seats in the Southern states.

After eight years of mostly pro-slavery Democratic presidents, a number of Northern abolitionist Democrats had left the party by 1860 to join the Republicans. Still, some of the most prominent Democrats at the time, such as Stephen A. Douglas, remained and led the party through a tough four-year period after the election of James Buchanan.

In April 1860, the Democratic National Convention convened in Charleston, South Carolina. The main idea of the convention was to nominate the next presidential candidate to run for the party in autumn. By that time, the number of extreme pro-slavery members outnumbered the moderate and abolitionist members of the party. And since the convention was being held in Charleston, which was a Southern city, it was mainly attended by pro-slavery party members. Still, Douglas was the front-runner for the Democrat nomination, despite the fact that he was considered to be a member of the more moderate wing. He was perhaps the most distinguished member of the party, having worked extensively on the passing of the Kansas-Nebraska Act.

However, the Fire-Eaters vehemently opposed his nomination. They had prepared an extremely pro-slavery platform to be endorsed during the election. Among other points, it included clear support of the Dred Scott decision, a point that was instantly opposed by the Northern abolitionist Democrats. The abolitionists claimed that if such a platform was adopted, they would lose support in pivotal states, such as New York or Pennsylvania, making it almost impossible to win the election. Instead, a more moderate platform was adopted by a vote of 164 to 138, and it did not include the extremely pro-slavery parts. The Fire-Eaters protested. Led by William Lowndes Yancey from Alabama, they walked out of the convention.

In total, fifty delegates from the Southern states left the Charleston convention, leaving those who remained unable to reach a consensus regarding the nomination of the next candidate since a two-thirds majority was needed. Douglas received 145.5 of the 253 votes cast and led the six other candidates for nomination; however, he still needed 56.5 more votes to be officially elected as the party's presidential candidate. In the end, the convention did not reach a consensus and adjourned to meet in six weeks in Baltimore to discuss the matter again.

The Democrats convened in Baltimore, Maryland, on June 18th, 1860, to nominate their candidate. However, 110 Southern delegates still boycotted the assembly, led by the Fire-Eaters, who did not attend it at all. The rest just walked out of the convention once they learned that the pro-slavery points would still not be included in the party's platform. The remaining Democrats were forced to resume the convention in the absence of the Southern delegates. Douglas managed to get the required two-thirds. However, the remaining delegates realized the severity of the situation and the fact that it would be near impossible to work with the Southern delegates. Still, they nominated Douglas as the Democratic presidential candidate for the 1860 election.

By that point, the extreme pro-slavery wing of the party had set up their own convention in Richmond, Virginia, on June 11th. When the Northern Democrats met in Baltimore, some Southerners decided to join them, but they left the assembly disappointed and returned back to Richmond, where they planned to nominate their own presidential candidate. Unsurprisingly, the first thing the Southern wing did was adopt the pro-slavery platform that had been rejected by the rest of the party. After unanimous approval of the platform, they nominated Vice President John C. Breckinridge as their candidate to run for president.

Although the whole situation was rather unusual and everybody recognized the problems associated with it, President Buchanan's administration was forced to accept two Democratic nominees. Buchanan had to endorse Breckinridge since he was the vice president; if he didn't, it would have been catastrophic for his administration's image. The president hoped that because of his endorsement, Breckinridge would win the electoral votes of his home state, Pennsylvania, which was a pivotal state in achieving victory in the election.

The sectional divides in the Democratic Party proved to be fatal for the party's future. Despite dominating the political landscape for the better part of the last twenty years, the Democrats were not able to deal with the problems between the Northern and Southern members of the party. Everyone knew that this split and the nomination of two candidates would be very difficult to overcome. Both camps were banking on getting electoral support in the North and South but failed to realize that their chances of winning the election were slimmer than ever. The newly formed Republican Party had gained the voters' attention by early 1860.

Republicans Nominate Lincoln

Things were looking up for the Republicans, whose numbers had only grown since the 1856 election. Unlike the Democrats, the Republicans were not sectionalized on the matter of slavery—well, at least not in the way the Democrats had been for decades. All Republicans opposed the expansion of slavery in the new territories acquired by the United States. However, some called for its complete abolition. This opinion separated the more moderate Republicans from the radicals, although the divide was not as extreme as the pro- and anti-slavery divide in other parties. In general, the Republicans opposed the practice of slavery, believing it to be harmful in the long term for the country's development. The main thing the party had to decide was which candidate would represent their views in the presidential race.

The Republicans held their convention in Chicago right after the failure of the Democratic convention in Charleston in May of 1860. In total, there were eight candidates that were running for the nomination. Out of them, four had perhaps the best chances: William H. Seward, the governor of New York who was considered to have been the main favorite; Salmon P. Chase, the governor of Ohio who had long opposed slavery; former Representative of Missouri Edward Bates, a conservative on the slavery issue and a slave owner himself; and, finally, Abraham

Lincoln, the former representative of Illinois who had made quite a name for himself during the Lincoln-Douglas debates in 1858 but was not considered to have much of a chance against the likes of Seward.

The convention started out differently from what some had predicted. From the very beginning, it became clear that the big three—Seward, Chase, and Bates—had almost split the party since all three proposed very different party platforms that opposed each other. Due to his enthusiastic speech that supported the concept of nativism, Seward was seen as a radical on the anti-slavery matter. Although he did not mention the total abolition of slavery, Seward was perhaps misunderstood by his colleagues, causing him to lose a lot of supporters. Chase, on the other hand, voiced his unyielding anti-slavery views, which attracted a lot of radical abolitionists in the party. However, he did not have as much past experience and prestige as Seward, making his marketing as a potential candidate difficult. In addition, he did not have much support from the former Whig delegates of the party since he had been a former Democrat. Finally, Bates did not get much love from the majority of the party because he supported the expansion of slavery in the new territories, something that was considered unacceptable by most delegates.

This situation was well utilized by Abraham Lincoln, who, despite not being a clear favorite to win the nomination, had made quite a name for himself. Lincoln had long stated his anti-slavery views. In 1858, he spoke out on the matter on several occasions, including during the Kansas-Nebraska crisis in 1854 and after the Dred Scott decision. He had also gained quite a lot of popularity in Illinois, the state where he resided and pursued his political career in the House of Representatives.

Although Lincoln had always been actively involved in the political processes of his state, the biggest breakthrough of his career was perhaps the famous Lincoln-Douglas debates in 1858 when Lincoln and Stephen A. Douglas, who were both up for election as the representative of Illinois, toured the state and engaged in a series of seven debates on the matter of slavery. Lincoln, who was still relatively unknown outside of his state and firmly opposed the expansion of slavery in the new territories, challenged a veteran politician, Douglas, who advocated for popular sovereignty. Thanks to Lincoln's innate talent and charisma during his speeches, as well as his memorable posture and height of 6'4", Lincoln was able to effectively mesmerize his audiences and, in many instances, was named the informal victor of the debates. Although he ultimately lost the race, it was a close battle. The events of 1858 made him a favorite of the Illinoisans, who would assemble in the thousands to watch him give speeches.

Abraham Lincoln

Having delivered an amazing speech three months before in New York, in which he carefully described the Republicans as the party where true American virtues were valued, Lincoln's views were well known inside of his party. The Cooper Union speech had been a massive success for Lincoln, who had not intended to use the platform to promote himself as a potential candidate. Instead, he wanted to give a thorough, honest run-down of his thoughts on crucial issues he believed needed to be addressed. The fact that the Republican convention was held in his home state was even more beneficial for Lincoln, let alone the fact that his three main opponents had not gained a significant edge over him for the spot of a nominee.

Although Lincoln did not attend the convention in person, he gained second place on the first ballot. Seward led the ballot, as predicted, but he could not manage to get the majority of the votes. In the second round, Lincoln saw a significant increase in his votes, going from 102 to

181 delegates, although he still trailed Seward by three votes. By the third ballot, it was clear that Lincoln had gained the most support in the party, as he led Seward by more than fifty votes. Since a two-thirds majority was required to get the final nomination, a fourth ballot was held, and Lincoln was able to defeat Seward, gaining 349 votes in total and becoming the Republican presidential nominee for the 1860 election. Maine Senator Hannibal Hamlin was selected to run alongside him as vice president.

Election Results

In addition to Stephen A. Douglas and John C. Breckinridge from the Northern and Southern Democrats, respectively, and Abraham Lincoln from the Republicans, there was one other candidate who ran and managed to gain electoral votes. Former Tennessee Senator John Bell represented the Constitutional Union Party, which had been created by conservative Whigs after the collapse of their party. The former "Know-Nothings," members of the infamously xenophobic and nativist (Native) American Party that had operated in the country since 1848, were also involved in the Constitutional Union Party. ("Native" was dropped from the party's title in 1855.) After the creation of the Republican Party and the subsequent collapse of the Whigs, many of the former Whigs became members of the American Party, which stood against the immigration of Roman Catholic Europeans. The party believed they posed a threat to the economic and social prosperity of the Protestant United States. The Know-Nothings initially met in secret in New York City, and when asked about their secretive organization, they would often answer that they knew nothing, hence the name.

By 1860, the American Party had largely lost traction, and its members instead joined the upcoming Constitutional Union Party, which stressed the need to follow the US Constitution and follow the country's legislation. Due to the party's relative silence on the slavery issue and its members' conservative-leaning opinions, the Constitutional Union Party was particularly popular in the slave-owning South.

These four candidates clashed in the 1860 election. The Republicans and the Northern Democrats held a more anti-slavery stance, while the Southern Democrats and the Constitutional Unionists were more pro-slavery. Thus, in a way, there were two separate elections. The free North had to choose between anti-slavery Lincoln or Douglas since choosing openly pro-slavery candidates would be out of the question.

The opposite went for the Southern voters, who had to make a selection between either Breckinridge or Bell, as voting for a clearly anti-slavery candidate would potentially impose direct changes to their lifestyles.

Due to these highly unusual circumstances, it should come as no surprise that there were some irregularities in the voting procedure. For example, Lincoln was not even on the ballot in ten of the Southern states and did not receive a single vote in 121 counties out of 145. Still, after the election ended on November 6th, 1860, Lincoln emerged victorious, thanks to the electoral college system of the United States.

Amassing just short of 40 percent of the country's popular vote, Lincoln got 180 electoral votes, all of them coming from states north of the Mason-Dixon Line, the Midwest, California, and Oregon. Comparatively, Douglas managed to gain the second-highest number of popular votes, coming in at about 29.5 percent, but he only carried two states—Missouri and New Jersey—which accounted for just twelve electoral votes. Breckinridge came third in the popular vote with just over 18 percent but second in the electoral vote, managing to gain seventy-two and winning in eleven states. Finally, Bell pulled a real rabbit out of his hat by gaining the least popular votes but still getting more electoral votes than Douglas and carrying three states.

The 1860 election still has one of the highest voter turnouts in the history of the United States, coming in at just over 81 percent. There were six states with a margin of victory under 5 percent and four with under 1 percent, making it one of the closest elections in the country's history. All four candidates had a genuine chance to win the election due to the electoral college, so it is not surprising that the final results further aggravated the political climate of the country. Abraham Lincoln, who did not even have 40 percent of all votes, was elected president of the United States.

Chapter 6: Outbreak of the War

In 1860, the American people elected Abraham Lincoln as the president of the United States. Lincoln knew he would have to serve in an already hostile and extremely complex environment and realized he had to carefully plan every move that he wanted to make. Unsurprisingly, the first weeks after the election saw the country become more destabilized and divided, leading to the outbreak of an armed conflict between the Northern and Southern states.

The South Secedes

Although Abraham Lincoln earned the title of the "Great Emancipator" when he signed the Emancipation Proclamation on January 1ˢᵗ, 1863, he did not initially support the full abolition of slavery. Lincoln recognized just how much the Southern states were dependent on slavery. It was the heart of the South's economic and social life, and even though Lincoln had a clear anti-slavery stance, he knew the damage abolition would bring to the Southerners would be very difficult to overcome. What he and most of the Republican Party stood for, at least in 1860, was that slavery was an inherently plagued practice and that its expansion into new territories of the United States would be detrimental to the country's future in the long term.

Lincoln and others proposed a slow, gradual development of the country's economy so it would not be as reliant on slave labor. However, since the South was so used to slavery, it was very difficult to get this message across to the slave owners who had built up their fortunes thanks to slave labor.

So, when Lincoln became president, he faced immense opposition in the South. Not a month had passed after his election that the thoughts of secession, ones that had just been threats by radical Fire-Eaters in Congress, started to become more like a reality. Soon, the whole South was talking about seceding from the Union due to their discontent with the newly elected president. Believing that Lincoln and his administration posed a direct threat to slave owners, word spread quickly in the slave states that the only sensible thing to do was to leave the Union and organize as a separate country.

This sentiment was partially amplified by a speech James Buchanan gave while still serving as president. In his speech, Buchanan recognized the hostile environment in the country and stressed that the Union depended on public cooperation. He urged the two sides of the opposition to come to terms with each other since it would be the only way to preserve the unity within the country. Crucially, however, he said that if states peacefully chose to leave the Union that Congress had no constitutional right to use force to bring them back.

In a daring and shocking move, South Carolina called a state convention on December 20th, 1860, and four days later adapted the South Carolina Secession Declaration, unanimously voting to leave the Union. The authors of the declaration underlined the fact that a natural divide between the Northern and Southern states had been created. They also stressed the importance of slavery and mentioned that the North had demonstrated unjust, hostile actions against the Southern population, something which they believed was unconstitutional. An example of an unconstitutional action was the North's opposition to the Fugitive Slave Act.

Five other states—Mississippi, Florida, Georgia, Alabama, and Louisiana—followed the secession of South Carolina in January. Texas approved the decision to secede in early February and held a referendum, which also voted in favor of secession on February 23rd, 1861. Each of these states passed similar declarations, focusing on the North's unconstitutional past and the election results of 1860, which did not convey the opinion of the majority. The representatives of these states then resigned their positions in Congress and returned to their home states.

All of this happened in a time span of just two months, making it very difficult for the government, which was in the process of transitioning to a new president, to react accordingly to the situation. The truth was that secession had only been perceived as a threat before, not as something that would actually take place. There was nothing mentioned specifically on the matter of secession in the Constitution, leaving Congress unable to provide a quick and effective response. Not only that, but the supporters of secession actually believed the exact opposite, quoting the Tenth Amendment on states' rights, which says that any power that is not granted to the US federal government by the states or is not prohibited to the states by the Constitution is a right to be decided by the state in question or its people. This was a huge factor and one of the main arguments regarding the legality of the Southern states' secession from the Union.

The seceded states proceeded to meet on February 4th, 1861, in Montgomery, Alabama, a month before Lincoln's official inauguration. There, they agreed to form a new provisional government and officially formed the Confederate States of America on February 4th. The government picked Jefferson Davis, a former Mississippi representative, as president and Alexander H. Stephens of Georgia as vice president, forever changing the history of the United States.

Efforts for Reconciliation

The Confederate States of America counted seven Southern states in total by March, a number that would eventually grow to eleven by July with the states of Arkansas, Tennessee, North Carolina, and Virginia. After organizing a new government in February, they took total control of the resources present in each state, including a significant portion of the US Army, which was stationed in Texas. David E. Twiggs, a general of great experience who was in charge of the Texan army, decided to join the Confederates and became the commander of the Confederate forces.

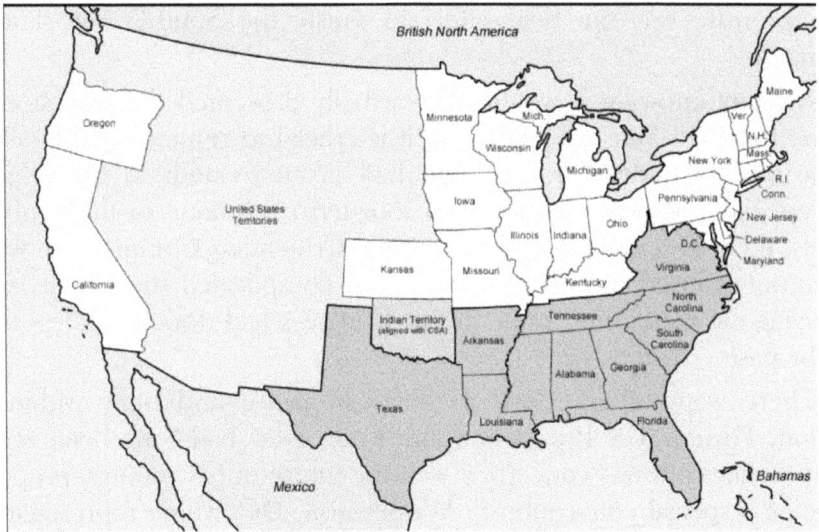

The Confederate States of America.

Golbez, CC BY-SA 3.0 <https://creativecommons.org/licenses/by-sa/3.0>, via Wikimedia Commons https://commons.wikimedia.org/wiki/File:CSA_1861-07-02_to_1861-10-31.png)

We have already mentioned that the federal government's response to secession was quiet, largely due to a transitional period in Congress where Buchanan's administration was getting replaced by Lincoln. Despite the fact that some recognized the severity of the situation, only some chose to act.

One of the first efforts to avoid or solve the secession crisis was the Crittenden Compromise, a proposal by Constitutional Unionist John J. Crittenden from Kentucky. Crittenden proposed that Congress guarantee the permanent status of slavery in the United States and its territories. In addition, Crittenden included points that focused on reinstating the Missouri Compromise line, as well as a stricter Fugitive Slave Act that would be enforced in the same way throughout the country. The proposal was presented to Congress on December 18th, just two days before South Carolina unanimously voted at its state convention to leave the Union.

It is clear from first glance that the proposal would be met with fierce opposition from the Northern congressmen. Crittenden basically proposed that Congress give up all of its legislative powers to regulate slavery and give the South total control over the matter. Lincoln and his party were particularly against its passing, and since they held the majority, they killed the bill as soon as possible. The Crittenden

Compromise was the final effort to satisfy the South's long-standing demands.

Nobody knows if it would have actually prevented the secession, let alone the Civil War. In hindsight, it is crucial to remember that all the measures the federal government had taken to address the issue of slavery did not provide successful long-term solutions to the problem. Thus, there is reason to believe that the Crittenden Compromise would have only caused more polarization and complicated the matter more, delaying the issue once again, just as Congress had done countless times in the past.

There were other efforts to maintain peace and unity within the Union. Former US President John Tyler, who had long been retired from politics but was concerned with the future of his country, proposed holding a special convention in Washington, DC, where representatives from both Southern and Northern states would convene and discuss the matter of secession. The representatives of all states were encouraged to attend, but the Deep South did not send any delegates, believing that the convention would not produce any important results and because they were planning to convene themselves to form a new provisional government. Thus, in total, fourteen free and seven slave states attended the convention, which was held on February 4th, just as the Montgomery convention was underway.

Now known as the Washington Peace Conference of 1861, the convention included 131 politicians who drafted a document with a similar purpose to the Crittenden Compromise. The bill aimed to reinstitute and extend the Missouri Compromise line to the Pacific Ocean and proposed to only acquire future territories with a majority vote from both the Southern and the Northern states. It also included constitutional amendments that would prevent Congress from legally interfering with the matter of slavery in the states where it existed and new, stricter laws regarding fugitive slaves.

The document drafted in Washington was almost exactly the same as the one proposed by Crittenden one and a half months before. Thus, it never saw the light of day. In the Senate, it was overwhelmingly rejected with twenty-eight votes against and only seven for.

The failed efforts to reconcile with the seceded states were followed by Abraham Lincoln's inauguration on March 4th, 1861. The whole nation awaited the president's speech, eager to find out what he would say about the Southern states that had ceased almost all contact with the North. "Legally void" is the phrase Lincoln used in his inaugural address to refer to the secession, claiming that despite the fact the states declared they had left, their decision had no effect in reality. Then, he once again repeated his stance on slavery, stating that he had never stood for abolishing slavery in the states and territories where the practice was legal but that he had always opposed its expansion in the newly acquired territories. Crucially, Lincoln underlined the fact that he would never use force to invade the South to make them rejoin the Union. However, what he did state was that he would use force against the Southern states if they seized control of the federal property located in their possessions. This included everything from mints to military forts and reserves. The president believed that he had a moral and legal obligation to do this since he had been chosen as the president of the United States by the people, binding him to all of these duties. Finally, Lincoln highlighted that he would do everything in his power to restore the "bonds which had held the Union together."

The Attack on Fort Sumter

The tensions between the two sides reached an all-time high. Even before Lincoln's inaugural address, in which he pledged to use force to defend federal property in the seceded states, both sides knew that an armed conflict was inevitable. However, neither side dared to strike first. The hostilities between South Carolina and the US Army nearly broke out at the beginning of the year over Fort Sumter, which was located at the entrance of Charleston Harbor.

At the time of South Carolina's secession, Fort Sumter was not fully finished, but it was fit to answer any threats. Instead, Fort Moultrie, a much older fort also located at the harbor, was manned. Its garrison was commanded by Major Robert Anderson. The state's authorities knew that taking control of the forts was pivotal for any sort of success in the coming conflict. They had eyed both forts since December, something that had not gone unnoticed by Anderson. He realized that if the situation got worse, he and his men would stand no chance at Moultrie. Anderson sabotaged the guns at the fort and, under cover of night, secretly moved his men to Fort Sumter on December 26th.

For the next month, Governor Francis W. Pickens engaged in fierce talks with Buchanan and his administration to order Anderson and his men to surrender Fort Sumter to South Carolina, claiming that the existence of an armed fort by hostile forces was harmful to the state's security. Buchanan responded that Fort Sumter was the property of the United States government and that Major Anderson was entitled to move his forces from one US Army fort to another. This infuriated Governor Pickens, who ordered state troops to proceed with seizing all other federal assets in South Carolina. His men also made sure that no one went in or out of the fort, depriving those in Fort Sumter of supplies. At the end of January, Governor Pickens once again contacted President Buchanan and demanded the fort's surrender. He received a negative response.

The tensions between the men at Fort Sumter and the South Carolina secessionists would not escalate for another four months. Lincoln's administration was aware of the pressing situation and was working on a solution. If the crisis in Charleston was not enough, a similar situation was happening in Fort Pickens in Florida, where Union men were surrounded by hostile secessionists. Lincoln was reluctant to act first, realizing that he might have been considered the aggressor, something that would have had negative implications for his presidency. In Lincoln's Cabinet, William H. Seward, who had now assumed the position of secretary of state, advised the president to order the troops to retreat, but Lincoln disagreed.

On the other side of the border, where the Confederate States of America had already been established, Confederate President Davis was in the same dilemma as his counterpart, acknowledging the fact that taking the fort was crucial but that acting first was not an option. A delegation from the South visited Washington with an offer to buy all the federal property in the seceded lands and to make peace with the Union, but Lincoln denied the delegates, stating that engaging in any sort of negotiations would mean that he acknowledged that the Confederacy was a sovereign nation, something that was unacceptable to him.

By early April, Fort Sumter had almost completely run out of supplies, but the spirits among the men in the fort were still relatively high. Anderson had eighty-five soldiers who could fight but about fifty or so other noncombatant men with him, making the situation even worse. Lincoln was aware of this and communicated with Pickens on April 6th, telling him that a relief ship with no soldiers or ammunition would deliver food and other necessary supplies to Fort Sumter. Crucially, Lincoln made contact with Pickens as the US governor of South Carolina, not the Confederate provisional government. This move is recognized to be perhaps the first of Lincoln's many diplomatic triumphs during the course of the Civil War.

Lincoln's message was discussed by President Davis and his advisors. After much consideration, a crucial decision was made, despite some opposition from Davis's cabinet. Davis ordered the commander of the Confederate forces in South Carolina—Pierre "P. G. T." Beauregard—to once again demand the surrender of Fort Sumter. In the event of a negative response, Beauregard was to proceed with an assault on the fort before the supply ship got to it.

Early in the morning of April 12th, the first shot of the Civil War was fired on Fort Sumter, the first out of four thousand upon the fort. Anderson and his men, who were outgunned and outnumbered, knew the end was near but still put up a fight. Fort Sumter fell the next day, with no casualties on either side. Anderson was forced to agree to surrender as it was a desperate situation.

The North grieved the loss of Fort Sumter, and everyone was waiting for Lincoln's response. On April 15th, two days after the fort's surrender, Lincoln named the secession of the Southern states an "insurrection." In addition, he called all states to assemble a voluntary force consisting of seventy-five thousand men to serve for three months, a decisive action that rallied the public and concentrated their efforts. Volunteers enlisted by the thousands, quickly meeting the president's demands, and prepared for an armed conflict. America was now at war, but it was at war with itself.

Border States

Despite the fact that the attention of Congress and Lincoln's administration was divided between trying to come up with a plan to reconcile with the South and dealing with the crisis of Fort Sumter, other important issues remained. One very important question that needed to be answered was what would happen to the slave states that had not yet chosen to secede from the Union. During the attack on Fort Sumter, the Confederate States of America still consisted of the Deep Seven. However, there were eight other slave states that still had to make their decisions.

These states were divided on the matter. Half of these states made their decisions soon after Lincoln's actions regarding Fort Sumter. Beginning in May 1861, Virginia, Arkansas, Tennessee, and North

Carolina all seceded from the Union and were accepted by the Confederacy. The population of these states was heavily dependent on slavery and saw the election of Lincoln and the Republicans as a direct threat to their everyday lives.

The other four states—Maryland, Delaware, Kentucky, and Missouri— were more hesitant. Although slavery was allowed in these states, the public was much less one-sided. Instead of choosing to remain or secede, these states left it to the public to decide what they wanted. As a consequence, Maryland, Delaware, Kentucky, and Missouri have come to be known as border states since none of them seceded from the Union but existed in a weird symbiotic relationship with both the North and the South.

In Missouri, a state convention was assembled on whether to hold a referendum, a decision much like the one that had been taken in Texas. Unlike Texas, the referendum demonstrated overwhelming support for remaining with the Union.

Maryland, whose territories surrounded Washington, DC, was in a much trickier situation. Despite its proximity to the capital, there was more support for secession. But giving up Maryland to the Confederacy would mean that the war effort would come knocking right at the door of the Union's capital, and Lincoln was not prepared enough for that kind of pressure. Maryland's legislature voted in favor of remaining with the Union, but the same resolution also mentioned that it would not get involved in the war, shutting down the crucial railroads that connected the North with the South. Lincoln responded by declaring martial law and making sure that all anti-Union officials and members of the Maryland General Assembly were arrested. His troops then quickly took control of the state. During the war and after its completion, Lincoln would be criticized for his actions, which some have deemed to be dictatorial or undemocratic.

In Delaware, things were decided in a much easier way. Despite the fact that slavery was permitted, the state was hardly reliant on it. Since 1860, the North had made quite an effort in trying to integrate Delaware's economy into its own. The general assembly opposed secession. The general public sentiment also reflected this decision, as average citizens were not slave owners and would rather see the conflict end through peaceful means. The fact that Delaware was deep into Northern territory also may have influenced the decision since it would have been much harder for the Confederacy to defend Delaware.

The situation proved to be the most explosive in Kentucky. Several different opinions existed on what exactly to do, but the state finally passed the legislation on assuming neutrality in May, declaring that it would continue to be neutral if neither side invaded it. Throughout the course of the war, both the Union and the Confederacy saw Kentucky as one of their own, and Kentuckians enlisted in both armies. After the Unionists gained additional seats in the state election in the summer of 1861, the Confederacy was only supported by a small minority of state officials. The Confederate forces did invade Kentucky but were met with fierce opposition from the Unionists, who did not give an inch to the invaders and managed to cling onto the most valuable parts of the state, including its capital, Frankfort. Throughout the war, the Confederacy recognized Kentucky as one of the Confederate states and even included it in the final version of the flag. President Lincoln personally noted on different occasions just how pivotal holding Kentucky was for the Union and the defensive effort in the war.

Chapter 7: America at War

Now that we have covered the preluding events of the Civil War, it is time to jump right into the action. This chapter will focus on examining the strengths and weaknesses of the Union and the Confederacy throughout the Civil War and cover some of the main strategies each side employed.

Was the US Prepared for War?

Despite the fact that the United States had yet to be defeated in a foreign war after gaining independence, it is safe to say when looking at the country's military resources in the 1860s that it was *not* prepared for war, let alone a war with itself. It had a standing military of about sixteen thousand soldiers—a tiny number when compared to the great empires of Europe in the 19th century. Yet, in 1812, the United States had managed to hold off the British, and in the 1840s, it had decisively defeated Mexico, despite the fact that the Mexican Army far outnumbered the US Army. So, where exactly did their secret lie?

The sixteen thousand men already ready for service were dispersed around the country in small numbers; Major Anderson and his soldiers at Fort Sumter are just one example. They were stationed everywhere, from fortified Native American territories to the harbors. The Founding Fathers had based the country's military philosophy on mustering up militias when there was a need for them during wartime. The militia system was based solely on voluntary service; states would supply men who wanted to fight. After the end of the war, these men would normally disperse, returning back to their lives, if possible, with only a minority continuing formal training and service.

On paper, the North was far more capable militarily than the South. More than twice the number of Southerners lived in the North, and about half of the Southerners were slaves. This gave the Union a significant edge manpower-wise. In a long, dragged-out war of attrition, it theoretically could have relied on this edge to achieve victory. And due to the South's reliance on the agrarian lifestyle and slavery, the North had far more industrial capabilities to produce weapons. Fewer than 20,000 manufacturing plants were located south of the Potomac River, while the North had about 100,000 at its disposal.

Despite this apparent disadvantage, the Confederacy hoped to put up a good fight, banking on the possibility of foreign aid from Europe, mainly from France and Britain. Engaging in what has come to be known as cotton diplomacy, the Confederate government requested aid from the Europeans and threatened to block cotton exports as a leverage factor. However, partially thanks to the efforts of Secretary of State Seward, who duly notified the Europeans that recognizing the Confederacy would mean antagonizing the Union government, and partially due to the fact that the Europeans could get their cotton from Asia, cotton diplomacy failed. Confederate President Davis and his government were perhaps too hopeful that Europe would interfere in the war and were disappointed when they learned they would be alone.

Although the Confederacy was outgunned and outmanned against the Union, the Confederates had high morale. They were united around the infamous "Southern cause," a notion that the Southerners had to achieve victory against the tyrannical North, which tried to limit the sacred Southern institutions, most importantly slavery. It was a typical narrative of David versus Goliath, with David, in this case, being the Confederacy. This idea had existed in the South before the start of the war but was amplified to higher degrees throughout the war by Confederate politicians.

What is important to realize is that the two sides had chosen completely different approaches to the war. This became more evident as the war entered its first stages. Davis and the Confederates knew they were at a numerical disadvantage and chose a more defensive tactic. Davis hoped the long southern coastline would make it impossible for the Union to completely blockade the South. A slower approach guaranteed that the Confederates would be able to defend their territories more cohesively and not be distracted by an offensive and find themselves at a disadvantage.

Some historians argue that the decision to adopt a defensive approach might have been fatal for the Confederates from the very beginning. Immediately after the events at Fort Sumter, it might have been better to organize a concentrated attack on the Union's positions when the North would have least expected it and, therefore, might have been less prepared. When paired with the dragged-out approach adopted by Lincoln and his team, this move seems more logical.

In what is referred to as the Anaconda Plan, the Northern high command envisioned the defeat of the Confederacy by a complete naval and land blockade of the South, followed by a concentrated attack along the Mississippi River—right at the heart of the South.

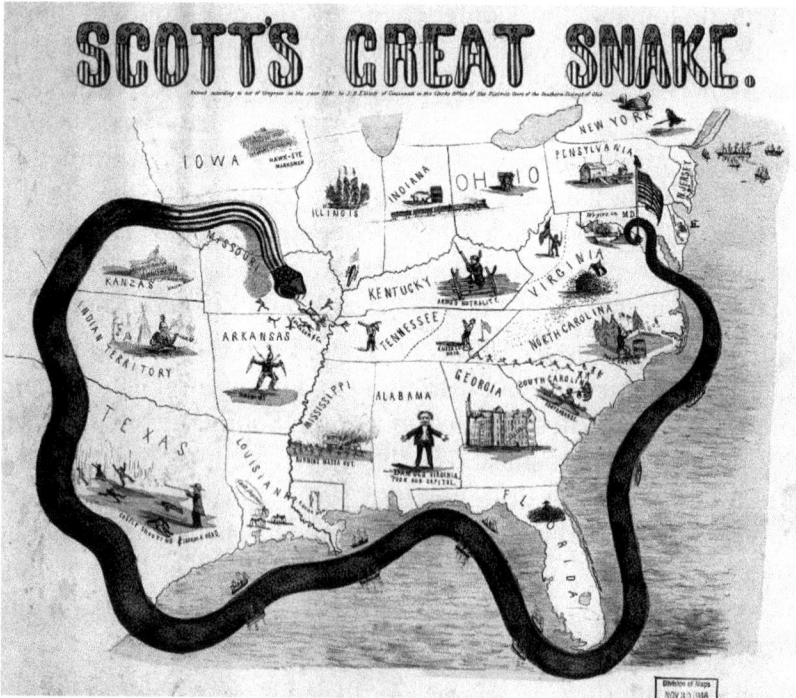

The Anaconda Plan.
https://commons.wikimedia.org/wiki/File:Scott-anaconda.jpg

The Fight for West Virginia

The attack on Fort Sumter was a cold shower for the Union and contributed to the growth of anti-Southern (or rather anti-secessionist) sentiment, which had existed in the country since December 1860. Out of the sixteen thousand or so soldiers in the army, more than half of them were located in the western part of the country at the time of the attack. It seemed unlikely that they would join up with the seventy-five thousand or so volunteers President Lincoln had called upon from the Northern states. Still, before the mustering of volunteers was completed, fighting between the Union and Confederate troops broke out in early June. The Union forces attempted to take control of the western part of Virginia, which was more pro-Union than the rest of the slave state.

Virginia had seceded from the Union in May and had been admitted by the Confederacy on May 7th. At the time, about 30 percent of its population were slaves, but they, along with the majority of slave owners, were concentrated in the eastern part of the state. In the west, pro-Unionists were discontent with the decision to secede from the Union. To use the situation to the Union's favor, Major General George B. McClellan, who was the leader of the assembled Union forces in Cincinnati, Ohio, marched to western Virginia with a pretty sizeable force of about twenty thousand men. His opposition was not ready. Confederate Colonel George A. Porterfield was in charge of the Confederate force stationed in northwestern Virginia but was not aware that an attack was imminent.

In what became the first land battle of the American Civil War, McClellan's three thousand or so men converged on the town of Philippi. They were able to rout a much smaller Confederate force of about eight hundred men, forcing them to retreat south to the town of Huttonsville. The whole encounter was more of a skirmish rather than an all-out battle, but it still counted as a victory for the Union Army, which was able to establish a somewhat favorable position in western Virginia. There were only about thirty casualties in total, but Philippi was almost completely destroyed after hours of shelling by the Union forces.

After the triumph at Philippi, McClellan and his men were praised by Northern newspapers for their bravery. McClellan was able to follow this up with two additional victories in western Virginia. A month later, at the Battle of Rich Mountain, McClellan's forces were able to inflict about three hundred casualties to the Confederate forces while suffering only forty themselves. They chased down the retreating opposition to Carrick's Ford, where they also emerged victorious, concluding the first set of battles fought in Virginia.

McClellan's efforts were quickly recognized by the Union high command, and his three quick victories were a factor behind his promotion to commander of the Army of the Potomac. The success of the Union forces was also crucial in the secession of pro-Union Virginians from their state. The anti-slavery state of West Virginia eventually separated from Virginia and aided the Union throughout the war.

The First Battle of Bull Run

An interesting characteristic of the war is that the capitals of the two sides—Washington for the Union and Richmond for the Confederacy— were very close to each other, separated by only about one hundred miles. Richmond was one of the richest and most prosperous Southern cities, so the Confederates chose to move their capital to the city after Virginia joined the Confederacy on May 7th. Because of this rather unusual situation, the tensions surrounding both sides started circulating early on. The largest parts of both armies were gathering near Washington and Richmond, and the cities' inhabitants sensed that, sooner or later, they would be under attack.

Union Brigadier General Irvin McDowell was in charge of the thirty-five thousand volunteers who had assembled at Washington. Despite the fact that the Anaconda Plan had been proposed by US General in Chief Winfield Scott, McDowell was tasked to lead the attack on enemy positions. The Confederates, who were commanded by P. G. T. Beauregard, had encamped about twenty-six miles south from Washington at the pivotal Manassas Junction, which played an important role in terms of rail connectivity to the east. Beauregard was in charge of about twenty thousand men and assumed a defensive position at Manassas. In addition, a smaller Confederate force of about twelve thousand men was encamped nearby, ready to reinforce in case of emergency.

On July 21st, McDowell, knowing that he had a numerical advantage over the enemy and succumbing to the social and political pressure in Washington, led his men against Beauregard. An additional force of eighteen thousand men commanded by Major General Robert Patterson was tasked to delay the reinforcements at Harpers Ferry.

Initially, McDowell's troops saw great success, managing to outmaneuver the enemy and weaken its left flank. However, the upper hand was quickly assumed by the Confederates, thanks to an inspiring rally from Thomas "Stonewall" Jackson—a Confederate general who earned his nickname due to this battle. Despite experiencing heavy artillery fire, Beauregard's men were able to contain McDowell, while the Confederate reinforcements, which had managed to break through Patterson's resistance, arrived just in time to outflank the Union Army. Union volunteers, who had relatively low morale because of inexperience, decided to flee and save their lives. McDowell was forced to retreat back to Washington, causing a city-wide panic because of his defeat.

The encounter became known as the First Battle of Bull Run in the North, while the Southerners referred to it as the Battle of First Manassas. It was a tough defeat to swallow for the North, which lost about 2,900 men compared to the South's 2,000. Fortunately for the Union, Beauregard's men were too exhausted to chase the retreating soldiers. Thus, the two sides interpreted the battle's outcome differently.

After the loss, the Union approach became more careful instead of assuming a proactive role and using its numerical advantage to the fullest to overwhelm the enemy forces. As for the South, the situation was not that different. The Confederacy saw the victory as hard proof that despite a numerical disadvantage, the Southern soldiers were more resilient than the Northerners. They were swept up in the idea that the "Southern cause" was far more important than what the Union was fighting for, giving them a natural advantage over their enemy and, as a consequence, making them overestimate their own capabilities.

Army of the Potomac

The defeat at the First Battle of Bull Run was devastating for Lincoln, who had hoped for a decisive action by the end of July but had only gotten a relatively small victory in western Virginia. As he called for more volunteers to bolster the army's numbers and replenish the loss the Union had suffered, he also made changes to the high command. General Winfield Scott, the long-standing general in chief, was replaced in November by Major General McClellan, who earned his spot due to his quick victories over the summer. Although the overall plans laid by

Scott remained intact, the experienced veteran had to be relieved due to his poor health.

Just five days after the Union's defeat at Manassas, McClellan started the transformation of his corps into the Army of the Potomac, the part of the Union Army during the Civil War that would take part in the military operations in the eastern campaigns. In the first months as the new general in chief, the number of volunteers grew to include more than 100,000 men, who, unlike the troops that participated in the First Battle of Bull Run, were substantially drilled and equipped. McClellan's main goal was to raise discipline, which would allow for more resilience on the battlefield.

Despite this, McClellan still faced some opposition from the Republican-dominated Congress, partially due to the fact that he was a Democrat. Congress was aware of the enemy's close proximity, as they had not only remained in Manassas but also occupied the territory near the town of Centreville, Virginia. In addition to having a bad reputation with Congress for sometimes demonstrating impolite and indelicate tendencies, McClellan also found himself in a personal feud with President Lincoln. After McClellan recovered from an illness in late January 1861, Lincoln ordered him to organize an attack on the Confederate positions in Virginia. McClellan disagreed, believing that the volunteers were still not fit for battle, despite the fact that they had greatly improved their capabilities after his arrival. Still, Lincoln's decision was final, and McClellan was obliged to advance on the enemy in late February.

Chapter 8: The War Grows

In the beginning, many in the North predicted the conflict would last no more than a couple of months. This was especially true after McClellan's early victories in western Virginia. However, by the end of 1861, as substantial efforts to put a dent into the Confederacy's defense proved unsuccessful, the approach from both the North and the South drastically changed.

The Peninsular Campaign

Acting on orders from the upper chain of command, Union General in Chief McClellan led his men in yet another offensive. In February, President Lincoln's main concern was the Confederate Army stationed at Centreville, Virginia, about thirty miles south of Washington. The president had perhaps overestimated the threat the Confederate forces could have posed to the Union's capital, which was heavily defended and contained a sizeable garrison.

At first, Lincoln ordered McClellan to attack Centreville. However, before the operation could be started, the Confederates retreated farther south, deeming the attack useless. Instead, McClellan's attention was focused on the Confederate capital of Richmond. McClellan finally managed to gain Lincoln's approval for an offensive after proposing to organize an attack from the East Coast by first landing at Fort Monroe through an amphibious assault and then marching his troops northeastward, all the way up the Virginia Peninsula to finally reach Richmond.

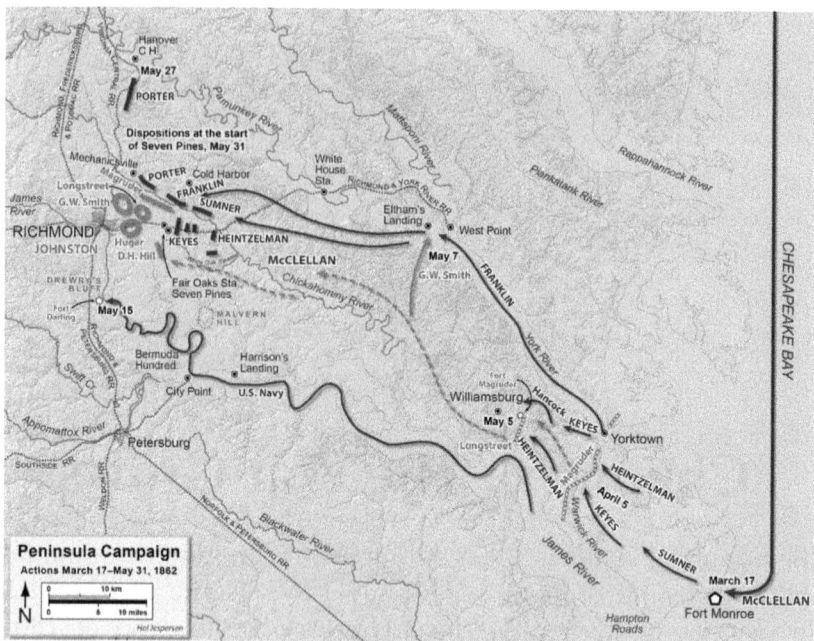

The Peninsular Campaign.

Despite the soundness of the plan, nothing went as smoothly as the Union high command had desired. One big detail to remember is that McClellan was relieved from the position of general in chief once the operation started, partially because of his feud with Lincoln and the Republicans but also because Lincoln hoped he could divert his whole attention to leading his campaign. President Lincoln assumed the position of general in chief and, together with his Cabinet, personally led the war effort until he could find a suitable replacement.

As for the Peninsular Campaign itself, the initial plans to land at Fort Monroe and converge on the town of Yorktown, both from the land and from the York River, failed. The Union forces faced several delays and were even confronted by Confederate vanguards in smaller skirmishes that cost them days. Finally, McClellan's troops reached the city. After a long siege, they forced the Confederates to give up their positions in early May.

Confederate Commander Joseph E. Johnston fell back to a more defensive line at Williamsburg, but McClellan quickly caught up and forced another confrontation, where the Union soldiers emerged victorious once again. Finally, after breaking through the defensive lines under tough conditions, McClellan found himself a target for a Confederate counterattack at the Battle of Seven Pines. There, Commander Johnston hoped to isolate McClellan's flank and surround the advancing Union forces. But after gaining a small advantage at first, he was forced to fall back, succumbing to the superior Union artillery.

The final outcome at Seven Pines favored neither side. The Confederate resistance had significantly slowed McClellan's momentum, who was forced to take a break before continuing his advance. On the other hand, Johnston was wounded during the battle and replaced by General Robert E. Lee—a man who had been serving as a military advisor to Jefferson Davis before stepping up to take control of the Confederate Army of Northern Virginia. In the long run, both outcomes proved to be terrible for the Union since Lee proved to be its toughest opponent in the war and greatly slowed the initiative that had been seized by McClellan during the Peninsular Campaign.

By the end of June, McClellan's forces had made headway into the Confederate territories. At the same time, fighting was unfolding in western parts of Virginia, mainly in the Shenandoah Valley, where Union corps under the command of Major General McDowell tried to converge on Richmond. However, the Confederates fiercely defended themselves against the Union troops that tried to cross the Potomac River. The Confederates gained several victories and seized a lot of valuable loot, like small arms and ammunition, in the battles of Front Royal and Winchester. Since the Confederates had thwarted the Union advance in the Shenandoah Valley, Stonewall Jackson, who was in command of the defending troops, turned his attention to the east to reinforce Lee.

This decision turned out to be crucial. Lee waited for almost a month for McClellan to attack. So, in the meantime, he gathered up his defenses in the southern and southeastern parts of Richmond and was ready to put up a fight with an additional couple of thousand soldiers. He organized a counterattack on June 26th, trying to further stall out McClellan's advance and make the Union forces run out of supplies so they would be forced to retreat. The ensuing battles lasted for about a week and are referred to as the Seven Days Battles. In a well-organized, concentrated assault, Lee was able to utilize the surprise factor and achieved victory after victory. He first pushed the Union forces back at Mechanicsville and at Gaines' Mill on June 26th and 27th, which was followed by another set of victories at Savage's Station and Frayser's

Farm by June 30th and Glendale and Malvern Hill by July 1st. Lee was able to reclaim a lot of lost ground.

Lee was proudly celebrated in the South, while the Northern high command was furious with McClellan, who they believed had thrown away the advantage they had achieved. In hindsight, it was a rather peculiar situation since, despite suffering some defeats, McClellan was still somewhat close to Richmond. Who knows, perhaps with more effort and reinforcements, he could have been able to reach the Confederate capital, but this was not something that neither he nor the high command believed to be feasible.

The truth of the matter is that McClellan already had an infamous reputation in the Union, and the fact that he requested more reinforcements to continue the campaign was perceived as another one of his unrealistic demands. In total, McClellan had lost more than fifteen thousand men throughout the campaign, while Lee had suffered about twenty thousand casualties. Although McClellan's early efforts had been successful, Lee had retaliated. Lee still had a lot to prove on the battlefield, and the war was nowhere near over. Instead of continuing the advance up the peninsula, Lincoln ordered a retreat to consolidate the forces and plan a new attack.

The Second Battle of Bull Run

After the unsuccessful Peninsular Campaign, Lincoln appointed Henry W. Halleck to the position of general in chief, which had been left open for months. McClellan was still the commander of the Army of the Potomac, but many of his troops eventually ended up under the command of John Pope in the newly formed Army of Virginia. The main idea behind the Army of Virginia was to have an additional force Lincoln could rely on, as McClellan had proven to be increasingly difficult to work with. Instead of attempting to recreate the previous offensive from the east, Pope's forces would try to converge on Richmond from the north and west.

Confederate Commander Lee envisioned a different development of the war. Although McClellan was still on the peninsula, Lee had become aware of his dwindling reputation among the members of the high command and decided to allocate fewer resources to keep his forces at bay. He recognized that Pope's Army of Virginia, which was marching to Gordonsville to start a new offensive on Richmond, had completely split from McClellan, who was on the other side of Virginia. Lee wanted to seize the opportunity and quickly strike Pope's position, hoping to take him out with a concentrated attack that would leave the Union even more disoriented.

With this in mind, he sent Stonewall Jackson with about fourteen thousand men to stop Pope at Gordonsville before the two Union armies could join up. He planned to follow up with even more reinforcements to crush Pope's forces. The initial plan worked. Stonewall Jackson was able to contain most of Pope's forces at Manassas, near the site of the original Battle of Bull Run, forcing Pope to make an aggressive move without waiting for more reinforcements.

In late August, Pope engaged with Jackson's forces in what has come to be known as the Second Battle of Bull Run but could not achieve a significant advantage, as Stonewall Jackson lived up to his reputation as a great defender. After holding off the Union Army, Jackson's job was done, and Lee, along with Confederate Brigadier General James Longstreet, arrived just in time to flank Pope. They routed his men, inflicting more than thirteen thousand casualties while, in turn, suffering only about nine thousand.

Invasion of Maryland

Having gained several consecutive victories, first against McClellan in June and then against Pope in August, Lee was determined to achieve more. This time, he planned to go on a full offensive and use the momentum to push his success by invading Maryland—a border state where Lincoln had declared martial law to enforce order and subdue anti-Republican tendencies. Lee hoped to achieve several victories in Maryland to motivate it to join the Confederacy, something that would have been detrimental to the Union. If Maryland joined the Confederacy, the security of Washington, DC, would come under question. Capturing the pivotal Baltimore and Ohio Railroad would also cut off a major supply line to the Union capital.

After learning of Lee's advance to Frederick, Maryland, Lincoln desperately thought of an effective answer as he slowly noticed panic build up within the Northern public. McClellan's operation from the peninsula had been fully recalled, with Lincoln tasking him with coming up with a response. Having finally joined up with the rest of Pope's troops, McClellan did what he did best: make sure that his men were fully capable of fighting and reconsolidated his position. However, he also demonstrated his main weakness once again: he was too hesitant to take decisive action against Lee because he overestimated the South's military capabilities.

This became even more evident when McClellan was notified of Lee's future plans after his men accidentally found a Confederate piece of paper that depicted the intended campaign. Instead of utilizing the element of surprise and picking off the smaller Confederate forces one by one, McClellan decided to wait for nearly a day and only managed to confront a larger Confederate force that had assembled at South Mountain on September 14th, 1862. There, after some skirmishes, Lee ordered his men to retreat to assume a more favorable defensive position at Antietam Creek near Sharpsburg, where he awaited a Union attack.

Robert E. Lee
https://commons.wikimedia.org/wiki/File:Robert_Edward_Lee.jpg

At Antietam Creek, Lee was joined by Stonewall Jackson's reinforcements, and the two Confederate commanders, along with General Longstreet, put up one of the best defensive efforts of the whole war. Antietam Creek was a rather irregular location to attack and gave the defenders an advantage, as they could use the small rivers to their favor. Nevertheless, a long front line was established, and early on September 17th, McClellan ordered his men to attack. Most of the fighting took place in the center at an area called "Bloody Road," where McClellan's forces broke through. However, Confederate reinforcements from the flanks, where less of the action was concentrated, quickly moved to the center to drive the Union forces back to their original front lines.

Crucially, additional reinforcements arrived at the same time for both armies, further contributing to the deadlock that had been created after hours of fighting. A deciding factor in the battle was, once again, McClellan's indecisiveness. The Union commander wrongly assumed the Confederates' strength and was reluctant to send in all of his soldiers to overwhelm the defenders despite having the numerical advantage. Lee and the Confederates, on the other hand, had been fully committed to the battle and fought until they were forced to retreat after realizing they did not stand a chance in a prolonged confrontation.

About twenty-three thousand men fell at the Battle of Antietam, which earned its infamous status as the single bloodiest day of the Civil War. The Confederates lost a bit more than ten thousand men, while the Union suffered about thirteen thousand casualties. However, these numbers are even more impressive when considering the fact that McClellan's forces outnumbered Lee's army two to one, coming in at about eighty-five thousand men to Lee's thirty-six thousand. Despite the Confederate retreat, the Union was not fully able to capitalize due to McClellan's distorted perception of the South's strength. Still, the Confederate offensive into Maryland was over, and Lee's main army was driven back to Virginia.

Fiasco at Fredericksburg

Although most of the Confederate forces had managed to retreat, Antietam was perceived by the Union high command as a victory. For the next few weeks after the end of the battle, Lincoln and his war council repeatedly urged McClellan to pursue the retreating Confederates, but the latter always refused, stating he was afraid to overextend his men and unwilling to chase Lee since he did not know his full strength. This back-and-forth lasted until the end of October. President Lincoln finally relieved McClellan of his duties as the commander of the Army of the Potomac and assigned Ambrose E.

Burnside as the new leader. He had previously been in charge of one of the companies at Antietam but failed to achieve anything meaningful throughout the course of the battle. The Union high command was hoping to at least have someone whom they could rely on to follow their orders.

This approach from Lincoln and his Cabinet worked, and Burnside launched a follow-up offensive aimed to make an advance straight to Richmond. His freshly reinforced army counted some 120,000 men. Theoretically, it was designed to overcome any resistance the South could dish up simply because of its numerical superiority. Burnside's plan envisioned a quick crossing of the Rappahannock River and outmaneuvering Lee's army to get to the relatively undefended Confederate capital. At first, it seemed as if the plan was going to work, but Burnside's army was delayed for weeks because the special pontoon bridges—the ones that float on water and are used by armies to quickly cross rivers—did not arrive due to logistical issues. This delay gave Lee and his men time to encamp on the other bank of the Rappahannock and set up defenses near the town of Fredericksburg.

Battle of Fredericksburg.
https://commons.wikimedia.org/wiki/File:Battle_of_Fredericksburg,_Dec_13,_1862.png

Pressured by the Union high command, Burnside proceeded to establish crossing points and crossed the river to the other bank, where Lee and his men were waiting with heavy artillery fire, having assumed the high ground on the nearby heights south of the city. However, if there is one thing military history has clearly demonstrated is that the defenders are always favored during river crossings. Burnside ordered his men to head right into the open arms of the Confederates, who were more than happy to pick off waves after waves of hopeless Union soldiers. On December 15th, 1862, after about five days of fighting, Burnside realized that he had made a fatal mistake. He ordered his men to retreat back across the Rappahannock River and accepted defeat.

The loss at Fredericksburg was detrimental to the Union Army's morale. The army suffered about thirteen thousand casualties to the Confederates' five thousand, marking one of the most decisive Union defeats in the war. And to add insult to injury, Burnside suffered another fiasco in the weeks following the Battle of Fredericksburg during a desperate flanking maneuver on Lee's forces.

In harsh winter conditions and lacking effective communication channels, Burnside was not able to achieve his goals for the whole of January, seeing a rising number of desertions and a lack of trust from the commanders directly under him. This caused President Lincoln to relieve Burnside from the position of the commander of the Army of the Potomac on January 25th, 1863, replacing him with the more experienced Joseph "Fighting Joe" Hooker. The two sides went into a temporary stalemate over the winter of 1863.

The Emancipation Proclamation

Ironically enough, the Union's lack of success on the battlefield was completely different from the crucial developments of late 1862 and early 1863 off the field. The instrumental Emancipation Proclamation— one of the most iconic documents in the history of the United States—was signed on January 1st, 1863, by President Lincoln, declaring all slaves living in seceded states to be freed. The signing of the Emancipation Proclamation was not only a huge social and moral victory for Lincoln and the Union but also a great strategic move.

The slavery issue became even more pressing for both sides. The Confederacy was dependent on slave labor, which was the main catalyst of its economy. The Union, on the other hand, had seen a vast increase in the number of fugitive slaves who had escaped from the South, seeking shelter and safety, afraid that with the secession of the Southern states, their chances of gaining freedom were non-existent. This factor, in addition to Southern reliance on slavery, was recognized by President Lincoln, but he was still hesitant to issue an emancipation bill or abolish the practice altogether. Mainly, Lincoln was afraid that in case of emancipation, the instrumental slave-owning border states might rebel against the Union and join the Confederacy. Slaves were also considered the property of their owners and thus were protected by the Constitution, something that would have been very difficult to change.

However, with Congress passing the First Confiscation Act in August of 1861, allowing Union soldiers to confiscate the property of the Confederate soldiers, the margins on the right to property, as mentioned in the Constitution, became thinner. In other words, with the First Confiscation Act, the Union troops were permitted to claim the slaves who had previously been in the defeated Confederates' possession.

The Union soldiers liberated hundreds of slaves throughout the course of the first two years. It put a dent into the South's production. With the majority of white Confederates enlisted in the army, every slave who would do the work for them in factories and fields mattered even more than before. Famously, Union General and politician Benjamin F. Butler referred to the slaves that would be seized during the campaigns as "contrabands," declaring that they would not be returned to their previous owners under any circumstances. The name stuck, and for the rest of the war, the escaped slaves were increasingly referred to as contrabands.

The First Confiscation Act and the increased number of fugitive slaves prompted Congress to abolish slavery in the District of Columbia in April 1862. The slave owners in the area received monetary compensation for the income they would lose. Still, DC was the easiest place to negotiate emancipation, followed by the US territories.

The situation was not quite as simple when it came to the border states, whose representatives met Lincoln on separate occasions to discuss the terms of potential emancipation. Lincoln offered monetary compensation to the slave owners of Missouri, Kentucky, Maryland, and Delaware but to no real success. These states had largely operated on their own since the start of the war, and Lincoln had to get them on board before he could make such an impactful decision. As the talks fell through, Lincoln was forced to draft a new version of the Emancipation Proclamation, which would eventually take effect from January 1ˢᵗ, 1863. The proclamation stated that starting in the new year, all slaves in the territories not under the control of the Union were free.

It was a monumental step for Lincoln and his administration, something that would not only give the moral high ground to the North but also incentivize slaves living in oppression in the South to break free from their owners and cause further harm to the South's economy. Crucially, Lincoln had used smart wording to indicate that the Emancipation Proclamation did not include the border states since they were still technically under the Union's control. It only affected the states that had seceded, where the practice of slavery was the most deeply rooted.

The Emancipation Proclamation was declared right after the Battle of Antietam. Despite mixed results, it was conceived by the Union high command as a victory. The implications of the Emancipation Proclamation were huge, and everyone waited for January to see what effect it would have on the slave population of the South. Historians note that the signing of the Emancipation Proclamation was one of the reasons behind Europe's decision not to support the Confederacy against the Union. The practice of slavery was frowned upon by the major powers of Europe at this time.

The immediate effects of the Emancipation Proclamation are evident. One important point of the document was that freed slaves and already freed African Americans could now serve as soldiers in the war on the side of the Union. Before 1863, African Americans and whites were not allowed to serve together in the US Army or Navy, although they were permitted to join the ranks in emergency situations like in the War of 1812. In total, about 200,000 black soldiers entered the war on the side of the Union, twenty thousand of whom joined the navy. They made up approximately 10 percent of all Union forces by the end of the war, and many of them had escaped their Southern masters to fight, just as Lincoln had envisioned.

The role played by African Americans in the Civil War is truly immense. They were instrumental in the battles that occurred as the Northern effort became more concentrated down the Mississippi, in Louisiana, and in South Carolina. It must have been a great sight to see those who had struggled for so long for their liberty to finally have a realistic chance to fight for it. Still, despite joining the Union Army in large numbers, the African Americans could not escape segregation, which they had faced all their lives. They were paid less than their white counterparts, were organized in separate "all-black" regiments, and had limited direct contact with white leadership. Their regiments were commanded by white officers since they rarely ascended in the ranks. The sense of "Negrophobia" that had always characterized Northern society showed itself once African Americans poured into the army. Although they were fighting for the same cause, the Northern soldiers' innate racism was something the African Americans had to bear with for the rest of the war.

The Trans-Mississippi

Along with the Eastern Theater of the Civil War, which historians refer to as the military action that unfolded mainly in Virginia and the surrounding areas, fighting between the Union and the Confederates took place in other parts of the country, one of which was the Trans-Mississippi Theater, where the war effort was more disorganized than in the east.

Several small-scale skirmishes and guerilla warfare were already present in the region, which spanned the territories west of the Mississippi River, mainly in the states of Missouri, Arkansas, Louisiana, and modern-day Oklahoma. It is important to remember that at the beginning of the war, both sides were quite unsure of the main goals set by their respective high commands. Thus, the fighting took place mainly to test and weaken the opposition rather than to have a decisive effect.

A more cohesive campaign in the Trans-Mississippi was organized by Confederate Commander Henry Sibley, who led his force of around 3,5000 men to New Mexico and managed to capture the cities of Albuquerque and Santa Fe by late March 1862. Sibley's intended objective was to reach California, as the control of the rich state would give many opportunities to the Confederate government. However, Sibley was forced to retreat back to Texas with heavy casualties after he was confronted by Edward Canby at the Battle of La Glorieta Pass.

Meanwhile, more concentrated encounters had taken place in the border states northeast of New Mexico. President Lincoln was well aware of the important role the border states, especially Kentucky and Missouri, played in the war and was prepared to divert most of his resources to defend the territories. At the first major battle between the two sides at Wilson's Creek, Missouri, around five thousand Union soldiers suffered a defeat against a much larger Confederate force, which managed to briefly seize control of the southern part of the state in August 1861. The North, however, was not willing to give up Missouri without a proper fight. After reinforcing the numbers under Brigadier General Samuel R. Curtis, the Union dealt a decisive blow to the Confederates at the Battle of Pea Ridge in March 1862. Before March 1862, neither side had the resources necessary to continue fighting in Missouri, as most actions at the time were taking place in Virginia due to the attempted Northern campaign to capture Richmond.

Farther east in Kentucky, fighting broke out when the Confederates violated the state's neutrality, assuming a commanding position by capturing Columbus. Led by General Albert Sidney Johnston, the Confederates convinced the anti-Union population of Kentucky to secede from the state and organized a provisional government, which admitted Kentucky into the Confederacy in December 1861. However, the long front line the Confederates had established proved to be difficult to maintain since they simply did not have enough manpower. Seizing the opportunity, the Union forces were able to break through, first at Mill Springs on the right flank of the Confederate line in January and then at Fort Henry and Fort Donelson in the center about a month later. By capturing these two important forts, the Union had virtually gained control of the Cumberland River, which was the main point of defense for the Confederates.

The Union forces under Ulysses S. Grant were able to drive the Confederates out of both Kentucky and northern Tennessee, suffering only about three thousand casualties while inflicting more than fifteen thousand to the enemy. The battles at Fort Henry and Fort Donelson are considered to be the first meaningful victories of the Union in the war, despite the fact that in the Virginia Theater, McClellan and others had seen some successes before this.

Ulysses S. Grant

By the end of March 1862, Confederate General Johnston had given up his positions in Kentucky and retreated back to Tennessee to regroup, awaiting a new opportunity to strike. This opportunity presented itself to Johnston early in April when the Union forces under Ulysses S. Grant and William Tecumseh Sherman decided to capitalize on their previous victories and advance over the Tennessee River. They knew that reinforcements under Don Carlos Buell would soon arrive from Nashville, where they had seen little resistance and had captured the Tennessean capital. However, as it turned out, Grant was walking right into Johnston's trap.

At the Battle of Shiloh, which started on April 6th, a Confederate force of about forty thousand troops ambushed Grant and the Union forces, driving them back by nightfall. Although Johnston hoped to have crushed Grant's army before the arrival of the reinforcements, he was fatally wounded in the leg. The person who assumed command, General P. G. T. Beauregard, was not quick enough to follow up on the initial successes, allowing Buell to save Grant with an additional twenty thousand fresh troops, which arrived on the battlefield early on April 7th. Now at a numerical disadvantage, Beauregard was forced to retreat to Corinth, Mississippi, but had still inflicted considerable casualties to the Union forces, about thirteen thousand men in total, while suffering ten thousand casualties himself.

The Battle of Shiloh was one of the most pivotal early encounters in the Trans-Mississippi campaigns, allowing the Union forces to gain an initial advantage and control large territories in Kentucky and Tennessee. This headway was crucial for the capture of the Mississippi River, which had been one of the original objectives of the Union high command. By capturing and holding the river, the Confederacy would have been split in half, with Texas, Arkansas, and Louisiana being disconnected from the rest of the Southern states in the east. After the relative success at Shiloh and the far less fruitful campaigns in Virginia, the Union's attention shifted to taking control of the Mississippi.

However, the Confederates were not keen on giving up fighting in the west. Beauregard, who was not favored by Jefferson Davis, was eventually replaced by Braxton Bragg as the commander of the Southern forces in the Trans-Mississippi. Acting on Davis's direct orders, Bragg split the army, leaving about twenty thousand men in defense of Mississippi, and ventured out to deal a blow to the Union in Kentucky, starting a campaign known as the Confederate Heartland Offensive. He moved north through Chattanooga with about thirty thousand soldiers and eventually joined up with the Confederate Trans-Mississippi Department under Edmund Kirby Smith, who had additional eighteen thousand men or so at his disposal.

The Confederate campaign was largely successful, gaining significant ground against the disunited Union forces. For instance, with just five thousand men, Smith and the Confederates were able to decisively defeat the Union Army regiments at Richmond, Kentucky, in late August. However, in early October, the Confederate Army came across a larger Union force under Commander Don Carlos Buell at Perryville, where the two sides engaged in fierce combat for two days. Both sides suffered heavy casualties at about four thousand each, but in the end, Buell and his men stopped Bragg's advance, forcing him to retreat back over the border to Tennessee.

Despite the Union's incapacity to properly punish the numerically inferior enemy, the encounter at Perryville largely determined Kentucky's fate, with the Union gaining firm control over it. In addition to Bragg's retreat from Kentucky, Federal (another name for the Union) forces under William S. Rosecrans were able to overcome the Confederate force that had split off from Bragg at the start of his campaign at Iuka, Mississippi, and later at Corinth, contributing to the weakening of the Confederate positions in the Trans-Mississippi Theater. By late October, the Union forces had assumed a commanding position in the fight for Tennessee, and by the end of the year, in the Battle of Stones River, they were able to gain a close victory against the Confederates. Having suffered about 13,000 casualties to Bragg's 11,700, Commander Rosecrans cemented the Union's control over both Kentucky and Tennessee and eliminated a major point of contention between the two sides.

All in all, the year 1862 proved to be very successful for the Union cause in the Trans-Mississippi since the fight for the border states was largely won thanks to the efforts of commanders Grant, Buell, and Rosecrans. The Confederates had been deprived of resources to use in the war and were forced to retreat from Kentucky and Tennessee farther south to the state of Mississippi, where they put up a final stand at Vicksburg.

Perhaps it is now best to take a look at a very important factor that contributed greatly to the Union's successes in the war, especially in the Trans-Mississippi Theater: the superior Union Navy. With it, the Federals had been able to seize control of the pivotal city of New Orleans in April 1862, something that became a thorn in the side of the Confederate war effort.

Union Naval Supremacy and the Capture of New Orleans

The Union's crucial advantage over the Confederacy did not actually come on the field. It came at sea, as the Northern navy was significantly larger and, therefore, more capable. President Lincoln was also lucky to have a very wise and experienced man as his secretary of the navy, Gideon Welles, a veteran Democrat-turned-Republican. Welles had an ability to correctly understand the most pressing situation and led the Union naval effort throughout the war. Under Welles, the number of men enlisted in the navy increased from nine thousand to about sixty thousand throughout the war, something that greatly contributed to the Northern war effort. With more men and resources, the Union Navy was able to maintain a blockade of the large Confederate coastline, which stretched for about 3,5000 miles—something that had been perceived impossible at the start of the conflict and, in the minds of the Confederates, gave the South a natural advantage over the North.

On the other hand, the Southern navy was not nearly as developed. In fact, compared to the number of ships, guns, and men available to the Northern sea effort, the Confederate Navy was almost laughable at the start of the war. It was thanks to Confederate Secretary of the Navy Stephen Mallory that the Southern coastline was able to hold off the Northern barrages for as long as it did. After the outbreak of the conflict, Mallory commissioned the building of new warships, sent out agents to foreign countries to try and buy ships and sailors to man them, and even paid locals who owned ships to equip them and make them ready for war. For most of the war, the Confederate sea effort was concentrated on disrupting the Union's maritime trade and commerce, with Southern raiders with smaller, faster ships being a thorn in the side of the Union.

An important characteristic of naval warfare during the Civil War is that it coincided with the development of marine military technology, which allowed for new, more resilient, and effective ship designs to emerge throughout the mid-1850s. The new steam engines made naval travel far easier and faster. In addition, the "ironclad" type warship is perhaps one of the most influential inventions of the 19th century, characterized by the use of reinforced iron casemates, which protected the body (the hull) of the ship. They became the most prominent type of warship in the Civil War and were even used in other parts of the world since they dominated the seas and were able to outdo older ships with wooden hulls.

The ironclads were used by both sides in the first naval battle of the Civil War on March 9th, 1862, at Hampton Roads, Virginia, where the Confederates, with the stolen northern ironclad *Virginia*, were able to decimate the wooden Union warships before the arrival of a Union ironclad, *Monitor*. The strength of the ironclads was demonstrated throughout the battle, especially when *Virginia* managed to hold off a whole fleet of wooden warships while suffering insignificant blows.

In addition to coastal warfare on the high seas, a significant part of the Union Army also operated on the Mississippi River, which allowed smaller-scale ironclads to be deployed and utilized as additional support to the army that operated on the field. The wide basin of the Mississippi made transportation by ships easy and efficient, especially considering just how much importance the North assigned to the control of the basin. However, seizing control of the upper course of the river would not be enough to achieve the goal envisioned by the Anaconda Plan. To successfully maintain dominance in the Trans-Mississippi and split off the western Confederacy from the east, the Union high command knew that capturing the city of New Orleans was instrumental.

New Orleans had been one of the largest and fastest-growing cities in the country for decades by the time the war broke out. It was the only city in the South with well over 100,000 citizens and the center of the Southern slave trade. In addition, it was located on the lower end of the Mississippi River and provided a gateway to the Gulf of Mexico and, thus, the Atlantic Ocean. In short, New Orleans was one of the most important cities the Confederates held at the start of the Civil War, holding not only material but also immense symbolic importance, something that had been well realized by the Union high command.

However, getting to New Orleans overland was never considered, despite the fact that the Union Army had seen quite substantial successes in their Trans-Mississippi campaign. The most sensible thing was to task the navy with getting to New Orleans from the sea and establishing temporary control over it before the army could reach it. It was a prime target, an obvious one even, but as it turned out, it was not nearly as well defended as it should have been.

In January 1862, once the war was well underway but before it could really kick off in the Trans-Mississippi, the Union high command put Captain David Farragut in charge of the West Gulf Blockading Squadron, which consisted of four heavy warships, about a dozen-and-a-half smaller gunboats, and twenty mortar boats. Farragut was tasked with taking New Orleans, something which he delivered immaculately. After sailing up to the city's entrance from the south, he came across two fortifications on the Mississippi: Fort Jackson and Fort St. Philip, both of which were firmly built and housed Confederate artillery. They were located on each bank of the river, with an underwater boom—a strong chain designed to keep the vessels from entering narrow points—stretched in between.

After reaching the city on April 16th, Farragut had to fight for a week to break through the forts' defenses, as well as a relatively small fleet defending the city. Confederate Major General Mansfield Lovell, who was in charge of the men in New Orleans, was forced to evacuate the city, knowing that the rest of the defenses were not designed to hold off an amphibious assault and that the Union fleet would soon be reinforced by the army. Thus, he loaded whatever supplies he could gather and fled to Camp Moore and Vicksburg to set up a final Confederate stand in the west. Captain Farragut faced no more resistance, with the forts surrendering on April 28th. He had captured New Orleans, a prized possession of the Confederacy, a city that embodied the spirit of the South, dealing an excruciating blow to the Confederate war effort in the west. On May 1st, Union Army regiments arrived in New Orleans and peacefully occupied the city.

However, the fight for the Trans-Mississippi was not quite over.

Chapter 9: The War in 1863

After almost two years since the secession of the seven Deep South states, the subsequent formation of the Confederacy, and bloody fighting between the two sides, nobody was still quite sure who had the upper hand in the war. Lincoln's more aggressive approach to the Civil War, caused by his belief that he had every right to protect the unity of the Union, had been somewhat effectively thwarted in Virginia, where the majority of fighting had so far unfolded. The two sides had entered into a stalemate, with neither of them having assumed an advantageous position. In the Trans-Mississippi, however, the Union forces significantly weakened the Confederate opposition, having driven them back from Kentucky and Tennessee. They had captured New Orleans and effectively achieved what had been intended from the very start of the conflict: control over the river and a separation between the eastern and western parts of the Confederacy.

The Vicksburg Campaign

Having taken control of the Lower Mississippi with the capture of New Orleans, one final location the Union needed to cement was its dominance of the city of Vicksburg, which was sometimes referred to as the "Gibraltar of the West" due to the important role of "conductor" it played on the river. It was another prized possession of the Confederates. And with New Orleans gone and the Union troops achieving success in the border states of Missouri and Kentucky, Vicksburg remained the only major connecting point between the western and eastern Confederate states. For this reason, it was heavily fortified and garrisoned, and the defenses were actually able to hold off the Union forces, which had set their eyes on the city in late December 1862.

The early efforts to capture Vicksburg had proven ineffective. Ulysses S. Grant, who was leading the main contingent of the Union forces on land and had maritime support from Admiral Farragut, tried to salvage the situation by attempting to take the city during the Bayou Expeditions in early 1863. However, these expeditions could not gain a significant enough headway to give the North an advantage over the defenders. Frustrated, Grant finally decided to launch one final offensive on Vicksburg, which involved a daring move of crossing the eastern bank of the Mississippi, where the city was located, to its southern flank while being supported by the Union gunboats that would pass the city downstream. The plan was risky because once the gunboats under Admiral David Dixon Porter passed the city and provided artillery support, they would require time to come up the stream to reinforce Grant and his men, leaving them potentially undefended.

In late April 1863, Grant landed south of Vicksburg at Bruinsburg, Mississippi, continuing his move eastward with about thirty thousand men and overcoming a relatively small Confederate resistance at Port Gibson, Raymond, and then Jackson—the capital of Mississippi—all in just the span of two weeks. By mid-May, Grant had seized control of Jackson and cut off the Confederate forces there from joining up with the rest of the army in Vicksburg. Next, he turned west to finally approach the city, achieving even more victories in skirmishes at Champion Hill and Big Black River Bridge until reaching Vicksburg on May 18th. He was finally within striking distance of Vicksburg, but instead of advancing right away with an assault, Grant waited for a couple of weeks, encircling the city to ensure it ran out of supplies. Eventually, he gained more reinforcements, almost doubling his numbers, while Confederate Commander John C. Pemberton inside the city was slowly losing his men due to attrition and desertion.

Vicksburg surrendered on July 4th, 1863, with the Union forces finally taking control of the whole Mississippi River in the coming weeks, giving President Lincoln a sigh of relief and turning the course of the war once again in favor of the Union.

Anti-War Opposition in the North

When the year 1863 rolled around, President Lincoln had nothing to worry about when it came to the Civil War, at least on paper. The war effort had been going strong for about two years, and even if the Union did not see significant successes against the South in Virginia, the situation was drastically different in the west. Domestically, however, even the naked eye could see that things were not as in order as Lincoln would have liked.

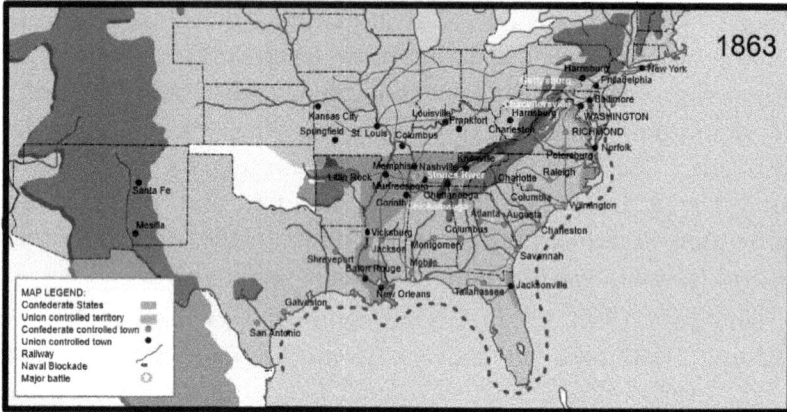

Overview of the American Civil War.

Due to the ambiguous results in Virginia throughout the autumn of 1862, as well as the recent signing of the Emancipation Proclamation, which had angered many anti-abolitionist Democrats, the president was facing a severe political crisis. The public, led by those Democrats who had opposed the war since the very beginning, either wanted decisive results or an end to the whole thing. It was very difficult for Lincoln and his team to effectively communicate to the ordinary Northern citizen that the military campaigns, despite not producing a clear-cut advantage for the Union in the east, were nevertheless successful in the Trans-Mississippi. It was becoming clear that Lincoln needed to get his house in order if he had any ambition of ending the already dragged-out war and gaining the final victory.

Democrats who were referred to as "Copperheads" by their Republican counterparts led the anti-war opposition. They had been named after a type of poisonous snake. The Copperheads gained much traction in the Union over the autumn. They had gained even more grounds to protest with the passing of the Emancipation Proclamation, believing that the freeing of so many enslaved people would harm the country in the long term. They were mainly comprised of more conservative-leaning groups who believed that Lincoln and the Republicans were violating the Constitution on a daily basis by overexercising their powers. A big number of them were Irish and German immigrants who had come under severe discrimination from the largely Protestant and, in many cases, nativist US public. The Copperheads united around the principle of "The Union as it was, the Constitution as it is," signaling their discontent with the way President Lincoln was handling things but also stating that they condemned the secession of the Confederacy.

In the end, the Copperheads were not able to grow their numbers significantly enough to pose severe problems to Lincoln and his administration, but they did protest almost every decision Congress made throughout the war. In the mid-term elections, although the Republicans had lost some seats, they still managed to gain a convincing majority in both of the legislative bodies of the country and were thus virtually free to pass any new bill they supported. For example, during the war, Congress introduced a new paper currency, which was cheaper to make. The currency slowly started to replace the minted coinage, something the Copperheads thought went against the Constitution. The income tax, among other things, was also protested by the anti-war Democrats.

Chancellorsville and Gettysburg

The decisive action in the east that the anti-war opposition had been asking for would take place in Virginia in the coming months. Lincoln had appointed a new commander to the Army of the Potomac, Fighting Joe Hooker, who, over the winter, had managed to grow the number of his men to about 130,000. The Northern army in the east dwarfed whatever the Confederates had to offer. By comparison, Confederate General Lee only had about sixty-two thousand men at his disposal, and if we take into consideration the array of supply shortages that had plagued his army over the past couple of months, he was at a serious disadvantage.

The stage was set for the continuation of hostilities once the winter cold blew in. After disappointing results at both Antietam and

Fredericksburg, Lincoln was hoping to achieve success in the east to calm the protesters back home and show that, in spite of the war dragging on more than anybody had predicted, the Union was still too strong to be overcome by anything the Confederacy could throw at it.

Hooker started his Chancellorsville campaign in the spring of 1863, hoping to capitalize on his numerical advantage and deal a blow to the Confederates at Fredericksburg, the control of which was vital to allow for the safe passage of the Union forces over the Rappahannock River. Hooker hoped to pull off a flanking maneuver, passing the Rappahannock several miles northwest from Fredericksburg, and attack the Confederate forces from the western part of the town. This part of his plan was successful, as the bulk of the Union forces—just short of 100,000 men—crossed the nearby Rapidan River and positioned itself on the Confederate flank. Only a minor portion of the Union Army crossed the river east of Fredericksburg to distract the enemy.

However, to his surprise, Hooker was met with the majority of Lee's troops, which had practically abandoned the town to defend against Hooker's troops that had just crossed the river. Frustrated, Hooker had to order a general retreat westward to the woods of Chancellorsville on May 1st, 1863, while the rest of the Union forces that remained in the eastern part of Fredericksburg were contained by the Confederates. Positioning at Chancellorsville was not ideal because the superior Union artillery was useless in awkward terrain and wilderness, as they blocked its line of sight. As if that was not enough, Lee was quick to follow up with the Union retreat, sending a portion of his forces around Hooker's main line. Commanded by Stonewall Jackson, the Confederate flanking force brilliantly maneuvered its way in the woods of Chancellorsville and burst through the Union's rear on May 2nd, although Commander Jackson was accidentally shot by his own men and died days later.

After hearing of the flanking maneuver's success, Lee ordered the rest of his troops to attack Hooker's front line, converging on all sides and eventually pushing the Union forces back over the Rappahannock River by May 6th. The Union troops that had landed on the eastern side of Fredericksburg were also repelled, marking a decisive Confederate victory at the Battle of Chancellorsville.

The battle had produced a devastating outcome for the Union, with over seventeen thousand casualties to the Confederacy's twelve thousand. This victory boosted the Confederates' morale through the roof, and many people on both sides believed that General Lee was one of the brightest military minds in the history of the United States. His decisive action and clever strategy had yielded successful results for the Southern cause once again, while the North was left empty-handed and disappointed at a pivotal moment in the war. However, as time would show, the victory at Chancellorsville perhaps caused overconfidence in Lee, if not among the whole Confederate Army, prompting the general to embark on a daring campaign to invade the Union for the second time.

It took about a month of preparing for Lee to cross the Rappahannock in early June and invade the Union territories. At that time, the Union forces had retreated farther up north to reinforce and resupply, and the high command was debating what to do next. Historians believe that Lee made this daring decision because he had overestimated the anti-war sentiment in the North. With a quick invasion of the free states, Lee hoped to disrupt whatever plans the Union might have had and encourage the anti-war Copperheads to push for the end of hostilities. However, in reality, the Copperheads represented the opinion of the minority. Most Northerners were inspired and assured by Lincoln and his administration that the Union had a commanding position in the war. They fully believed in the Northern cause. Although they hoped that the war would be over quickly, they were also determined to see the South defeated because they believed the Southern states had unjustly seceded from the Union. Thus, overconfident in the capabilities of his men and banking on several hypothetical outcomes, Lee marched north, still managing to catch the Union high command off-guard.

Heading northwest from Fredericksburg up the Shenandoah Valley, Lee hoped to envelop his forces and surround the bulk of the Union troops on the eastern coast. His movement was mirrored subtly by Hooker and his troops, who were positioned at a distance. They were close enough to engage if necessary but also waited for a bolder advance of the Confederates to assume a more defensive position. The two sides engaged in several skirmishes during Lee's advance throughout early June, first at Brandy Station, then at Winchester, where the Confederates emerged victorious and captured about 4,000 troops while only losing 250 themselves.

Lee continued his march northward, perhaps trying to find a suitable time and place to break through and converge on Washington, but the Union troops were always in a position to intercept. After more small-scale encounters between the two sides, Hooker resigned his position as the commander of the Army of the Potomac after a disagreement with the high command on the matter of additional reinforcements, which he did not receive. In late June, he would be replaced by George Gordon Meade.

By that time, Lee and the Confederates had crossed the border of Pennsylvania. Some of their corps were even stretched all the way northeast up to Harrisburg on the Susquehanna River. The state was swept up in an all-out panic after Lincoln notified the governor of potential Confederate strikes on major towns like Philadelphia and Harrisburg. The president also requested more volunteers to respond to the imminent threat, and defenses were organized in the big cities to hold off a Confederate attack until the main army could reinforce them. Fearing Lee's intentions, the Union high command also ordered a small force of about thirty-two thousand men under Major General John A. Dix to threaten the Confederate capital of Richmond, which had been left relatively undefended, as the vast majority of the Southern troops were with Lee in Pennsylvania.

On June 30th, after about a month of the Union forces chasing Lee's army north of the Rappahannock, the two main armies were dangerously close to each other. A day later, on July 1st, the two sides would engage in the most famous battle of the American Civil War near the town of Gettysburg, Pennsylvania. Gettysburg acted as a gateway to the Confederate forces. If they took control of the town, they would be able to converge on Washington from the north. Thus, the two armies met in the skirmish. Both sides knew of the battle's importance.

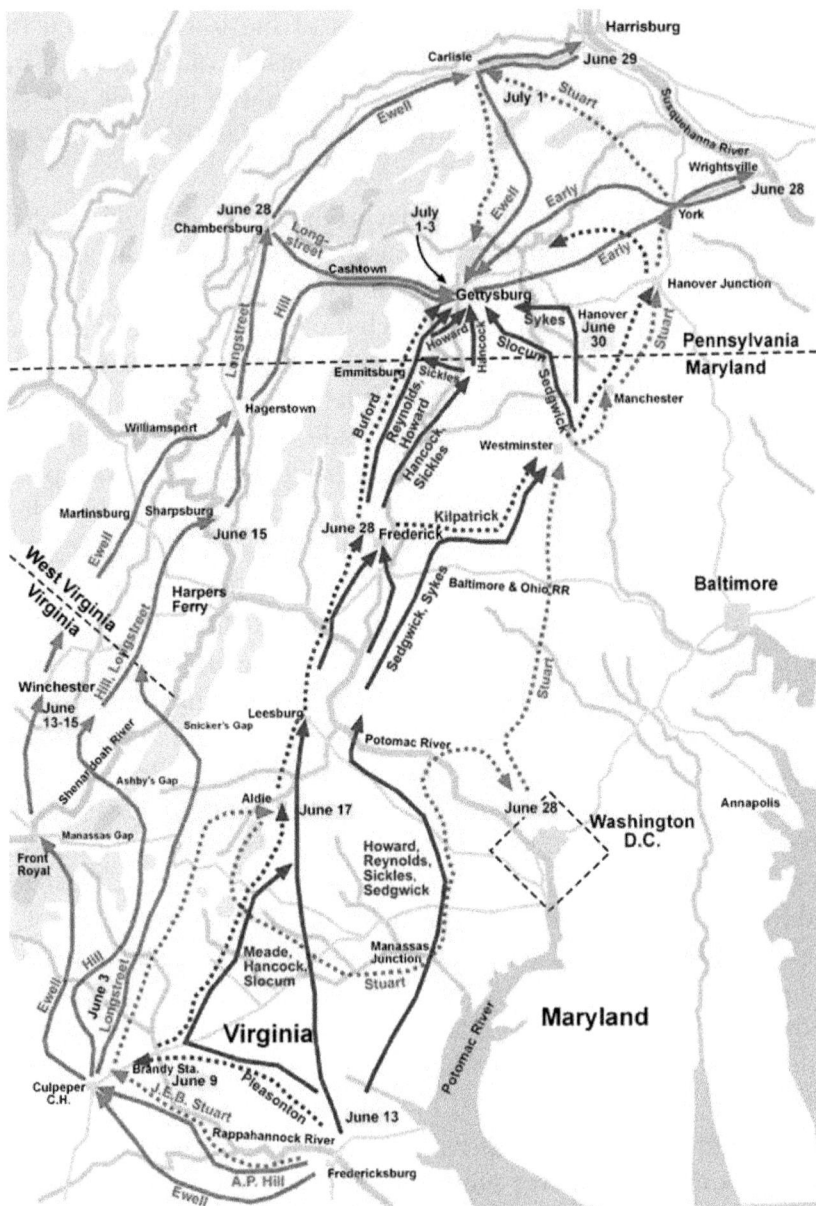

Gettysburg campaign.

https://commons.wikimedia.org/wiki/File:Gettysburg_Campaign_(original).jpg

On the first day of battle, a force of no more than thirty thousand Confederate troops defeated a much smaller Union resistance of about eighteen thousand men commanded by John F. Reynolds. After hours of fighting, the Union forces realized they were being overwhelmed and were forced to retreat, first to the streets of the town and then to the defensive location of Cemetery Hill, just outside of Gettysburg in the south. There, the leftover Union troops met up with the bulk of General Meade's army and awaited the further advance of the Confederates, who had now taken partial control of the town.

On July 2nd, with both armies having been significantly reinforced, Meade organized his ninety-five thousand or so troops in a defensive position, making use of the high terrain, which gave an advantage to the Union artillery. Lee did not try to match the Union front line; instead, he ordered a concentrated attack on Meade's left flank. Led by Confederate General James Longstreet, the Confederates were able to push the Union defensive line farther back but could not fully break through the left flank. Meade was quick to reorganize his defenses to make up for the numerical disadvantage on the left flank and established a new defensive line. The Confederate attack was repulsed.

July 3rd turned out to be decisive for the course of the battle. As Meade's defensive position was proving to be difficult to crack, Lee ordered more than ten thousand men to charge the left center of the Union frontlines. It was an all-out infantry attack, which could likely go either way. Commanded by General George E. Pickett, this move, which began in the afternoon, became known as Pickett's Charge. Although Meade's men were first softened up by artillery, they were shocked that such a large contingent of troops was hurtling right at them with bayonets, especially considering the fact they had the high ground. Despite the hand-to-hand combat going in favor of the Confederates, the Union troops managed to hold their positions. The Confederate soldiers had appeared to have charged to their deaths. They were already missing hundreds by the time they reached the enemy. It was a tragic sight, brothers killing brothers with whatever they could find, even their bare hands.

Eventually, after the massacre had settled, Lee called off the attack and retreated with whatever men were left from the deadly charge. The retreating troops were relentlessly gunned down by Union artillery, and the North finally sighed in relief as the Confederates returned to their positions.

The three days of fighting were equally catastrophic for both sides. The total casualty toll stands anywhere from forty-five thousand to fifty-five thousand. After the Confederate retreat late on July 3rd, Lee decided to give up Gettysburg and retreat to assume a defensive position of his own, confident that Meade would follow up with a counterattack. However, the Union commander, thinking that his forces were exhausted after so much fighting, chose to hold his position—a decision for which he has been criticized by both his contemporaries and historians. Although the Union forces were not in the greatest shape to continue a long-term campaign, a quick follow-up assault on Lee's remaining troops might have sealed the deal in terms of the Confederates' strength to continue the war effort. Still, Meade should be respected for not sending more of his men on an ill-prepared offensive, as it would have only caused the loss of more lives. In the following weeks, smaller Union forces made sure the Confederate Army of Northern Virginia was fully out of Northern territory and had crossed the border back into Virginia.

The Battle of Gettysburg is perhaps the most widely known battle of the Civil War. It remains the bloodiest battle of the war, and although both sides suffered heavy casualties, it is considered a Union victory. General Meade was able to almost flawlessly defend the pivotal town of Gettysburg from falling under the control of the Confederates and forced Lee and his men to abandon their offensive on Union territories. The events that transpired at Gettysburg greatly influenced the development of the war. The Confederates had to suffer a rather disappointing result while having come so close to victory. President Lincoln, on the other hand, could finally present the victory at Gettysburg as not only another valiant effort of the Union soldiers but also as proof to the anti-war opposition that the war was going in the North's favor. Although the war was still far from over, the fatalities suffered by the Confederates, including many veteran soldiers who had greatly developed their skills over the course of the war and different valuable officers who had also demonstrated their various strategic capabilities, would prove to be impossible to overcome.

The Fight for Tennessee

In the summer of 1863, the momentum of the war shifted heavily in favor of the Union. In the east, Meade had been able to drive back the invading Confederate Army of Northern Virginia at Gettysburg. The remarkable efforts of General Grant and Admiral Farragut led to the Union forces taking control of the Mississippi River, further weakening the opposition. Although the war had dragged on for longer than Lincoln had hoped in the beginning, most of the original goals of the Anaconda

Plan had been achieved. The Confederacy was split into two down the Mississippi, and the naval blockade was paying off dividends. It was apparent that as time went by, the South was doomed to run out of resources to effectively continue the war effort. However, despite the lack of resources, the strength and resilience of the Confederate soldiers, who were motivated by the Southern cause, would be demonstrated once again.

After the defeat of the Confederates at Gettysburg and Grant's successful Vicksburg campaign, the fighting would slowly shift eastward from the Mississippi to the central Confederate territories. Thanks to the efforts of Commander Rosecrans, the Union had already established control over Kentucky and most of Tennessee, with the next main objective being the town of Chattanooga, located on the Tennessee River in the southern part of the state. Capturing Chattanooga would eliminate another major center of the South. It was also a crucial railway connector. It was a natural target for the North, something that had been realized by the Confederate high command, which had tasked General Bragg with the defense of the territory with more than forty thousand soldiers. After General Lee's unsuccessful offensive, a portion of the Confederate Army of Northern Virginia was transported to Chattanooga to reinforce Bragg and make sure that Rosecrans and the Federals would not break through. Out of the three main Union armies, Rosecrans had the most natural path to the city. Having encountered Bragg before at Stone River, he was tasked with capturing the important Tennessean town.

Coming fresh off his success at the Tullahoma campaign, Rosecrans continued to chase down the Confederate troops and drive them back to the other side of the river. However, Bragg, having just been reinforced by the contingents from Lee's army, decided to adopt an active approach and tried to cut off Rosecrans's men. Thus, after a whole month of being chased throughout central and southern Tennessee, Bragg confronted the Union Army southeast of Chattanooga in mid-September at a location called Chickamauga Creek. In a two-day battle, thanks to a miscommunication error on the side of the Union and to the battle being one of the rare instances where the Confederates were not actually heavily outnumbered, Bragg was able to rout Rosecrans and force him to retreat to Chattanooga, where the Confederate commander had the Northern army almost entirely encircled. It was one of the few victories the South gained in the western campaign, but it still inflicted serious casualties on both sides: more than eighteen thousand on the side of the

Confederacy and about seventeen thousand on the side of the Union.

Rosecrans found himself now trapped in Chattanooga, besieged by Bragg, who, despite his previous victory, did not have enough resources to force a fight with the Union forces in the city. During the next few weeks, the latter tried to cut off the Union's supply lines in Chattanooga, perhaps hoping that either he would get reinforced or that Rosecrans would give up. However, it was all in vain. After hearing of Rosecrans's defeat at Chickamauga Creek and realizing the possible consequences that could follow the army's surrender, Lincoln quickly tasked the other commanders with relieving the entrapped Rosecrans. First, an additional twenty thousand men, under the command of Major General "Fighting Joe" Hooker of the Army of the Potomac, were immediately sent by rail to reinforce Commander Rosecrans. In addition, Ulysses S. Grant, who was also appointed as the commander of the newly established Union Military Division of the Mississippi, which incorporated all the armies in the western theater, headed east from Vicksburg to Chattanooga in late September. Arriving in the Tennessean city on October 22nd, Grant was determined to keep the city and not give it up under any circumstances, even if it meant vicious fighting.

With the arrival of reinforcements, the balance of power swung in favor of the Union. Grant, who had assumed command of the united force, now outnumbered Bragg's Confederate Army by about ten thousand. Although there were still supply problems, Grant launched an offensive on the besieging Confederates in late November and was able to defeat them at the battles of Orchard Knob and Lookout Mountain. By November 25th, the Union forces were able to capture the strategically important Missionary Ridge near Chattanooga, gaining the high ground and forcing Bragg to issue a full-on retreat. The Confederates retreated to Chickamauga, where they utilized the rail to flee to Georgia. The fight for Tennessee was over, with the Union suffering about 5,800 casualties to the Confederacy's 6,600.

After gaining firm control of Chattanooga, the Union stripped the Confederacy from a lot of its core territories. The deadlock still existed in the east, with the front lines having changed inconsequentially after the start of the war. But thanks to the efforts of General Grant and the rest of the forces who fought in the west, the North now controlled all of the Mississippi Basin, the crucial border states of Missouri and Kentucky, and Confederate territories east of the Mississippi, including the states of Mississippi, a large part of Louisiana and Arkansas, and all of Tennessee.

Only the modern southeastern states were still under the Confederates' control, but there, too, existed a myriad of problems that were linked with the war effort.

Davis and the Southern government diverted the majority of the country's resources, everything from food to clothes to the army, leaving the Southern population upset and on the verge of starvation. The South was also quickly running out of men, and new conscription laws, which first required all capable men aged eighteen to thirty-five to enlist, were later extended to all men aged between seventeen and fifty. This caused the wealthier Southerners, who had no intention of fighting, to hire replacements who could serve instead of them, causing even more anti-war sentiment among the commoners. They often called the conflict "a war of the rich, but the fight of the poor."

With the Southern economy collapsing, its population greatly upset, and the Union pressing forward at a steady pace, it was only a matter of time until the North gained a decisive advantage and emerged victorious from the Civil War, a detail that was realized by both sides by the end of 1863.

Chapter 10: The Final Campaigns

The year 1863 had proven to be the most decisive in the war, with the Union assuming a clear advantage over the Confederacy by achieving important victories on all fronts. In the east, General Meade and the Army of the Potomac were able to successfully drive the Confederate offensive back at Gettysburg, dealing a catastrophic blow to the Southern war effort and punishing Confederate General Lee for his overconfidence and overzealousness to invade the Northern territories. In the west, through the efforts of Ulysses S. Grant, the Union had gained a significant advantage and achieved the original intended goal of the war by splitting the South into two along the Mississippi River and making it more difficult for it to continue the war. Then, despite initial setbacks at Tennessee and Mississippi, the Union forces managed to overcome the Confederate defenses and gain control of some of the key Southern states, giving them direct access to the Confederate heartland. Finally, the superiority of the Northern fleet at sea and the effective naval blockade it had maintained for much of the war had reduced the Southern economy to dust and further pressured President Jefferson Davis to come up with an effective response.

The Overland Campaign

After Chattanooga, no major campaigns were immediately started by both sides, as they decided to wait out the winter in their respective camps and replenish their losses. President Lincoln had noticed Grant's successes and liked him for his resilient personality and outlook on the war. So, in early 1864, Lincoln appointed Grant as the new general in chief, replacing Halleck. The new general in chief visited the capital in the spring of 1864 to discuss his strategy and the intended objectives for the Union forces. Having left the command of his forces in the west to William Tecumseh Sherman, Grant did not assume direct control of the Army of the Potomac himself, leaving Meade in his position.

From the very beginning, Lincoln and his Cabinet trusted Grant to deliver, and Grant would be actively involved for the remainder of the war in all of the military developments, which earned him great popularity among his contemporaries. Eventually, he would become the eighteenth president of the United States.

Realizing the Union's advantageous position, Lincoln and Grant hoped to deal fatal blows to the South from all sides. The Army of the Potomac would start an offensive against the main Confederate force under Lee and try to take Richmond. Simultaneously, the newly appointed commander of the western armies, Major General Sherman, would lead his men to Georgia with the objective of capturing Atlanta. Union Commander Franz Sigel was tasked with attacking the crucial fields in the Shenandoah Valley. Nathaniel Banks would split off from Sherman to take control of Alabama. And finally, the Union forces under George Crook were tasked with taking control of the Confederate supply lines in West Virginia. Together, these armies should overwhelm anything the South could provide. It was the first instance in the war that the Union forces would conduct a coordinated offensive on all fronts. Often referred to as the "Overland Campaign," it marked the successful culmination of the Union war effort.

The Overland Campaign started in early May, with Grant leading the Army of the Potomac over the Rappahannock River in Virginia, approaching Wilderness Tavern west of Chancellorsville. Lee noticed Grant's movements and was quick to react, confronting the Union Army on May 5th. The Battle of the Wilderness lasted for two straight days. The Confederates were able to use the surprise factor in their favor and inflicted about 18,000 casualties to Grant's 110,000-strong force (the Confederates only had about 60,000 men with them). This maneuver forced Grant to assume a defensive position, and he ordered a retreat, despite the fact that the South did not gain a convincing victory.

The Union general decided to pull away from the battle and lick his wounds while continuing his march southeast. He would be met with Confederate forces at Spotsylvania Court House. The two sides engaged fiercely on May 7ᵗʰ with their cavalry regiments, with both trying to gain a more advantageous position for the ensuing battle. In the following days, Lee unsuccessfully tried to outflank Grant's front line, although it did seem like the Confederates were gaining the upper hand despite their inferior numbers. By May 12ᵗʰ, a Confederate offensive made a slight gap in the Union defenses, but General Grant was quick to focus his reinforcements on containing the breakthrough while maneuvering the remainder of his army to create a new front line on the eastern side of the battlefield.

When the fighting ended on May 19ᵗʰ, neither side had gained anything valuable. Although Grant suffered another eighteen thousand or so casualties in the battle, he had many more men at his disposal to continue his campaign. The Confederates, who had lost no more than twenty thousand men since the start of Grant's offensive, did not press forward, fearing that further losses would be detrimental in the long term.

After the events at Spotsylvania, Grant decided to continue his advance southeast, racing Lee's men to the Confederate capital of Richmond. The two forces mirrored each other's movements and slowly made their way to Richmond, engaging multiple times over the next few weeks. The Confederates were able to utilize the Virginia railroads, which were not accessible to the Union, to match Grant's movements and deny them a closer approach to Richmond a couple of times, like at North Anna and Totopotomoy Creek. Lee would always be there first, forcing Grant to fight in unfavorable conditions. In early June, as the fighting had shifted farther south and was dangerously close to the capital, Grant crossed the Pamunkey River and confronted the Confederates at Cold Harbor, which lay just northeast of Richmond.

By that point, Grant had lost about fifty thousand men during his campaign, but he had also taken the fight to Lee and posed a real threat to Richmond. The Confederates at Cold Harbor assumed favorable defensive positions, having entrenched themselves and set up artillery. For two days, several separate Union attacks were repelled by the defenders, who were putting up a good fight despite being outnumbered. Then, on June 3ʳᵈ, Grant ordered a massive frontal assault on the Confederates—a move that has been deemed borderline suicidal by historians. Engaging with his 2ⁿᵈ, 6ᵗʰ, and 18ᵗʰ Corps early in the morning fog, the Union forces were forced to charge through difficult terrain. They became stuck in the mud and swamps, making them an easy target for the entrenched Confederates. Up to twelve thousand Union men died in the battle, which was finally recalled by Grant once he realized the South was not about to break as he had hoped.

After being forced to leave the battlefield without the results he had hoped for but having softened up the Confederate forces, Grant decided to continue his movement southward. He aimed to reach the town of Petersburg, Virginia, on the Appomattox River. Still, Lee was adamant about confronting Grant at every possible opportunity that presented itself. His troops, exhausted from the constant marching and fighting, still continued to defensively mirror the Union forces and stop them from gaining access to crucial locations, including Petersburg, which they defended fiercely. The Confederates held off the Union attacks from June 9th to June 18th at the outskirts of the town, not allowing them to take control of Petersburg, which would cut off a crucial supply line to Richmond and open up the southern capital for a Union offensive.

With more than eight thousand Union men lost in the encounters at Petersburg and fearing that further losses would demoralize his troops, who had seen enough action over the course of May and June, Grant decided to settle for a long and tiresome siege of Petersburg in late June. By then, he had realized he could not gain the upper hand on Lee, as his attempts to outflank the Confederates had proven ineffective. Constructing a long trench line while not fully surrounding Petersburg, Grant besieged the Army of the Potomac for nine months, beginning in late June 1864. The Overland Campaign had not yielded the results he had initially hoped for, perhaps because the Confederates realized that giving up ground near Richmond would be fatal for them. Still, despite Grant's relatively unsuccessful effort to capture Richmond, he was counting on the other armies operating in the west to pressure the Confederate defenders to give up.

Into the Confederate Heartland

As Grant attempted to break through Lee's forces and get to Richmond, Commander Sherman, now in charge of the western armies, was closing in on Atlanta. Fielding more than 110,000 men, Sherman's forces outnumbered whatever resistance the Confederacy could offer in this theater. Commander Johnston was in charge of the Confederate Army in the west, but he only commanded about half the men available to Sherman, giving the North a clear advantage once again.

The campaign to capture Atlanta greatly resembled Grant's efforts. The Union Army marched south from Chattanooga while being matched by the Confederates at every step of the way. After heading south from Dalton, Georgia, light skirmishes broke out between contingents of the two armies throughout early May at Resaca and Adairsville. Johnston knew he had the numerical disadvantage and did not opt for a full-on large-scale fight. Sherman, just like Grant, was trying to outflank the defenders and often sent large portions of his forces on daring maneuvers, but the gradual Confederate retreat made it impossible to catch the Southerners and force them into a head-to-head battle.

This constant cat-and-mouse game arguably favored neither side, but Sherman was still inching forward. The situation was so frustrating that in late June, after countless smaller raids by the Confederate cavalry, Sherman ordered a massive full-frontal assault at Kennesaw Mountain. His impatience proved to be deadly for the Union, as thousands fell victim to the Confederate soldiers' guns. The Confederates had assumed a defensive position up a slope and largely free-fired for most of the battle. Sherman called off the attack eventually, and the Confederates decided to retreat back to Atlanta to organize a final defense. Still, despite these setbacks, the Union forces moved forward at a slow and steady pace.

After the battle at Kennesaw Mountain, Commander Sherman was in reach of Atlanta and had the manpower to lay siege to the city. Confederate Commander Johnston realized the severity of the situation and contacted Jefferson Davis to tell him that fighting for Atlanta would be a lost cause since the Union was just too strong to defeat fully. The answer from Davis was just what one might expect; Johnston was relieved from his command and replaced by John B. Hood, a veteran of the war who had fought at Gettysburg and Chickamauga. One of his legs had been amputated, and his arm was permanently damaged after being shot. Hood, unlike Johnston, was not about to give up without a last stand and decided to sally out from the city and engage Sherman's army on a couple of different occasions.

The newly appointed Confederate commander was unable to stop the Union's advance, despite putting up a fierce fight in each of the battles, first at Peachtree Creek, then at Atlanta, then Ezra Church, and, finally, after being driven back from the outskirts of the city, at Jonesboro. Sherman managed to take control of Atlanta by late August, and the Confederates were forced to abandon the city on September 1ˢᵗ, calling for an evacuation. After taking Atlanta, Sherman decided to wait for a little bit to give his men time to rest and fix the supply issues he had been facing throughout his march. He split off a number of his troops and sent them to Nashville to repel a Confederate attack. Then, Sherman enquired about the situation in the other theaters of war. Around a month and a half later, he embarked on what has been deemed his "March to the Sea."

On November 15th, Sherman took his forces from Atlanta to the east with one goal in mind: to reach the Atlantic coast of Georgia and lay waste to every possible Southern resource on his way. During his thirty-seven-day journey from Atlanta to the town of Savannah, Sherman and about sixty-two thousand Union soldiers covered nearly three hundred miles and destroyed important industrial and agrarian holdings in Georgia. The Union soldiers went after nearly everything, from farms to railroads, and made sure that one of the most pivotal states of the Confederacy had nothing left to contribute to the Southern war effort. Their actions also had a grave psychological impact on the Southern population, which witnessed the relentless destruction of resources. Although Sherman had instructed his soldiers not to touch private property unless provoked, many of them ran rampant with the possibility of demonstrating their power to ordinary Southern citizens. Hundreds of slaves, seeing that the Union Army was close, ran off from their masters and joined the forces.

Sherman's March to the Sea
https://commons.wikimedia.org/wiki/File:F.O.C._Darley_and_Alexander_Hay_Ritchie_-_Sherman%27s_March_to_the_Sea.jpg

The March to the Sea is often classified as an instance of "total war"—an approach to war that favors the idea that one should do everything in their power to gain an advantage over the enemy. Sherman, as well as Grant, are thought to have been firm believers in total war. Although no civilians were reportedly killed during Sherman's brutal march, Georgia suffered irreparable damage to its economy, and Georgians personally hated Sherman for what he had done to the state. The March to the Sea remains one of the most dreadful events of the American Civil War and is a great example of the extent the two sides were willing to go to gain an advantage.

The Fall of Virginia

Having rampaged through Georgia before reaching the Atlantic coastline, Sherman was in position to transfer his troops north and close in on Virginia from the south, while Grant and the Army of the Potomac simultaneously attacked from the north. This would mark the Union's final large-scale military campaign in the war and would conclude the original plan that had been agreed upon by Grant, Lincoln, and the rest of the Union high command during Grant's visit to Washington. By the end of 1865, the Union controlled not only the disputed border states but also large parts of Tennessee, Louisiana, Mississippi, Arkansas, and Georgia. The Confederacy's days were numbered. Their territories were divided, and their armies were scattered in different areas and lacked resources.

Like the March to the Sea, Sherman and his sixty thousand or so men destroyed everything of military value on their way through the Carolinas. Historians argue that this measure was not nearly as necessary as it was in Georgia and that it was only taken to have a further psychological effect on the Southern forces. Many Northerners, including the ones in Sherman's army, believed that South Carolina was responsible for the start of the conflict since it had been the first state to secede from the Union and encouraged the others to join. Thus, when Sherman started to move toward Columbus, South Carolina, in early January 1865, he ordered his men to bring destruction upon the state.

The Confederates had significantly fewer men. The Confederate Army of the Tennessee, battered from constant unsuccessful engagements, numbered fewer than ten thousand men by the spring of 1865 and could not put up a fight against Sherman and his mighty Union force. Several skirmishes broke out between the opposing forces during the late winter, such as the one at the Rivers' Bridge in early February, but it was clear from the beginning that the Federals were too strong to be stopped. On February 17ᵗʰ, Columbus surrendered to Sherman, and the city of Charleston was evacuated by the Southerners. In Columbus, hundreds of slaves and captured Union soldiers were freed, and Sherman's men lavishly celebrated their triumph, something that resulted in a fire that spread throughout the center of the city before it was contained, destroying much of Columbus in the process. While some argue that the fire was accidental, others claim that it was an act of vengeance from the Union troops—an act to demonstrate the North's superiority over the South.

Sherman pushed northward to North Carolina, where he fought a series of battles against the Confederate forces throughout March. After these initial encounters, the town of Fayetteville was captured on March 11ᵗʰ. After the Battle of Bentonville about ten days later, Sherman had eliminated all Confederate resistance in the area, pushing the remnants of the Southern army to Virginia. The Union armies were now at the southern doorstep of Virginia.

Meanwhile, in Virginia, the Union siege of Petersburg was still underway. The Northern forces had established a very long front line, from the southern part of Petersburg all the way to Richmond, and outnumbered the enemy two to one. They wanted to stretch the Confederate forces thin. The siege, which lasted for nine months, proved to be very difficult for General Lee and his fifty thousand or so men. The Union forces had virtually cut off all important railroad access points to Richmond and Petersburg, and Sherman's victories in the south meant that it was only a matter of time before Virginia would run out of supplies and fall to the North. The Confederates could not gain any significant advantage in the skirmishes that broke out during the nine-month period along the front lines. Instead, Grant was slowly waiting out Lee. Grant did not want to commit a lot of men to storm the cities, knowing that it would cost the lives of thousands.

In a desperate attempt to drive the Union forces back, Lee gathered up the majority of his men and ordered them to engage in a concentrated attack on one of the defensive Union locations at Fort Stedman. Lee realized that inaction would only be signing his death warrant, especially with the Union forces under Philip Sheridan slowly approaching to reinforce the siege from the south. Thus, in late March, he trusted the command of around ten thousand men to Major General John B.

Gordon and tasked him to try and break through the Union defenses at Fort Stedman, south of Petersburg, which would, in theory, give the Confederate forces a headway to organize more cohesive offensives and maybe even take back control of the railroads.

However, the assault proved to be inconsequential for the Southern cause, as the Confederates suffered about four thousand casualties while not achieving anything of significance. On March 25th, as fighting at Fort Stedman had ceased, it became clear to Lee that he stood no chance. On April 1st, the Union forces followed up their success at Fort Stedman with a complete victory at the Battle of Five Forks. The Union soldiers were ready to converge on Petersburg.

On April 2nd, Lee ordered a general retreat from both Petersburg and Richmond, evacuating the cities and fleeing southwest along the Appomattox River, although this was in vain. Grant chased the remnants of the Confederate forces for about ninety miles, finally catching up to them at Amelia Court House and cutting off their only path to flee.

On April 9th, in what became one of the most important events in American history, Confederate General Lee was forced to meet with the Union high command at Appomattox Court House, where he surrendered the Army of Northern Virginia to Grant. A preliminary ceasefire between the two sides was signed, marking the beginning of the end for the Confederacy.

Chapter 11: Aftermath

With Lee's surrender at Appomattox Court House on April 9th, 1865, the Confederacy's days were numbered. Technically, the war was not officially over, as the remnants of the Confederate Army were still at large in several different locations.

The War Ends

Although Lee surrendered the Army of Northern Virginia to Grant on April 9th, the fighting between the Confederates and the Federals did not cease right away. A number of smaller Southern forces were still scattered around the country and were hoping to put up a final stand against the Union. Still, much of the fighting after April was pointless and yielded no results whatsoever for the Confederacy.

The word of Lee's surrender spread throughout the United States, reaching the ear of Major General Johnston, who was in charge of the Army of the Tennessee—the second-largest Confederate force after Lee's. Following Lee's surrender, Union cavalry units from General Sherman's army quickly reached Johnston and offered him the chance to surrender, additionally proposing peace terms to take to President Davis. Davis and his Cabinet refused the proposed agreement because they thought it was too humiliating for the South and ordered Johnston to put up a last stand—an order that was smartly refused by Johnston, who chose to save his men and surrendered to Sherman in late April.

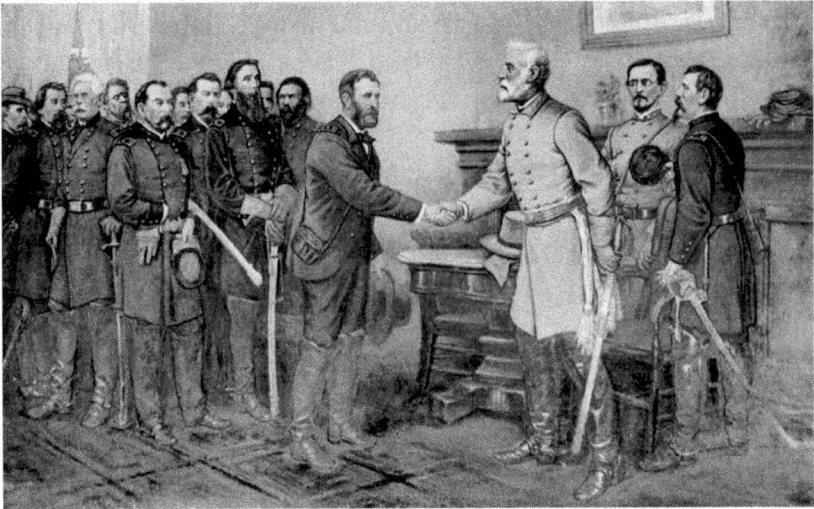

Lee's surrender

By signing the agreement, all the troops in the Confederate states east of the Mississippi were given up, and the fighting largely ceased in this part of the country. The Confederate forces under Lieutenant General Richard Taylor in Alabama—about ten thousand men—surrendered on May 4th. This was followed by the capture of President Davis in Georgia, whose government had crumbled in the face of the Union victory and had lost all legitimacy by April. Davis had been on the run since the evacuation of Richmond in early April. Since then, he had traveled south with the remnants of his government, trying to evade the Northern forces, but he eventually realized that his fate had been sealed. On May 9th, a month after Lee's surrender at Appomattox Court House, Davis and his men were captured by the Union forces, who, by that time, suspected that he had instigated the assassination of President Lincoln a month before. He was taken to Fort Monroe in Virginia, where he spent the next two years.

Despite these events, the fighting had not ceased west of the Mississippi, where Confederate Lieutenant General Kirby Smith was in control of the South's final army. However, since Lee's surrender, his army had been slowly disintegrating. Three days after the capture of Jefferson Davis, the final land battle between the Union and the Confederacy unfolded in Texas, where about 600 Union troops under Colonel Theodore H. Barrett engaged with about 350 Southerners under the command of Colonel. John Ford. Although the fighting in Texas had stopped by then, the relatively inexperienced Barrett ordered an assault on the Confederate force and suffered a close defeat at the Battle of Palmito Ranch. As one can imagine, this engagement was inconsequential. Confederate Lieutenant General Smith surrendered his force on May 26th.

Interestingly, the last Confederate surrender would take place in modern-day Oklahoma, which had been declared "Indian Territory" during the Civil War. About a month after Smith's surrender, Confederate Brigadier General Stand Watie—the first Native American to serve as a commander in the Civil War—finally gave up his forces, which largely consisted of Native American fighters, at Fort Towson.

The American Civil War was finally over.

A New Age

While the last of the Confederate forces were surrendering throughout the country, important events were transpiring in the North.

President Lincoln's Emancipation Proclamation, which had gone into effect on January 1st, 1863, had proven extremely effective. As we have already discussed, thousands of slaves left their masters and fled northward, even joining the Union Army in the fight for their freedom. This had catastrophic effects on the Confederacy's economic and social life and contributed to the North's victory.

Since 1863, Lincoln had spoken on a number of occasions about the gradual abolishment of slavery as a whole, something that sparked debate among the Democrats and the Republicans. Slavery was still in full effect in the four border states since Lincoln knew that upsetting these slave-owning states with emancipation would make them hostile toward the Union. When Lincoln had first run for president, his party platform clearly stated that the Republicans opposed the expansion of slavery to the newly acquired territories of the US, not its complete abolishment. This had been misunderstood by the slave-owning South, which blamed Lincoln for deliberately trying to sabotage their lives and enforce the tyranny of the North. For a similar reason, many Northern Democrats, who had historically opposed the complete abolishment of slavery, feared the material disadvantages it would bring to millions of people. Some outright believed that God had made blacks purposefully inferior to whites. Regardless, the abolishment of slavery moved up on the

Republican agenda, and in-party consultations had already started to discuss the matter.

In late 1863, Representative James Mitchell Ashley of Ohio proposed a new constitutional amendment that would end slavery in the United States. This proposal saw overwhelming support from the party. In February 1864, led by the efforts of radical abolitionist Republicans Charles Sumner of Massachusetts and Thaddeus Stevens of Pennsylvania, an amendment proposing the permanent abolishment of slavery was submitted to the Senate. Two months later, in April 1864, the Senate easily passed the new amendment by a vote of thirty-eight to six, gaining the required two-thirds majority. The amendment was now up for the House of Representatives to vote on, which needed three-fourths of all votes.

In June, a new problem presented itself to Lincoln and the Republicans—the House rejected the new amendment, with ninety-three votes in favor and sixty-five against. Thirteen additional votes were needed to pass the amendment, and with the Democrats overwhelmingly opposing it and the new presidential elections just around the corner, it seemed as if the matter would be forever stalled.

What followed next was months of clever political maneuvering by Lincoln and his colleagues to assure they would gain enough support for the amendment in the House. The first major event was Lincoln's reelection in the autumn of 1864. In his platform, he stated that he supported abolition, something that guaranteed his victory. After his reelection and as the Union was gaining a demonstrable advantage in the war, Lincoln envisioned the passing of the new constitutional amendment as an assurance that his fight against slavery would not be in vain. Perhaps the president feared that the Emancipation Proclamation, which he had passed during wartime, would be deemed unjust or get reversed after the end of the war.

Thus, determined to have the proposed abolishment added to the Constitution, Lincoln devised a plan to gain as much support from Congress as he could, knowing that, come spring of 1865, many of the existing congressmen would be gone. Many were "lame ducks," meaning their replacements had already been elected. Lincoln identified these lame ducks, mostly Democrats, and hoped to convince them to vote for the amendment before they left office.

The president tasked Secretary of State Seward with this job, and the latter delivered. In the span of three months, he approached the outgoing Democrats and offered them assurances in the form of government jobs after their leave of office in return for their votes. By then, a few Democrats had already publicly stated they were in favor of the amendment, something that facilitated the process a bit for Seward. Still, Seward, acting on Lincoln's direct orders, outright bribed a handful of Democrats and did everything in his power to get them to vote for the amendment. Although President Lincoln's involvement in the process has never been truly identified, Senator Stevens, the author of the amendment, stated, "The greatest measure of the nineteenth century was passed by corruption aided and abetted by the purest man in America."

In a hurry to pass the amendment before the end of the war, Lincoln pushed the House to vote on it on a number of occasions. Finally, on January 31ˢᵗ, 1865, the House convened to vote on the matter. The session had an unusually large audience, mostly people of color who had been allowed to attend the sessions after emancipation. In a close vote, the Republicans managed to get 119 votes from the representatives—just two more than what they needed to achieve a two-thirds majority. Along with all of the Republicans, fourteen Democrats voted in favor, including those convinced by Seward. Freedom had triumphed.

The new Thirteenth Amendment read: "Neither slavery nor involuntary servitude, except as a punishment for crime whereof the party shall have been duly convicted, shall exist within the United States, or any place subject to their jurisdiction." It was a historic day for the United States and the democratic world. The attendees rejoiced in Congress, with some being reduced to tears, and city-wide celebrations started in Washington. Slavery had finally been abolished.

The Assassination of President Lincoln and the Reconstruction

Chronologically, the Thirteenth Amendment was followed by the victorious Union campaigns in Georgia, the Carolinas, and Virginia. By early April, it was clear the war would be over soon, and everyone in the North breathed a sigh of relief. On April 9ᵗʰ, Lee surrendered the largest Confederate force to Grant, starting a chain reaction that eventually led to the complete defeat of the Confederacy. However, President Lincoln, the man who had engineered both the military victory in the Civil War and perhaps the greatest achievement of American politics in the 19th century, did not live long enough to see the end of the conflict.

On April 14th, just five days after Lee's surrender, President Lincoln was shot at Ford's Theater in Washington, DC. His assassin, a well-known actor named John Wilkes Booth, shot the president in the head while the latter was attending the play *Our American Cousin*. The assassination was part of a larger underground conspiracy plan to undermine the North in the war and gain public support for the Southern cause. Lincoln died the next morning in the Peterson House opposite the theater, but the plan to murder the rest of the leaders in the Union failed, with Secretary of State Seward being only wounded and Vice President Andrew Johnson's assassin never reaching his target.

The assassination of Abraham Lincoln.
https://commons.wikimedia.org/wiki/File:Lincoln_assassination_slide_c1900_-_Restoration.jpg

John Wilkes Booth evaded the authorities for twelve days until he was finally found and shot in Virginia, just south of the Rappahannock River. The rest of the conspirators, who had devised an elaborate plan to extend the Confederacy's fight in the war, were subsequently captured and hanged.

As America mourned Lincoln's death, Vice President Andrew Johnson was sworn in as president, just hours after Lincoln had passed away. As the seventeenth president of the United States, Johnson had arguably just as difficult a task to accomplish as Lincoln: to lead the country through the period immediately after the war, something that, in the face of Lincoln's untimely death, seemed even harder.

The period of recovery after the war would come to be known as the Reconstruction. In fact, the Union government had started thinking about the Reconstruction in 1863 after Lincoln passed the Emancipation Proclamation. Lincoln and his administration proposed the so-called "Ten Percent Plan," which proposed the election of new governments in seceded states if one-tenth of their population swore loyalty to the federal government. However, in 1863, the plan was not that developed, and it certainly did not address many of the problems that would arise once the conflict effectively came to an end. Mainly, there was the question of what exactly to do with all the freed slaves after emancipation had been applied to all of the territories. With no more slavery in the country, were the freed slaves allowed to vote? Did they have the same rights?

Immediately after Johnson became president, he started the initial stage of the Reconstruction, often referred to as the Presidential Reconstruction, which lasted for about two years. He pardoned most of the seceded Southerners except those who had held positions of power in the Confederate government and restored their pre-war properties to them, except for their former slaves, of course. Then, he laid out the plan for the organization of local governments in the former seceded states. Johnson required that they accept the abolition of slavery and reject the secession. In return, he repealed their debt and gave them relative freedom in forming their new state legislatures.

However, despite these measures and the fact that a lot of the Southern population were former slaves, the anti-black sentiment had persevered in the South. The states enacted the so-called "Black Codes," which were laws that forced the newly freed slaves to sign labor contracts with whites. The Black Codes essentially replaced traditional slavery in the Southern states, limiting the social and economic options of the emancipated population and requiring them to continue living in conditions that were similar to the ones they had during slavery.

The new Southern laws sparked a series of protests, including in Congress, where Radical Republicans Stevens and Sumner—two of the authors of the Thirteenth Amendment—proposed that the newly created local Southern governments be dismantled and new ones that respected the equality of all citizens and not treat the freed African Americans as slaves be established. Despite the soundness of their argument and the fact that most African Americans in the South were struggling under the Black Codes, President Johnson opposed the idea, perhaps due to his personal opinions on the matter of race and beliefs on states' rights.

Over time, especially after the congressional elections of 1866, the Northern voters showed overwhelming support for the Radicals Republicans' proposals. The Reconstruction entered a new period, often called the Congressional Reconstruction. After 1867, the Radical Republicans led the effort to reorganize the Southern states and end the injustice of inequality that had existed there for ages. Congress passed the Fourteenth Amendment a year later, a crucial piece of legislation that granted citizenship to almost everyone born in the United States (barring women and Native Americans), guaranteeing that people of color were just as much American as the whites. In the following years, as the formerly seceded states were gradually readmitted to the Union and had all of their rights reinstated, the Reconstruction proved more beneficial than in its first two years, making sure that the Civil War was truly over.

In the long run, the Northern Republicans were able to lead the Reconstruction efforts and ensured that the gap between the North and the South was reduced significantly in all aspects, especially in regard to education. The federal government sponsored the construction of free public schools and universities and also helped the South rebuild its economy around agriculture, which proved to be possible to maintain even though there were no more slaves to work the fields. New manufacturing factories and railroads popped up all over the former Confederate territory with the aim of modernizing all of America as quickly as possible. In addition, the South soon became actively involved in the country's politics, something that had been one of the federal government's priorities to make sure that the Southerners felt like they were not marginalized. The Fifteenth Amendment granted African Americans the right to vote, a natural progression after emancipation and citizenship. Soon, more and more African Americans became involved in politics, and some were even elected to Congress.

Eventually, the Democrats gained control back in the South, passing the infamous Jim Crow laws, which were also passed in the North. These laws made life more difficult for African Americans. For instance, poll taxes and literacy tests discouraged African Americans from voting. This meant African Americans could not serve on juries or run for office, which practically guaranteed that things would not change any time soon.

In the end, the Reconstruction, although flawed in some regards, was a very influential period of American history, lasting up until the year 1877 when Congress officially pulled the remainder of its troops from the Southern territories. It achieved its main purpose of ending the secessionist sentiment in the Southern states and making them feel as if they were part of the same nation as the North. On the other hand, the emancipated African Americans, although formally declared equal to the white citizens, continued to be discriminated against for nearly one hundred more years. It would not be until the civil rights movement of the 1960s that the American public finally addressed the disenfranchisement that had persevered in the country for much longer than it should have.

Conclusion

The American Civil War remains one of the most influential events of the 19ᵗʰ century. It stands out as one of the most iconic due to the significant part it played in contributing to form a more democratic, free world. No one really knows what would have happened if the Confederacy had emerged victorious in the conflict. Although historians debate the possibility of a Southern victory, it has to be said that the South put up a much better fight than what everyone expected at the beginning of the war. The "Southern cause," a concept that might have seemed too abstract for outsiders, was deemed as something worth fighting for by each Confederate, who, despite being outnumbered at almost every instance, believed they were not on the wrong side of history.

The Civil War is perhaps the best example of what can happen in a country that is divided due to different interpretations of the country's foundations. In the early 19ᵗʰ century, more and more Americans recognized that a society built on the practice of slavery could not fully flourish and act as a beacon of democracy in the world. The divide between the North and the South thus became steeper and steeper. The two sides developed differently for decades, almost to the point that each was its own separate country by the time the war came about. This level of polarization proved to be fatal for the United States, a country that learned the hard way of what can follow if one constantly avoids a problem. For decades, US politicians tried to deal with slavery, but they never succeeded in finding a long-term solution.

Still, the modern United States was forged from these mistakes, and many significant improvements were the byproduct of the bloody war that cost the lives of more than one million Americans, including innocent citizens. The Thirteenth, Fourteenth, and Fifteenth Amendments were the first steps toward an America that truly guaranteed liberty and equality of all peoples against the law, regardless of their race. Abraham Lincoln, the man who led the Union through one of the toughest times in American history, is rightfully credited for his achievements, and it is not hard to see why he is adored by almost everyone. Who knows how he would have led the country after the war? What further improvements would he have been the author of if it weren't for his untimely death?

Just like with everything else concerning the Civil War, it is difficult to judge the path the US took after the end of the war. The Reconstruction era is regarded to have helped the country depolarize after the Civil War. Many of the policies and legislation introduced during this time reintegrated the South back into the Union. Congress tried to justly approach the problem of racial inequality with the Fourteenth and Fifteenth Amendments, but discrimination persisted for nearly a century, and many argue that it still continues today. The years from the end of the Reconstruction to the 1960s are often seen as one of the most shameful periods in US history.

In conclusion, the American Civil War was a conflict rooted not just in political differences between the Northern and Southern states but also in the different cultures and societal structures of the two sides. The country disintegrated into the bloodiest war in its history while the rest of the world was going through the process of modernization and rapid industrialization. In the end, the North, led by President Abraham Lincoln, triumphed. However, the Civil War's ultimate victory would be achieved about a hundred years later with the triumph of the civil rights movement.

If you enjoyed this book, a review on Amazon would be greatly appreciated because it would mean a lot to hear from you.

To leave a review:

1. Open your camera app.
2. Point your mobile device at the QR code.
3. The review page will appear in your web browser.

Thanks for your support!

Here's another book by Enthralling History that you might like

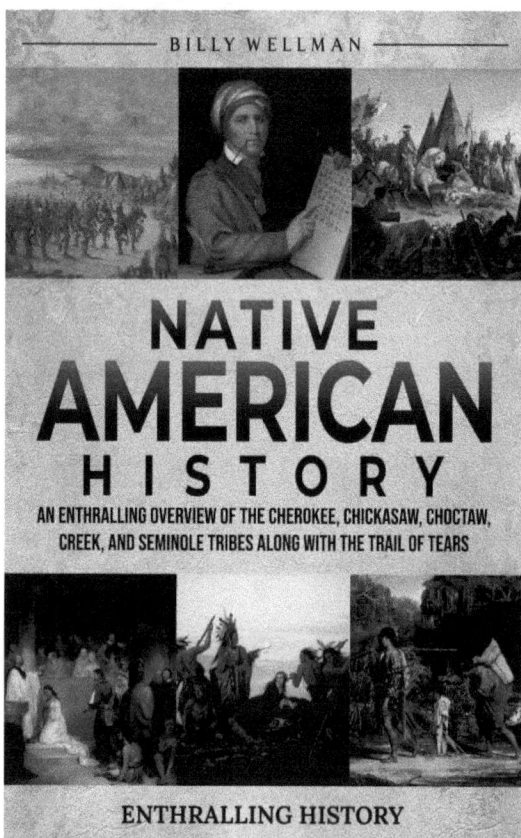

Free limited time bonus

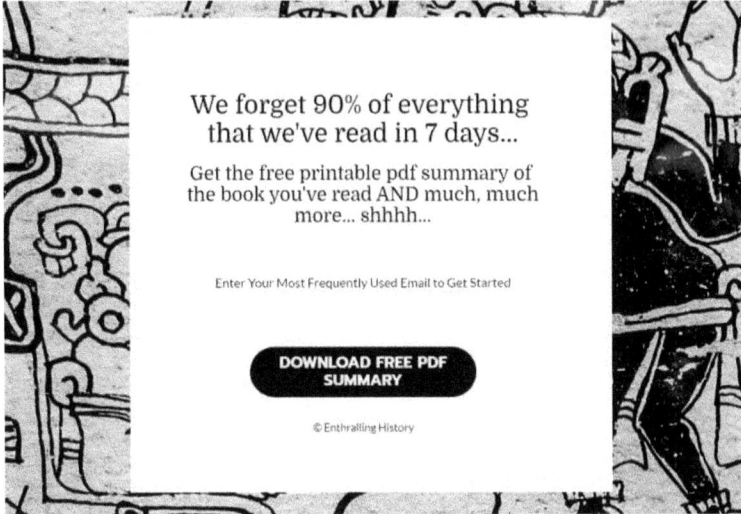

We forget 90% of everything that we've read in 7 days...

Get the free printable pdf summary of the book you've read AND much, much more... shhhh...

Enter Your Most Frequently Used Email to Get Started

DOWNLOAD FREE PDF SUMMARY

© Enthralling History

Stop for a moment. We have a free bonus set up for you. The problem is this: we forget 90% of everything that we read after 7 days. Crazy fact, right? Here's the solution: we've created a printable, 1-page pdf summary for this book that you're reading now. All you have to do to get your free pdf summary is to go to the following website: **https://livetolearn.lpages.co/enthrallinghistory/**

Or, Scan the QR code!

Once you do, it will be intuitive. Enjoy, and thank you!

Sources

https://www.history.com/topics/exploration/francisco-vazquez-de-coronado

https://www.history.com/topics/colonial-america/thirteen-colonies

https://www.history.com/this-day-in-history/new-amsterdam-becomes-new-york#:~:text=Following%20its%20capture%2C%20New%20Amsterdam%27s,Island%2C%20Connecticut%20and%20New%20Jersey.

https://www.britannica.com/event/American-Revolution

https://www.history.com/news/american-revolution-causes

https://www.loc.gov/classroom-materials/united-states-history-primary-source-timeline/american-revolution-1763-1783/british-reforms-1763-1766/

https://www.nps.gov/subjects/americanrevolution/timeline.htm

https://www.worldatlas.com/articles/major-battles-of-the-american-revolutionary-war.html

https://www.battlefields.org/learn/articles/10-facts-founding-fathers#:~:text=Fact%20%231%3A%20These%20seven%20men,John%20Jay%20and%20James%20Madison.

https://www.whitehouse.gov/about-the-white-house/our-government/the-constitution/

https://history.state.gov/milestones/1776-1783/articles

https://www.mtsu.edu/first-amendment/article/1448/bill-of-rights#:~:text=To%20ensure%20ratification%20of%20the,fourths%20of%20the%20state%20legislatures.

https://www.usa.gov/branches-of-government#item-214500

https://www.history.com/topics/us-presidents/george-washington#america-s-first-president

https://www.britannica.com/event/Louisiana-Purchase

https://www.history.com/topics/19th-century/war-of-1812

https://www.digitalhistory.uh.edu/disp_textbook.cfm?smtID=2&psid=2986

https://www.battlefields.org/learn/war-1812/battles/tippecanoe

https://www.history.com/topics/native-american-history/trail-of-tears

https://www.thecanadianencyclopedia.ca/en/article/northwest-territories-and-confederation

https://www.encyclopedia.com/history/dictionaries-thesauruses-pictures-and-press-releases/oregon-treaty-1846

https://history.state.gov/milestones/1830-1860/texas-annexation

https://www.nps.gov/civilwar/facts.htm#:~:text=The%20Union%20included%20the%20states,Abraham%20Lincoln%20was%20their%20President.

https://www.history.com/topics/american-civil-war/vicksburg-campaign

https://www.nps.gov/articles/a-short-overview-of-the-battle-of-antietam.htm

https://www.historynet.com/battle-of-fredericksburg/

https://www.history.com/news/7-things-you-should-know-about-the-battle-of-gettysburg

https://www.ducksters.com/history/civil_war/border_states.php

https://www.archives.gov/publications/prologue/2010/spring/newnation.html

https://www.pbs.org/wgbh/americanexperience/features/grant-impeachment/

https://guides.loc.gov/chronicling-america-spanish-american-war

https://www.ushistory.org/us/44b.asp

https://www.khanacademy.org/humanities/us-history/rise-to-world-power/age-of-empire/a/the-progressive-era#:~:text=The%20period%20of%20US%20history,progress%20toward%20a%20better%20society.

https://www.smithsonianmag.com/history/when-roosevelt-and-jp-morgan-fixed-coal-mine-strike-180975311/

https://www.history.com/news/the-strike-that-shook-america

https://www.pbs.org/tpt/slavery-by-another-name/themes/progressivism/

https://www.khanacademy.org/humanities/us-history/the-gilded-age/american-west/a/the-dawes-act

https://www.loc.gov/classroom-materials/immigration/native-american/removing-native-americans-from-their-land/

https://www.mnhs.org/fortsnelling/learn/us-dakota-war#:~:text=The%20Fort%20Snelling%20Concentration%20Camp&text=In%20December%20soldiers%20built%20a,a%20hospital%20and%20mission%20station.

https://www.historytoday.com/archive/months-past/end-great-sioux-war

https://www.legendsofamerica.com/warren-wagon-train-raid/

https://www.pbs.org/wgbh/americanexperience/features/carnegie-biography/

https://www.khanacademy.org/humanities/us-history/rise-to-world-power/us-in-wwi/a/the-league-of-nations#:~:text=The%20League%20of%20Nations%20was,opposition%20from%20isolationists%20in%20Congress.

https://www.history.com/topics/roaring-twenties/roaring-twenties-history

https://www.history.com/this-day-in-history/truman-doctrine-is-announced

https://www.history.com/topics/world-war-ii/marshall-plan-1

https://www.khanacademy.org/humanities/us-history/postwarera/postwar-era/a/start-of-the-cold-war-part-2

https://en.wikipedia.org/wiki/Third_World#Development_aid

https://www.history.com/topics/black-history/martin-luther-king-jr-assassination#king-assassination-conspiracy

https://www.jfklibrary.org/learn/education/teachers/curricular-resources/elementary-school-curricular-resources/ask-not-what-your-country-can-do-for-you

https://study.com/academy/lesson/culture-of-1960s-america.html

https://www.history.com/news/vietnam-war-origins-events

https://www.britannica.com/topic/oil-crisis

https://www.worldbank.org/en/about/history/the-world-bank-group-and-the-imf

https://www.history.com/this-day-in-history/helsinki-final-act-signed

https://www.history.com/news/jimmy-carter-camp-david-accords-egypt-israel

https://en.wikipedia.org/wiki/1979_oil_crisis#Effects

https://www.american-historama.org/1945-1989-cold-war-era/iran-contra-affair.htm

https://www.history.com/topics/1980s/iran-contra-affair

https://www.encyclopedia.com/history/encyclopedias-almanacs-transcripts-and-maps/malta-summit

https://www.nps.gov/articles/start-treaty-1991.htm

https://history.state.gov/departmenthistory/short-history/firstgulf

https://www.britannica.com/event/Persian-Gulf-War

---

https://millercenter.org/president/clinton/domestic-affairs
https://srebrenica.org.uk/what-happened/bosnian-war-a-brief-overview
https://time.com/5120561/bill-clinton-monica-lewinsky-timeline/
https://www.pbs.org/wgbh/pages/frontline/shows/kosovo/etc/cron.html
https://www.georgewbushlibrary.gov/research/topic-guides/global-war-terror
https://www.history.com/this-day-in-history/baghdad-falls-iraq-war
https://www.acorns.com/learn/investing/what-caused-great-recession-of-2008/
https://obamawhitehouse.archives.gov/the-record/economy
https://www.cms.gov/Regulations-and-Guidance/Legislation/Recovery
https://millercenter.org/president/obama/foreign-affairs
https://www.cnn.com/2014/09/23/politics/countries-obama-bombed/index.html
https://www.vox.com/policy-and-politics/2017/1/17/14214522/obama-lgbtq-legacy
https://en.wikipedia.org/wiki/Paris_Agreement
https://doggett.house.gov/media/blog-post/timeline-trumps-coronavirus-responses
https://www.cnn.com/2021/04/28/politics/president-biden-first-100-days/index.html

American Battlefield Trust. (2024, February 15). Bunker Hill. Retrieved from Battlefields.org: https://www.battlefields.org/learn/revolutionary-war/battles/bunker-hill.

American Battlefield Trust. (2024, February 15). Fort Ticonderoga, May 10, 1775. Retrieved from American Battlefield Trust: https://www.battlefields.org/learn/maps/fort-ticonderoga-may-10-1775.

American History Central. (2024, February 10). The Suffolk Resolves. Americanhistorycentral.com. Retrieved from Suffolk Resolves Summary 1774: https://www.americanhistorycentral.com/entries/suffolk-resolves/.

American History Central. (2024, February 4). The Navigation Acts. Retrieved from Americanhistorycentral.com: https://www.americanhistorycentral.com/entries/navigation-acts/.

Battlefields.org. (2024, February 20). Waxhaws. Retrieved from Battlefields.org: https://www.battlefields.org/learn/revolutionary-war/battles/waxhaws.

Battlefields.org. (2024, January 23). 10 Facts: The Continental Army. Retrieved from Battlefields.org: https://www.battlefields.org/learn/articles/10-facts-continental-army.

Battlefields.org. (2024, February 21). Brandywine. Retrieved from Batlefields.org: https://www.battlefields.org/learn/revolutionary-war/battles/brandywine.

Battlefields.org. (2024, February 20). Camden. Retrieved from Batlefields.org: https://www.battlefields.org/learn/revolutionary-war/battles/camden.

Battlefields.org. (2024, February 21). Germantown. Retrieved from Battlefields.org: https://www.battlefields.org/learn/revolutionary-war/battles/germantown.

Battlefields.org. (2024, February 20). Horatio Gates. Retrieved from Battlefields.org: https://www.battlefields.org/learn/biographies/horatio-gates

Battlefields.org. (2024, February 20). Siege of Savannah. Retrieved from Battlefields.org: https://www.battlefields.org/learn/revolutionary-war/battles/savannah.

Battlefields.org. (2024, February 25). Siege of Yorktown. Retrieved from Battlefields.org: https://www.battlefields.org/learn/revolutionary-war/battles/yorktown.

BBC.com. (2024, February 17). Philosophers Justifying Slavery. Retrieved from Ethics guide: https://www.bbc.co.uk/ethics/slavery/ethics/philosophers_1.shtml.

Bill of Rights Institute. (2024, February 17). Thomas Jefferson and the Declaration of Independence. Retrieved from Billofrightsinstitute.org: https://billofrightsinstitute.org/essays/thomas-jefferson-and-the-declaration-of-independence.

Bill, R. (2021, August 4). The Northern Campaign of 1777. Retrieved from Nps.gov: https://www.nps.gov/fost/blogs/the-northern-campaign-of-1777.htm.

Boston National Historical Park. (2024, February 15). Dorchester Heights. Retrieved from Nps.org: https://www.nps.gov/places/dorchester-heights.htm.

Boston National Historical Park. (2024, February 11). Samuel Adams: Boston's Radical Revolutionary. Retrieved from National Park Service: https://www.nps.gov/articles/000/samuel-adams-boston-revolutionary.htm

BritishBattles.com. (2024, February 14). Battle of Lexington and Concord. Retrieved from Britishbattles.com: https://www.britishbattles.com/war-of-the-revolution-1775-to-1783/battle-of-lexington-and-concord/.

Colonial Williamsburg. (2024, February 11). William Pitt's Defense of the American Colonies. Retrieved from Slaveryandremembrance.org: https://www.slaveryandremembrance.org/Almanack/life/politics/pitt.cfm.

Cronin, A. (2015, April 3). Untangling North Atlantic Fishing, 1764-1910 Part 2: Anglo-American Treaties Regarding the Fishery, 1783-1818. Retrieved from Massit.org: https://www.masshist.org/beehiveblog/2015/04/untangling-north-atlantic-fishing-1764-1910-part-2-anglo-american-treaties-regarding-the-fishery-1783-1818/.

Editors, H. (2024, February 21). British Abandon Philadelphia. Retrieved from History.com: https://www.history.com/this-day-in-history/british-abandon-philadelphia.

Eisenhuth, C. (2024, February 10). The Coercive (Intolerable) Acts of 1774. Retrieved from Mountvernon.org: https://www.mountvernon.org/library/digitalhistory/digital-encyclopedia/article/the-coercive-intolerable-acts-of-1774/#:~:text=The%20Coercive%20Acts%20were%20meant,particular%20aspect%20of%20colonial%20life.

Ellis, J. J. (2024, February 4). John Adams. Retrieved from Britannica.com: https://www.britannica.com/biography/John-Adams-president-of-United-States.

Encyclopedia.com. (2024, January 30). Franco-American Alliance. Retrieved from Britannica.com: https://www.britannica.com/event/Franco-American-Alliance

Famguardian.org. (2024, February 26). The Definitive Treaty of Paris 1783. Retrieved from Fanguardian.org: https://famguardian.org/PublishedAuthors/Govt/USTreaties/DefinitiveTreatyOfPeace1783.pdf.

Founders Online. (2024, February 10). The Final Hearing. Retrieved from Founders Online: https://founders.archives.gov/documents/Franklin/01-21-02-0018.

Franklin, Benjamin. (2024, February 10). Benjamin Franklin in His Own Words. Retrieved from Loc.gov: https://www.loc.gov/exhibits/franklin/franklin-break.html.

Hallowed Ground Magazine. (2018, December 18). Revolution on the Frontier. Retrieved from Battefields.org: https://www.battlefields.org/learn/articles/revolution-frontier.

Hattem, M. (2024, February 26). Newburgh Conspiracy. Retrieved from Mountvernon.org: https://www.mountvernon.org/library/digitalhistory/digital-encyclopedia/article/newburgh-conspiracy/.

Hickman, K. (2019, June 13). American Revolution: General Thomas Gage. Retrieved from Thoughtco.com: https://www.thoughtco.com/general-thomas-gage-2360620.

History.com. (2023, June 21). Treaty of Paris. Retrieved from History.com: https://www.history.com/topics/american-revolution/treaty-of-paris.

History.com. (2024, February 21). George Washington Crosses the Delaware. Retrieved from History.com: https://www.history.com/this-day-in-history/washington-crosses-the-delaware.

History.com Editors. (2009, October 27). Boston Tea Party. Retrieved from History.com: https://www.history.com/topics/american-revolution/boston-tea-party.

History.com Editors. (2009, June 13). Townshend Acts. Retrieved from History.com: https://www.history.com/topics/american-revolution/townshend-acts.

History.com Editors. (2023, June 21). Battle of Yorktown. Retrieved from History.com: https://www.history.com/topics/american-revolution/siege-of-yorktown.

History.com Editors. (2024, February 11). British Parliament Passes Unpopular Tea Act. Retrieved from History.com: https://www.history.com/this-day-in-history/parliament-passes-the-tea-act.

Horan, Katherine. (2024, February 10). First Continental Congress. Retrieved from Mountvernon.org: https://www.mountvernon.org/library/digitalhistory/digital-encyclopedia/article/first-continental-congress/#:~:text=One%20of%20the%20Congress%27s%20first,and%20to%20raise%20a%20militia.

Howe, W. (2024, February 1). William Howe Goes His Own Way. Retrieved from Clements.umoich.edu: https://clements.umich.edu/exhibit/spy-letters-of-the-american-revolution/stories-of-spies/howe-goes-his-own-way/.

Hurst, N. T. (2020, March 17). Made in American. Retrieved from Colonialwilliamsburg.org: https://www.colonialwilliamsburg.org/trend-tradition-magazine/spring-2018/made-american/.

Jstor.org. (2024, February 18). Foreign Intervention ... in the American Revolution. Retrieved from Jstor.org: https://daily.jstor.org/intervention-american-revolution/.

Keesling, D. K. (2024, February 21). Valley Forge: A Place of Transformation for the Continental Army. Retrieved from Thepursuitofhistory.org: https://thepursuitofhistory.org/2022/10/24/valley-forge-a-place-of-transformation-for-the-continental-army/.

Kiger, P. J. (2023, July 11). How Thomas Paine's "Common Sense" Helped Inspire the American Revolution. Retrieved from History.com: https://www.history.com/news/thomas-paine-common-sense-revolution.

Lee Resolution (2022, February 8). Lee Resolution. Retrieved from National Archives: https://www.archives.gov/milestone-documents/lee-resolution.

Longley, R. (2020, October 14). Committees of Correspondence: Definition and History. Retrieved from Thoughtco.com: https://www.thoughtco.com/committees-of-correspondence-definition-and-history-5082089.

Makos, I. (2021, April 13). Roles of Native Americans during the American Revolution. Retrieved from Battlefields.org: https://www.battlefields.org/learn/articles/roles-native-americans-during-revolution.

Maloy, M. (2024, February 21). The Battle of Freeman's Farm: September 19, 1777. Retrieved from Battlefields.org: https://www.battlefields.org/learn/articles/battle-freemans-farm-september-19-1777.

Mark, H. W. (2024, January 25). Battle of Long Island. Retrieved from Worldhistory.com: https://www.worldhistory.org/article/2359/battle-of-long-island/.

Mark, H. W. (2024, February 1). New York and New Jersey Campaign. Retrieved from Worldhistory.com: https://www.worldhistory.org/article/2364/new-york-and-new-jersey-campaign/.

Mary Stockwell, P. (2024, February 21). Baron Von Steuben. Retrieved from Mountvernon.org: https://www.mountvernon.org/library/digitalhistory/digital-encyclopedia/article/baron-von-steuben/.

massmoments.org. (2024, February 15). Henry Knox Brings Cannon to Boston. Retrieved from massmoments.org: https://www.massmoments.org/moment-details/henry-knox-brings-cannon-to-boston.html.

McGee, S. (2023, August 25). 5 Ways the French Helped Win the American Revolution. Retrieved from History.com: https://www.history.com/news/american-revolution-french-role-help.

Mobley, C. (2006, September 24). Hundreds of African-Americans Campaigned for the King during 1779 Struggle for Savannah. Retrieved from Savannahnow.com: https://www.savannahnow.com/story/news/2006/09/25/hundreds-african-americans-campaigned-king-during-1779-struggle-savannah/13826035007/.

Mount Vernon. (2024, February 11). The Coercive (Intolerable) Acts of 1774. Retrieved from Mountvernon.org: https://www.mountvernon.org/library/digitalhistory/digital-encyclopedia/article/the-coercive-intolerable-acts-of-1774/#:~:text=The%20Coercive%20Acts%20were%20meant,particular%20aspect%20of%20colonial%20life.

Mountvernon.org. (2024, February 21). 10 Facts About Washington's Crossing of the Delaware River. Retrieved from George Washington's Mount Vernon: https://www.mountvernon.org/george-washington/the-revolutionary-war/washingtons-revolutionary-war-battles/the-trenton-princeton-campaign/10-facts-about-washingtons-crossing-of-the-delaware-river/.

Museum of the American Revolution. (2024, February 18). Spain and the American Revolution. Retrieved from Amrevmuseum.org: https://www.amrevmuseum.org/spain-and-the-american-revolution.

National Geographic. (2024, February 17). Signing of the Declaration of Independence. Retrieved from Education.nationalgeographic.org: https://education.nationalgeographic.org/resource/signing-declaration-independence/.

National Park Service. (2024, February 18). The Clinton-Sullivan Campaign of 1779. Retrieved from Nps.gov: https://www.nps.gov/articles/000/the-clinton-sullivan-campaign-of-1779.htm.

National Park Service. (2024, February 21). Henry Clinton. Retrieved from Nps.gov: https://www.nps.gov/people/henry-clinton.htm#:~:text=Sir%20Henry%20Clinton%20replaced%20Sir,to%20face%20the%20rebellious%20Americans.

NCC Staff. (2021, May 24). 10 Fascinating Facts About John Hancock. Retrieved from Constitutioncenter.org: https://constitutioncenter.org/blog/10-fascinating-facts-about-john-hancock.

NPS.gov. (2021, January 25). Battle of the Capes. Retrieved from Yorktown Battlefield: https://www.nps.gov/york/learn/historyculture/battle-of-the-capes.htm.

Orrison, R. (2024, January 3). Native American Impact on British War Strategy in Southern Campaign. Retrieved from Battlefields.org: https://www.battlefields.org/learn/articles/native-american-impact-british-war-strategy-southern-campaign.

Oxford Learning Link. (2024, February 11). Document-Edmund Burke, Excerpts from "Conciliation with the Colonies." Retrieved from Learnnglink.oup.com: https://learninglink.oup.com/access/content/schaller-3e-dashboard-resources/document-edmund-burke-excerpts-from-conciliation-with-the-colonies-1775.

Paine, T. (2024, February 17). Thomas Paine, Common Sense, 1776. Retrieved from Billofrightsinstitute.org: https://billofrightsinstitute.org/activities/thomas-paine-common-sense-1776.

Paine, T. (1776). The American Crisis. Retrieved from Library of Congress: https://www.loc.gov/resource/cph.3b06889/.

Powell, J. (1996, September 1). Charles James Fox, Valiant Voice for Liberty. Retrieved from Foundation for Economic Freedom: https://fee.org/articles/charles-james-fox-valiant-voice-for-liberty/.

Revolutionarywar.us. (2024, February 21). Southern Theater. Retrieved from Revolutionarywar.us: https://revolutionarywar.us/campaigns/1775-1782-southern-theater/.

Revolutionarywar.us. (2024, February 21). The Battle of Kings Mountain. Retrieved from Revolutionarywar.us: https://revolutionarywar.us/year-1780/battle-kings-mountain/.

Revolutionary-war-and-beyond.com. (2024, February 24). Admiral Howe's Fleet Arrives at Staten Island. Retrieved from Revolutionary-war-and-beyond.com: https://www.revolutionary-war-and-beyond.com/admiral-howes-fleet-arrives-staten-island.html.

Rosenfield, R. (2024, February 21). Princeton. Retrieved from Battlefields.org: https://www.battlefields.org/learn/articles/princeton.

Ruppert, B. (2016, August 4). How Article 7 Freed 3000 Slaves. Retrieved from Allthingsliberty.com: https://allthingsliberty.com/2016/08/how-article-7-freed-3000-slaves/.

Rust, R. (2023, April 14). The Powder Alarm of Massachusetts in 1774. Retrieved from Americanhistorycentral.com: https://www.americanhistorycentral.com/entries/powder-alarm-1774-massachusetts/.

Scythes, J. (2024, February 21). Conway Cabal. Retrieved from Mountvernon.org: https://www.mountvernon.org/library/digitalhistory/digital-encyclopedia/article/conway-cabal/#:~:text=The%20Conway%20Cabal%20refers%20to,with%20Major%20General%20Horatio%20Gates.

Sprague, D. (2023, January 24). American Revolution and Canada. Retrieved from Thecanadianencyclopedia.ca: https://www.thecanadianencyclopedia.ca/en/article/american-revolution.

The Paul Revere House. (2024, February 14). The Real Story of Paul Revere's Ride. Retrieved from Paulreverehouse.org: https://www.paulreverehouse.org/the-real-story/.

Triber, J. E. (2024, February 4). Britain Begins Taxing the Colonies: The Sugar & Stamp Acts. Retrieved from Nos.gov: https://www.nps.gov/articles/000/sugar-and-stamp-acts.htm.

Tsaltas-Ottomanelli, L. G. (2023, November 15). Black Loyalists in the Evacuation of New York City, 1783. Retrieved from Gothamcenter.org: https://www.gothamcenter.org/blog/black-loyalists-evaculation-zy4la.

UKessays.com. (2024, February 17). Aristotle's Views on Slavery. Retrieved from UKessays.com: https://www.ukessays.com/essays/politics/slavery.php.

Washington, G. (2024, February 26). Newburgh Address: George Washington to Officers of the Army, March 15, 1783. Retrieved from MountVernon.org: https://www.mountvernon.org/education/primary-source-collections/primary-source-collections/article/newburgh-address-george-washington-to-officers-of-the-army-march-15-1783/.

Wigington, P. (2018, November 29). What Were the Navigation Acts? Retrieved from Thoughtco.com: https://www.thoughtco.com/navigation-acts-4177756.

William P. Kladky, P. (2024, February 15). Continental Army. Retrieved from Mountvernon.org: https://www.mountvernon.org/library/digitalhistory/digital-encyclopedia/article/continental-army/.

Wirt, William (ed. 1973). Give Me Liberty or Give Me Death. Retrieved from Colonial Williamsburg: https://www.colonialwilliamsburg.org/learn/deep-dives/give-me-liberty-or-give-me-death/.

Zeidan, A. (2024, February 4). Stamp Act Congress. Retrieved from Britannica.com: https://www.britannica.com/topic/Stamp-Act-Congress.

Zielinski, A. E. (2021, November 17). What Was the Stamp Act Congress and Why Did It Matter. Retrieved from Ameicanbattlefields.org: https://www.battlefields.org/learn/articles/what-was-stamp-act-congress.

Arnold, J. R., & Wiener, R. (2011). *American Civil War: The Essential Reference Guide.* ABC-CLIO.

Cleland, R. G. (1916). "Jefferson Davis and the Confederate Congress." *The Southwestern Historical Quarterly, 19* (3), 213-231. http://www.jstor.org/stable/30237274.

Collier, P., & Hoeffler, A. (1998). "On Economic Causes of Civil War." *Oxford Economic Papers, 50* (4), 563-573. http://www.jstor.org/stable/3488674.

Gallagher, C. (2007). "When Did the Confederate States of America Free the Slaves?" *Representations, 98* (1), 53-61. https://doi.org/10.1525/rep.2007.98.1.53.

Gienapp, W. E. (1992). "Abraham Lincoln and the Border States." *Journal of the Abraham Lincoln Association, 13*, 13-46. http://www.jstor.org/stable/20148882.

Gunderson, G. (1974). "The Origin of the American Civil War." *The Journal of Economic History, 34* (4), 915-950. http://www.jstor.org/stable/2116615.

Hassler, W. W. and Weber, Jennifer L. (2022, April 20). *American Civil War. Encyclopedia Britannica.* https://www.britannica.com/event/American-Civil-War.

Horwitz, J., & Anderson, C. (2009). "THE CIVIL WAR AND RECONSTRUCTION." In *Guns, Democracy, and the Insurrectionist Idea* (pp. 118-136). University of Michigan Press. https://doi.org/10.2307/j.ctv3znzcm.9.

Kingseed, C. C. (2004). *The American Civil War* (Ser. Greenwood guides to historic events, 1500-1900). Greenwood Press.

Krug, M. M. (1973). "Lincoln, the Republican Party, and the Emancipation Proclamation." *The History Teacher*, *7*(1), 48-61. https://doi.org/10.2307/491202.

Peck, G. A. (2007). "Abraham Lincoln and the Triumph of an Antislavery Nationalism." *Journal of the Abraham Lincoln Association*, *28*(2), 1-27. http://www.jstor.org/stable/20149114.

Reynolds, D. E. (1970). "Union Strategy in Arkansas during the Vicksburg Campaign." *The Arkansas Historical Quarterly*, *29*(1), 20-38. https://doi.org/10.2307/40030703.

SHEEHAN-DEAN, A. (2011). "The Long Civil War: A Historiography of the Consequences of the Civil War." *The Virginia Magazine of History and Biography*, *119*(2), 106-153. http://www.jstor.org/stable/41310737.

Sickles, J. (2007). "THE CAPTURE OF JEFFERSON DAVIS." *Military Images*, *28*(6), 4-19. http://www.jstor.org/stable/44034528.

Surdam, D. G. (1996). "Northern Naval Superiority and the Economics of the American Civil War." *The Journal of Economic History*, *56*(2), 473-475. http://www.jstor.org/stable/2123979.

Wallenfeldt, J. H. (2012). "The American Civil War and Reconstruction: 1850 to 1890 (1st ed., Ser. Documenting America: The Primary Source Documents of a Nation, vol. 1). Britannica Educational Pub. in association with Rosen Educational Services.

Welling, J. C. (1880). "The Emancipation Proclamation." *The North American Review*, *130*(279), 163-185. http://www.jstor.org/stable/25100834.

9 798887 653952